D1268940

DISCARDED

THE
UNIVERSITY OF WINNIPEG
PORTAGE & BALMORAL
WINNIPEG, MAN.   R3B 2E9
CANADA

CATHOLIC THOUGHT AND PAPAL JEWRY POLICY 1555-1593

Volume V in the **Moreshet** Series, Studies in
Jewish History, Literature and Thought

KBG
.S76

CATHOLIC THOUGHT AND PAPAL JEWRY POLICY 1555-1593

by Kenneth R. Stow

THE JEWISH THEOLOGICAL SEMINARY OF AMERICA
NEW YORK 1977

© Copyright 1977
The Jewish Theological Seminary of America

Library of Congress Cataloging in Publication Data

Stow, Kenneth R.
  Catholic thought and papal Jewry policy, 1555-1593.

  (Moreshet; 5)
  Bibliography: p.
  Includes index.
  1. Susannis, Marquardus de, d. 1578. De Iudaeis. 2.
Jews—Legal status, laws, etc. (Canon law) 3. Catholic
Church—Relations—Judaism. 4. Judaism—Relations—
Catholic Church. I. Title. II. Series: Moreshet (New
York); 5.
Law   262.9   76-55307
ISBN 0-87334-001-9

Distributed by KTAV Publishing House, Inc.
New York, New York 10013

Manufactured in the United States of America

To my parents

CONTENTS

CONTENTS

TABLE OF ABBREVIATIONS

KEY TO ROMAN AND CANON
LAW REFERENCES

Canon law—edited by E. Friedberg, *Corpus Iuris Canonici*—will be
cited, as will be Roman law also, by the traditional abbreviations.—For example,
Gratian's *Decretum:*

> Part 1:   D.1,c.1 (Distinctio 1, canon 1)
> Part 2:   C.1,q.1,c.1 (Causa 1, quaestio 1, canon 1) Causa
>   33, q.3 is known as *De Penitentia.* It is divided into
>   distinctions and canons.
>   D.1,c.1, *de pen.*
> Part 3:   D.1, c.1, *de cons.* (Dist. 1, can. 1, *De Consecra-*
>   *tione*)

Decretales of Gregory IX (*Liber Extra*): X.1,1,1 (*Lib. Extra,*
     Book 1, title, 1, canon 1)
Liber Sextus of Boniface VIII: *Sext.* 1,1,1 (same as *Decretales*)
Constitutiones of Clement V: *Clem.* 1,1,1 (same as *Decretales*)
Roman law—edited by Krueger-Mommsen, *Corpus Iuris Civilis*—
     Inst. 1,1 (*Institutes,* book 1, title 1)
     D. 1,1,1 (*Digest,* book 1, title 1, law 1) (ff.=D. in medieval
     citations)
     C. 1,1,1 (*Code,* and same as Digest)
     Nov. 1 (Novels, #1)
N.B., the editions of both Roman and Canon law are arranged ac-
     cording to the above system, and texts may be located by means
     of it.

PREFACE
AND INTRODUCTION

ONE OF THE MOST PERPLEXING issues with which the student of
medieval Jewish history must deal is that of the status of the Jews in
Western Christendom. On the surface it appears a simple matter.
The Jew was the deicide condemned to a marginal, if permitted,
existence. The Church sought to separate him from all significant
contact with Christians, as well as to restrain his exploitative economic behavior. To the secular leadership the Jew was an economic
resource, but one which was easily expendable should it outlive its
usefulness. The simplicity of these definitions is perhaps the source
of their great appeal—one feels tempted to say charm. Their exacti-
tude is another matter.

All our definitions of medieval life and society have in recent
years undergone redefinition. In particular, a number of works dealing with medieval legal theory have succeeded in reconstructing the
finer details of the shape of medieval society; and, more important,
they have elicited the conception contemporaries held at different
times during the Middle Ages of the right order and nature of their
society. It is, then, quite understandable that the picture of the
status of the Jew requires redefinition. Equally so, there is sufficient
reason to expedite this task by employing the same tools used in the
case of medieval society in general.

Yet with the exception of the essays of Vittore Colorni and
Walther Holtzmann,[1] medieval legal thought about the Jews has

---

1. V. Colorni, *Legge ebraica e legge locale* (Milan, 1945), and *Gli Ebrei
nel sistema del diritto comune* (Milan, 1956); and W. Holtzmann, "Zur päpstlichen
Gesetzgebung über die Juden im 12 Jahrhundert," in *Festschrift Guido Kisch*
(Stuttgart, 1955), pp. 217–35.

been generally ignored by modern scholars. Colorni has surveyed some of this thought in his discussion of Jews as citizens, in his discussion of Jewish legal and jurisdictional autonomy, and in his sketch of the overall place of the Jews in the system of Italian common law. Holtzmann's article traces the sources of the most prominent canons of the major medieval textbook of Church law, Gratian's *Decretum* (1144), which apply to the Jews. A thorough study of medieval legal thought about the Jews thus remains to be produced. As a first step toward such a study, the following examination of the synthetic legal tract of Marquardus de Susannis, the *De Iudaeis,* has been made. Additionally, an index of the legal sources of the *De Iudaeis* has been appended to this examination. These sources include approximately 150 laws and canons and 400 interpretations (some cited repeatedly) drawn from 100 different commentators. Together, these sources comprise the bulk of medieval thought on the legal status of the Jews.[2] Working from this index, the thorough study which is so much needed may eventually be completed.

But since most of history is filled with paradox, the *De Iudaeis,* which provides the basis for this present attempt at redefinition, is a product of the period of the Catholic Reformation. And the actual society spoken of will also be that of the later sixteenth century in Italy. Yet was not one of the significant acts of the Catholic Church at this time the reedition and publication of the medieval Canon law in what came to be known as the *Editio Romana* of Gregory XIII? And in the realm of legal study as a whole, was not the most typical product the synthetic tract, which gathered together and summarized the fruits of the legislation and commentary of previous centuries on specific topics? Accordingly, a legal tract on the status of the Jews written in 1558, which is what the *De Iudaeis* is, would not only define the legal status, or at least the ideal legal status, of the Jews at that moment, but it would also hold the materials to permit future definitions of the legal position of the Jews during earlier centuries.

---

2. This statement is, of course, limited to legal thought based on Roman and Canon law; it does not take into consideration such as Germanic, French, or English law.

Quite logically, then, the study of the Jews in medieval society, as revealed by contemporary legal sources, should begin with the *De Iudaeis*. Put simply, it tells us where to look.

The composition of the *De Iudaeis,* however, was no mere coincidence. It appeared nearly simultaneously with the bull *Cum nimis* of Paul IV, which, as will be seen, takes a revolutionary approach to the question of Jewry law. Only, this new approach can be, indeed has been, totally overlooked—because before the *De Iudaeis* is read, it is possible to skip over the crucial phrases found in the bull itself. My belief is that the *De Iudaeis* was written to preclude just this possibility. It is for this reason that the tract is so inviting. Not only is it the starting point for the study of the Jews in the thinking of medieval Roman and Canon lawyers—that is, for the redefinition of current views on the status of Jews in medieval society—but in itself it provides a perfect case in point, namely, that from the examination of this legal material it truly is possible to obtain conclusions which are not only more accurate, but, indeed, more convincing. Through the *De Iudaeis* the policies of Paul IV and his successors may be seen unerringly.

To provide a background and setting for the understanding of these new policies, a brief synopsis of the history of Italian Jewry will be helpful.[3] The oldest settlement of Jews in Italy was that of Rome, going back to the period of the Caesars. While it never went out of existence, it was not the most prominent Jewish community either in the early or the later Middle Ages. Through the eleventh century, the center of culture and leadership was the south in Sicily and in the region of the later Kingdom of Naples. The *Megillat Yuḥasin* of Ahimaaz ben Paltiel describes in vivid colors the transmission of traditional Jewish learning and culture from the older Palestinian and Babylonian centers and its subsequent digestion and embellishment at the hands of his ancestors, men who distinguished

---

3. For more information on the history of the Jews in Italy, see C. Roth, *A History of the Jews in Italy* (Philadelphia, 1946), M. A. Shulvass, *Jewish Life in Renaissance Italy* (Hebrew), (New York, 1955), S. Simonsohn, *Toldoth ha-Yehudim be-Dukhsuth Mantovah,* 2 vols. (Jerusalem, 1962-64), and A. Milano, *Storia degli Ebrei in Italia* (Turin, 1963).

themselves as scholars, communal judges, and equally as poets. In the twelfth and thirteenth centuries a number of luminaries appear at the Sicilian court, including such as Jacob Anatoli, known for his achievements in Aristotelian and Jewish philosophy. Sicilian Jewry was also known for its mastery of the art of cloth dyeing, for the practice of which it possessed a state-given monopoly. This artisanry likely typified most of Jewish economic life in all areas of settlement up to this time. In the later thirteenth and fourteenth centuries, the Roman community rises to a degree of cultural importance through the writings of such as Judah Romano, known for his philosophical studies and translations, and Emanuel HaRomi, whose rhymed prose fables and poetry, most notably the *Notebooks* (*Maḥberoth*), have variously been compared with the works of Boccaccio and Dante. Schools at Rome also went back into the earlier Middle Ages, their most famous product being the *Arukh,* a Talmudic lexicon, composed before 1101 by R. Natan b. Yehiel. It may further be safely said that the Jews at Rome had always played an important role as intermediaries and negotiators between various Jewish communities, including those outside Italy, and the papacy.

A turning point is perhaps to be identified in the slow settlement of the northern half of the Italian peninsula, commencing approximately in the mid to later thirteenth century, by individual Jews or by small groups. To this time, Jews had either shunned this region or had been prevented from settling there. Some cities, like Genoa, never really allowed what could be called a permanent Jewish settlement. What characterized these new settlements was that they usually arose as a result of a *condotta,* a contract, which stipulated that a Jew would be permitted to open a "store," that is, a loan-bank, in return for which the Jew agreed to remain in the city for a specified number of years. At its expiration date, the *condotta* was normally renegotiated and renewed, in a manner similar to the *condotta* given to the war-captain *condottiero.* Sometimes, however, the expiration of the *condotta* was exploited as an opportunity to get rid of the Jew(s), should such a notion have entered the minds of the town citizenry. These loan-bank–based settlements grew in number during the Renaissance period. In the larger cities, they also served as an entry wedge for the eventual growth of a sizable community.

By the mid-fourteenth century, the bulk of Italian Jewry was setled in central and northern Italy. Indeed, after 1492, when the Jews were expelled from Spanish Sicily, and 1511, when they were expelled from the then Spanish kingdom of Naples, there were no Jews in Italy except in the north and in the Papal States. While most large cities had Jews living in them, the most important communities were Rome, Mantua, and Venice. There was also a sizable group of ex-converts from Spain and Portugal in Ancona.

Further reinforcement for these communities came in the fourteenth and fifteenth centuries, when, partly as a result of flight from persecution, and partly as one element of the larger German commercial migration southward, German Jews came to settle in northeastern Italy. They added characteristically Ashkenazic (German Jewish) elements to both culture and economy. At the end of the fifteenth century a third element entered, Jews—along with Jews reconverted from Catholicism—fleeing after the 1492 expulsion from Spain. Italian Jewish society was now tri-cultural, and the breadth of that culture was remarkable. It included not only traditional rabbinic learning, but extended to belles-lettres, linguistics, philosophy, mysticism, and medicine.[4]

Most noteworthy of the products of this Jewish culture are the clearly discernible parallels and contacts between them and the products of secular Italian culture. Thus, it is not surprising that Judah Abravanel composed his *Dialoghi d'Amore* (late fifteenth century), a treatise on the philosophical (Platonic) aspects of love, in Italian, or that the physician David de Pomis (sixteenth century) wrote a Latin essay, the *Enarratio Apologica,* which displays a knowledge of Roman and Italian common law. Abravanel, moreover, together with Johannan Alemanno and Elijah del Medigo, was closely involved with the philosophical humanist circle surrounding Pico della Mirandola in Florence. Similarly, the historiography of Azariah de

---

4. For more detailed information on Italian Jewish culture, see esp. C. Roth, *The Jews in the Renaissance* (Philadelphia, 1959), passim, and particularly chaps. 4–6 and 13, and Milano, *Storia,* chaps. 8 and 9.

Rossi (*Me'or 'Eynayim,* 1579) reflects the nascent source critique and the first attempts to understand ancient events on their own terms, and not solely in terms of the moral lesson they conveyed, which characterized the best secular historiography of his day. Perhaps most illustrative, by 1475 two Hebrew books had already appeared in print, and by 1488 Gershon Soncino had brought out the *editio princeps* of the Hebrew Bible.

What proved the greatest stimulus for this culture, and likely also provided an important attraction pulling non-Italian Jews to migrate to Italy, was the relative freedom of movement and security of existence enjoyed there. This freedom is reflected in the fact that not only were Jews influenced by Italian culture, but Christians too felt free to learn from Jews. From the later fifteenth century numbers of Christians began to study Hebrew, even rabbinics, although not, to be sure, with the purpose of converting to Judaism. Most notably, Elijah del Medigo and Elia Levita served as teachers of Pico and Cardinal Egidio da Viterbo respectively. This is not the place to discuss at length the fruits of these cross-cultural contacts. But the preceding paragraphs do assuredly demonstrate that Jews had been able to integrate themselves into Italian culture and society in a way never surpassed and far from the norm in the course of Jewish history in Latin Europe. The one significant problem Jews in Italy had encountered was the preaching of certain Franciscans during the course of the fifteenth century: Bernardino da Siena (active 1405–44), Giovanni da Capistrano (1420s and 1430s), Bernardino da Feltre (1480s), and Bernardino da Busti (1490s). These men had literally rabble-roused against the Jews, calling them the enemies of Christianity and the robbers of Christians through usury. This incendiary preaching was certainly responsible in no small measure for the growth of a negative popular view of the Jews—one expressed most strongly, as will be seen, by de Susannis himself. Jews at times became the subject of suspicion, and ultimately were accused, as at Trent in 1475, of ritually killing Christian children. Still, this negative view did not bring fundamental alterations in the patterns of Jewish life and culture. Indeed, the leadership of Italian society, most notably the papacy, often spoke strongly in defence of the Jews. Martin V, for instance, issued letters in 1422 and 1429 denouncing unambiguously the uncanonical incitations on the part of the Franciscan preachers.[5]

In the light of these last remarks, the policy launched by Paul IV in 1555 comes as a shock—as it also shocked contemporary Jews. As a result of this new policy, which was, as will be seen, zealously and consistently furthered by Paul IV's successors, Italian Jewry in the latter half of the sixteenth century found itself shut within the walls of ghettoes and shorn of the cultural, economic, and personal privileges it had normally enjoyed.

The process of ghettoization had actually begun in 1516 in Venice. It was not, as is sometimes believed, a phenomenon of earlier medieval Europe, at least in a formal sense and as a widespread practice. The ghetto, as the Italian origin of the word indicates,[6] was an Italian institution. But while Venice may have taken the lead, it was Paul IV's action which created the ghetto in its most pejorative aspect and led directly to the establishment of other ghettoes. The ghetto in Venice, at least in its early decades, seems to have functioned primarily as a device for regulating residence, although the psychologically depressing effect it undoubtedly exercised on its inhabitants was surely great. Even so, Jewish commercial and cultural life in Venice remained largely intact and thriving through the seventeenth century. The Roman ghetto, on the other hand, brought with it a host of additional restrictions, which even before the sixteenth century ended, had choked off nearly all creativity on the part of Roman Jewry. Within a few decades this fate was shared by the Jewries of the many other Italian cities that slowly followed the lead of the papacy on both ghettoes and restrictions. Paul IV's 1555 bull, *Cum nimis,* thus marks a watershed with respect to internal Jewish life in Italy. Jewish writings from the later decades of the sixteenth century reflect, more often than not, only despair and pessimism. By the mid-seventeenth century, the flourishing culture described above had ground to a halt. It would not come to life again

---

5. For the texts of these letters, see M. Stern, *Urkundliche Beiträge über die Stellung der Päpste zu den Juden* (Kiel, 1893), pp. 30 f. and 38 f.

6. See Milano, *Storia,* pp. 525 f.

until the mid-nineteenth century, as late as 1870 in Rome, when the ghettoes were at long length abolished.

Cum nimis also posed a threat of a unique nature to the very existence of the Italian Jews. For 1555 proved a departure from a tradition of a papal-Jewish relationship that had consistently rested on the notion that while the Jews were to be restricted and to be prohibited from causing damage to the Christian faith, they were also to be allowed to live freely in Christian lands and to practice their Judaism, irrespective, in fact, in spite of their unwillingness to accept Christianity. It is, therefore, worth glancing at the outlines of that relationship, as it developed from the late-sixth-century papacy of Gregory the Great.[7]

The history of the relationship between the Jews and the papacy is not, of a certainty, the history of the Church and the Jews in the broadest sense of the term *Church.* Various bodies or individuals, who collectively comprised the Church, approached the Jews from often radically opposing points of view. Bishops in seventh-century Spain sought to rid Spanish society of Jews through forced conversion, while their counterparts in the eleventh-century Rhineland tried, albeit unsuccessfully, to save Jews from the same fate, and outright slaughter too, during the First Crusade. The accusations of sorcery and black magic made by the late-eleventh-century abbot, Guibert of Nogent, clash with the willing use of Jewish economic skills and fruits by numerous monasteries, including St. Denis, which in the later eleventh and twelfth centuries held a royal grant to collect the rents and taxes which normally would have gone into the royal treasury. Similarly, in the mid-thirteenth century, Thomas of Aquinas presented a balanced picture of toleration and restriction, while his contemporary, the theologian Duns Scotus, favored removing Jewish children forcibly from their parents to save them through baptism. Nevertheless, as the formal executive and legislative—and

---

7. For a more complete description of papal Jewry policy, see E. Synan, *The Popes and the Jews in the Middle Ages* (New York, 1965). S. Grayzel, *The Church and the Jews in the Thirteenth Century* (Philadelphia, 1933), and idem, "The Papal Bull *Sicut Judaeis,*" in *Studies and Essays in Honor of A. Neuman,* ed. M. Ben-Horin et al. (Leiden, 1962), pp. 243–80.

theological—center of the Church, it was the papacy which established what, for want of a better word, may be called the official policy toward the Jews. And it was to the papacy that Jews, from all the countries of Latin Europe, turned in times of crisis and threat to secure guarantees against attacks.

In a *de facto* sense, the traditional papal policy originated in the administrative decisions made by Gregory the Great (590–604) concerning those Jews who lived on papal estates. In these decisions he applied the principle, laid down in the Theodosian Code,[8] that while the Jews were to enjoy the protection of law, they were not to exceed the privileges the law granted them. Gregory's formulation, preserved in his letters,[9] was adopted by Calixtus II in 1119 when he was called upon to issue a bull of protection for Roman Jewry. And Calixtus' letter, in turn, became the basis for similar letters issued by nearly every medieval pope,[10] absorbed into the Canon law,[11] and known appropriately as the *Constitutiones pro Iudaeis*.[12]

The key clauses in these constitutions—which, it must be noted, emphasized restrictions no less than privileges, and therefore made room for, if they did not actually presuppose, a whole body of such restrictions—stated:

> . . . Just as license ought not to be granted the Jews to do in their synagogues more than the law permits them, just so they ought not to suffer curtailment in those (privileges) which have been conceded them. That is why, although they prefer to remain hardened in their obstinacy rather than acknowledge the prophetic

8. C.T. (*Code of Theodosian*), bk. 16, title 8, laws 18 and 20.

9. For this text in translation, see J. R. Marcus, *The Jew in the Medieval World* (Philadelphia, 1937), p. 113.

10. X.5,6,8 *sicut*.

11. The text of Innocent III's *Constitutio*, for example, repeats Clement III's bull verbatim. Innocent III himself states in *Licet* that he is adhering to the practice of Calixtus III, Eugenius III, Alexander III, Clement III, and Coelestine III.

12. The *Constitutiones pro Iudaeis* are known as the *Sicut Iudaeis* bulls because they all begin with, or contain a clause opening with, these words. See S. Grayzel, "The Papal Bull *Sicut Judeis*," pp. 243–80, for a full discussion of these bulls, and esp. p. 244, where Grayzel notes that *Sicut* was issued by six popes in the twelfth century, by ten in the thirteenth, by four in the fourteenth, and by three in the fifteenth.

words and the eternal secrets of their own Scriptures, that they
might thus arrive at the understanding of Christianity and Salvation, nevertheless, in view of the fact that they begged for our
protection and aid, and in accordance with the clemency that
Christian piety imposes, we . . . grant their petition and offer them
the shield of our protection.[13]

The constitutions then continued by upholding the principle, also
found in the Theodosian Code, that Jews may live unmolested in
Christian lands and may freely observe the rituals of Judaism.[14]
Christians were furthermore admonished to refrain from the use of
force in converting Jews to Christianity, while the Jews in turn were
instructed to observe the precepts and abide by the restrictions of
Jewry law.

But, as is at once apparent from the second clause (beginning
with, "that is why, although"), the constitutions also laid down a
policy on conversion. It was clearly most desirable, but the basic
privilege of toleration was to be granted irrespective of current Jewish acceptance of Christianity. Rather, as other papal letters which
touch the subject of conversion elaborate, it was not even to be expected in the near future, nor was any definite action proposed, let
alone a formal program, to bring large groups or the mass of the
Jews into the Christian fold.

In 1205, for instance, in a bull concerning Jewish usury and
Jews serving as witnesses, Innocent III wrote to the king of France
that:

It does not displease the Lord, but it is, rather, acceptable to Him,
that, under Catholic kings and Christian princes, lives and serves
the dispersion of the Jews, whose remnant, *at length,* will be
saved.[15]

---

13. This translation is taken from the bull *Licet* of Innocent III (Sept. 15,
1199) as found in Grayzel, *The Church and the Jews,* p. 93. The Latin text is
found on p. 92 in Grayzel. See also A. Potthast, *Regesta Pontificum Romanorum,*
2 vols. (Berlin, 1875), no. 834.

14. C.T. 16,8,21.

15. Potthast, no. 2373; Grayzel, *The Church,* p. 104. *Etsi non displiceat,* Jan.
16, 1205: "Non displiceat Domino, sed ei potius sit acceptum ut sub catholicis

As far as Innocent III was concerned, large-scale or mass conversion would occur only "at length," in the distant future. He gave no indication that it was a goal to be achieved through current programs.

In 1236 Gregory IX granted privileges to two recent converts from Judaism. In this grant he stated:

> Even though we open the womb of paternal piety to all who come to the Christian faith, since we are fondly disposed toward the salvation of all men, nevertheless, we embrace with particular love converts from Judaism.[16]

He said nothing, however, about acting or establishing policy, to insure the conversion of more Jews. Further, on September 5, 1236, in response to the massacre of twenty-five hundred Jews on the pretext that they refused baptism, Gregory IX wrote to the prelates of France that such acts must not go unpunished, for:

> From their [the Jews'] archives, testimony of the Christian faith appears; and, as the prophet testifies, if they were as the sands of the sea, their remnant, at length, will be saved, . . . because the Lord will not forever spurn His people.[17]

Thus, while Gregory desired conversion, it was his implicit assumption that mass conversion was a matter of prophecies to be fulfilled sometime in the future. Indeed, further along in the same letter

---

regibus et principibus christianis vivat et serviat dispersio Iudaeorum, cuius tunc tandem reliquie salve fiant." N.b., Grayzel translates *tandem* as "end of days." In support of Grayzel's translation, see pp. 242–73, infra, where the doctrine that the mass conversion of the Jews will occur at the time of the Second Coming is discussed at length. See also pp. 130–48, infra, where the presence of this doctrine in the *De Iudaeis* is discussed.

16. L'Auvray, *Les Registres de Gregoire IX,* 3 vols. (Paris, 1899–1908), no. 3144; or Grayzel, p. 222. *Etsi universis,* May 5, 1236: "Etsi universis qui ad fidem veniunt Christianam aperiamus paterne viscera pietatis cum salutem omnium affectemus carius tamen amplectimur de Judaismo conversos."

17. Potthast, no. 10243; Auvray, no. 3308; or Grayzel, p. 226. *Lachrymabilem:* ". . . ex archivis ipsorum Christianae fidei testimonia prodierunt, et propheta testante, si fuerint velut arena maris, ipsorum tandem reliquie salve fient, . . . quoniam non repellet in sempiternum Dominus plebem suam; . . . non sunt ad baptismi gratiam, nisi sponte voluerint, compellendi. . . ."

he noted that none are "to be compelled to the grace of baptism unless they seek it voluntarily." Yet he added nothing about a program to seek such voluntary converts.

In contrast with this attitude of passivity, on August 4, 1278, Nicholas III published *Vineam sorec.*[18] This bull was sent to Dominicans and Franciscans in various locations,[19] instructing them that the papacy freely seeks labors, "Pro illius populi (Iudaei) obcaecatione," and ordering them to preach the Gospel to the Jews. It thus seems that Nicholas was making a serious effort to convert Jews. Why he was doing so is an open question, although he may have been responding to a request made by the Dominicans and Franciscans themselves. These two orders, particularly in Spain, were engaged in active missionizing. There is, however, nothing in *Vineam sorec* to indicate that Nicholas III himself was intent on altering the policies of his predecessors on the subject of conversion.[20] For he may have ordered the friars to preach; but he revealed a lack of commitment and a firm policy in that he did not compel the Jews to attend these sermons. He merely requested that the friars inform him if Jews stayed away, and he would then think of a remedy.[21]

Still, Nicholas III was undoubtedly making some conversionary efforts. And it is possible that ten years later, Nicholas IV was at least retaining the spirit of his predecessor when he referred to the Church's hope for the illumination of the Jews and forbade attacks on Jews, which he considered counter-productive to conversion. But here, despite the allusion to conversionary hopes, Nicholas IV was in actuality returning to the traditional passive expectation. Conversion was not to be hindered; it was, on the contrary, to be welcomed. But nothing specific was to be undertaken to forward it.[22] Simi-

---

18. *B.R.*, 4:45 f.

19. P. Browe. *Die Judenmission in Mittelalter und die Päpste* (Rome, 1942), pp. 28–31.

20. Ibid., pp. 28–31. This bull is also the only evidence which Browe adduces relating Nicholas III to conversion.

21. *B.R.*, 4:45: "Sed si forte, quod absit, aliqui ex ipsis in eorum obstinata perfidia perdurantes . . . ne tui . . . vocem audiant . . . nobis rescribere non omittas, ut circa pertinaces huiusmodi, sicut expedire videbimus."

22. *Orat mater Ecclesia* (1288), in E. Langlois, *Les Registres de Nicolaus IV*

larly, John XXII spoke of conversion in *Cum sit absurdum* (June 19, 1320),[23] but only with the object of securing the material well-being of individual converts. And in 1365 Urban V renewed the *Constitutio pro Iudaeis* in his bull *Sicuti Iudaeis,* employing the same formula used by his predecessor, "Although, etc." [24]

In 1425, however, in the proemium of *Sedes Apostolica pietatis,* which orders the Jews to wear a distinguishing habit, Martin V inserted a new phrase. He declared that Christian piety receives the Jews in Christian lands, and "it is known to sustain them with the hope that they convert." [25] This phrase undeniably conveys a greater sense of immediacy of expectation than does the mechanically repeated prophecy of ultimate salvation found in earlier bulls. It even implies a possible connection between the privilege of toleration and the movement of the Jews toward Christianity. Nevertheless, Martin V never acted in accordance with this implication. He was not even consistent in implementing the edicts of the bull in which it was found. Soon after, he exempted the Jews of Ferrara from its requirements.[26] A certain proof that Martin V in no way intended to pursue conversion systematically appears in a letter he wrote in March 1422 in response to complaints by Jews that they had suffered injury as a result of Dominican and Franciscan sermons which called for the complete isolation of Jews from Christians. Such sermons must cease, he wrote, for through them "cause is given to those Jews who would perhaps convert to the Christian faith, if they were treated

---

(Paris, 1886), p. 93: "Orat mater pro subducendo velamine . . . ut . . . Christum illuminate agnoscant, . . . propter quod ipsa ecclesia non tolerat . . . , ut Iudaeos iniuriis . . . (Christiani) afficiant . . ."

23. *B.R.,* 4:294. See also the translated excerpts from all of John XXII's Jewry bulls printed by Grayzel, "References to the Jews in the Correspondence of John XXII," *Hebrew Union College Annual* 23 pt. 2 (1950–51): 37–80. None of these bulls initiate efforts to seek converts.

24. *B.R.,* 4:523.

25. *B.R.,* 4:718: "Illos sub spe conversionis eorumdem noscitur sustinere."

26. Cf. infra, the analysis of *De Iudaeis* pt. 1, chap. 4, and the *consilium* of R. Fulgosius presented there. Cf. also the excerpts from eighty-four letters pertaining to Jews issued by Martin V in F. Vernet, "Le Pope Martin V et Les Juifs," *Revue des Questions Historiques* 51 (1892): 409–23. None of these letters initiate efforts to promote conversion.

with piety and humanity, to remain strong in their perfidy . . ." The
Jews as a whole, he added, would convert only in the distant future
(tandem).[27] Clearly, this letter expresses the conclusion of the late-
sixth-century Gregory the Great, who had written that kindness
alone would encourage conversions.[28] But Gregory had also supported conversionary preaching.[29] Martin V, in opposition, had
ordered the cessation of sermons, which may possibly have had
some conversionary value.[30]

The policy of passive expectation, of hope but little else, continued for the next 125 years. With Paul IV, however, all this would
change radically; and it is because of this change that I have brought
so many examples from his predecessors to demonstrate their lack
of activity when it came to the question of pursuing conversion.
Quite the opposite, all of Paul's IV's actions concerning Jews were
predicated on their conversionary efficacy. Indeed, and truly crucial,
while Paul IV did not go so far as to stipulate that should the Jews
fail to convert, they would cease to be tolerated—albeit he suggested
as much, and albeit two of his successors, Pius V and Clement VIII,
did go that far on a limited scale—he did reverse the stand of all
previous popes on the issue of the link between toleration and conversion. Henceforth Jews would be tolerated so that they could be
constantly and actively pressed to convert. From the time of Paul IV
and during the succeeding three hundred years, the papacy would
indeed pursue an active missionary policy, and with no small success. In this way the policy of Paul IV did most certainly threaten
Jewish existence.

---

27. O. Raynaldus, *Annales Ecclesiastici,* ed. J. D. Mansi (Lucca, 1752),
8:560, prints this letter, but without the above-cited clause, which appears in the
copy found in Stern, *Urkundiche Beiträge,* p. 32. Perhaps the time of composition
of the *Annales,* the later sixteenth century (it concludes with the year 1557), when
Jewry policy was the precise opposite of that espoused here, explains this dele-
tion. "Daturque materia Iudaeis ipsis, qui se forsan ad Christianam fidem converterent, si pie et humane tractarentur, in eorundem perfidia perdurandi . . ."
(Mar. 10, 1422).

28. See B. Blumenkranz, *Les auteurs chrétiens latins du Moyen Age sur les
juifs* (Paris, 1963), #73, p. 78.

29. Ibid., #90, p. 84.

30. Cf. p. 379, infra, on the mendicant preachers and their sermons.

Paul IV also went beyond, if he did not actually reverse, the policies of his predecessors in the matter of the restrictions to be placed on Jews. This does not mean that he violated, by arbitrary limitations, the bounds of the canons restricting the behavior of the Jews. No pope, as surprising as this may seem, had ever gone that far. Nor does this mean that Paul IV was the first to apply the Jewry canons with rigor. The popes of the thirteenth century had applied them quite forcefully. But they had done so, on the one hand, in line with the need to establish norms which, following the *Constitutio pro Iudaeis,* would properly restrict the Jews to balance their broad grant of toleration. On the other hand, and perhaps more importantly, the canons dealing with the Jews were enforced as a part of the papacy's overall program of institutional and legal reform, which would, at last, establish the proper relationships between the many elements within the Church and bind them through a universally valid Church law.

Thus there should be no surprise in the fact that, with the exception of the rule concerning special Jewish garb, there is nothing concerning Jews in the conciliar edicts or the letters of the thirteenth-century popes that had not been previously edicted numerous times, in the decrees of regional councils or in the canons of local Church law collections from the sixth century and on. Even the decree of the 1215 Fourth Lateran Council on Jewish dress is not, as is normally thought, a part of a new program to segregate Jews, but a new means—borrowed from long-standing Muslim practice at that—to prevent the insult to baptism which was incurred when a Jew and a Christian had sexual relations.[31] From the time of the Theodosian and Justinianic Codes, the gravest offense a Jew could commit against Christianity was insult.[32]

---

31. On insult resulting from sexual relations, see infra, p. 93f. To the possible objection that I have omitted mention of the attack on the Talmud, I reply that the major concern for the papacy there was blasphemy, an old source of irritation with Jews. More important, a great deal of doubt must arise concerning the degree of papal involvement in the whole episode. The papal letters dealing with the Talmud in the 1240s all display only the vaguest knowledge of what the Talmud was, and in all cases are basically responses to what had been reported from Paris.

32. See esp. chap. 4, infra, for a full discussion of this point.

Yet the thirteenth-century papacy was also highly involved in the eradication of heresy, and it would be foolhardy to suggest that this project had no repercussions vis-à-vis the Jews. But the eradication of heresy may only be fully understood as a part of the overall papal reforms. The same must be said of the papal policy toward the Jews. The thirteenth century marks a culmination and not a beginning. The thirteenth-century popes were now scrupulously applying throughout the Church regulations that had developed locally and disjointedly in the course of the previous six or seven centuries.

What marked papal policy toward the Jews, then, was a basic consistency in observing the principle of toleration, but equally in demanding that the Jews submit to canonical regulations. It was only in the early fifteenth century that the pattern became somewhat erratic. From that point on, nearly every one of the popes appears culpable of arbitrary reversals of course, especially toward the Jews of Italy, vacillating between clear-cut dispensations from canonical regulations, on the one hand, and overly severe applications of the same canons, on the other—usually with no palpable explanation for the shifts. The height of laxity came in the early sixteenth century, with popes like Leo X employing Jewish physicians and even granting them the right to hold teaching positions at various universities. Italian Jews moved about nearly free from the social limitations on fraternization prescribed by the canons. Furthermore, while it is true that there were certain signs which pointed to an imminent change as the Church began to reexamine itself in the light of the upheavals of the early sixteenth century, the tolerable conditions of Jewish life under papal regulation prevailed nearly unscathed up to 1555 and the issuance of the bull *Cum nimis* by Paul IV.

What *Cum nimis* did, however, was not merely to put an end to the inconsistencies and leniencies of the previous century and a half. It did not merely reestablish the rigorous enforcement of prior regulations. *Cum nimis* went beyond this, without introducing new legislation or violating older laws, by carrying the implications of existing canons to their ultimate limits. If Jews and Christians were not to fraternize, then the Jews must live in a ghetto. If Jews were not to be the masters of Christians, then they must not be allowed to own land within Christendom or to be dignified with titles of honor and nobility. These, and more—as will be seen.

Yet it was not alone this new level of restriction or the new attitude toward conversion that made the actions of Paul IV so revolutionary. Rather, it was the combination of these two in such a way as to create a truly conversionary policy that brought about the radical break. The details of this new turn, the way in which new attitudes and new restrictions were combined to create the new policy, will be at the center of the following study.

A word of caution is, however, in order. This study seeks to understand the new policy of Paul IV and a large body of the contemporary literature that amplifies on it—in particular, the *De Iudaeis* of Marquardus de Susannis, whose contents have made it possible to see the intrinsic unity and integrity of everything else to be discussed. This study does not purport to be a reexamination of the history of later-sixteenth-century Italian Jewry, nor a political history documenting the day-by-day prosecution of the new papal policy. Bulls of other sixteenth-century popes are brought in only to show that Paul's IV's decrees were not shots in the dark, heard once to disappear and be forgotten seconds later. Rather, they introduced fundamental changes, which represent the end of a tradition that had commenced with Gregory I in the sixth century and was now, one thousand years later, to be replaced with a new one. Indeed, as will be seen, Paul IV's successors did not abandon his programs, but enhanced and elaborated on them. To understand the basic lines and the motivation behind such a major turn has seemed to me a sufficiently broad scope for this study. This is especially so considering that this understanding has demanded a rigorous introduction to the whole problem of the Jews in medieval law.

A second caution is perhaps equally appropriate. Since the Jewry policy of later-sixteenth-century popes quite obviously is but one part of the overall restructuring which occurred within the Catholic Church of that time, any discussion of the motivations behind that policy will, of necessity, reflect on the overall motivations impelling contemporary popes to act as they did. Yet if this discussion does raise issues concerning the nature of the Reformation Church, it will do so only incidentally, and with no purposeful intent of making a statement about that Church. The purpose behind this study is to examine the relationship between the Jews, the sixteenth-century papacy, and medieval law.

All responsibility for what I will say in this study is, of course, mine. But I must thank with the greatest of feeling those who helped and encouraged me in the course of my work. Professor Gerson Cohen of the Jewish Theological Seminary has guided me from the inception of this project and has tirelessly reread the manuscript and given valuable aid. The manuscript, at various stages of preparation, has also been read with helpful comments by Professors Zvi Ankori, Isaac Barzillay, Robert Somerville, and Arthur Schiller of Columbia University and by Professor Amos Funkenstein of UCLA. Sound advice has also been offered by Professor John Mundy of Columbia. To the staffs of the libraries and archives at Columbia University, the Jewish Theological Seminary, Union Theological Seminary, the Hebrew University, the Vatican, the Vicariate of Rome, and the City of Udine, I owe my deepest gratitude. Special thanks are owed to Mrs. Harriet Catlin of the Jewish Theological Seminary, who was most gracious in overseeing the many details of publication. The National Foundation for Jewish Culture was also kind enough to help me twice in the course of my research. My greatest appreciation goes to my wife, Sandra, who labored with me and gave me unending support at those moments when it was most needed.

KENNETH R. STOW
The Jewish Theological Seminary
April 1975   of America

PART ONE

The New Policy

CHAPTER I

THE NEW POLICY

JULY 17, 1555 HAS TRADITIONALLY been designated as a major turning point in the history of Judaeo-papal relations. On this date the newly elected pope, Paul IV (G. P. Carafa),[1] issued the bull *Cum nimis absurdum.*[2] Besides renewing all the restrictions established by previous papal Jewry legislation, this bull also required, for the first time in the Papal States, that all Jews live in an enforced ghetto, that they sell all their real property to Christians, and that they limit their commercial activity with Christians in the sphere of the necessities of life (i.e., food and clothing) to the selling of second-hand clothes (*strazzaria*).[3] These provisions and restrictions were put into effect, and over the next fifty years they became standard within the Papal States, to endure for more than three hundred years. The issuance of *Cum nimis* thus brought to an end the poli-

---

1. Gian Pietro Carafa was elected pope on May 23, 1555. *Bullarium Diplomatum et Privilegiorum Sanctorum Romanorum Pontificum, Taurensis Editio,* ed. F. Gaude (Augustae Taurinorum, 1860), 6:499. Hereafter cited as *B.R.*

2. Ibid., 6:498–500.

3. Ibid., pars. 1 and 9. Par. 9 has usually been interpreted to mean that the commercial activity of Jews was restricted to dealing solely in used or second-hand clothing; e.g., I. Sonne, ed., *Mi-Pavolo ha-Revi'i 'ad Pius ha-Ḥamishi* (Jerusalem, 1954), p. 11. However, the wording of this clause: "Iudaei . . . sole arte strazzariae . . . contenti, aliquam mercaturam frumenti . . . aut aliarum rerum usui humano necessarium facere . . . nequeant . . . ," argues for my more restricted interpretation. In support of this interpretation, cf. Marquardus de Susannis, *De Iudaeis et Aliis Infidelibus* (Venice, 1558), pt. 1, chap. 4, pars. 9–13.

cies of generally mild treatment which the Jews living under direct papal dominion had almost invariably enjoyed.[4]

Paul IV's policy toward the Jews has regularly been explained[5] as an outgrowth of the repressive measures that typified the Catholic Restoration.[6] It is asserted that just as the Church used such measures to protect Catholic orthodoxy by erecting a barrier between Catholics and Protestants, so too the Church, and Paul IV in particular, sought to protect Catholic orthodoxy by erecting a barrier between Catholics and Jews.[7] Yet, as has been cogently argued, the Catholic Restoration ought not be seen merely as a series of repressive measures taken by the Church to defend itself against Protestantism.[8] The Catholic Reformation was both a reaction to enable the Church to deal with a changing world order and a movement

---

4. On the vicissitudes of the Jews living under papal rule, which were marked by frequently granted dispensations from the more rigorous ordinances of canon Jewry law (see n. 9, infra), alternating with occasional attempts at rigorous enforcement, cf. S. W. Baron, *A Social and Religious History of the Jews*, 2d ed. (Philadelphia, 1957–70), vols. 4, 5, 9, & 14 (hereafter cited as *SRH*); and L. Erler, "Die Juden des Mittelalters: Die Päpste und die Juden," *Archiv für Katholisches Kirchenrecht* 53 (1885): 1–70, for a synthetic treatment of this subject, based on the interpretation of medieval bulls dealing with Jews; and also E. Rodochanachi, *Le St. Siège et les Juifs* (Paris, 1891). For the Jews in the Papal States immediately preceding 1555, see especially C. Roth, *The Jews in the Renaissance (Philadelphia,* 1959), passim, and M. Shulvass, *Jewish Life in Renaissance Italy* (Hebrew) (New York, 1955), passim.

5. The various studies that deal with the Jewry policy of Paul IV are: *SRH*, 14, chap. 1; A. Berliner, *Geschichte der Juden in Rom* (Frankfurt, 1893), 2:111 ff., U. Cassuto, *Gli Ebrei a Firenze nell'età del Rinascimento* (Florence, 1918), pp. 90–95; A. Milano, *Il Ghetto di Roma* (Rome, 1964), pp. 71–76; E. Rodochanachi, *Le St. Siège;* C. Roth, *Renaissance;* idem, *The History of the Jews in Italy (Philadelphia,* 1946). pp. 296–98; M. Shulvass, *Jewish Life,* pp. 195–98; S. Simonsohn, *Toldoth ha-Yehudim be-Dukhsuth Mantovah* (Jerusalem, 1962–64), 2:18–20; I. Sonne, *Mi-Pavolo;* and H. Vogelstein, *Rome,* trans. M. Hadas (Philadelphia, 1940), pp. 267–69.

6. For this term, see Baron, *SRH,* 14, chap. 1. It has been adopted because of its neutrality. However, in appropriate places the terms *Counter-Reformation* and *Catholic Reformation* will be applied.

7. See esp. Sonne, *Mi-Pavolo,* pp. 9–10, 26–31.

8. W. Bouwsma, *Venice and the Defence of Republican Liberties* (Berkeley, 1968), pp. 296 ff. Bouwsma claims that the repression of the Counter-Reformation was the outward symptom of a Church which had fallen victim to the disease of insecurity and hoped to cure itself of this disease by means of repressive measures.

of inner restructuring and renewal. Nowhere is this argument more valid than in the case of the Jewry policy[9] initiated by Paul IV and pursued by the remaining popes of the Catholic Restoration. The goal of this policy, I hope to show, was not to segregate Jews from Catholics; it was, rather, to convert the Jews *en masse*.

That the sixteenth-century papacy had organized a mission to the Jews on a greater scale than ever before is not a new discovery. Although Browe, in his overall survey of medieval proselytizing efforts directed toward the Jews, does not explicitly compare sixteenth-century missionary activity with the activity of previous centuries, his list of later-sixteenth-century missionary endeavors leaves no doubt that the papacy was never more intent on converting the Jews than it was in that period.[10] By its very title, *Ursprung und Anfängstatigkeit der ersten Päpstlichen Missioninstituts, ein Beitrag zur Geschichte der katholische Juden und Mohammedanermission im sechzehnten Jahrhundert*,[11] K. W. Hoffmann's book indicates that in the sixteenth century the papacy developed conversionary machinery on a previously unknown level. And the text of the book supports the claim of its title. Both Hoffmann and Browe, however, fail to see that conversion was not only a major part of papal Jewry policy in the later sixteenth century, but it was the core to which all of Jewry policy was united.

The centrality of a conversionary goal is revealed most clearly in the bull *Cum nimis* itself, and especially in its proemium.

> *Since it is absurd and improper that Jews*—whose own guilt has consigned them to perpetual servitude—*under the pretext that Christian piety receives them and tolerates their presence, should be ingrates to Christians, so that they attempt to exchange the servitude they owe to Christians for dominion over them; we*—to whose notice it has lately come that these Jews, in our dear City

---

9. This is an adaptation of Kisch's term *Jewry law*. Jewry law and Jewry policy refer to policies applied to the Jews, in distinction to Jewish law and Jewish policy, meaning laws and policies devised and applied by the Jews themselves.

10. P. Browe, *Die Judenmission in Mittelalter und die Päpste* (Rome, 1942), passim, and esp. pp. 39–50.

11. Munster, 1923.

and in some other cities, lands, and places of the Holy Roman
Church, have erupted into insolence: they presume not only to
dwell side by side with Christians and near their Churches, with
no distinct habit to separate them, but even to erect homes in the
more noble sections and streets of the cities, lands, and places
where they dwell, and to buy and possess fixed property, and to
have nurses, housemaids, and other hired Christian servants, and
to perpetrate many other things in ignominy and contempt of the
Christian name—*considering that the Roman Church tolerates
the Jews in testimony of the true Christian faith and to the end
[ad hoc, ut] that they, led by the piety and kindness of the Apostolic See, should at length recognize their errors, and make all
haste to arrive at the true light of the Catholic faith,* and thereby
[*propterea*] to agree that, as long as they persist in their errors,
they should recognize through experience that they have been
made slaves while Christians have been made free through Jesus
Christ, God and our Lord, and likewise recognize that it is iniquitous that the children of the free women should serve the
children of the maid-servant,—*and, desiring to make sound provisions* as best we can—with the help of God—*in the above
matter,* we *sanction,* by this our perpetually valid constitution,
that [ghettoes be established, etc.].[12]

---

12. *B.R.,* 6:498: "Cum nimis absurdum et inconveniens existat ut iudaei,
quos propria culpa perpetuae servituti submisit, sub praetextu quod pietas christiana
illos receptet et eorum cohabitationem sustineat, christianis adeo sint ingrati, ut,
eis pro gratia, contumeliam reddant, et in eos, pro servitute, quam illis debent,
dominatum vendicare procurent; nos, ad quorum notitiam nuper devenit eosdem
iudaeos in alma urbe nostra et nonnullis S.R.E. civitatibus, terris et locis, in
id insolentiae prorupisse, ut non solum mixtim cum christianis et prope eorum
ecclesias, nulla intercedente habitus distinctione, cohabitare, verum etiam domos
in nobilioribus civitatum terrarum et locorum, in quibus degunt, vicis et plateis
conducere, et bona stabilia comparare et possidere, ac nutrices et ancillas aliosque
servientes christianos mercenarios habere, et diversa alia in ignominiam et contemptum christiani nominis perpetrare praesumant, considerantes Ecclesiam
Romanam eosdem iudaeos tolerare in testimoniam verae fidei christianae et ad
hoc, ut ipsi Sedis Apostolicae pietate et benignitate allecti, errores suos tandem
recognoscant, et ad verum catholicae fidei lumen pervenire satagant, et propterea
convenire ut quamdiu in eorum erroribus persistunt, effectu operis recognoscant
se servos, christianos vero liberos per Iesum Christum, Deum et Dominum
nostrum effectos fuisse, iniquumque existere ut filii liberae filiis famulentur an-

To paraphrase, Paul IV has stated that since it is absurd that Jews acquire dominion over Christians, he has sanctioned the following edicts, "considering" first, that the Church tolerates the Jews so that it can lead them to convert; second, that conversion will, or at least should, follow upon the Jews' assent and agreement that the prophecies of Jewish servitude[13] have been fulfilled.[14] Both by its syntax and in context, the first of these ideas reveals that in Paul IV's estimation, Church Jewry policy must have as its on-going basis the pursuit of the conversion of the Jews. For Paul IV stated that he is issuing the following edicts considering—as the basis for issuing them—that the goal of toleration is conversion. He did not state, moreover, that the Church tolerates the Jews *because* they will eventually convert; rather, he stated that the Church tolerates the Jews

cillae. Volentes in praemissis, quantum cum Deo possumus, salubriter providere, hac nostra perpetuo valitura constitutione sancimus quod de cetero. . . ."

To insure the enforcement of this bull, Paul IV issued letters on Aug. 19, 1555 (see *ASV, Arm.* 42, vol. 6, #183), and Aug. 26, 1556 (see *ASV, Arm.* 42, vol. 8, #375), the first calling for general implementation and the second for the implementation of the clauses forbidding private property.

13. The image to express Jewish servitude used here by Paul IV is that of Ishmael the son of Hagar, the serving-maid, and Isaac, the son of Sarah, the mistress and free-woman. Paul IV selected this particular image, which is based on the statement of Paul in Gal. 4:24–25, because, as will be seen momentarily, he had modeled *Cum nimis* in part on the canon *Etsi,* which also used this image to express the concept of Jewish servitude. But this image was only one of many interchangeable ones, the most well known being that of Esau and Jacob (based on Rom. 9:12), used to express this concept. Since, moreover, Gen. 25:23 (cited in Rom. 9:13) spoke of the elder (Esau, Ishmael, etc.) serving the younger (Jacob, Isaac), and the elder became identified with the synagogue and the younger with the Church, these images together were considered prophecies of Jewish servitude to the Church. For a detailed exposition of this matter, see G. D. Cohen, "Esau as Symbol," in *Jewish Medieval and Renaissance Studies,* ed. A. Altmann (Cambridge, 1967), pp. 31–38, and esp. 32–34.

14. In detail, the clause can be read: The Church tolerates the Jews to the end that they agree (i.e., assent) that as long as they remain Jews, they must recognize through experience that the prophecies of servitude have been fulfilled. The emphasis is on "agree" (assent). They must not only recognize that they are *servi,* they must also assent to the fact that they must so recognize their condition. In other words, the Church tolerates the Jews so that it can lead them to agree that the prophecies of servitude have been fulfilled. And structurally such assent is assumed either to precede or be concomitant with their conversion.

so that (*ad hoc, ut*) they can be led to convert, thereby indicating
an on-going commitment to conversionary activity. Then, when he
introduced the second idea and proceeded to issue edicts which do
indeed make the Jews experience servitude, he was surely indicating
that while he did intend to end Jewish dominion over Christians,
he was pursuing this intention only as a means to reaching his ultimate goal. And that was to gain the conversion of the Jews by making them assent to the fact that the prophecies of servitude had indeed been fulfilled. Apparently—although it is impossible to explain
why on the sole basis of the legal restrictions themselves, for after
all, the Church had demanded for centuries that the Jews must live
in "servitude," that is, in an inferior status to Christians—Paul IV
believed that by fixing the Jews in an all-encompassing status of
servitude, he would convince them that the prophecies of servitude
(and thence every other prophecy about Christ and about the
punishment of the Jews for rejecting Christ) had been fulfilled; at
which point the Jews would convert.

To insure that nobody would miss the intent of *Cum nimis,*
Paul IV relied not only on the actual wording of his text, but he
carefully modeled it on the canon *Etsi Iudaeos.*[15] This canon, orig-

---

15. *Corpus Iuris Canonici,* ed. E. Friedberg (Leipzig 1879 and 1881),
X.5,6,13. (Henceforth, all citations to canon *and* civil law will, as usual, refer to
location only. The texts of the canons may be found in Friedberg, and the texts
of the civil laws may be found in P. Kreuger and Th. Mommsen, eds., *Corpus
Iuris Civilis* [Berlin, 1905–28].) For a full text of the letter from which *Etsi* is
taken, cf. Friedberg, ibid.; A. Potthast, *Regesta Pontificum Romanorum,* 2 vols.
(Berlin, 1875), no. 2565; or S. Grayzel, *The Church and the Jews in the Thirteenth Century* (Philadelphia, 1933), pp. 114–117: "Etsi iudaeos, quos propria
culpa submisit perpetuae servituti, pietas christiana receptet et sustineat cohabitationem illorum, ingrati tamen nobis esse non debent, ut reddant Christianis
pro gratia contumeliam et de familiaritate contemptum, qui, tanquam misericorditer
in nostram familiaritatem admissi, nobis illam retributionem perpendunt [so that
they have become as a serpent in our laps . . . in that they have committed such
delicts as employing Christian wet nurses, etc.]. . . . Alia insuper contra fidem
catholicam committunt, propter quae fidelibus est verendum, ne divinam indigna-
tionem incurrant, quum eos perpetrare patiuntur indigne, quae fidei nostrae
confusionem inducunt. . . . Inhibemus ergo districte, ne de cetero nutrices vel
servientes habeant christianos, ne filii liberae filis famulentur ancillae, sed tan-

inally a decree of the Fourth Lateran Council of 1215, had been absorbed into the 1234 *Decretals* of Gregory IX, the official book of Church law, still valid in 1555. The manifest correspondence between the old law and the new edict naturally invited readers of *Cum nimis* to compare it with the canon. Both *Cum nimis* and *Etsi* hold that Christian piety allows Jews to live in Christian lands, that the Jews' guilt consigns them to servitude, and that it is a gross breach for Jews to offend Christianity and to hold it in contempt in return for Christian kindness. *Cum nimis* combines all the offenses of the Jews under the heading of unlawful usurpation of authority and dominion over Christians, although it also renews the prohibition against Jews employing Christian nurses and servants. Jewish use of Christian nurses and servants is the main complaint of the canon, although it too speaks of *alia detestabilia*. The striking parallels of content and formulae indicate that *Cum nimis* has intentionally repeated the canon *Etsi*. But there is also a significant difference between the two. *Etsi* prescribes that Jews may not have Christian servants or nurses, "lest the sons of a free woman should be servants to the children of a slave. Rather, as slaves reprobate to God, in Whose death they evilly conspired, they should recognize through experience, at all events, that they are the slaves of those whom the death of Christ made free." The aim of *Etsi* was only that the Jews become aware of the fact of their servitude, to the end that they do not become presumptuous and try to acquire dominion over Christians. Its doctrine, moreover, was law. Therefore, when *Cum nimis* employed precisely the same words but added the preceding clause—that the Church tolerates the Jews to the end that they convert,[16] and therefore agree, etc.—it had altered an official legal formula and doctrine. And because of the overall congruity of the bull and the canon, it was impossible for the legists or canonists who read the bull to miss the complete shift of purpose.

---

quam servi a Domino reprobati, in cuius mortem nequiter coniurarunt, se saltem per effectum operis recognoscant servos illorum quos Christi mors liberos, et illos servos effecit . . ." (Innocent III, July 15, 1205).

16. See infra, p. 10 f., for a discussion of this clause.

The Jews were not merely to recognize the fact of their servitude for the purpose of self-restraint,[17] but they were to recognize in their servitude the fulfillment of the prophecies of servitude, and therefore, as a result of this recognition, they would convert.

But while through the incorporation of the words of *Etsi* Paul IV may have emphasized his policy shift, as well as indicated how Jews were to arrive at the knowledge of Christian truth, the real novelty in *Cum nimis* is the clause which states that the Jews are tolerated "so that" (*ut*). This becomes immediately apparent when it is realized that *Cum nimis* belongs to the category of bulls known as the *Constitutio pro Iudaeis*. As discussed in the Introduction, these constitutions, reissued by nearly every pope in the Middle Ages, set forth the basic condition that the Jews would be tolerated so long as they abided by the restrictions imposed upon them. *Cum nimis* does precisely this. However, it was also seen that these constitutions set down a theory concerning conversion, namely, that conversion was a matter for the distant future, that by implication there was no need to establish conversionary programs, and most important that toleration was in no way linked to Jewish acceptance of Christianity. Conversion and toleration were entirely separate matters. Thus the constitutions invariably contained the clause: we are prepared to tolerate the Jews, although (*licet*) they prefer to remain in their hardheartedness.[18] *Cum nimis,* as a constitution, should also have contained this *licet* clause. It does not. In place of "tolerated although" (*licet*) comes "tolerated to the end that" (*ad-hoc, ut*), a most emphatic clause of purpose. For Paul IV there was no discontinuity. Toleration—indeed, in the overall context of *Cum nimis,* every privilege and restriction touching the Jews—had been granted solely for the purpose of leading the Jews to convert. With this clause of purpose, then, Paul IV was announcing that he had reversed a centuries-long tradition. His intention was to establish a Jewry policy predicated solely upon its conversionary efficacy.

---

17. In fact, by directing his entire Jewry policy toward actively seeking the mass conversion of the Jews, Paul IV had made a radical break with all of past papal Jewry policy, not only with the traditional interpretation of the doctrine of servitude. Cf. supra, p. ix–xiv, to illustrate this point.

18. Cf. supra, p. ixf.

In launching an all-out campaign to convert the Jews *en masse,* Paul IV was not alone. His immediate predecessors had clearly been moving toward the same views. In 1543, four days before he issued the bull establishing the Roman *Domus catechumenorum,*[19] a residence and training center for recent converts from Judaism, Paul III wrote to the Roman Jewish community:

> To the Jewish community . . . that you should recognize the way of truth, and (having then recognized it) observe it; so that continuously discerning kindness and clemency on our part and on the part of the apostolic throne, you should at some time turn to the way of truth.[20]

Nearly identical wording appears in the bull *Cum sicut accepimus,* issued by Julius III on June 9, 1551.[21] Nor are these two items isolated. There are as many as sixty-three letters from the period of Paul III and Julius III which contain similar statements. These letters renew individually the privileges accorded by the papacy to the various Jewish communities within the pontifical states, in return for the agreement of those communities to pay the taxes levied on them.[22] Of particular interest in these letters, especially with reference to post-1555 Jewry policy, is the precise wording of their conversionary statements, which became almost formulaic, and the context in which these statements are found. To the Jews of the Romagna, Paul III wrote on February 13, 1544:

> May you recognize the way of truth, and having done so, may you observe it. (We have learned that you have promised to pay your taxes). Therefore, wishing to deal with you in the manner of a pious father, so that regularly perceiving our generosity you at some point acquire a wiser spirit, we approve each and every

---

19. Cf. infra, pp. 51ff., on the *domus* and its importance.

20. *Archivio della Comunità di Roma, Bolle e editti Papali,* secs. 13–18, ITc: "Universitate Hebraeorum . . . via veritatis agnoscere, et agnitam custodire, ut nostrae et apostolicae sedis mansuetudinem atque clementia sepius agnoscentes, ad viam veritatis aliquando redeatis. . . ." (no pagination).

21. *Comunità di Roma,* ITc.

22. The letters are to be found in *ASV Arm.* 40–42.

privilege, charter, exemption, and immunity (you have previously received).[23]

These privileges specifically include the rights *not* to wear a distinguishing badge, not to have children taken to be baptized against the will of their parents, to have contracts honored by Christians, and to locate dwellings freely among the Christians of the province.

This letter, and the many others like it, thus seems to propose the same goal as *Cum nimis.* To the extent that the letter looks forward to conversion, this is true. After that, the gap between the letter and *Cum nimis* is huge. The obvious difference is that the earlier letters seek to attain their end through expansive concessions and canonical exemptions, in complete opposition to *Cum nimis.* A second and more crucial difference is to be found in the formulae of the letters. They propose to treat the Jews with generosity, so that (*ut*) they convert. *Cum nimis* declared that the Jews were tolerated, so that (*ut*) they convert. Thus Paul IV had modified not only the formulae of *Etsi* and the *Constitutio pro Iudaeis,* but he had also abruptly and conspicuously transformed the formula and methods of his immediate predecessors.[24] What this transforma-

---

23. Arm. 41, lib. 29, #90: ". . . viam veritatis agnoscere et agnitam custodire. . . . Nos propterea volentes vobiscum more pii patris benigne agere ut nostram mansuetudinem sepius agnoscentes ad saniorem spiritum aliquando redeatis, omnia, etc. . . ."

24. In actuality, the   formula, tolerated *ut,* appeared twice prior to *Cum nimis.* However, in *Cum sicut nuper* (May 29, 1554), the bull of Julius III ordering the burning of the Talmud (cf. infra, p. 56f.), it is clear that the formula was inspired, if not composed, by Carafa. The earliest appearance of the formula occurred in a 1540 letter of the papal chamberlain, G. A. Sfortia, renewing the privileges of the Jews of Romagna. He wrote that the Church "Hebreos inter Christicolas conversari tolerat, ut aliquando resipiscant et verae fidei lumen sequantur" (see Stern, *Urkundliche Beiträge,* p. 82, #81). Nevertheless, while this may be the precise origin of the new formula, one must ascribe both the origin and the use in this instance to accident. The formula would not appear again until 1554. But from that point it would invariably be employed without change. It is likely that Paul IV discovered Sfortia's letter and decided that its formula, tolerated *ut,* suited his own purposes exactly. Even if Sfortia did use the formula intentionally, it remained for Paul IV both to understand it and to appreciate its possibilities. Then, curiously enough, Sfortia himself reverted to its use in letters he composed as the chamberlain of Pius IV. See infra, n. 41.

tion signified is that while his predecessors may have begun to hope for conversion, Paul IV was intent on actually achieving it. He would not rely on what were in effect barely more than pious expressions, as had Paul III and Julius III; he would begin with the very question of toleration itself.

The decision of Paul IV to go against the past and to exert relentless conversionary pressure was accepted by all his sixteenth-century successors. Each of the bulls they issued pertaining to the Jews sustains the policy of Paul IV, either by reedicting it or by elaborating on it. On February 27, 1562, Pius IV, Paul IV's successor, issued the bull *Dudum a felicis.*[25] Its proemium states that the Jews were disturbed because some men had interpreted the edicts of Paul IV even more harshly than Paul IV himself had intended. Accordingly, *Dudum*'s edicts require the cessation of these excesses. What is more, they also appear to ease the repressive measures of *Cum nimis.* For this reason it is likely that historians who evaluate Judaeo-papal relations on the basis of the degree of severity with which popes enforced Jewry law have judged Pius IV as a pope whose policy was favorable to the Jews.[26] To understand the Jewry policy of a given pope, however, demands both an examination of his entire Jewry policy—not just of his enforcement of specific edicts—and also that this examination be made within the scope of his overall policies. The pope who called the third meeting of the Council of Trent would hardly have pursued a Jewry policy which was "favorable" to the Jews. Indeed, no pope ever thought of his policy as "favorable" or "unfavorable" to the Jews.

The policy of Pius IV was, in reality, a continuation of that of his predecessor.[27] Indeed, on July 8, 1560 he had issued, through the Papal Camera, a letter "confirming" the bull of Paul IV *contra Hebraeos.*[28] As for *Dudum,* despite certain minor mitigations, it

25. *B.R.,* 7:167–71.
26. See, e.g., Baron, SRH, 14:44–45.
27. This fact has also been noted by Sonne, *Mi-Pavolo,* pp. 156–57. However, Sonne bases his judgment only on specific changes or continuities in the edicts of *Dudum.*
28. *ASV, Div. Cam.* 200, f.36. This letter is headed "Confir. Bulle Pauli iiii contra Hebraeos," and the specifics of its contents do basically just that.

maintains the restrictions introduced by *Cum nimis.* Its provisions
are, more than anything else, adjustments to that bull designed to
meet immediate needs without canceling any of its basic stipulations.
Perceiving this, Pius V, Pius IV's successor, thought it worthwhile
to remark that the "concessions" found in *Dudum* were made for
"urgent cause." [29]

These concessions were mainly commercial. Jews were permitted to engage in commerce outside the ghetto, and their commercial activity could again extend to the purveying of foodstuffs.[30]
There were also some refinements of the regulations on lending and
pledges.[31] So, too, the persons and legal rights of the Jews were
guaranteed, a provision which by no means reversed, but supported,
the policy of conversion. By insuring the Jews' legal protection,
Pius IV was attempting to demonstrate to them that they were being
restricted only in matters that reinforced their status of servitude.[32]
They should not be laid open to arbitrary or illegal acts which would
surely obscure papal goals. These protective clauses were, therefore, directed against the excesses referred to in the proemium. In
addition, the Jews were exempted from wearing a distinctive habit
while on a journey,[33] the rents on their homes in the ghetto were
fixed to prevent gouging,[34] and they were to receive payment for the
real property they had been forced to sell in 1555.[35] The bull also
established a statute of limitation for crimes Jews had committed in
the time of Paul IV. This statute was probably included to avoid
indiscriminate vindictiveness for the part played by Jews, along with
most of the Christians of Rome, in the riots which followed Paul IV's

29. *B.R.,* 7:439: "Non obstantibus omnibus . . . privilegiis, indultis, et
litteris . . . per . . . Pium Quartum . . . ex quavis, etiam urgentissima et onerosa,
causa." What is important is that with this assertion Pius V indicates that *Dudum*
did not change the policy of *Cum nimis;* it only modified the earlier bull *ex causa.*
30. *B.R.,* 7:167, pars. 1, 2, and 11.
31. Ibid., pars. 7, 10, 12.
32. Cf. infra, pp. 161–68.
33. *B.R.,* 7:167, par. 1.
34. Ibid., par. 6. This clause, in part, led to the development of the *ius
gazaga,* which created a state of assured possession and fixed rents for ghetto
dwellings. Cf. Baron, *SRH,* 14:52–53.
35. *B.R.,* 7:167, par. 7.

death.[36] Furthermore, the bull stated that the Jews were bound by the statutes of Rome, except where they had concessions and privileges. Here Pius IV simply meant that in certain types of litigations, Jews could be judged in accordance with Jewish law.[37] *Dudum* reversed *Cum nimis* in only one point. It gave the Jews permission to own real property which did not exceed fifteen hundred gold ducats in value. Paul IV's exclusion of Jews from the ownership of real property was not based on any specific law, however, but was a quasi-legislative act of princely prerogative.[38] By reversing Paul IV on this issue, Pius IV was only invoking the same prerogative; he was not issuing a major exemption or dispensation from law. Thus *Dudum* effected no radical change in the restrictions which *Cum nimis* had imposed on the Jews.

More important, Pius IV not only sustained the practical machinery of Paul IV's policy, he also espoused its purpose. The proemium of *Dudum* begins with the inscription: "Pope Pius IV, to all Jews living in Rome, that they recognize the way of truth, and having recognized it, observe it," [39] and it continues: *"Considering that the Church tolerates the Jews* . . . and concedes many things to them, *so that,* led by Christian kindness, *they* recognize their error, and *at length convert* to the true light, which is Christ . . .

36. Ibid., par. 8. On these riots see the diary of A. Massarelli for Aug. 19 and 20, 1559 (S. Merkle, ed. *Concilii Tridentini Diariorum,* which is vol. 2 of *Concilium Tridentinum* [Freiburg, 1911], p. 333). It is usually accepted that the Jews in Rome played a part in the riots. See, e.g., Duruy, *Le Cardinal Carafa,* p. 305, where he notes that when the head of the statue of Paul IV was dragged through the streets, a Jew received general applause for placing a Jews' hat on it. There does, however, exist a first-hand report which raises questions about the role the Jews played in the riots. This report is found in the diary of Firmani, who noted, for Aug. 20, 1559, that the "people," not the Jews, placed the *biretum zagulum more Hebraeorum* on the head which had been severed from the statue (Merkle, op. cit., p. 516).

37. *B.R.,* 7:167, par. 5. Cf. *De Iudaeis,* pt. 2, chap. 4, passim, on the subject of the observance of Jewish law.

38. Cf. infra, p. 174.

39. *B.R.,* 7:167, proemium: "Pius Papa IV universis et singulis utriusque sexis Hebraeis in alma urbe commorantibus, et commorari solitis, viam veritatis agnoscere, et agnitam custodire." Cf. *Exponi nobis* of Paul V, Aug. 7, 1610 (*B.R.,* 11:629), which begins with the identical words, thus indicating that they had become an established formula by that date.

we concede . . . ." [40] These two statements echo Paul IV precisely; the provisions of the administrative *actio* clauses that follow are intended to precipitate the conversion of the Jews. Hence *Dudum* is nothing more than Pius IV's extension and refinement of Paul IV's program.

Nor was *Dudum* the only locus of such statements on the part of Pius IV and his officials. Two formularies of the Papal Camera and Curia from this period include a number of documents addressed to Jews. Each of these documents contains in its prefatory material an assertion identical or similar to the following:

> To you, so and so, Hebrew, may you recognize and then observe the true faith, we grant the following, because the Holy Mother Church, in testimony of the orthodox faith, tolerates Hebrews to dwell among Christians so that at some point they come to their senses, and having cast off the Jewish blindness, they embrace the true faith of Christ. [41]

More directly, in a letter of January 23, 1560 providing for the support of converts, Pius IV explicitly announced that he was taking this action following in the footsteps of Paul IV, who saw in such support an important inducement for the encouragement of conversion. Indeed, he added, we are most desirous of using this means to invite and lead those who are not members of the Catholic faith, and Jews in particular, to enter into the bosom of the Holy Mother Church. [42] Thus in *Dudum,* as well as in his other declarations concerning Jews, Pius IV was purposefully continuing the policy of

----

40. *B.R.,* 7:167, proemium: "Ut christiana benignitate allecti, errorem suum recognoscant, et ad verum, quod est Christus, lumen tandem convertantur . . . concedimus . . ."

41. *ASV, Instr. Misc.,* 7480, *Forma Procedendi in Romana Curia,* and 7481, *Formularium Card. Camerarii,* neither with pagination or dates, contain nine documents on Jews. "Tibi Josepho danielis hebreo incole civitatis Interamne vere fidei agnitionem et observantiam. Humilibus nostre tuo nuper nobis porrecti precibus mox attendentes quod sa. mater ecce. in testimonium orthodoxe fidei Hebreos tolerat inter Christicolas versari ut aliquando resipiscant et Judaica cecitate abiecta veram Christiani fidem amplectantur. . . ."

42. *Copie delle Bolle* relating to the *Domus cathecumenorum, Archivio del Vicariato,* Rome, *Fond. Pia Casa dei catecumeni e neofiti, Filze* 121 (hereafter,

Paul IV. Any deviations from the specifics of that policy must be perceived as extensions or refinements, and not as contradictions.

Whatever the conditions were which caused Pius IV to make such refinements of *Cum nimis,* Pius V believed they no longer applied.[43] On April 19, 1566, in the bull *Romanus Pontifex,* Pius V reissued *Cum nimis* in full,[44] and thus both renewed and indicated his assent to Paul IV's policy. He also elaborated on it. Whereas *Cum nimis* applied only to the Papal States, *Romanus Pontifex* explicitly extended the provisions of 1555 to all Jews, wherever they lived, and it concomitantly prescribed that secular princes must aid in enforcing its regulations.[45]

To insure the enforcement of *Romanus Pontifex,* and to put an end to Jewish circumvention of the decree against ownership of real property, Pius V issued a second bull, *Cum nos nuper,* on January 19, 1567.[46] First he threatened the Jews with the forcible distraint of any real property they did not dispose of immediately.[47] Then, and most significantly, he appointed Cardinal Michael Saracen, the head of the *Domus catechumenorum,*[48] to enforce this and all other regulations prescribed by *Cum nos nuper* and *Romanus Pontifex,*[49] thereby centralizing the prosecution of Jewry policy in the hands of the official whose prime duty was overseeing conversion. This act makes matters quite clear. So far as Pius V was concerned, both *Romanus Pontifex* and *Cum nos nuper* were instruments of a conversionary policy.

Copie delle Bolle): ". . . Nos igitur qui omnes gentes a Cattolica fide alienas ac presertium Hebreos ceteris longe pertinaciores ad Sancte Matris Ecclesie gremium propositis premiis invitare et allicere cupimus huiusmodi supplicationibus. . . ."

43. See supra, n. 29.
44. *B.R.,* 7:438–40; par. 1 cites *Cum nimis, in toto.*
45. Ibid., pars. 2 and 5.
46. *B.R.,* 7:514–16.
47. Ibid., par. 3.
48. Established in 1543, see infra, p. 52.
49. *B.R.,* 7:514–16, par. 5. On this centralization of control, see esp. the article of Ch. Dejob, "Documents tirès des papiers du Cardinal Sirleto," *Revue des Études Juives* 9 (1884): 77–91. As will be seen shortly in the discussion of the functions of Cardinal Sirleto, this centralization of control became a matter of fixed policy.

The following statement of Pius V, contained in the proemium to the bull *Sacrosanctae Catholicae Ecclesiae* (November 29, 1566), which mandated the expansion of the facilities for housing recent converts, thus comes as no surprise. Presiding, he said, over the Catholic faith, outside of which there is no salvation, we see, among those for whom we sorrow in their infidelity,

> The people of the Hebrews, and we suffer the sharpest pangs and it moves us singularly with pity when we realize that this people [which you, God, chose is now most pertinaciously desisting from the Lord, and thus has purchased for itself eternal damnation]. Nor indeed have we left undone anything in our power which we consider advantageous for leading them from the path of error to the way of sure redemption. This and more, especially after we had been raised to the office of the Highest Apostolate, we have not for a moment desisted from teaching, from exhorting, from admonishing, experienced as we are, to the end that we lead as many of them as we can to the faith of Christ. Nor have all our labors, by the grace of God, been to no avail; for many indeed of both sexes have accepted the Christian religion, regenerated at the sacred font, some indeed of the first of these perfused with the salutary water by our own hands. And innumerable others, following their example, have become such a multitude that we must expand the facilities established for them by Paul III.[50]

In short, in his dealings with the Jews, conversion was Pius V's primary concern.

This concern of Pius V was both maintained and broadened by

---

50. *Copie delle Bolle* (no pagination): ". . . Hebraeorum gens et acerbissi-mum nobis dolorem inurit et misericordia commovet singularem dum recolimus populum hunc [once chosen and now damned] . . . neque sane quicquam praeter-mittimus quantum quidem in nobis situm est quod ad eos ab erroris semita in redemptionis salutis viam reducendas pertinere arbitramur. Itaque et alias, et maxime posteaquam ad summum Apostolatus officium promoti fuimus nunquam destitimus docendo, hortando et monendo conniti, ut eorum quamplurimus ad Christi fidem adduceremus neque omnes irriti Dei benignitate labores nostri fuerunt quando et satis multi utriusque sexus sacro fonte regenerati nonnulli etiam ex primariis a nobis ipsis salutari aqua perfusi Christianam Religionem sus-ceperunt, et alii quamplures eorum exemplum secuti ad tantam multitudinem pervenerunt, ut iam [we must expand].

his successor, Gregory XIII. In the proemium of *Vices eius* (September 1, 1577),[51] Gregory XIII stated that the apostolic concern had to extend to every part of the world.

> So that *we do not cease to appeal* with all our strength, and also to hope, for not only the repentance of heretics and schismatics but also *for the conversion and true salvation* of those who perish miserably walking in the darkness of infidelity.[52]

Therefore, he continued, "We have ordered some time ago, that on each Sabbath in a specified oratory in Rome, Christ be preached and announced to the Jews." [53] In addition, a college for neophytes is to be established:

> So that from those [who have lately converted] shall come forth workers suitable for the work of the Gospel, who will be able to preach the mysteries of the Christian faith in every land where Jews and other infidels dwell.[54]

Gregory then appointed a number of men to be the protectors of this college. One of them was Cardinal Sirleto, who was at this time not only supervising the operation of the *domus* but was also engaged in overseeing the enforcement of the edicts of *Cum nimis.*[55] In other words, the centralized control initiated by Pius V had be-

---

51. *B.R.,* 8:188–91.

52. Ibid., proemium: "Ut [not only the repentance of heretics and schismatics,] sed eorum, qui, in infidelitatis tenebris ambulantes, misere pereunt, praesertim iudaeorum, conversionem veramque salutem exoptare, ac totis viribus quaerere non cessemus."

53. Ibid., par. 1: "Nos iampridem singulis diebus sabbati in certo oratorio in alma urbe iudaeis Christum . . . annunciari et praedicari iussimus."

54. Ibid., par. 2: "Ut ex eis [who have lately converted] prodeant operarii ad opus Evangelii idonei, qui . . . in omnibus terrarum orbis partibus, in quibus iudaei et infideles degunt, christianae fidei mysteria . . . praedicare possint."

55. Ibid., par. 6. On the activity of Sirleto, see the article of Dejob, cited supra, n. 49. In addition, the following documents, *BAV. Vat. Lat.* 6189 ff. 687, 772, 788, 805, 811, and 819, and *Vat. Lat.* 6792 ff. 81, 89, 106, 109–15, and 170, all illustrate how Sirleto actually did coordinate the many aspects of Jewry policy by such acts as fining Jews who transgressed papal regulations on the one hand, and by insuring the collection of *domus* payments on the other.

come an integral part of Jewry policy. As for the college itself, Gregory displayed his zeal for its development and success by issuing at least five additional bulls providing for its financial stability.[56]

The true beginning of the use of sermons as a conversionary device must be dated from September 1, 1584.[57] In the bull *Sancta mater ecclesia,* Gregory XIII elaborated on the idea of *Vices eius.* Terribly moved by the plight of the Jews, he declared, "Each day we consider whence more opportune provisions can be made for their conversion and salvation." [58] Therefore, he continued, adhering to the practice of Nicholas V and other popes (none of whom ordered any measure which more than faintly resembles the edicts of this bull),[59] all prelates, in whatever land, art to appoint a suitable

---

56. *Copie delle Bolle: Quae ad commodum,* Apr. 8, 1578; *Quemadmodum agricola,* Sept. 11, 1578; *Decet providum,* Feb. 5, 1579; *Cum sicut accepimus,* Feb. 5, 1583; and *Ex injuncto,* May 15, 1583.

57. *B.R.,* 8:487–89.

58. Ibid., proemium: "In dies semper aliquid excogitamus, unde eorum conversioni et salutati opportunius provideatur, ipsique ad intelligentiae viam . . . valeant pervenire."

59. The history of preaching to the Jews is discussed at length in Browe, *Judenmission* pp. 13–55. In the forefront of this activity, especially in the thirteenth century, were the Dominicans. And the Jews were, at times, forced to attend their sermons (Browe, pp. 17–21, 26–32). The Dominicans were also involved in the thirteenth and again in the early fifteenth century in seeking converts through disputations (Browe, pp. 65–68). In 1312, at the Council of Vienne, a decree was issued at the urging of Ramon Lull (this decree was incorporated into the canons. Clem. 5, 1, 1), which ordered that two chairs in Hebrew, Arabic, and Chaldean be established at the Universities of Paris, Oxford, Bologna, and Salamanca for the purpose of training preachers so that they could deliver conversionary sermons to *all* infidel groups in the infidels' own language. This decree remained virtually a dead letter. There are hardly any records about its implementation at Oxford, Bologna, and Salamanca, and Paris appears to have never had more than one instructor of Hebrew at a time, usually a converted Jew (Browe, pp. 273–74). The one place where Hebrew was assiduously studied in the thirteenth century was the Dominican school in Spain (Browe, pp. 271–72). As for direct efforts at organizing preaching on the part of the papacy itself—and it is specifically the actions of the papacy which are under review here—before the mid-sixteenth century the only instances of papal initiation or approval of preaching to the Jews are 1245 by Innocent IV, 1278 by Nicholas III, 1415 by Benedict XIII, and 1447 by Nicholas V (Browe, pp. 19, 29, 26, and 36 f.). The initiative by Benedict XIII will be discussed at length in the last chapter of this volume. Innocent IV actually did no more than approve an order of King

man to preach the Gospel to the Jews in their synagogues on each Sabbath, preferably in Hebrew.[60] The Jews are to be taught the truth of the Catholic faith, the nature of their desolation, and the error of their messianic hopes and beliefs. They must be especially informed of the "mendacious" interpretations of the rabbis. In addition, these sermons are obligatory. Weekly attendance by at least one-third of the Jews above the age of twelve in any community is mandatory, or else all contact with Christians will be forbidden.[61] Most interesting is the fact that Gregory specifically instructed that the Jews be reminded of their desolation. He undoubtedly hoped that through preaching, the experiential lessons of such bulls as *Cum nimis* and *Romanus Pontifex* would be verbally reinforced.

Gregory XIII's successor, Sixtus V, is another of the popes

Jaime I of Aragon. As for Nicholas V, Raynaldus, in his *Annales Ecclesiastici*, ed. J. D. Mansi (Lucca, 1752), 9:509–10, notes that on January 13, 1447 Nicholas V gave permission to René of Anjou, king of Sicily, to force the Jews of Provence, on pain of confiscation of goods, to attend sermons four times a year. However, Browe believes that whatever happened, such preaching was short-lived. Moreover, as for Nicholas V's motives, Browe claims that Nicholas V's policy toward the Jews was based completely on convenience, because it was full of reversals. Keyser, in his article "Papst Nikolaus V und die Juden," *AKKR,* 53 (1885): 209–20, differs. He believes that Nicholas was following the traditional line of tolerance and that he did so consistently. Even so, the policy was not conversion. Yet Gregory XIII could have used Nicholas V's bull (which, says Kayser, is unprinted), as a model. But the difference between granting permission for forced preaching in Provence and instituting it by papal initiative in Rome is very great. There was, however, one papal initiative. That was made by Nicholas III. Yet his bull *Vineam sorec (B.R.,* 4:45 f.) of Aug. 4, 1278 bears no resemblance to *Sancta mater ecclesia.* Whereas the latter establishes forced preaching in specific places at specific times, *Vineam sorec* merely orders the Franciscans to preach, and adds that if the Jews will not listen, the friars should inform the pope, who will think of a remedy. The real beginning of papally directed forced preaching was perhaps in 1568 at the order of Pius V (Browe cites this date with no note, p. 41). According to Browe, Pius V was imitating Ch. Borromeo, who had begun such preaching in Milan in 1561 and 1565 (for Borromeo's order, see Hardouin, *Acta Consiliorum* [Paris, 1714], 10:724–26; or J. D. Mansi *Nova et Amplissima Collectio Sacrorum Conciliorum* [Paris, 1902], 34: cols. 96–97). It appears, then, that if Gregory XIII was indeed "adhering to the practice" of his predecessors, those predecessors were the thirteenth-century Dominicans, and it was their practice that he was reviving.

60. *B.R.,* 8:487, par. 1.
61. Ibid., par. 2.

whose policy is described as favorable, for he reversed Pius V's order
of 1569, which expelled the Jews from all the cities of the Papal
States except Rome and Ancona.[62] He also gave permission for the
republication of the Talmud, albeit in a censored version and with
the name *Talmud* removed.[63] Nevertheless, the demand for censorship proved too rigorous, and the Talmud was not republished.[64] Indeed, Sixtus V's Jewry policy continued the basic lines of the
program in effect since 1555. His specific mitigations, which are
found in the bull *Christiana pietas* (October 22, 1586)[65] are explicitly modeled after those of Pius IV.[66] But those mitigations, as
seen above, did not alter the main thrust of Paul IV's policy. Moreover, in the light of his bull *Quae ordini ecclesiastico* (September 4,
1589),[67] which established separate prisons for Jews and Christians
to prevent scandals from arising because of overfamiliarity between
Jews and Christians, it is unlikely that Sixtus V would have had a
policy favorable to the Jews.

---

62. *Hebraeorum gens,* Feb. 26, 1569. *B.R.,* 7:740 f.

63. A. Yaari, *Srefat ha-Talmud be-Italiah* (Tel-Aviv, 1954), p. 12, claims that
Sixtus V did indeed give permission to publish the Talmud. However, the text of
Christiana pietas, the source for this claim (*B.R.,* 7:786 f.), says: "Tutti li libri
Ebraici." It does not specify the Talmud. And in an article in *Jewish Quarterly
Review* 1:113–21, "A Breve of Pius IV," M. Radin argues that Sixtus V had
no intention of permitting the publication of the Talmud, only of other Hebrew
books, as in fact was the case with Pius IV. Indeed, even according to Yaari,
the Talmud was not published in Italy after 1553 (pp. 7–12). Furthermore, the full
text in *Christiana pietas* states: "Possino tener tutti li libri Ebraici, spurgati che
siano o vero purgati che nell'avenire saranno dalle blasfemie contro Santu, e con
la mutazione delli nomi, secondo fu gia nel Concilio Tridentino e da Pio quarto
et di parere di Pio V allora cardinale Alessandrino, stabilito ed ordinato, come
appare nell'indice, e per scritture del secretario di detto concilio." This statement
suggests a uniform papal policy toward Hebrew books.

64. On Julius III's action, which was likely based on the theory, contrary
to that which argued for burning the Talmud, that the Jews could be convinced
of Christian truth through the supposed Christological references found in the
Talmud, see K. Stow, "The Burning of the Talmud in 1553, in the Light of
Sixteenth Century Catholic Attitudes toward the Talmud," *Bibliothèque d'Humanisme et Renaissance* 34 (1972): 457 f.

65. *B.R.,* 8:786.

66. Ibid., par. 1, where he stresses that he is adhering to the memory of Pius
IV, while par. 15 specifically derogates the constitutions of Paul IV and Pius
V which are not in accord with *Christiana pietas.*

67. *B.R.,* 9:121.

That Sixtus V pictured his edicts as conforming to the program of the previous thirty years is evident from the proemium of *Christiana pietas*. Christian piety, Sixtus states, permits Jews to dwell among Christians;

> So that [the faithful will remember the passion of the Lord] and *so that these Hebrews,* impressed by such piety, *will recognize their errors,* and will arrive at the true light of clarity, which is Christ.[68]

"Whence" (*Unde*), he continues, thus indicating that the following provisions are intended to foster the end described in the proemium, "we concede" (*concedimus*) the following.

While some of the bull's provisions mirror those found in Pius IV's *Dudum,* such as the permission to deal freely in foodstuffs, *Christiana pietas* basically fixes the rules and living conditions for the Jews whom Sixtus V had invited to resettle the various localities of the Papal States. The most significant of these conditions touches the matter of jurisdiction, restating in expanded and more precise terms the position of the bull *Cum sicut accepimus,* issued by Julius III on February 22, 1550.[69] *Cum sicut* ruled that jurisdiction in both criminal and civil cases involving the Jews in Rome belonged solely to the pope's Roman vicar. (Paul IV probably considered this ruling recent enough to make its repetition in *Cum nimis* unnecessary.) In *Christiana pietas,* Sixtus V pronounced that:

> The resident bishops in the cities and in other places, and the governors or principal ministers of the lands or castles respec-

---

68. *B.R.,* 8:786, proemium: "Ut . . . ipsique hebrei, huiusmodi pietate compuncti, suos agnoscant errores, ad verum lumen, quod est Iesus Christus, perveniant claritatis."

69. *B.R.,* 6:404. Most revealing of the fact that the Jews of Rome had indeed lost jurisdictional autonomy is the bull of Paul V, *Exponi nobis* of Aug. 7, 1610 *(B.R.,* 11:629). The Jews, "cupientes circa dotes mulierum in melius reformare," had turned to the pope to get this change in Jewish legal practice approved. He noted: "Nonnulla capitula, ordinationes et reformationes super iis condidistis . . . [And] ut firmius subsistant et ab omnibus inviolabiliter observentur, apostolicae nostrae confirmationis patrocinio communiri summopere desideratis . . . [after these new ordinances] a vicario in spiritualibus generali . . . approbata fuerunt."

tively shall be competent judges and shall administer justice in litigations which arise between the Hebrews themselves, as well as between Jews and Christians.[70]

This clause abrogates Jewish jurisdictional autonomy. And as will be seen from the relationship drawn by the *De Iudaeis* between the abrogation of jurisdictional autonomy and conversion,[71] this clause furnishes strong evidence that the goal of Sixtus V's Jewry policy was conversion.

Similar evidence is furnished by the clause which orders all Jewish men to attend sermons six times a year.[72] In a following clause, however, Sixtus V allows Jewish physicians who have been licensed by the papacy to freely minister to Christians. Yet, like Pius IV, Sixtus V may have made this exception to meet a pressing need.[73] It does not cancel the thrust of Sixtus V's program as a whole.

The conversionary bent of later-sixteenth-century Jewry policy is summarized in the bull *Caeca et obdurata,* issued by Clement VIII, the last pope of the century, on February 25, 1593.[74] In the proemium Clement VIII repeats the now standard formula, that faithful Christians *"receive and tolerate the Jews,* in kindness, in testimony of the true faith, and in memory of the passion of the Lord, *so that they may repent."* [75] This assertion appears, however, in the middle of a protest against the *enormes excessus* practiced by the Jews. In particular, rather than convert, the Jews have continued their criminal behavior.

The next four paragraphs describe not only how these excesses

---

70. *B.R.,* 8:786, par. 7: "Li vescovi residenti nelle città e nelli altri luoghi, li governatori o vero ministri principali delle terre o castelli rispettivamente siano giudici competenti, e nelle liti che verteranno sia tra essi ebrei, come tra essi e cristiani, amministrino la giustizia."

71. See infra, chap. 7 passim, pp. 149 ff.

72. *B.R.,* 8:786, par. 10. The reduction in number from seventeen required sermons a year to six was perhaps a consequence of the lack of suitable preachers.

73. Ibid., par. 11. See *De Iudaeis,* pt. 2, chap. 7, par. 10 (infra, p. 114), on the matter of exemptions from the normal prohibition against the use of Jewish physicians by Christians.

74. *B.R.,* 10:22.

75. Ibid., proemium: "Eos in testimonium verae fidei, et in memoriam passionis Dominicae, atque ut tandem resipiscant, benigne tolerant et recipiunt."

had arisen but also how various regulatory measures had affected
the matter of conversion. Clement VIII first refers to the edicts of
Paul IV[76] and then to their renewal (*innovavit*) by Pius V, who also
had to abrogate *plura indulta et privilegia* which the Jews had obtained in the meanwhile. What is more, Pius V ultimately felt constrained to order the perpetual exile of the Jews from all the Papal
States except Rome and Ancona.[77] But the Jews,

> As time progressed, attempted, little by little, to loose themselves
> from these chains, and, by chance, they extorted certain tolerations
> from our other *predecessors, who thought that the generosity of
> Christian piety should not be denied the Jews if they were to lead
> the Jews from their darkness* to the recognition of the true faith.
> But afterward, in a way completely opposite from the pious mind
> and intention of these predecessors, the Jews perversely abused
> these tolerations to such an extent that [by violating the divine,
> natural, and human laws against usury, they impoverished and
> defrauded Christians].[78]

Hence, Clement VIII believes, "this nation must be expelled *in
toto.*" [79] Nevertheless, "lest once this nation is expelled, it betakes
itself to the other nations which do not know Christ and moves
farther from the way of salvation promised by the prophets for the
remnant of Israel," the Jews should be allowed to remain in the
major cities, Rome, Ancona, and Avignon, where their actions may
be closely monitored.[80]

Accordingly, for the Jews who will live in Rome, Ancona, and

---

76. Ibid., par. 1.

77. Ibid., par. 2; cf. pp. 34 f., infra, on Pius V's expulsion edict.

78. Ibid., par. 3: "Successu temporis paulatim ab huiusmodi vinculis se
eximere attentarunt, et forsan ab aliis praedecessoribus nostris, qui ut eos ab
eorum caligine ad agnitionem verae fidei allicerent, mansuetudinem christianae
pietatis non denegandam eis censuerunt, aliquas super hoc tolerantias extorserunt.
Quibus postmodum, contra piam eorumdem praedecessorum mentem et intentionem,
prave abutentes, eo tandem sunt progressi, ut [they violated the divine and
natural, let alone human, laws against usury, etc.]"

79. Ibid., par. 4: "Huiusmodi nationem . . . omnino expellendam."

80. Ibid., par. 4: "Ne a nobis prorsus eiecta, ad gentes, quae Christum non
norunt, divertat, atque a via salutis reliquiis Israel prophetico ore promissae
longius recedat . . ."

Avignon, Clement VIII approves (*approbamus*) and renews
(*innovamus*) the constitutions of Paul IV and Pius V and cancels
the privileges of Pius IV and Sixtus V which eased the strict limits
imposed by Paul IV and Pius V.[81] The Jews in the remaining parts
of the Papal States he expels, on three months notice, with the threat
that failure to depart within that time-limit will result in the confiscation of property and consignment to galley slavery.[82] These Jews
may, however, settle in Rome, Ancona, and Avignon:

> Since we hope that those especially, who are under our close
> observation, will be tempered from their evil doings by the terror
> of punishment and that, now and then, others will more easily
> recognize the light of truth.[83]

In sum, Clement VIII has unmistakably weighed each of the
various directions taken by Jewry policy during the preceding forty
years in terms of conversionary efficacy. The privileges granted by
Pius IV and Sixtus V are eschewed not as violations of a policy
of rigid segregation, but as a poor method of seeking conversion,

---

81. Ibid., par. 5.
82. Ibid., par. 6.
83. Ibid., par. 6: "Si ad dictas potius civitates quam alio se recipere maluerint
. . . quia illos praesertim, qui nostro et huius Sedis conspectui proximi sunt,
poenae formidine a maleficiis temperaturos atque interdum aliquos lumen veritatis
facilius agnituros speramus." Baron, *SRH,* 14:56–57, expresses some doubt that
this expulsion took place, and suggests that it was *de facto* canceled by the bull
Cum superioribus mensibus of July 2, 1593 (see Stern, *Urkundliche Beiträge,*
#157,, p. 164), in which Clement VIII invited Jews, because he had seen "Ex
Hebraeorum commercio plurimum utilitas statui nostro," to come to the various
cities of the Papal States to carry on trade: "accedere, vendere, mercari, . . . et
negotiari." Baron's conclusion is perhaps built on his translation of the above
phrase: "to dwell, trade, or negotiate." But it is hard to conceive of *accedere* as
meaning "to dwell," especially in the context here, where it means "to enter on a
temporary basis." More important, twice in the bull Clement VIII states: they may
come "dummodo nullo modo in eis domicilium habere vel contrahere possint . . .,"
and "non habeant permanens domicilium." It seems fairly indisputable that the
expulsion did take place and that it was not canceled shortly afterward. Indeed, I
have found no document from the succeeding years of Clement VIII's pontificate
which suggests such a cancellation. Cf., moreover, n. 197, infra, for a text of Clement VIII which indicates quite clearly that the expulsion of 1593 had never been
canceled.

because they ultimately encouraged Jewish abuses. The decision to expel the Jews reflects despair over their failure to convert. Experience teaches, says Clement in explanation of this decision, that the Jews do much that is detrimental, and that it is possible to hope for little that is good from them.[84] And in context "good" means not probity, but principally conversion. Nevertheless, the expulsion is limited, because expulsion prevents the fulfillment of the prophecy that the Jews will ultimately embrace Christianity. In other words, Clement VIII recognized the discontinuity between expulsion and a policy whose end is immediate mass conversion. Moreover, his hope that after living under the closely enforced restrictions enacted by Paul IV and Pius V, some of those Jews who had been tempered from their evildoing would convert, identifies him squarely with the policy of his two predecessors. Making the Jews recognize their servitude will lead them to the baptismal font.

The extent of Clement VIII's commitment to a conversionary Jewry policy is best illustrated in his letter of July 9, 1604 to the Roman Jewish community:

> We, *desiring of the Jewish Community* of Rome *that it recognize the way of truth* and then observe it, therefore . . . release and pardon you and each member of the Community of whatever transgressions excesses or delicts, excepting, however, homicides [counterfeiting, sacrileges, *lèse majesté,* and infractions against the Inquisition], done or committed by you up to the present day.[85]

Clement VIII is here granting Roman Jewry the privilege known as the *Absolutio,* which was not infrequently given Jews by secular rulers to save them from arbitrary treatment at the hands of such as the craft guilds.[86] That is, the *Absolutio* was not originally con-

---

84. Ibid., par. 4: "Apud quos experientia docuit eam multo plus detrimenti afferre, quam boni ab ipsis sperari queat."

85. *Comunità di Roma,* ITc: "Della università degli Ebrei di Roma volendo conoscere la strada della verità e conosciuta custodirla . . . , per tanto . . . voi et ogni persona della vostra Univ'a da qualsivoglia trasgressione, eccessi, e delitti eccettuati però gli omicidi . . . sino nel presente giorno per voi fatti e commessi . . . assolviamo, e liberiamo . . ."

86. Cf. Simonsohn, *Mantovah,* 1:78–79, on the development of the *Absolutio.*

ceived of as a conversionary device. Clement VIII's wording, however, transforms the *Absolutio* into precisely that. But what is more,
he had been preceded in doing this by both Paul III and Julius III.
Indeed, it was their grants of the *Absolutio* which were cited earlier
in demonstration of their conversionary intentions.[87] And the wording of their texts differs only slightly from that found in the letter
of Clement VIII.

Perhaps because the idea of a conversionary policy was still
embryonic, Paul III provided no word or phrase to explicitly link
his declaration of conversionary hopes with the actual grant. Julius
III, on the other hand, stated that he grants the *Absolutio* because he
wishes to deal kindly with the Jews so that (*ut*) they come to recognize Christian truth.[88] In this context the *Absolutio* is justifiable as
a conversionary device. But Clement VIII definitely associated himself with Paul IV's argument that restriction, not kindness, promotes
conversion. Hence, while Clement must have felt impelled for some
reason to grant the *Absolutio,* even if it contradicted the temper of
his actual program, he explicitly asserted, at the same time, that it
was a conversionary device. As far as he was concerned, every aspect
of his Jewry policy, at least in theory, must be associated with the
pursuit of conversion.

The contents of the bulls and letters of the later-sixteenth-
century popes thus argue strongly that the repressive papal Jewry
policy of that period had a conversionary motivation. Three items,
however, seem to oppose this conclusion: the papal persecutions of
Marranos at Ancona; the expulsions of Pius V and Clement VIII;
and the fact that contemporary Jewish writings that speak of papal
repression do so only in vague terms (with the exception of accounts
of the episode at Ancona), making scarcely any references to the
specifics of papal policy and to conversion in particular.

The persecution of Marranos at Ancona[89] has been cited[90] as

---

87. Cf. p. 11f., supra.
88. *Comunità di Roma,* ITc, Julius III, June 9, 1551: ". . . nos volentes . . .
benigne vobiscum agere, ut . . . ad saniorem spiritum aliquando redeatis, vos
[grant the *Absolutio*]."
89. In April of 1556 twenty-four Marranos from Ancona were burned, and

evidence that the goal of later-sixteenth-century papal Jewry policy was the separation of Jews and Catholics to protect Catholic orthodoxy. This has been done because Paul IV's general edict, *Cum nimis,* has been linked with his assault on these Marranos, an association which on the one hand reflects a general tendency to view Marranos as Jews, and on the other hand stems from the fact that the Marranos of Ancona had been living openly as Jews for many years. Nevertheless, to discuss Jews and Marranos together can lead to severe distortions, especially if the discussion concerns Jews and Marranos in the light of Church policy. In the eyes of the Church, Marranos are heretic Christians, and not Jews.[91] Paul IV, in particular, considered the Anconitans Marranos.[92] In a letter of April 30, 1556, he instructed the Inquisition that certain Portuguese who had settled in Italy (Ancona) should be condemned and punished as apostates. These Portuguese may have denied that they had ever been baptized, but it was common knowledge that no Jews had lived in Portugal for sixty years.[93] Hence, Paul IV clearly distinguished the Anconitan Portuguese from Jews. Their repression may not be considered a part of his Jewry policy.

Even if these Anconitans were considered Jews—as they were by other sixteenth-century popes—their fate had no bearing

---

a number of others were made galley slaves. Cf. esp. Baron, *SRH,* 14:39 ff., and Sonne, *Mi-Pavolo,* pp. 19–100, in which Sonne has published an important chronicle of these events. Cf. also the report to the doge and the Senate of R. Navagero, the Venetian ambassador at Rome during most of Paul IV's pontificate, found in Rawdon-Brown, *Calendar of State Papers, Venetian* (London, 1881), vol. 6, #463, p. 419. Navagero reports twelve burnings and forty-two sent to the galleys (April 25, 1556).

90. See supra, n. 7.

91. Cf. *De Iudaeis,* pt. 1, chap. 1, par. 5, where de Susannis explicitly distinguishes between Marranos and Jews. See the discussion in Baron, *SRH,* 14:35 f; for the attitudes of the sixteenth-century popes, including Paul IV, toward these Anconitans.

92. Cf. *ASV, Arm.* 42, vol. 6, #140, July 26, 1555, where Paul IV accuses separately of unwarranted usury the Jews of Ancona and the Judaizing Portuguese Christians living there.

93. *BAV, Ottob.* 2532, fol. 72ᵛ: ". . . quoscunque Portugeses . . . in Italiam venisse, ubi reperantur esse Iudaei, sive iudaizasse, condemnentur tanquam Apostatae a Fide, prout de iure similes Apostatae condemnari, et puniri debent. . . ."

on Jewry policy as a whole. The Anconitans whom Paul IV attacked belonged to a group which had received special treatment since at least 1543.[94] And this group continued to be so treated throughout this period, because many of its members were not formally subjects of the Papal States, but of the Turkish Empire.[95] It was, indeed, the response of the Turkish fleet, which put to sea in great force immediately after the burnings of 1556, that caused Paul IV to suspend his assault on the Anconitan Marranos after the initial burnings.[96] As for the Marranos who had come to Ancona directly from Portugal, they benefited by inclusion in the privileges given to the Turkish subjects,[97] privileges which are contained in bulls issued by Paul III, Pius IV, Pius V, and Gregory XIII.

Dudum emanarunt of Gregory XIII (February 23, 1573)[98] is an explicit renewal of the earlier privileges, and hence displays not only the nature, but also the consistency, of the papal policy toward the Anconitans. *Dudum* begins by citing in full the letter of Pius V. This letter is itself a literal repetition of the letter of Pius IV. And

94. For the bull of Paul III of Feb. 5, 1543, see M. Stern, *Urkundliche Beiträge über die Stellung der Päpste zu den Juden* (Liel, 1893), #99, pp. 95 f.

95. There is no doubt that some of the Marranos at Ancona were Turkish subjects. Joseph HaKohen, *'Emeq ha-bakh'a, ed.* M. Letteris (Cracow, 1895), p. 135, attests to this when he says: נטה לאנקונה מתורגמה הבאים האנוסים על וגם קו פאולו (cf. the Spanish trans. by P. L. Tello, *Emeq Ha-Bakha De Yosef Ha-Kohen* [Madrid, 1964], p. 232). Cf. C. Roth, *The House of Nasi: Doña Gracia* (Philadelphia, 1948), p. 135; and infra, n. 96.

96. Navagero in *Rawdon-Brown,* 6, #463, p. 419 (Apr. 25, 1556): "So I understand, letters have been written to stay the execution until further orders; it being said that the report of the Turkish fleet's putting to sea in great force has caused this countermand, lest with pretext it comes to Ancona, and they [the pope and the curia] regret having gone so far" (trans. from Italian). See also the letter sent from Suleiman to Paul IV protesting the treatment of his subjects residing in Ancona, printed in Baron, *SRH,* 14:39. As for Jewish citizenship in general, see *De Iudaeis,* pt. 2, chap. 1.

97. See Roth, *Doña Gracia,* pp. 135–37, and esp. 135, where he states that Paul III issued a letter "encouraging New Christians to share in the safe conduct [previously] granted to foreign merchants"; and see also *SRH,* 14:36, where Baron makes no suggestion that the Anconitan privileges given by Paul III and Julius III drew a distinction between Turkish and Portuguese Marranos.

98. *B.R.,* 8:32–39.

Pius IV, in turn, declares that he is following the edict of Julius III. *Dudum* concludes by reaffirming the clauses of the previous letters. Most significant is the obvious differentiation made between the Anconitans and other Jews. *Dudum* is specifically directed: "Pro parte Hebraeorum, Turcarum, Graecorum et aliorum utriusque sexus mercatorum partium Orientalium." [99] It also intends to solidify the distinctions between the Italian and non-Italian Jews, as the clause that permits the non-Italians to build their own synagogue makes clear:

> Paul III conceded to the said Hebrews, Turks, Greeks, and other Orientals, for their comfort and for the satisfaction of their souls, the permission to erect one school, that is, synagogue, for their immovable will, in that very place of the ecclesiastical state where they reside. Their synagogue belongs fully to these Orientals; such that no other Hebrew or body of Hebrews . . . may control or be superior in that synagogue. [100]

Furthermore, as seen above, the papacy canceled Italian Jewry's privilege of jurisdictional autonomy. In *Dudum* the "Oriental" Jews are, on the contrary, granted this privilege, albeit in an indirect way:

> In the cases of these Hebrews [etc.] . . . in which their interests are at stake, . . . no official may intervene; but any penalty in these causes ought to be fixed by the governor of these Anconitans or his judges and the consul of these Orientals or his substitute. [101]

---

99. Ibid., par. 4.

100. Ibid., par. 4: "[Paul III] concesserat dictis Hebraeis, Turcis, Graecis et aliis orientalibus ut liceret eis, pro eorum commoditate et animi satisfactione, unam scholam seu synagogam ad eorum voluntatem amovibilem, in unoquoque loco status Ecclesiastici, in quo ipsos residere contingeret, erigere, quae sua ipsorum orientalium libera esset; ita quod nullus alius Hebraeus aut alia universitas Hebraeorum . . . in ipsa schola seu synagoga imperium seu superioritatem haberet. . . ."

101. Ibid., par. 7: "Et quod in causis ipsorum Hebraeorum [etc.] . . . in quibus de eorum interesse ageretur, tam in civilibus quam in criminalibus, nullus officialis se intromittere posset, sed omnis dictarum causarum commissio fieri deberet per gubernatorem Anconitanum seu illius iudices et consolem ipsorum Orientalium aut eius substitutum. . . ."

These "Orientals," moreover, were exempt from the taxes required of other Jews:

> And the said Orientals [etc.] are not included in the imposition of tenths, twentieths, and other burdens, ordinary and extraordinary, imposed temporarily on the Hebrews and by the Hebrews.[102]

However, despite these special and distinguishing privileges, which prove beyond a doubt the exemption of the "Orientals" from the restrictions leveled on the Italian Jews, *Dudum* does conclude on the following note:

> *Hoping that through long conversation with Christians,* the grace of the Holy Spirit cooperating, *they may at length be able to arrive at* the recognition of *the true faith,* inclined to their supplications in this matter, we approve and confirm the letters and decrees [of our predecessors.][103]

Basic to the conversionary policy of Paul IV and his successors is the prohibition of free intercourse with Christians.[104] The exact opposite is actually encouraged in the case of the Anconitans. More surprising, such free intercourse is said to promote conversion. What first became apparent in the case of the *Absolutio* now becomes crystal clear. The popes were in agreement that all Jewry policies, at least in theory, had only one legitimate end, namely, conversion.

There was, however, one area in which there was a corre-

---

102. Ibid., par. 9: "Dictique Orientales [etc.] . . . sub decimarum, vigesimarum et aliorum onerum, tam ordinariorum quam extraordinariorum, impositionibus, Hebraeis et per Hebraeos pro tempore impositis non comprehensi." In particular, by "per Hebraeos" this clause probably refers to the tax which each Jewish community had to raise, as a community, to support the *domus;* see the bull *Dudum postquam* of Mar. 23, 1556, in which Paul IV ordered these payments (*B.R.,* 6:509); see also the full discussion of this tax in Rodochanachi, *Le St. Siège,* pp. 229–40.

103. Ibid., par. 14: "Sperantes per diuturnam eorum cum Christianis conversationem, Spiritus Sancti cooperante gratia, ad agnitionem verae fidei tandem pervenire posse, illorum supplicationibus in hac parte inclinati, litteras et capitula praedicta [of previous popes] approbamus et confirmamus."

104. Cf. the canons cited in *De Iudaeis,* pt. 1, chap. 4, esp. par. 12.

spondence between the policy toward Jews and the policy toward Marranos. In common with the other Jewry bulls of the period, *Antiqua Iudaeorum Improbitas* of Gregory XIII (July 1, 1581)[105] affirms that the Church tolerates Jews in order to convert them:

> The Church, which, laboring for their conversion, mercifully receives them and sustains their cohabitation along with its own sons, has always strived with pious zeal, to lead them to the light of truth.[106]

Its *actio* (administrative) clauses, nevertheless, are intended not to foster new conversions, but to halt the problem created because "the Jews have not desisted from multiplying daily their horrendous crimes against the Christian religion." [107] Accordingly, the inquisitors are instructed to prosecute the following offenses:[108] denying the unity of God,[109] invoking demons,[110] teaching Christians to commit *nefaria*,[111] blaspheming Christ,[112] convincing a Christian to leave Christianity and/or to become a Jew,[113] convincing a catechumen to renege on his conversion,[114] knowingly receiving or aiding heretics,[115] possessing heretical books, or Talmuds,[116] causing offense to the host,[117] and forcing Christian nurses to pour their milk into latrines on the day they receive the Eucharist.[118] In addition, all

---

105. *B.R.,* 8:378–81.

106. Ibid., proemium: "[The Church] quae, pro eorum conversione laborans, eos misericorditer excepit, atque in cohabitatione una cum filiis suis sustinuit, ad veritatisque lumen allicere pio semper studio conata est."

107. Ibid., proemium: "[The Jews] non desinunt in religionem Christianam horrenda facinora quotidie magis agere."

108. Ibid., par. 1.

109. Ibid., par. 2.

110. Ibid., par. 3.

111. Ibid., par. 4.

112. Ibid., par. 5.

113. Ibid., par. 6.

114. Ibid., par. 7.

115. Ibid., par. 8.

116. Ibid., par. 9. The Talmud's blasphemies are its crimes.

117. Ibid., par. 10.

118. Ibid., par. 11. This too is blasphemy.

privileges and immunities ever granted to "Marranos and apostates" in the Papal States are abrogated.[119]

Antiqua's main purpose was probably dual: first, to stop Jews from aiding Marranos, and second, to prevent Jews from helping converts return to Judaism.[120] *Antiqua* also proposed to halt Jewish blasphemy. None of its provisions, however, refers to *Cum nimis* or its successor bulls. If those bulls were directed toward regulating relations between Jews and converts, it is certain that Gregory XIII would have at least mentioned them in *Antiqua*. Popes continually cited previous bulls as precedents for the bull they were in the process of issuing. In other words, *Antiqua* does not reflect on the policy instituted by *Cum nimis*.

The second apparent obstacle to the conclusion that papal policy was conversion-oriented is the expulsions ordered by Pius V and Clement VIII. Clement VIII's bull of expulsion, *Caeca et obdurata,* has already been discussed. Pius V's bull, *Hebraeorum gens,*[121] the prototype of *Caeaca et obdurata,* is almost identical to it and requires no detailed examination.[122]

In neither bull do the popes simply order the expulsion of the Jews. Rather, both popes first repeat the standard formula that the Church tolerates the Jews so that it can convert them, and then

---

119. Ibid., par. 15. This clause in no way means that Gregory XIII was about to embark on a unified policy toward both Jews and Marranos. It may signal the cancellation of the special privileges of the Anconitan Jews. Or it may signal a renewed attack on Marranos.

120. The bull, of course, refers to clandestine efforts to bring converts back to Judaism. On overt efforts to do the same, see A. Milano, "L'impari lotta della comunità di Roma contro la casa dei catecumeni," *La Rassegna Mensile di Israel* 16 (1950): 355–68.

121. Issued on Feb. 26, 1569. *B.R.,* 7:740–42.

122. One important difference: Clement VIII allowed Jews to migrate to Rome and Ancona; Pius V restricts residence (par. 2), "Eos solos Hebraeos qui nunc eas habitant." That Pius V actually implemented this restriction is made clear by Clement VIII in a letter of Jan. 20, 1605, *Alius per nos (Com. di Roma,* ITc), where he states: "Pius V Hebraeos eiusmodi ab universo Stato Ecclesiastico, alma urbe et civitate Ancona dumtaxat exceptis, ubi solos Hebraeos, qui tunc eos habitabant permisit tolerandos, expulerat." However, while offering no proof, both Roth, *Italy,* p. 307, and Milano, *Il ghetto,* p. 77, claim that many Jews entered Rome and Ancona in 1569.

proceed to agonize over the question of expulsion. Both not only express a definite unwillingness to resort to expulsion, but they also display their hope and expectation for the conversion of the Jews remaining in Ancona and Rome. Such expressions suggest that both popes viewed expulsion as an obstacle and a measure of despair rather than a desideratum.[123] In addition, both list crimes that the Jews have allegedly committed. Clement VIII specifies that the Jews oppress Christians through usuries. Pius V accuses the Jews of receiving stolen goods, of precipitating base offenses with honest women, and worst of all, of dealing in magic and incantations, thereby leading the weak to Satan and seizing their goods in the process.[124] Now, *Cum nimis* and some other bulls did speak of offenses, of Jews who sought social equality and even superiority. But these in no way correspond to the crimes recounted here. Thus, expulsion was not an alternative method for the achievement of at least the regulatory aims of *Cum nimis,* or of any other regulatory bull.

Why, then, did two popes resort to expulsion? Two outside sources and one note from actual events provide possible solutions to this question. First, these bulls of expulsion may have been intended as threats to blackmail the Jews into converting, although as threats to be implemented if the blackmail failed. If so, both popes were likely employing the tactic of giving the Jews the choice of conversion or expulsion.[125] An immediate stimulus for using this

---

123. See n. 80, supra. See also *B.R.,* 6:740, proemium.

124. *B.R.,* 7:740, proemium. The list fills twenty-four lines; e.g., "Omnium perniciosissimum est, sortilegiis, incantationibus magicisque superstitionibus et maleficiis dediti, quamplurimos incautos atque infirmos Satanae praestigiis inducunt. . . ." There is no way to prove that these crimes were or were not committed. However, according to law (cf. *De Iudaeis,* pt. 1, chap. 7, par. 4), Jews could be expelled only if they had committed grievous crimes. Thus Pius V may have fabricated the accusations in order to make his expulsion edict legal.

125. See Browe, *Judenmission,* p. 243, where he asserts that these two popes were employing this tactic. See also Browe, pp. 242–43, for a discussion of the history of this tactic. He claims that it was employed in England, France, Germany, and Spain, but always by secular rulers and most often for the purpose of forcing the Jews to make a large payment in order to free themselves from the expulsion edict, and that only in Spain did such an edict result in numerous conversions. Cf., however, S. Grayzel, "The Avignonese Popes and the Jews,"

tactic had been provided by Francisco de Torres. In 1555 he wrote to the inquisitors that the Jews should be threatened with expulsion if they refused to attend conversionary sermons. Should they persist in their refusal, then the threat should be implemented. The expulsion order itself, he added, would have the power of inducing conversions.[126] The fact that in at least one town, Viterbo, the priors were under Pius V's orders to pay twenty-five scudi to Jews and one hundred scudi to Jewesses who would convert rather than be expelled suggests that Pius V was influenced to some degree by de Torres' advice.[127] Indeed, in 1555 Pius V was the chief inquisitor, and hence one of the men to whom de Torres' book was directed.

Nevertheless, the stated apprehension of both Pius V and Clement VIII that expulsion would hinder conversionary efforts, and the lack of any explicit reference by either pope to an actual choice of conversion or expulsion, makes it impossible to assert without qualification that they viewed their expulsion orders as a conversionary device.[128] Thus, another possible explanation of these orders must be adduced.

In the 1513 *Libellus ad Leonem Decem* of P. Quirini and P. Justiniani, Leo X is advised that if his policy does not succeed in converting the Jews within a certain time, then he should expel them.[129] This advice likely derived from the theory, found for ex-

---

Historia Judaica 2 (1940): 10, who makes the interesting hypothesis that each of the expulsions from France in the fourteenth century resulted in a large number of conversions.

126. *Francisci Torrensis de sola lectione legis . . . et de Iesu in synagogis . . . annunciando. Ad reverendiss. Inquisitores. Libri Duo* (Rome, 1555), p. 150: "Date ergo iudaeis optionem, aut recedant a nobis, aut dienceps Synagogis satanae ne utantur nisi ad lectionem legis et prophetarum . . . , [and except for those times when] surgat Christianus aliquis [who will preach the Gospel to them]"; and pp. 159–61: "Hos non compelletis, sive eiiciendo, sive ex lege in synagogis redarguendo, ut intrare velint? [Did not the Spanish expulsion compel many to enter!]"

127. A. Milano, "Sugli Ebrei a Viterbo," *Scritti Sull'Ebraismo in Memoria di Guido Bedarida* (Florence, 1966), p. 145.

128. Cf. Baron, *SRH*, 14:47–48, where he describes Pius V's expulsion order only as the culmination of that pope's repressive measures and makes no suggestion that Pius V's intent was conversionary.

129. Paulus Justiniani and Petrus Quirini, *Libellus ad Leonem Decem*, in *Annales Camaldulenses*, ed. J-B. Mittarelli and A. Costadoni (Venice, 1793), 9: cols. 612–719; for expulsion, col. 625.

ample in the writings of John Chrysostom and Joachim of Flora, that many Jews would first join the camp of Antichrist and then convert after his defeat at Armageddon.[130] Quirini and Justiniani probably reasoned that those Jews who would not convert after a period of active papal proselytizing were the ones destined to join forces with Antichrist. And for the mortal safety of all, it was preferable that they be expelled forthwith.

There is no question that Pius V was influenced by the *Libellus*. According to Jedin, Pius V's liturgical reforms were an outgrowth of that tract.[131] So too was his appointment of a committee to reedit the texts of Canon law.[132] Hence it is likely that Pius V, as well as Clement VIII after him, was also influenced by the *Libellus* in the matter of the conversion, and possible expulsion, of the Jews. Thus the enigma of the expulsions may be plausibly explained. Whether Pius V and Clement VIII were using the tactic of offering the choice of conversion or expulsion, or whether they were influenced by the *Libellus,* their expulsion edicts were but a facet of a conversionary policy.

The third apparent obstacle to the conclusion that later-sixteenth-century Jewry policy was conversion-oriented is the relative absence of explicit references to the specifics of this policy in contemporary Jewish writings. Yet for this scarcity of references there is good cause. On the one hand, Jews were simply cowed into extreme reticence by the threat of reprisal or the destruction of their writings by the Papal Inquisition. Two examples suffice to explain this situation.

---

130. Ibid., col. 625. There they write that those Jews who have not converted should, as "morbidas oves a Christianis gregibus ita omnino separari." The term *morbidas oves* smacks of the following: John Chrysostom, "Homily Thirty-Three on Hebrews," in *The Nicene and Post-Nicene Fathers,* ed. P. Schaff (New York, 1906), 14:515: "[The Jews expect another messiah] and, having deprived themselves of Him that is, will fall into the hands of Antichrist"; and Arsenio Frugoni, ed., *Adversus Judaeos di Gioacchino da Fiore* (Rome, 1957), p. 48: "Inde est quod, effectus cecus secundum maiorem sui partem, recepturus est Antichristum."

131. H. Jedin, *A History of the Council of Trent,* trans. E. Graf, 2 vols. (St. Louis, 1957–61), 1:130.

132. Ibid., p. 128.

On February 4, 1559, the chief inquisitor and future Pius V, Cardinal Ghislieri, wrote to the duke of Ferrara, complaining about the circulation of a pamphlet clearly written at Ancona and praising those who were burned there in 1556. The author, who is reported to be residing at Ferrara, should be punished, and the archepiscopal vicar of Ferrara should assume the responsibility of confiscating and burning all copies of the pamphlet.[133] Soon after, the duke of Ferrara wrote to Ghislieri, informing him that the order had been carried out.[134] According to David Kaufmann,[135] the pamphlet in question is the sixteen-page poem, *Shilte Giborim,* of Jacob b. Joab of Fano, written in 1556. The first fourteen pages of the poem contain a misogynous diatribe; the last two, however, record what Fano saw when he passed through Ancona on his way to Ferrara in April of 1556 and witnessed the execution of twenty-four Marranos. Fano even lists their names.[136] Arguing in favor of his hypothesis, Kaufmann notes not only the content of the poem, as well as Fano's demonstrable itinerary and place of residence in the spring of 1556, but also—and this is crucial—the great rarity of complete copies of the poem.

In 1568, in order to obtain evidence corroborating the charges of the convert Alessandro Foligno that rabbinic writings in general, and the *Shilte Giborim* of R. Isaiah Trani in particular, attack Christianity as idolatory, the Inquisition at Bologna arrested R. Yishmael Hannina of Ferrara.[137] As R. Yishmael himself records in a personal memorial of his encounter with the Inquisition, written shortly after his release from prison,[138] he was not the only one inter-

---

133. A copy of this letter appears in C. Feroso, *Gli Ebrei portoghesi giustiziati in Ancona sotto Paolo IV* (Foligno, 1889), p. 211.

134. Ibid., p. 212.

135. D. Kaufmann, "Les Martyrs d'Ancone," *REJ* 11 (1893): 149–53.

136. The full text of the poem has been published by Neubauer in *Letterbode* 10 (1884): 124 ff. The pamphlet was originally printed at Ferrara in May 1556 by Abraham Usque.

137. For a general description of this incident, see the unsigned article, "Inquisitionsverfahren gegen die Juden in Bologna in Jahre 1568," *MGWJ* 20 (1871): 378–81.

138. A. Jellinek, ed.,‏ ‏חקירות על עניני הנוצרים, תשובות על העלילות של הכומר‏
‏אליסאנדרו בבולוניאה בחודש נובימ' ,ורבים מהיהודים הנתפשים בבולוניא הודו ע"י יסורין."‏

rogated. "And many of the Jews who were imprisoned in Bologna confessed to their [the Inquisition's] charges as a result of torture." [139] But as for R. Yishmael himself: "When the inquisitor interrogated me about this, he brought me to a place where royal prisoners suffer rope torture. . . . They bound my hands with cords and began to draw me with the rope. Then I said, 'Let me down'; and the face of the inquisitor grew bright, as he thought that I too wanted to confess." [140] Once cut down, however, R. Yishmael refused to confess and stated that repeated torture would yield the same result. Should he break down and confess under torture, he went on, he would at the first opportunity declare his confession invalid, because it had been gained under duress. The inquisitor, on hearing this, "steamed with rage, and anger burned within him. He reviled and cursed me bitterly, and ordered his servants to cast me into a prison more evil and vile than the first, a cramped place with no room for one who is standing to stretch himself to his full height or for one who is sitting to stand. There I remained three weeks; but he did not continue to interrogate me any more . . ." [141]

Thus, the absence of explicit Jewish descriptions of papal policy is in part the product of anxiety. If Jews wrote too explicitly, their works might be burned. If they spoke too openly, they might themselves share a fate similar to that of R. Yishmael Hannina.[142] However they understood it, then, Jews were certainly not going to make bold-face statements on the nature or the specifics of papal policy. To do so was simply too dangerous. These anxieties even led to such

---

Ha-Shaḥar 2 (1870): 17–23. Most of this record contains R. Yishmael's replies to the Inquisition, which are noteworthy for their skillfulness and cleverness. At the end he reports on his own trials.

139. Ibid., p. 22: „ורבים מהיהודים הנתפשים בבולוניא הודו ע״י יסורין.‟

140. Ibid., pp. 22–23: „וכאשר חקרני החוקר על זה הביאני במקום אשר אסירי המלך מקבלים החבל . . . אסרו ידי בעבותים והתחילו למשך אותי בחבל. אך אמרתי הורידוני וצהבו פניו של החוקר בהאמינו שהייתי רוצה להודות גם אני . . . ‟

141. Ibid., p. 23: „עלה עשן באפו וחמתו בערה בו וחרף וגדף אותי במאד מאד ויצו את עבדיו להשימינו בבית כלא אחר רע ומר מן הראשון, מקום צר אשר אין דרך לעמוד, ושם ישבתי שלשה שבועות ולא יסף עוד לחקור אותי . . . ‟

142. Cf. Baron, *SRH*, 14:133–39, on self-imposed constraints on writing resulting from the fear of censorship.

DISCARDED

paradoxes as the following statement of David del Bene, which refers to the implementation by local authorities of the papal decree ordering the burning of the Talmud.

In his *Sefer Khis'oth le-Veth David,* he goes on at length, decrying the attitude toward Jews and their treatment in Muslim lands. In contrast, he praises the kindness and generosity of Christian rulers. But he ends this praise saying: "And if in these [Christian] regions . . . permission is not given by the rulers of the land to retain the Talmud in our hands, and if with difficulty they have permitted what they have permitted, for they are gracious kings, there should be no wonder that the production of books in these parts today is just not a common occurrence." [143] The sarcasm is unmistakable as Del Bene impugns a point of Christian policy outright. The real "gracious" kings are the Muslim sultans, and those who treat the Jews poorly are the Christians.

Indeed, but one distinct reference to papal conversionary activity appears in a book composed in the sixteenth century. Recording the death of Julius III, Joseph HaKohen declares in his *'Emeq ha-Bakh'a*:[144] "Let the mountains break forth in joyous song, for Julio del Monte, the pope, who wished to lead us to apostasy, is dead . . ." How did he expect to achieve this end? "By burning our glorious books." [145] As will be seen below, HaKohen was quite correct. The burning of the Talmud was a component of conversionary policy. Nevertheless, this brief reference truly proves the point about anxiety and reticence in expression. The *'Emeq HaBakh'a* was not published, but remained in manuscript until 1852.[146]

As for other references to conversion or conversionary pressure, they are vague about its extent and completely silent about its source,

---

143. David Del Bene, *S. Khis'oth le-Veth David* (Verona, 1597), fols. 88–89 f. The citation itself is from fol. 94b: ‏,ואם בגלילותינו אלה . . . אין הרשות נתונה‏
‏מאדוני הארץ להחזיק תלמודינו בידינו ובקושי התירו מה שהתירו כי מלכי חסד המה, אין לתמוה‏
‏אם עשות ספרים היום בכאן מלתא דלא שכיחא . . .‏"

144. Jos. HaKohen, *'Emeq ha-Bakh'a*, ed. M. Letteris (Cracow, 1895).

145. HaKohen, *'Emeq*, p. 131:   ‏,פצחו הרים רנה כי מת יוליו די מונטי, האפיפיור‏
‏אשר דמה להדיחנו אשר שרף ספרי תפארתינו.‏"

146. Cf. M. M. Kasher, *Sarei HaElef* (New York, 1959), p. 349, #393, where he notes that the *'Emeq* was first published only in 1852.

although they may be most adamant in their statements of intention to combat it. The strongest of these statements is found in the polemic of Yair b. Shabbtai of Correggio, the *Herev Pifioth,* written sometime during the 1560s.[147]

> When I saw the upraised hand of the enemy of truth resting on the necks of the tenderhearted children of Israel, some of whom were so startled and unnerved by the lightning sharp order of their [Christian] arguments . . . that they were seduced by their deceits, . . . I said: "It is time to labor for the Lord, . . . to gird the avenging sword to avenge the covenant, . . . to go to war against the enemies of God and to save the souls of the unfortunate Jews, so that they do not surrender and fall . . ."[148]

In the same vein, the anonymous protagonist and author of the Hebrew transcription of a dispute held at Ferrara in 1617 attempts to minimize the value of the preaching and disputation which Yair b. Shabbtai found so upsetting.[149] His basic point, to be sure, is that the Christians have nothing of value to prove to the Jews.[150] Yet some wishful thinking about the cessation of such efforts, and indeed about their fruitfulness, is undeniably implicit in his conclusion that "those who have labored to dispute with the Jews and to bring proof that they are obligated to leave their Torah and to receive another one have labored in vain."[151] This claim is then reinforced

147. Yair b. Shabbtai, *Herev Pifioth,* ed. J. Rosenthal (Jerusalem, 1958).

148. Ibid., intro.: „בראותי תנופת יד אויבי האמת מונחת על צוארי בני ישראל רכי הלבב, שקצתם נבהלו נחפזו מברק שנון סדר טעגותיהם . . . עדי שנתפתו לכזביהם . . . אמרתי עת לעשות לד׳ . . . לחגור חרב גוקמת נקם ברית . . . לערוך מלחמה נגד אויבי ד׳ ולמלט נפשות יהודים האמללים שלא יכריעו ויפולו . . ."

149. MS Bodl. 2587 (Film # 22290, Hebrew University Library Division of Manuscript Photography). This *Vikuah* has also been published as *Vikhuah 'al Nitzhiuth ha-Torah* (Livorno, 1876). Citations here are from the MS.

150. The general theme of the *Vikhuah* is that Judaism is a true religion according to all philosophical theological standards. The antagonist, D. Alf. Caracciolo, had tried to prove the opposite. By removing the basis for Caracciolo's claim, the protagonist feels that he has demonstrated that Christian preachers are wasting their time. As far as he is concerned, there is no reason why Jews should convert.

151. Ibid., p. 17b: „לשוא עמלו הרוצים להתוכח עם היהודים ולהביא ראיון שהם מוכרחים להניח תורתם ולקבל תורה אחרת."

by constant repetition. Over and over the protagonist affirms that his opponent has in no way proved "that the Jews are obligated to receive their [Christian] religion and messiah." [152]

The 1588 *Enarratio Apologica* of David de Pomis attacks the problem of conversionary pressure from the opposite direction.[153] Ostensibly intended to refute charges leveled against Jewish physicians, in large part this book is devoted to the theme: "If you wish to defend religion poorly [that is, by repressing other religions and by driving their adherents to convert], it is not defended, but corrupted; for nothing is such a matter of free choice as is religion." [154] The intended audience, moreover, was the body of Italian secular princes, whose members had begun to capitulate to papal suasion by the 1580s and were increasingly enforcing the papacy's restrictive Jewry edicts.[155] De Pomis thus implores the princes to allow Jews to live freely with Christians, unhampered and without duress in their observance of Judaism. Certainly, he adds, to allow this poses no threat to Christianity. "For if Jews should be allowed the society of Christians, they would in no way be able to lead a Christian to Mosaic law, even if they wished to (which they most assuredly do not). Indeed, the contrary is true. Christians constantly turn Jews (through social intercourse) toward baptism." [156] Whether through pressure or through simple persuasion, de Pomis is conceding, there are always going to be conversions to Christianity in these times. At least allow such acts to result only from freely arrived at decisions.

There is little, however, to distinguish between these statements, all made after the initiation of the new papal policy, and that found in an anonymous Italian commentary on the Book of Job,

---

152. Ibid., p. 1a: (and also pp. 17b and 18a)

‫„שהיהודים הם מוכרחים לקבל את דתם ואת משיחם . . .”‬

153. David de Pomis, *Enarratio Apologica* (Venice, 1588).

154. Ibid., p. 80: "Si male Religionem defendere velis, iam non defendetur illa, sed polluetur; nihil profecto est tam voluntarium quam religio."

155. Cf. chap. 9, infra.

156. De Pomis, *Enarratio*, p. 82: "Et si societatem cum Christianis habuerint, Christianum nihilominus ad legem Mosis ducere, etiam si vellent (quod non concedimus) nequeunt, . . . Contra vero Christianus quotidie hebraeos (propter conversationem) ad baptismum vertit."

which dates from about 1540, prior to the new policy.[157] While this
commentary may lack some of the emotionalism present in the later
works, an emotionalism which is surely attributable to the fact that
over eight hundred Jews had converted to Christianity during the
later sixteenth century,[158] it nevertheless does address itself to the
same basic problem of conversionary preaching. Thus its author propounds that Job is a model of the Disputation between Israel and the
Nations. The Jew who reads Job will be strengthened to meet the
challenges and stresses he now faces.[159] "And they [the Christians] do
continuously challenge us. All day long in their temples they make
propaganda, speaking publicly, calling to our people. Some even go
into homes, at any time and at any hour, speaking their words to
every Jew." [160] The activity the anonymous author speaks of probably represents an unofficial movement within the Church in favor
of a conversionary policy which would become official after 1555.
Yet here, as with the later works, there is no way of knowing precisely what the author is writing about, because the specifics are
missing. This earlier work could just as easily have been written
after 1555, and the later works beforehand. It is, of course, possible
to surmise precisely what the authors of these works meant and to
what they were referring, but this may be done only with the help
of other sources. Alone they are insufficient. These men may have
known more, but if so they were unwilling to admit it.

Now, there are three items which do indicate some direct con-

---

157. See H. H. Ben-Sasson, "HaYehudim Mul HaReformatziah," *Proceedings
of the Israel Academy of Arts and Sciences* 5 (1970): 62–116.

158. Cf. A. Milano, "Battesimi di ebrei a Roma dal cinquecento all'ottocento," in *Scritti in Memoria di Enzo Sereni* (Jerusalem, 1970), pp. 140 f., where
he gives figures for baptisms in that period, and p. 148, where he notes what I believe the Jews of the time saw, namely, that heavy Christian pressure in the
form of restrictive edicts was a potent factor in increasing the number of conversions. As a comparative yardstick, it is well to note that the Jewish population
of Italy remained fairly stable throughout the period; about 22,000–30,000.

159. Ben-Sasson, "Hayehudim," p. 81, and p. 82, nn. 93 and 94.

160. Ibid., p. 82, n. 95: ‏„כמו שעושים תמיד כל היום בהיכליהם בפרסום רב,‎
‏בהשמיעם קול קריאתם על בני עמנו. גם יחידיהם בבתיהם בכל עת ובכל שעה אלה דבריהם על‎
‏כל יהודי."‎
Ben-Sasson's source is MS Adler, 1253, Jewish Theological Seminary.

nection between papal letters and conversion. The most striking of these comes in the circular letter sent sometime shortly before the 1569 expulsion by the community of Cori in the (Roman) Campagna to Italian communities outside the Papal States asking their financial aid to enable the two hundred or so members of the Cori community to move to Tiberias in the Galilee. Writing directly of the effects of the bulls of both Paul IV and Pius V, the author declares, perhaps with some exaggeration, that the oppressions were so severe in 1555 that:

> Anyone who was incapable of suffering or of sanctifying God's name [as a martyr] converted from our holy faith, until the converts were exceedingly numerous in that time, and those who remained were left with nothing except their body and soul.

And in 1568 again the pressures were so extensive that:

> We all wandered as sheep. Each of us went his own way to convert from the holy faith of God. Every day families important and unimportant, wise and intelligent, rich and poor converted. And they [the Christians], if they were not persecuting us, came to vex us, undermining and pressing, enticing the people of Israel to their belief.[161]

A bit less directly, but nonetheless distinctly, Immanuel of Benevento writes in the dirge prefacing his *Livyat Ḥen,* recounting the troubles which befell the Jews of Italy between 1554 and 1557:

---

161. For the complete letter, see Sonne, *Mi-Pavolo,* pp. 175–79.

באופן שמי לא היה בידו כח לסבל ולקדש את השם היו ממרים דתינו הקדושה,   עד שרבו כמו שרבו הממרים בזמן ההוא והנשארים לא נשאר להם בלתי אם גויתם וצורתם (גופם ונפשם, (p. 176

כי כלנו כצאן תעינו איש לדרכו פנינו להמיר דת האל   הקדושה,   שבכל יום ויום באים משפחות גדולים וקטנים חכמים ונבונים דלים ועשירים וממרים דתם, והם היו בעכרינו מסיתים ומדיחים מפתים אנשי ישראל אל אמונתם מלבד שרודפים אותנו (p. 177).

Relatives were made into strangers
    And many have become foreigners
Some passed over seas
    And as harts over mountains.[162]

In Hebrew "strangers" (*nokhrim*) and "foreigners" (*gerim*) also mean Christians and converts respectively. Hence, Isaiah Sonne has correctly interpreted these lines:[163] Immanuel is informing us here that the issuance of *Cum nimis* brought many Jews either to flee from the Papal States or to convert.[164] In a similar passage, but this time speaking directly of the 1569 expulsion decree of Pius V, Gedalya ibn Yaḥya states: "He ordered that within three months all Israel must depart from his dominions. . . . And such happened that not one remained, except the few who converted." [165] Ibn Yaḥya may have purposely understated the number of converts here. In view of the over eight hundred conversions between 1555 and 1600, there is room for doubt. But for the moment that is immaterial. What is of importance is that ibn Yaḥya, as well as Immanuel of Benevento, write only of effects, and not of purposes. They leave their reader guessing whether the conversions were something hoped for by Paul IV and Pius V, or merely an accidental and unplanned side effect. Even the Cori letter, while more suggestive than the other two passages, provides no direct evidence that the conversions themselves, or the activities of those Christians who pressed for conversions, were specifically intended or mandated by either Paul IV or Pius V.

---

162. This dirge is printed in Sonne, *Mi-Pavolo*, p. 115; lines 25–26:

ורבים הלכו גרים   קרובים נעשו נכרים
וכצביים על הרים   קצתם עברו ימים

The *Livyat Ḥen* was originally published at Mantua in 1557.

163. Sonne, *Mi-Pavolo*, p. 115.

164. Cf. L. Finkelstein, *Jewish Self-Government in the Middle Ages* (New York, 1924), pp. 26 and 30, on the subject of rabbinic ordinances concerning dealings with converts, including those whose conversion was not a matter of their own will.

165. G. ibn Yaḥya, *Shalshelet ha-Qabbalah* (Jerusalem, 1962), p. 277:

„צוה שמשך ג׳ חדשים כל ישראל יצאו ממלכותו בקנס אבידות הגוף והממון.   וכך נעשה שלא נשאר פרסה זולת מעטים שהמירו.‟

In all three of these passages, moreover, the impression is given that their authors were imprecise not so much because of their anxieties, as was likely the case elsewhere, but because of ignorance. Indeed, one is forced to ask at what point anxiety and fear ended and ignorance began, that is, how much did most Jews really comprehend about their situation and specifically about the intricacies of papal policy?

The problem here may be one of perspective. The three major chronicles of the period, the *Dibre ha-Yamim* of Benjamin Nehemiah b. Elnathan,[166] the *'Emeq HaBakh'a* of Joseph HaKohen, and the *Shalshelet ha-Qabbalah* of Gedaliah ibn Yahya all describe the bull *Cum nimis* in some detail. Yet they discuss the bull in the same paragraphs in which they write of the episode at Ancona.[167] This is, however, to be expected. For each of the three chroniclers was a Sephardi and quite understandably most caught up in the plight of other Sephardim, even to the point that he was unable to perceive the clear line separating the policy toward Jews and that toward the Anconitans.

These Sephardim were not alone in failing to discern things as they actually were. A large number of Jewish texts, mostly homilies, are concerned with the lot of all Jews, their suffering and redemption, and they are unanimous in seeing the Jews threatened with destructive pressures. Typical are the two Purim sermons (1553 and 1559) of Moses Almosnino.[168] God, he declares, once saved His people in time of trouble, and "so He will continue to do," until He finally brings redemption.[169] The identical sentiment is expressed

---

166. Benj. Neh. b. Elnathan, *Dibre ha-Yamim,* as published by Sonne in *Mi-Pavolo,* pp. 13–93.

167. Sonne, *Mi-Pavolo,* pp. 23–30; ibn Yahya, *Shalshelet,* pp. 276–77; and HaKohen, *'Emeq,* pp. 133–36. Cf. the recent Spanish trans. of this last: *Emeq Ha-Bakha De Yosef Ha-Kohen,* trans. and notes by Pilar Leon Tello (Madrid, 1964), pp. 230–35.

168. Biographical data is sparse or nonexistent for Almosnino, as well as for most of those cited on these pages. For many of them, however, some information, especially bibliographical, is available in Neppi-Girondi, *Toldoth Gdole Yisrael ve-Geone Italiah* (Trieste, 1853), and brief entries are often to be found in the *Encyclopaedia Judaica.*

169. The sermon was actually delivered in Salonika, but in its final written

repeatedly in the sermons of Samuel Yuda b. Meir Katzenellen-bogen,[170] Samuel Hagiz,[171] and especially Menahem Raba.[172] In a sermon for Sabbath *Zakhor,* Raba states: "Amalek and Samael have joined together at this time to destroy the memory of Israel, as did Esau." [173] But "on that day [of redemption] . . . He will blot out the name and memory of Amalek." [174] At Purim time Raba tells his listeners that their present situation is as delicate as that of Mordecai and Esther.[175]

Non-homiletic literature too contains similar thoughts. Judah Moscato, in his commentary on the *Kuzari,* the *Qol Yehudah,* speaks

---

form it appeared in Venice in *Sefer Ma'amatz Khoaḥ* (Venice, 1588), a collection of twenty-eight sermons. Sermon on *Parashat Zakhor*, p. 135a: „וכן ימשיך לעשות Ibid., second sermon on *Zakhor*, p. 140b.

„וכן היה העניין בימים ההם ובזמן הזה . . . וכן יהיה תמיד . . ."

170. Sam. Y. b. M. Katzenellenbogen, *Shtaim 'Esre Drashot* (Venice, 1588), for Sabbath *Naḥamu*, p. 51b: וכנגד . . . „האומות החזיקו היהודי בהיותו בגלות לאיש נבזה דעתם זה אמר הנביא . . . כי כל מי שהקב"ה חפץ בו מדכאו ביסורין; ומאהבתו את ישראל דכא אותם ביסורי גלות . . . " , „ימהר יחיש מעשיו ויזכנו . . . לימות המשיח." (52) And if the Jews observe all the commandments, then the redemption will quickly follow.

171. S. Hagiz, *Sefer Mvaqesh Adonäi* (Venice, 1596), a collection of sermons. For Sabbath *be-Shalaḥ*, p. 144, he speaks of the redemption at the Red Sea as the symbol of redemption for all time, and he immediately follows by speaking of the eschatological Gog and Magog. Later on, p. 176, in a sermon for *T'tzaveh*, he announces that even if the "Evil Edict" has now been decreed, God will still save His people. This "Edict" is almost certainly a synonym for contemporary papal policy.

172. M. Raba, *Beth Mo'ed* (Venice, 1605), a collection of fifty sermons. For Sabbath *Ḥanukhah*, fols. 103–6: the burning Hanukkah lamp should remind Jews of redemption. For the Fast of Esther, fols. 114–17: This fast is praiseworthy; it is of help in hastening the redemption. And in this time of troubles, Jews should not fear; for God will not forget them. For the day of Purim, fols. 117–19: All the enemies of the Jews are like Amalek; that is, they will be destroyed. If God once saved Israel, so He will so do again. For the various days of Passover, fols. 128, 141–46: The theme for each of these sermons is redemption.

173. Raba, *Beth Mo'ed*, fol. 112b: „ועמלק וסמאל נזדווגו עתה להכרית זכרם של ישראל, כמו עשו, והראיה כי עמלק וסמאל בגמטריא עשו פחות חמשה, שלא הגיעו להכרית שם ישראל, שהם חמש אותיות . . . "

174. Ibid., fol. 115a: „וביום ההוא . . . ימחה שמו וזכרו של עמלק . . . לפי שעמלק גרם לישראל כל הצער ובקש למנוע מישראל שלשת הכתרים. מלכות. תורה. וכהונה . . . ובחר עוד בישראל."

175. Raba, *Bet Mo'ed*, fol. 114a: „במקרה כשבא המן לערבם עירוב עצמי היינו שימירו דתם כדי להנצל מהמות . . . נזורו אחור מן הגוים ושבו אל ה' ובראש כלם מרדכי הצדיק."

of great trials, but equally of his assurance that God will never forsake His people.[176] In his mystically oriented *Sefer Ḥaredim,* Eliezer Aziqri writes that the people now suffers because it has yet to repent of its sins. Whence, "from time to time and from season to season there comes [divine] anger: expulsions, forced conversions, and drawn swords." [177] And Eliezer Nahman Foa, in his *Midrash be-Ḥidush,* a commentary on the Passover Haggadah, talks of the value of contemporary suffering, for by means of such, Jews become purified in preparation for their ultimate redemption.[178]

Yet none of these texts specifies the dangers it speaks of. What they seem to be reacting to is the whole collection of shocks and reverses the Jews had suffered in the past two hundred years, and which had now befallen the Jews of Italy too. Here again the problem is one of switching perspective. The edicts of 1555 were viewed as but another link in a chain of tragedies. This, after all, is the standpoint of Joseph HaKohen: Jewish history is to be retold by recounting a list of calamities. Furthermore, in their past dealings with the papacy, the Jews had known only one pattern. Popes were either heavy- or light-handed in their enforcement of restrictions. Paul IV, whose reputation with Christians too was one of severity, was another of those popes who would be harsh, perhaps extremely harsh, but no more. Indeed, this image of papal policy was further reinforced by the administrative shifts of Paul IV's successors. It is perhaps too much to think that most Jews would have been able to grasp the subtleties of *Cum nimis* and its formulae. What concerned them were its administrative and regulatory clauses, action and not theory.

---

176. The *Qol Yehudah* appears in the margins of Y. Halevi's *Kuzari, ed. princ.* (Venice, 1594), essay 5, p. 51.

177. E. Aziqri, *Sefer Ḥaredim* (Venice, 1601), which is a discussion of *Mitzvoth* pertaining to bodily acts, with a pronouncedly mystical bias. Intro., pp. 2–4: וימא . . . "ועדיין לא שבנו מטעויותינו ולכן נארך גלותנו ומצאנו צרות רבות ורעות רונז מעת לעת מפקידה לפקידה, גרושין ושמדות וחרבות שלופות; מי נתן למשיסה יעקב . . . הלא ה' זו חטאנו לו במצוות לא תעשה . . . ואין אנו בטוחים מגרושין ושמדות אחרות . . . "

178. E. N. Foa, *Midrash be-Ḥidush* (Tel-Aviv, 1965), pp. 7–8. This work was originally published at Venice in 1641. Despite the late date, however, it is surely reacting to the troubles of the later sixteenth century, besides those of the author's own time, which were but a continuation of the earlier ones.

Moreover, while on paper it has been possible to show a consistency in papal policy, actuality may have belied that. Aside from the changes in regulations, there were also the inconsistencies in the treatment of the Anconitans. It was these matters of daily practice which the Jews saw. What is more, the mechanisms of conversion themselves were established within the papal territories over a long period of time and in a somewhat haphazard way. The *Domus catechumenorum* preceded *Cum nimis* by twelve years, and the Talmud burning preceded it by two. Expulsions came fourteen and thirty-eight years later. And preaching was instituted only in 1584. Thus Jews, or at least those dwelling within the Papal States, may have sensed a growing conversionary pressure, as the various references they made to conversion indicate, but they were probably in the dark about an organized and coordinated effort.

As for the Jews outside the papal domains, their ignorance would have been even greater. The papacy may have implemented its theoretical policy, if in a somewhat disjointed way, within its own states, but it was never able to persuade the numerous local Italian rulers to follow suit. Even when these rulers acceded in such matters as Talmud burning, missionary sermons, and the ghetto, they did so only selectively and arbitrarily.[179] None of them ever adopted the papal program in its entirety.

There were some Jews, nevertheless, who were not totally ignorant of what was taking place, to wit, the statement of Joseph HaKohen about the burning of the Talmud. How knowledgeable these Jews were, however, must remain unknown, because of their anxieties and reticence about the results if they did speak out—with one notable exception.

On 16 August, 1555, the Roman Jewish printer, Elijah b. Emanuel da Nola, sent a business letter to the Flemish humanist Hebraist, Andreus Masius.[180] This letter contains a most unbusiness-like last paragraph: "The Jews here are in bad straits, because an-

---

179. Cf. chap. 9, infra.
180. The Italian original of this letter is to be found in J. Perles, *Beiträge zur Geschichte Aramaischen und Hebraischen Studien* (Munich, 1855), p. 219; and a Hebrew trans. in Sonne, *Mi-Pavolo,* pp. 108 f.

other bull has recently been published by His Holiness, from which it seems as if he wishes to force us to baptism . . ." [181] Had da Nola said this and no more, it would be absolutely certain that he was speaking of *Cum nimis,* which was issued only one month prior to the date of his letter.[182] There would thus be an explicit Jewish text indicating that Paul IV had launched a conversionary program. However, the letter continues: ". . . saying [in this bull] that any man who does not believe that Christ was born of the Virgin Mary and that Christ is not the son of God must depart the States of the Church within three months." [183] As far as I can tell, Paul IV issued no such directive, nor is there any evidence to suggest that he did. But it is possible that da Nola was passing on here not fact, but rumor—a rumor which arose among a number of Roman Jews in response to *Cum nimis.* Somehow these Jews had learned that Paul IV was intent on fostering conversion. But at the same time, the confused understanding of *Cum nimis* expressed by da Nola's letter reveals most strikingly that the precise dimensions, if not the actual existence, of the new papal policy were unknown. It is for this reason, more than for any other, that Jewish sources have so little to say on the subject of the papacy and conversion.

The program of the papacy did, however, exist. Two of its facets now remain to be examined: the *Domus catechumenorum,* and the burning of the Talmud, as well as the proscription and destruction of any rabbinic commentary or text, such as the *Alfas* or the *Mishneh Torah,* based on the Talmud.[184]

---

181. Perles, *Beiträge,* p. 219: "Qui li hebrei stanno molto travagliati per una altra bolla novamente uscita da sua santità, per laqual pare che sua santità vogli che ci batizano per forza . . ."

182. See Sonne, pp. 106 ff., for da Nola's two previous letters to Masius, of June 15 and June 29, 1555 respectively. Both antedate *Cum nimis,* whence there can be little doubt that in this letter of Aug. 15 he is referring to no other bull. Perles, p. 223, claims flatly that da Nola is speaking of *Cum nimis* in this August letter.

183. Perles, *Beiträge,* p. 219: ". . . (per forza) dicendo che qual sivoglia persona che non creda che Cristo non sia nato di Maria virgine et che sia figliolo di dio che tutti habiano di partirsi del tutto tenimento de la ecclesia fra termino de tre mensi."

184. That not only the Talmud, but all its commentaries, too, were burned is

In the 1540s two bulls were issued which brought the *Domus* into being. The first, *Cupientes Iudaeos,* issued on March 21, 1542 by Paul III, was intended to insure the material well-being and, indeed, betterment of converts.[185] Accordingly, it declares: "Cupientes Iudaeos et alios infideles quoslibet ad fidem catholicam converti," it is desirable that Jews should not hesitate to convert out of fear that conversion will result in impoverishment. Therefore converts must not suffer, as they usually did, confiscation of property at the hands of princes.[186] They must also acquire the full rights of citizenship. To insure sincerity and constancy, new converts must be carefully taught and kept apart from Jews. So too, they must be urged to marry those who are Christians by birth.

The concept of improved material well-being for converts was not new in 1542; it was already present in bulls dating from 1278[187] and 1322.[188] The reappearance of this idea immediately preceding the bulls beginning with *Cum nimis* both heralds their appearance and reveals growing interest in conversion on the part of the papacy. Moreover, establishing conditions favorable to the convert became a fundamental of the conversionary policy of the succeeding decades.[189]

---

seen in Stern, *Urkundliche Beiträge,* letters, # 105 (pp. 106–7), # 124 (pp. 132–34), and # 159 (p. 166), among others, where distinct reference is made to the sequestration, burning, or proposed censorship of various works, including, beside those mentioned above, the *Bet Yaacov,* the *Responsa* of R. Asher, and the *Sefer Mizvot ha-Gadol.* See also Milano, *Il Ghetto,* p. 216, where he notes that in May 1557 the Scola Tedesca was closed and its members fined because a copy of the commentaries of Abraham ibn Ezra was found there.

185. *B.R.,* 6:336 f.

186. Despite the illegality of the act (cf. p. 179, infra), princes had almost invariably confiscated the property of Jewish converts. The princes did so on the pretext that they were the legal owners of all Jewish property (see S. Baron, "Medieval Nationalism and Jewish Serfdom," in *Studies in Honor of Abraham A. Neuman,* ed. M. Ben-Horin et al. [Leiden, 1962], pp. 17–48, and esp. 32), or on the pretext that the convert was a rebellious vassal (Grayzel, *The Church and the Jews,* p. 19). Such confiscation was explicitly outlawed by X.5, 6, 5 (originally a decree of the Third Lateran Council), and by numerous other bulls (see, e.g., Grayzel, *The Church,* pp. 97 and 223, and idem, "The Avignonese Popes and the Jews," pp. 10 f.), but as *Cupientes Iudaeos* reveals, they had not ceased.

187. *Vineam Sorec,* issued by Nicholas III, Aug. 4, 1278, *B.R.,* 1:29.

188. *Cum sit absurdum,* issued by John XXII, June 19, 1320, *B.R.,* 4:294.

189. Cf. *De Iudaeis,* pt. 3, chaps. 2–9, and also infra, pp. 179f.

The stimulus for *Cupientes Iudaeos* came from Ignatius Loyola. Loyola considered converting the Jews an important part of his general missionary activity,[190] and his efforts toward that end were not restricted to lobbying for *Cupientes Iudaeos* alone. On February 19, 1543, Paul III issued the bull *Illius qui*. In its proemium he wrote:

> We should incessantly take upon ourselves diligent cares, so that Jews and infidels should be able to convert from their Hebrew blindness to the recognition of the light of truth, and so that, converted, they can be instructed in the Catholic faith. . . .[191]

Therefore, in response to the request of Ioannes de Iorano, rector of the church of St. John de Mercato, a *domus catechumenorum* is to be established in which recently converted Jews will reside and be instructed. It was not, however, Ioannes de Iorano who conceived of the *domus*. It was Ignatius Loyola.[192] In other words, by the 1540s there was an influential body within the Church, the Jesuits, which was moving the papacy toward a policy of conversion, and which had already succeeded in convincing the papacy to establish some of the apparatus of that policy.

Beside serving as a base for catechizing converts and for strengthening their Christian convictions, the *domus* also provided the papacy with a further means for promoting conversion. This is reflected in the series of edicts concerning the financial upkeep of the *domus*. The first such edict, *Pastoris eternis vices,* issued by Julius III on September 1, 1554,[193] required each synagogue in Rome

190. P. Tacchi-Venturi, *Storia della Compagnia di Gesù in Italia* (Rome, 1922–31), II, 1:152–53, and see also the sources cited there.

191. *B.R.,* 6:353–58, proemium: "Incessanter curis affligimur assiduis, ut iudaei et infideles ex eorum hebraica caecitate ad veri luminis agnitionem converti, ac conversi in catholica fide instrui. . . ."

192. On the *domus* in general, see K. W. Hoffmann, *Ursprung und Anfangstätigkeit des Ersten päpstlichen Missioninstituts: Ein Beitrag zur Geschichte der katholische Juden und Mohammendermission in sechsten Jahrhundert* (Münster, 1923), pp. 9–67, and esp. p. 9, where Hoffmann claims that Loyola modeled the *domus* on its English predecessor. Also on Loyola's involvement in the *domus,* see Tacchi-Venturi, *Storia,* 1:403, and the sources cited there. On the operations of the *domus,* see Milano, "L'impari lotta," and Dejob, "Documents . . . du Cardinal Sirleto."

193. *Comunità di Roma,* ITc.

to contribute ten ducats per annum to the *domus*. With the issuance of *Cum nimis*, the number of synagogues in Rome was reduced to one, and Julius III's financial scheme could not be continued. But Julius' principle of Jewish responsibility for *domus* finances was accepted by Paul IV, and he therefore ordered that the Jews should now support the *domus* through one collective payment.[194] Paul IV also extended this principle by requiring[195] the Jews to pay for the services of the convert Giacomo Giratino, whose task was to censor Hebrew books.[196]

According to both Julius III and Paul IV, these payments were justified because many of the residents of the *domus* had previously been on the charity rolls of the Jewish community. Very likely, however, both popes had an ulterior motive, which a letter of Gregory XIII (October 22, 1582) clarifies. The Jews, he wrote, had petitioned him to lower their payments to the Apostolic Camera, including that for the *domus,* and he was now acceding to their request:

> For the Community had approached him quite frequently, bemoaning that it was now cast into utter poverty, because many rich Jews had become Christians, and because it was already heavily burdened with debts.[197]

---

194. Ibid., ITc; cf. Stern, *Urkundliche Beiträge,* #110, p. 115, for *Ex operibus pietatis* of Paul IV, a letter of Mar. 20, 1556 to Ercole, duke of Ferrara, which repeats the essentials of *Dudum postquam,* and also notes the bull of Julius III (*Pastoris . . .*) as the basis for both *Dudum* and the present letter.

195. *Com. di Roma,* ITc: *Cum sicut accepimus,* Sept. 19, 1556.

196. On censorship in general, see Wm. Popper, *The Censorship of Hebrew Books* (New York, 1899).

197. *Com. di Roma,* ITc: ". . . et essendo detta Università ricorsa più volte da noi dolendoli esser jettata in grandissima povertà per causa di molti Ebrei ricchi fatti Christiani, e per haver ancora di presente molti debiti, ci siamo contentati, che pagando di presente [an amount which both sides have agreed upon]." Noteworthy here is the letter of Clement VIII of Jan. 1, 1605, *Alius per nos,* in which he notes that the 1593 expulsion, as well as that of Pius V in 1569, had diminished Jewish wealth to the point that the *Comunità* could not meet its financial obligations to the *domus.* The Archives of the *Comunità,* IZd, referred to below in the text, confirm the existence of this problem. It would seem then that the expulsions only served to heighten the financial predicament and, hence, conversionary pressures.

Aside from showing that papal conversionary policy had not been barren of results during the thirty or so years of its existence, this letter suggests the possibility that the levies on the Jews had themselves played a conversionary role.[198] Its wording indicates that the level of imposts had always been beyond the means of the community. Indeed, Gregory XIII agreed to lower the rates only when he realized that there was no hope of ever collecting in full. Rather than bankrupt themselves trying to pay these imposts, wealthy Jews, it would appear, had preferred conversion.

It was probably this end which Julius III and Paul IV hoped to achieve by demanding extravagant payments to the *domus*. So, too, they must have hoped that the despair resulting from the requirement of continuing to support those whose gratitude for communal charity had been expressed by conversion would itself encourage conversions. In short, the financial scheme established for the *domus* must have been construed as one aspect of the general policy of conversion through restriction and repression.[199] This financial scheme, moreover, continued for the next three hundred years. The records of the Roman Jewish Community contain document after document attesting to an unending financial struggle with the papacy on the subject of the *domus*.[200]

The attack on the Talmud and on rabbinic literature began with an order of the Inquisition. To insure the complete implementation of this order, Julius III issued the bull *Cum sicut nuper,* published on May 29, 1554.[201] It was in this bull that the crucial

------

198. Cf. p. 84f., infra, where de Susannis claims that it is legal to tax Jews in lieu of their conversion. It may be that this legal point is what underlay papal reasoning here.

199. Cf. p. 56f., infra, for the role of Julius III in the burning of the Talmud, where it becomes clear that by 1554, when he issued *Pastoris,* he had moved from his position of 1551, when, in *Cum sicut accepimus,* he had advocated kindness as a conversionary device.

200. *Com. di Roma,* IZd, *Nota di spese inviata dalla Casa dei Catecumini.* Additional material on the issue of payments may be found in the following documents pertaining to Cardinal Sirleto: *BAV, Vat. Lat.* 6189, fols. 772, 805, 811, and 819; and *Vat. Lat.* 6792, fols. 81, 89, and 106.

201. *B.R.,* 6:482. In fact, as the bull states, some copies of the Talmud had already been burned in the fall of 1553 at the order of the Inquisition. This bull mandates all remaining copies of the Talmud to be burned also.

formula of *Cum nimis* that the Jews "are tolerated by the Holy Mother, Church, so that at some time, led by our kindness and by the breath of the Holy Spirit, they convert to the true light of Christ," [202] made its first appearance. This formula, moreover, is the interior clause of a sentence which states that Jews, who are tolerated *ut . . .* , may freely retain only books that contain no blasphemies.[203] The juxtaposition of a statement indicating conversion as a goal with an order forbidding the possession of blasphemous books, whether they be the Talmud or any of its commentaries, implies that the possession of such books hinders conversion. And if this sentence is read in the light of *Cum nimis,* it is evident that the burning of the Talmud was the first actual step in the establishment of a Jewry policy completely directed toward conversion.[204]

Further evidence that Julius III intended the burning of the Talmud as a proselytizing measure is provided by the remark with which he prefaced *Cum sicut nuper.* He noted that although some copies of the Talmud had already been burned, he was disturbed because other copies still remained in existence, in defiance of the inquisitional order. On the one hand, the main body of the inquisitional order condemned the Talmud for its many blasphemies.[205] This condemnation fits in well with the usual explanation of the burning as the final result of a dispute which arose between the two Venetian publishers, M. Giustiniani and E. Bragadoni. Both had printed the *Mishneh Torah* of Maimonides, but both wanted to have a corner on the market. Hence each accused the other of publishing blasphemous material. To strengthen their claims they employed the

---

202. Ibid., 6:482: "A sancta matre Ecclesia tolerantur, ut aliquando mansuetudine nostra allecti ad verum Christi lumen, divino afflante spiritu, convertantur."

203. Ibid.: "Non permittentes de cetero eosdem hebraeos, (qui . . . tolerantur ut [etc.] . . .) a quibusvis [in the matter of their books] dummodo blasphemiam . . . non contineant, . . . vexari."

204. For a more thorough description of papal motives for burning the Talmud, and for a general discussion of contemporary Catholic opinions about the Talmud, see my article, "The Burning of the Talmud in 1553," pp. 435–59. Cf. also the remark of Joseph HaKohen, p. 40 supra.

205. For a full text of the Inquisition's order, see Stern, *Urkundliche Beiträge,* #100, p. 98.

converts Josef Moro Zarfati and Solomon Romano, who attacked the blasphemies of the Talmud before the Inquisition. Convinced by their attacks, the Inquisition ordered the Talmud burned.[206]

Undoubtedly this publishers' feud brought the matter of the Talmud to a head. The issue of censoring books as a measure to achieve purity of faith, however, had been a source of deep concern for Cardinal Carafa, the future Paul IV, long before 1554.[207] It was also the name of Carafa, then the chief inquisitor, which appeared at the head of the order to burn the Talmud. Thus it is not surprising that the introductory paragraph of the inquisitional order asserts that since the task of the Inquisition is to bring men to recognize the light of truth, that body must concern itself with the blind perfidy of the Jews. Therefore,

> We have considered that nothing would be more conducive to their illumination than if we were able to lead them away from their impious and inane doctrines to the scrutiny of sacred letters (which they falsely assert they study), where they would be able, to discover and know the hidden treasure of their salvation, God granting to us that the veil be removed from their hearts.[208]

Simply put, the Inquisition conceived of the burning of the Talmud as part of its required task of preventing false doctrine from blinding the Jews.

Julius III could hardly have been blind to the Inquisition's intention. Therefore, when he indicated that he was issuing *Cum sicut nuper* to enforce the inquisitional order, he was assenting not only to the action, but also to the intention of the Inquisition. He was, moreover, merely restating the intention of the Inquisition when he connected the prohibition of the Talmud with the notion that the

---

206. See esp. Yaari, *Srefat ha-Talmud be-Italiah,* pp. 7–8, and R. Rabbinowicz, Ma'amar 'al Hadpasat ha-Talmud, ed. A. Haberman (Jerusalem, 1952), p. 59.

207. Bromato, *Storia di Paolo IV* (Ravenna, 1748), 1:213 and 2:12.

208. Stern, *Urkundliche Beiträge,* p. 98: "Nil eorum illuminatione conducibilius fore arbitrati sumus quam si ipsos ab impiis et inanibus doctrinis avertentes ad sacras (quas se colere falso iactant) litteras scrutandas deducere possemus, ubi suae salutis absconditum thesaurum remoto ab eorum cordibus velamine, nobiscum Deo donante, invenire et agnoscere valerent."

Church harbors the Jews for the purpose of converting them. *Cum sicut nuper,* then, is no more than a reinforcement of the inquisitional order by a higher authority. The bull also reveals that Julius III identified with those who sought to burn the Talmud for conversionary purposes rather than with those who sought to protect Christians from the blasphemies the Talmud allegedly contained.[209] In

209. Cf. p. 285, infra, for a discussion of Benedict XIII's attack on the Talmud for the purpose of promoting conversion. Cf. also pp. 212f., infra, on de Torres' comments on Talmud burning and conversion. In distinction to the point of view of Benedict and de Torres, see the texts concerning the Talmud burning in thirteenth-century France, published by I. Loeb, "La Controverse de 1240 sur le Talmud," *Revue des Études Juives* 1 (1880): 247–61, 2 (1881): 248–70, and 3 (1881): 39–57. See also the bulls of Gregory IX and Innocent IV, along with the responses of Odo, bishop of Paris, pertaining to this burning, published by Ch. Merchavia, *The Church versus Talmudic and Midrashic Literature, 500–1248* (Jerusalem, 1970), pp. 446–52. The emphasis of the polemics and the letters is that the Talmud is full of blasphemies against Christ and must therefore be burned. However, Gregory's bulls of June 6, 1239 (Potthast, 10759), June 20, 1239 (Potthast, 10768), and Odo's letter of 1247 (Quetif-Echard, *Scriptores Ordinis Praedicatorum* [Paris, 1719–21], 1:128) all contain the phrase: "Cum igitur hec dicatur esse causa precipua, que iudaeos in sua tenet perfidia obstinatos." But as Merchavia notes (p. 228), Gregory probably knew little of the Talmud, if he knew it directly at all. Thus the phrase is an afterthought, and certainly does not indicate a conversionary policy. The inquisitional order of 1553, moreover, spoke positively: the burning would promote conversion. It also asserted its conversionary intention before speaking of blasphemies. In 1239 the order was reversed. In addition, Innocent IV did say on May 9, 1244 (Potthast 11376) that the Jews teach their children the Talmud, not the Bible, because they fear that from the Bible their children will perceive the truth of Christ. However, he had no conversionary expectations, for he opened his letter by asserting that "quorum [the Jews'] cordibus . . . redemptor noster velamen abstulit, sed in cecitate . . . manere permittit," thereby affirming that the time for the conversion of the Jews had not yet arrived (cf. Browe, *Judenmission,* pp. 306–10.). Hence in France the basic reason for Talmud burning was to purge blasphemies; in Spain the Talmud was burned to promote conversion. In Spain, moreover, attacks on the Talmud were further refined with the late-thirteenth-century *Pugio Fidei* of the Dominican, Raymund Martini, which sought to prove the truth of Christianity to Jews by citing Talmudic passages which supposedly contained Christological references. See Y. F. Baer, *A History of the Jews in Christian Spain* (Philadelphia, 1966), 1:167, 185, and 411, n. 54, and S. Lieberman, "Raymund Martini and His Alleged Forgeries," *Historia Judaica 5* (1943): 87–102, for opposing opinions on the authenticity of Martini's passages. The apparent contradiction between exploiting the Talmud to foster conversion and burning it to attain the same end was resolved, as seen in the work of de Torres. Borrowing from

addition, since Carafa was the moving force behind the inquisitional order, it is probable that it was he who induced the pope to issue the bull, and it is at least possible that it was also Carafa who drafted for the bull the new formula, "tolerated, *ut,*" which he would employ so conspicuously in *Cum nimis* when he became pope. In other words, the burning of the Talmud may be seen as the first step taken by Carafa in the erection of his Jewry policy. The next step would be the issuance of *Cum nimis.*

In summary, a study of the bulls issued by the popes of the later sixteenth century reveals that in radical distinction to their predecessors, these popes had established the promotion of mass conversion as the goal of their Jewry policy. Most previous popes had viewed conversion as an event which would occur simultaneously with the advent of the Second Coming. As their actions could in no way hasten the Second Coming, so too in no way could they hasten the conversion of the Jews. If popes did take steps to encourage conversion, these steps were peripheral to their Jewry policy as a whole. After 1555 conversion became central.

In order to attain the goal of mass conversion, the papacy instituted five programs. The first of these was the establishment of a *domus catechumenorum* in 1543. In 1553 the Talmud was burned. In 1555 the policy came into full flower with the issuance of restrictions which were intended to make the Jews assent to the fact that the prophecies had been fulfilled which predicted their punishment for rejecting Christ. In 1569, and again in 1593, an order of expulsion was issued, partly out of despair, but more probably intended to blackmail the Jews into conversion. Finally, in 1584, the Jews were required to attend missionary sermons.

From the bulls which established these programs it is possible

---

French thought, he asserted that the Church allowed the Jews to observe only that part of their law which was true, i.e., explicitly found in the Old Testament and prefiguring Christianity; the remainder, all rabbinical concoctions, should be burned. See pp. 212f., *infra.* On attacks on the Talmud as a *nova lex* which should be destroyed (French origin), and on the concept that Jews could be converted by citing the proper Talmudic passages to them (basically Spanish origin), see A. Funkenstein, "Changes in the Patterns of Anti-Jewish Polemics in the 12th Century" (Hebrew), *Zion* 33 (1968): 137–42.

to acquire a rudimentary understanding of both their nature and their specific functions. To understand the full scope of these programs, however, to explain why the papacy embarked on them when it did, and to prove beyond any question that the Jewry policy of the later-sixteenth-century popes did indeed have conversion as its goal, other tools are required.

PART TWO

The De Iudaeis

CHAPTER II

THE *DE IUDAEIS* AND ITS AUTHOR

THE *De Iudaeis et Aliis Infidelibus* of Marquardus de Susannis was first published in Venice in 1558.[1] Since the work praises the acts of Paul IV[2] and at one point refers to 1555, and at another to 1557, as the present year,[3] one may assume that it was composed during the first three years of Paul IV's pontificate. The place of composition was doubtless Udine (the capital of Friuli in the Republic of Venice), where de Susannis lived throughout his life. The book must have enjoyed great popularity, for it was reprinted four times: 1568, 1584, 1601, and 1613, the last three after de Susannis' death in 1578.[4]

---

1. Marquardus de Susannis, *Tractatus De Iudaeis et Aliis Infidelibus: Circa Concernentia Originem Contractuum, Bella, Foedera, Ultimas Voluntates, Iudicia, et Delicta Iudaeorum et Aliorum Infidelium, et Eorum Conversionem Ad Fidem* . . . Cum privilegio summi Pontificis Pauli IIII. & Illustriss. Senatus Veneti per annos XV. M D LVIII.

2. Ibid., dedication.

3. Ibid., pt. 3, chap. 1, par. 48 (1555), and par. 66 (1557).

4. R. Streit, ed., *Bibliotheca Missionum* (Münster, 1916), 1:34 (Venice, 1558); 45 (Venice, 1568); 64 (Venice, 1584); 119 (Frankfurt, 1601); 151 (Frankfurt, 1613). Of the sum total of five printings, I have examined four, those of 1558, 1568, 1584, and 1613. The 1568 printing contains many additions which are preserved in the 1584 printing, which appeared not as an individual volume, but as a part of the *Tractatus Universi Iuris* (Venice, 1584), 14:27–77. Since de Susannis died in 1578, 1584 offers the book in its final redaction. Almost all of the additions made between the first and final redaction are excursuses, which must be seen as footnotes because they deal with material that has no bearing on the declared subject of the work: Jews and infidels. More important, not one word of the original text is omitted in any of the three later printings examined, as I determined through comparison. There is, then, no reason why the original printing cannot be considered as accurate; and for reasons of convenience, all citations in the present work will be taken from the original printing.

According to de Susannis, the *De Iudaeis* is intended to be a handbook for judges in cases involving Jewry law.[5] That contemporary legists recognized the value of the work as a legal tract is clear. The 1584 *Tractatus Universi Iuris,* in which the *De Iudaeis* is included, is a major collection of late medieval legal tracts. In addition, Fichardus lists the *De Iudaeis* in his catalog of medieval lawyers and their works.[6] However, of the three hundred duodecimo pages that comprise the *De Iudaeis,* only two hundred are devoted to an exposition of legal matters. The remaining hundred pages contain a polemic whose purpose, as stated by de Susannis, is to convince Jews and other infidels to embrace Christianity.[7] Because of this polemic, contemporaries also considered the *De Iudaeis* to be a missionary tract.[8] In fact, the *De Iudaeis* is both a legal manual and a polemic. For that reason it is extremely valuable for understanding the Jewry policy of Paul IV.

The *De Iudaeis* is dedicated to Paul IV, who in de Susannis' opinion had properly restricted the Jews and had made every effort to convert the nations.[9] Conversely, the *De Iudaeis* was printed with the benefit of a papal privilege.[10] These two facts raise the question whether the *De Iudaeis* was an official work, written at the request of Paul IV. Unfortunately, most of Paul IV's papers were burned in the riot which occurred at his death,[11] and a direct answer may

---

5. *De Iudaeis,* pt. 1, intro. chap., intro. par.

6. Io. Fichardus, *Elenchus omnium auctorum sive scriptorum qui in iure tam civili quam canonico . . . claruerunt* (Frankfurt am Main, 1579), fol. 68v.

7. *De Iudaeis,* pt. 3, chap. 1, par. 81.

8. C. I. Imbonatus, *Bibliotheca Latino-Hebraica sive de Scriptoribus Latinis, qui ex Diversis Nationibus Contra Iudaeos vel de Re Hebraica Utrumque Scripsere,* which is vol. 6 of I. Bartoloccius, *Bibliotheca Magna Rabbinica* (Rome, 1694), all of which was printed under the auspices of the Congregation for the Propagation of the Faith. The *De Iudaeis* is cited by Imbonati on p. 157 and p. 530 under the heading of tracts *Adversus Iudaeos.* See also supra, n. 4, for Streit, who also calls the *De Iudaeis* a polemic.

9. *De Iudaeis,* dedication: "Iudaeorum licentiam, labem ac pestem pontificiae ditionis, urbium severis legibus repressisti, quodque iampridem a te tetrica, et incorrupta veterum Christianorum disciplina revocata, nunc . . . in ignotis prius orbis regionibus Christianae Reipub. fines . . . propagantur. . . ."

10. See supra, n. 1.

11. Pastor, *History of the Popes,* 14:260.

therefore be impossible. It is, nevertheless, highly unlikely that the man who considered the censorship of books to be of prime importance would have granted a privilege of publication to a book whose contents he could not sanction. Furthermore, in his *Cronaca d'Udine,* written sometime before 1570, Jacobo Valvasone il Vecchio wrote that the De Iudaeis "fu gratissimo a Paolo IV." [12] As a contemporary report, this statement is most valuable. It suggests at first hand that Paul IV not only approved of the book, but that he probably saw it as a reflection of his own ideas.

In addition, in the State Archive of Udine there are twenty to thirty papal letters written between the fifteenth and seventeenth centuries to members of the de Susannis family who served as canons at the Cathedral of Aquileia. The bulk of these letters are from Paul III and Pius IV to Marquardus' brother, Antonio, and his cousin, Cristoforo de Susannis. There is also a letter from **Paul IV** (1555) to the canons concerning privileges to be accorded to another brother of Marquardus', Giovanni-Battista de Susannis, in return for the services and significant donations given to Aquileia by the de Susannis family in the past. [13] In the light of these letters it is clear that the papacy, including Paul IV, was quite familiar with the de Susannis family as a whole, and with Marquardus' brothers in particular. Thus he doubtless knew Marquardus too, and his work as well. The privilege of publication and Valvasone's statement, then, can both be safely considered as reflecting Paul IV's actual esteem of the *De Iudaeis.*

One thing is certain, the *De Iudaeis* was extremely popular and well received. If not, it would not have been mentioned in Fichardus and reprinted in the *Tractatus* so soon after its initial publica-

---

12. Gian Giuseppe Liruti, *Notizie delle vite ed opere scritte dei Litterati del Friuli* (Venice, 1830), 4:174. Valvasone's chronicle itself, *Chroniche delle Città d'Aquileia, d'Udine, e della Cargna* (or shortened, *Cronaca d'Udine*), is cited by Liruti, 2:204. The reference for the remark about de Susannis is *Cronaca d'Udine,* 1:317. Valvasone's dates are 1499–1570.

13. Archivio di Stato di Udine, MS 2294, #1309, Raccolta del Torso, Archivio Susanna, Busta 76. De Susannis' own papers have been removed from the Archivio. Their obvious interest lies in the possibility of direct correspondence between de Susannis and Paul IV.

tion. One reason for this success was that a comprehensive synthesis of Jewry law had never before been constructed. So de
Susannis himself claims, and correctly, for his tract is the only one
on Jewry law mentioned by Fichardus and printed in the *Tractatus*.[14]
Nor was its success transitory. The last of its five printings appeared
fifty-five years after the first.[15]

In addition, and of particular interest, the Jew, David de Pomis,
twice cites de Susannis in his *Enarratio,* written for the duke of
Urbino and published at Venice in 1588.[16] In both cases the citation refers to the Jews' right to justice and is introduced to support
de Pomis' call for just that. Logic dictates that de Pomis would
have cited de Susannis to support his call only if the *De Iudaeis* was
at that time—just thirty years after its publication—commonly held
to be the authoritative synthesis of Jewry law.

That authoritativeness is demonstrable. As early as 1574, in
his annotated edition of Felynus Sandeus' *Commentaria in Decretales,* Brunori a Sole refers the reader to the *De Iudaeis* for a thorough discussion of matters which Sandeus treated only briefly in
his discussion of the *Decretal* title "De Iudaeis"[17] Furthermore, its

---

14. In truth, the *Tractatus* also lists Isidore of Seville, *Contra Iudaeos, valdis-
sime eorum errores confutans* (14: fols. 23–27), and Ludovici Montalti, *De Re-
probatione Sententiae Pilati* (14: fols. 8–23). The *De Iudaeis* is found in the same
volume, fols. 27–77. In addition, Fichardus, besides listing the *Contra Iudaeos*
and *De Fide* of Isidore of Seville, also notes the *De Iudaeorum Foenore* of Fr.
Sixtus Medices Venetus and the *De Iudaeorum Infantibus Baptisandi*s of Ulrich
Zasius, fol. 68v. Despite these citations, my statement in the text is correct, because none of these tracts attempts, as does the *De Iudaeis* alone, to deal with
all of Jewry law.

15. It is noteworthy that the Turin second official in charge of Jews, Jos.
Sessa, composed a *Tract. De Iudaeis* (Turin, 1712) because he wanted to add
items from the local law of Turin into a general Jewry law code for the use
of judges. There he relies heavily on de Susannis. The work is on the whole
similar to that of de Susannis, with the exception of the additions just mentioned
and a somewhat longer discussion of the regulations pertaining to baptism. It lacks,
however, the uniformly high quality of organization found in the *De Iudaeis*.
German lawyers too relied on the *De Iudaeis,* esp. in the seventeenth and eighteenth centuries. Cf. Georg Landauer, "Zur Geschichte der Judenrechtswissenschaft," *Zeitschrift für die Geschichte der Juden in Deutschland* 2 (1930): 261.

16. De Pomis, *Enarratio,* pp. 46 f. and 59 f.

17. Felinus Sandeus, *Commentariorum Felini Sandei Ferrariensis in Decre-*

inclusion in the *Tractatus,* which was published, as its title page states, by order of Gregory XIII, serves as a reliable indicator that officially speaking, the papacy viewed the *De Iudaeis* as a valuable —and of course orthodox—dissertation. But most important, the *Editio Romana* of the *Decretals*[18] contains marginalia added by its editors. And in his bull of approbation of the *Editio Romana,* Gregory XIII declared both the text and its marginalia to be authoritative.[19] For the titles "De Iudaeis" and "De Usuris" these notes refer the reader to the *De Iudaeis* The authoritativeness thus achieved by the sections of the *De Iudaeis* cited in these marginalia was in all probability eventually attained by the rest of the tract too.

The *De Iudaeis* is, then, a significant document. Accordingly, if an examination of the *De Iudaeis* reveals that the tract reflects the thought of Paul IV, the question must be raised, although it can never be answered, whether the *De Iudaeis* achieved its importance precisely because of that reflection.

Of de Susannis personally, little is known. Aside from contemporary references to the *De Iudaeis,* the only sources for a biography are a few not overly informative documents housed in the Biblioteca Comunale in Udine and some brief profiles of de Susannis found in locally produced biographical dictionaries of distinguished men from Udine.[20] Nevertheless, the sources provide sufficient information to permit the construction of a character sketch.

De Susannis was a member of an important Udinese family which had its origin in a certain Leonardus "Gingi" Waisinger, a

---

talium, Libros V . . . Benedicti a Vadis, Philippi Simonetae, Ioannis de Gradibus, atque Brunori a Sole adnotationibus (Venice, 1574).

18. See Friedberg, *Corpus Iuris,* 1:lxxci and 2:xli, for an introduction to this edition.

19. Ibid., 1:lxxix–lxxx, where Friedberg reprints Gregory XIII's bull of approbation of the "Editio Romana." On the subject of the marginalia which appear in the edition, the bull declares that some marginalia detrimental to the faith, which appeared in previous editions, have been excised, but: "Ipsum Decretum absque glossis a prefatis a nobis deputatis iam totum emendatum et correctum ac nonnullis annotationibus . . . una cum dictis Decretalibus . . . iam impressis recognita et approbata sit."

20. A collection, MS 2294, possessed by L'Archivio di Stato di Udine constitutes the Susanna family archive.

former member of the Teutonic Order, who had migrated to Udine in 1220, and whose descendants had possessed a patent of nobility since 1377.[21] The men of the family, as in the cases of Marquardus himself, his father, Cristoforo, and his grandfather, Marquardus,[22] frequently became jurisconsults. The prime function of these lawyers was the writing of legal opinions, known as *consilia* (responsa), sometimes for their clients, but often for judges too.[23] These *consilia,* especially if the jurisconsult was well known, were normally used by judges, who functioned without a jury, as the basis of their decision in a given case. The *consilia* of the most famous jurisconsults, for example Bartolus and Baldus in the fourteenth century, were incorporated into an unofficial body of legal precedents and carefully preserved. The jurisconsults themselves invariably bore the title of Doctor of Both Laws, referring to Roman and Canon law, if they held the full rank of lawyer (*advocatus*). Many of the functions of our contemporary lawyers were in de Susannis' day carried out by notaries, men of lesser rank than lawyers.

Lawyers were trained in both Roman and Canon law for a practical reason. The quasi-official, although uncodified, common law (*ius commune*) for all Italy was nearly identical with Roman law. Indeed, when a lawyer like de Susannis used the term *law* alone, he normally meant the Roman law. (The laws of Canon law were referred to as *canons.*) Courts relied on *ius commune,* in effect on the precepts of Roman law, when there were no local statutes pertaining to a specific matter. And that was often the case. On the other hand, certain issues, including marriage and testaments, were decided by Canon law exclusively, and in ecclesiastical courts. Clergy were always tried by these courts, at least in theory. There were also situations in which the boundary between common law and Canon law jurisdiction was not precise. Statutes from both laws had to be

---

21. MS Joppi 1236, Biblioteca Comunale di Udine, and Archivio di Stato, Udine, MS 2294, #1266, Racc. del Torso, Busta 18.

22. MS 2294 contains a genealogy of the family, called "Genealogie Joppi" by the Biblioteca Comunale. See also Liruti, *Notizie,* 4:174.

23. For more detail on the role of the jurisconsult, see P. Riesenberg, "The Consilia Literature: A Prospectus," *Manuscripta* 6 (1962): 3–22.

rationalized with each other to make an acceptable decision possible. Thus a lawyer had to be conversant with both Roman and Canon law. Indeed, the legal bases for any *consilium* are composed almost entirely of citations from these two laws. Needless to say, law was also an academic university subject, where it was studied for its theoretical values and where treatises and commentaries on it were composed. To be sure, treatises and tracts were composed outside the university walls too. Here again a student would need to know both laws, a point which will be well illustrated when de Susannis' tract itself is discussed.

Aside from their role as jurisconsults, the de Susannises were also active in civic government. Marquadus became a counselor of Udine in 1529, and a cousin, Pagano, held a similar post in the mid-1550s.[24] As is to be expected, other members of the family entered the clergy, including Marquardus' two brothers, Antonio and Giovanni-Battista, who, as noted above, served as canons at Aquileia.[25]

The exact date of Marquardus' birth is obscure. The genealogy in the Biblioteca Comunale gives 1578 as the year of his death, at the age of ninety.[26] In his biographical dictionary, Liruti claims Marquardus was born in the early sixteenth century.[27] The genealogy also seems questionable in the matter of Marquardus' marriage. It asserts that he did not marry until 1538. Following the dates of the genealogy, Marquardus then fathered nine children between 1538 and 1550, that is, between the ages of sixty and seventy-two.[28] As for the children themselves, some became jurisconsults, but none gained distinction.[29]

De Susannis received his legal training at Padua.[30] After at-

---

24. MS Joppi 640, n. 3, is a holograph by this Pagano, entitled "La Peste di Udine dall'anno 1556 al 1557." It describes the expulsion of the Jews from Udine on the charge that they were responsible for the plague.

25. "Genealogie Joppi."

26. MS Joppi 359 is Marquardus' will. It unfortunately contains no data except a formal division of his property.

27. Liruti, *Notizie,* 4:174.

28. "Genealogie Joppi."

29. Liruti, *Notizie,* 4:176.

30. Ibid., 4:176.

taining the degree of *doctoratus utriusque iuris*,[31] he returned to
Udine, where he spent nearly all of his life and achieved much success as a jurisconsult.[32] This rather uneventful life was interrupted in
1559. Possibly as an outgrowth of the publication of the *De Iudaeis*
in the previous year, de Susannis was called on to serve as an ambassador (for a purpose the sources do not indicate) for the Republic of
Venice.[33] He apparently performed his assignment well, for in 1563
he again represented the republic, for a period of eighteen months,
as a negotiator in a border dispute with Austria.[34] It was in connection with this mission that a most revealing remark was made about
de Susannis. In his 1564 report on this mission, Sebastiano Venier
wrote to the Venetian Senate that:

> The excellent Signor Marquardus de Susannis, so considered not
> only in Udine, *but in all Italy,* has left an income of five hundred
> scudi a year and more, just from *consilia* . . . and has come to
> serve Your Serenity.[35]

It was doubtless the *De Iudaeis* which was responsible for de Susannis' reputation.

De Susannis' next appointment was in 1565 as vicar for

---

31. According to the "Genealogie Joppi" he received the doctorate in
1543, which means that he was then fifty-five if he was born in 1488. This date
seems inaccurate.

32. Prospero Antonino, *Del Friuli ed in particolare dei Trattati da cui
ebbe Origine* (Venice, 1873), which contains the *Relazione di Sebastiano Venier,
Commissario a confini del Friuli ritornato di là,* Novembre, 1564. Venier reports to the Venetian Senate that Marquardus de Susannis "ha lasciato un guad-
agno di scudi cinquecento a l'anno, et piu, solo di consulti." p. 539. MS Joppi
1054 is a *consilium* in defense of Pompeo Palmense, a cleric accused of adultery. It reveals nothing pertinent to de Susannis' biography. The same can be
said for MS Joppi 1236, n. 15, which contains a series of contracts for the
purchase and sale of property by de Susannis.

33. Gio:Francesco Palladio, *Historie della Provincia del Friuli* (Udine,
1660), p. 178.

34. Ibid., p. 182, and Liruti, *Notizie,* 4:175.

35. Antonino, *De Friuli,* p. 539: "L'excellente Ser Marquardo Susanna, te-
nuto non solamente d'Udine, ma d'Italia, ha lasciato un quadagno de scudi
cinquecento a l'anno, et piu, solo di consulti . . . et è venuto a servir Vostra
Serenità . . ."

Io:Battista Contarini, the podesta of Padua.[36] He must have remained in Contarini's service for a long time, for in 1577 Contarini
granted him a villa in recognition of his meritorious labors on behalf
of the Cathedral of Aquileia.[37] In the same year as his appointment
as vicar, de Susannis published his second major work, the *De Celibatu,* dedicated to Pius IV.[38] This work is both a synthesis of the
laws of celibacy and a defense of that institution. Finally, in 1571
de Susannis wrote a short poem praising the victory over the Turks
at Lepanto and ascribing the success to the work of Pius V.[39]

From even this brief sketch two significant points emerge. First,
de Susannis was himself well known, and so too was the *De Iudaeis.*
Second, his family background, the events of his life, and the nature
of his writings, all devoted to advancing orthodox Catholic policies
and aspirations, argue strongly that in his book on the Jews, de
Susannis was writing in support of official teachings.

---

36. Gio:Giuseppe Capodagli, *Udine Illustrata* (Udine, 1665), p. 464, and
Liruti, *Notizie,* 4:174.

37. MS Joppi 1236 contains a document dated 1577 and signed by Io:B.
Contarini, which both makes this grant and praises de Susannis' labors.

38. *De Celibatu Sacerdotum non abrogando, TUJ,* 14: fols. 104–22.

39. Marquardus Susanna Turcarum Imperatori
   Aspice terribilem, Sydoes coeleste, Leonem
   Turce, ferox etiam quam sit in orbe Leo,
   Quam bene nunc mundi Quintus moderetur habenas
   Iste Pius, superos in sua vota trahens.
   Aspice, ut adversis obstet tibi fluctibus aequor
   Adverso, arma movens in tua fata, Deo
   Roma tuam et Venetis coniuncta Hispania, classem
   Perdidit, haec laeti sint monimenta, tui
   Niteris in vetitum, coelestia numina laedens,
   Imperium, perdet crux veneranda, tuum.
This poem is printed in Petrus Gherardus, ed., *In Foedus et Victoriam contra
Turcos . . . Poemata Varia* (Venice, 1572), which is a collection of poems cele-
brating the victory at Lepanto in 1571, p. 343.

CHAPTER III

DE SUSANNIS' LEGAL METHODOLOGY

THE *De Iudaeis* WAS UNIQUE among sixteenth-century legal works in subject matter. In genre it was but one of many tracts which attempted to create a composite overview of a given legal topic, such as donations, dowries, or wills, by collecting and harmonizing all the laws (Roman, Canon, local, and customary) and interpretations which dealt with that topic.[1] These tracts were not innovative, but synthetic.[2] Nevertheless, by structuring widely scattered sources and interpretations into a coherent body of law, they made it possible to apply the laws pertaining to a given topic with a previously unattainable logic and consistency.

Within the *De Iudaeis* there are three basic divisions. *Pars Prima,* based primarily on canons (Church laws), discusses the admission of Jews into Christian society and the establishment of their status in relation to Christians. *Pars Secunda* examines the status of Jews and Jewish law in Italian civil and criminal common law (that is, Roman law as applied in Italy). It also specifies how the Jews are privileged or restricted in the matters of citizenship and jurisdictions. Most of the conclusions here are substantiated by the citation of laws (that is, Roman law and local statutes), but appropriate canons are

---

1. Cf. de Susannis' own statement identifying his work with others of this genre: *De Iudaeis,* I, 1, intro.: "Satis constat quaestiones sive Tractatus qui de variis rebus . . . conscripti sunt. . . . Nam ubi tota res est collecta, ibidem facilius inveniri potest. . . . Et cum adhuc neminem viderim, qui de Iudaeis . . . materiam in opus speciale redegerit . . . non modo ad lites tollendas, sed etiam ad animarum salutem, ea ratione in primis adductus . . . ."

2. V. Piano-Mortari, *Ricerche sulla teoria dell' interpretazione del diritto nel secolo XVI.* (Milan, 1956), chap. 1, passim.

cited as well. *Pars Tertia* divides into two distinct parts. Chapters two to nine discuss the canons pertaining to converts to Christianity. Chapter one is the polemic. Almost devoid of legal issues, its identified sources are the Bible, the Fathers, theologians, and Christian and ancient pagan historians. It also contains, without citation, the ideas of many contemporaries. Significantly, the polemic contains the information revealing both why and for what purpose de Susannis wrote the *De Iudaeis*.

At this point, some observations about the methodology of medieval lawyers in general, and about the procedures of de Susannis in particular, are appropriate. Underlying medieval legal thought was the concept of the unity of law.[3] All law, which exists for the purpose of articulating justice,[4] derives from divine law, the law of God expressed in the Scriptures, and natural law,[5] the unwritten body of law elucidated by medieval theologians and jurists that delineates the basic rights of all men. In turn, divine and natural law specify the concrete precepts of the abstract ideal, justice.[6] Human law, positive law, must reflect those precepts.[7] Individual laws, then, were never pictured as self-sufficient entities, but as parts of a system. Legal interpretation—that is, the elucidation and determination of both the meaning and proper application of a law—strove to accurately fit a given law into a system whose end was justice.[8] Justice itself was seen as the virtue through which the divine order was realized.[9] Stated somewhat differently, the purpose of justice was "to

3. On this concept, see W. Ullmann, *The Medieval Idea of Law as Represented in Lucas de Penna* (London, 1946), esp. pp. 16 and 119; Francesco Calasso, *Medio Evo del Diritto, I. Le Fonti* (Milan, 1954), esp. p. 371; and Piano-Mortari, *Ricerche,* esp. p. 20.

4. Ullmann, p. 16; Piano-Mortari, p. 28.

5. Ullmann, p. 35: "Law is articulated Justice and is its practical execution," and p. 39; Piano-Mortari, p. 30.

6. Ullman, p. 16; Piano-Mortari, p. 24.

7. Piano-Mortari, pp. 10–11.

8. Ibid., pp. 131–37.

9. Ullmann, pp. 16, 35, 39–40; G. Le Bras, J. Rambaud, and Ch. Lefebvre, *L'Age Classique (1140–1378),* vol. 7 of *Histoire du droit et des institutions de l'église en Occident* (Paris, 1965), pp. 26–27.

direct human social life to the definitive pre-conceived end of man." [10]

The just quality of an individual law was calculated by measuring its *rationabilitas*,[11] this is, the degree of its conformity to natural reason.[12] Every just law had a *ratio* which united the law with natural and divine law,[13] and all law together possessed a *ratio iuris communis*.[14] It was on the basis of its *ratio* that each law was interpreted.[15] So important was the *ratio* that it could establish the interpretation of a law in a sense totally contrary to its literal meaning.[16] In other words, a law which did not in fact lead to justice was made to do so by positing for it a *ratio*, so that interpreted according to the sense of the posited *ratio*, it could be inserted into a just system of law.[17] For such laws, the *ratio* was deduced from extra-legal ethical premises.[18]

What has been said about legal methodology applies equally to legists (students of Roman law, but sometimes meaning all students of law) and canonists (students of Canon law).[19] The canonists, however, carried the idea of the rational unity of law to its extreme. Canon law, they asserted, must, like the Church, be one, holy, catholic, and apostolic.[20] So too they accepted Augustine's principle that justice consists in adhesion to the divine order,[21] which led them to conclude that the ultimate justification and goal of Canon law was the salvation of the soul.[22] Most later medieval lawyers were doctors of both Roman and Canon law (*utrumque ius*), however,

---

10. Ullmann, p. 17.
11. Piano-Mortari, p. 32.
12. Ibid., pp. 38, 73–80.
13. Ibid., pp. 80–91.
14. Calasso, p. 470.
15. Piano-Mortari, pp. 63–64.
16. Ibid., p. 30.
17. Ibid., pp. 36–37.
18. Ullmann, p. 24.
19. For the use of Roman law methodology by canonists, see Le Bras, *L'Age Classique*, p. 35.
20. Ibid., p. 43.
21. Ibid., p. 26.
22. Ibid., p. 43.

and this conclusion eventually gained general recognition: the goal of all law was salvation.[23]

It goes without saying that de Susannis, himself a doctor of both laws, accepted this conclusion, as well as all the other principles just discussed. The term *ratio* rarely appears in the *De Iudaeis,* yet the laws and interpretations found there clearly rest on specific *rationes.*[24] Moreover, the order of presentation reveals that the various laws, and their *rationes,* unite to form a unified system of law resting on a common *ratio.*[25] To be sure, de Susannis conceived of this system as just.[26]

In the exposition of particulars, de Susannis' usual procedure is to cite the (Roman) law or canon most applicable. If the matter is complex, commentary from various legal authorities is brought in to explain why the cited law is so applicable. Frequently, however, no law or canon stipulates how a matter is to be regulated. In such cases the regulation is often determined by the process of "extension."[27]

In certain instances lacking explicit legal regulation, however, the number of possible interpretations was, at least theoretically, unlimited. One of two methods are then used to arrive at a determination. Most often, de Susannis follows the *opinio communis* or the opinion of the most influential legal authorities, such as Bartolus or Baldus, on whose interpretations the "common opinion" was

---

23. See E. Cortese, *La Norma Giuridica* (Milan, 1962), pp. 1–33, 37–96, where he discusses the efforts made by medieval lawyers to make all law conform to, or at least compatible with, the religious imperatives of Canon law.

24. Cf. the analysis of *De Iudaeis,* pt. 1, chap. 4 (infra, pp. 93-96). There, incidentally, de Susannis does employ the term *ratio.* Cf. also the analysis of pt. 2, chap. 6, (infra, pp. 149f.).

25. Cf. esp. the analysis of pt. 2 (infra, pp. 116–24).

26. Cf. the analysis of pt. 2, chap. 5 (infra, pp. 149–52).

27. Cf. the summaries of *De Iudaeis,* pt. 1, chap. 3, pars. 8–15 (infra, p. 82) and pt. 2, chap. 3, pars. 3–12 (infra, pp. 105–06). *Extension* is a technical term which describes the operation of using a law which governs one situation to govern a second which is similar to the first, but for which there exists no law. On extension, see Piano-Mortari, *Ricerche,* chap. 4, pp. 63–130, and esp. pp. 108–22, 126, for a full discussion of *extensio iuris.*

usually based anyway.[28] "Common opinion" was construed as the consensus of the majority of the important commentators, and from the late fourteenth century and on, it was regularly considered binding.[29] Nevertheless, the "common opinion" was not absolutely binding, and a legist was free to make his own interpretations. De Susannis does so rarely, and then as a rule only to make minor adjustments. Yet at one point (in chapter six of *Pars Secunda*) he insists on a completely original determination in defiance of every major authority. This determination will demand close scrutiny.

De Susannis interpreted Roman law as it applies to the Jews from the standpoint of the medieval *mos italicus* school of legal study, rather than from that of the new *mos gallicus* school, which had arisen in France under the leadership of such men as Budé.[30] The latter school was distinguished by a philological-historical approach which sought to discover the meaning of Roman law not as it was applied in contemporary courts but as it had been applied in ancient Rome. Nevertheless, the procedures of the *mos gallicus* were not unknown to de Susannis. In one instance he quarrels with an interpretation of Alciatus' on the grounds that Alciatus had incorrectly identified the emperors to whom a law was attributed and, therefore, misconstrued the meaning the Roman themselves attached to that law.[31]

In *Pars Secunda,* de Susannis freely intermingles citations of laws and canons. This practice was not unusual. On the one hand, canonists had always admitted the validity, even in ecclesiastical affairs, of laws which complemented and supplemented the canons.[32]

---

28. Cf. the summaries, pt. 1, chap. 7, par. 4 (infra, p. 84); pt. 1, chap. 12, par. 4 (infra, p. 89); and pt. 2, chap. 2, par. 5 (infra, p. 105).

29. Piano-Mortari, pp. 155–62; and esp. W. L. Engelmann, *Die Wiedergeburt der Rechtskultur in Italien* (Leipzig, 1938), pp. 212–37, for a full discussion of "common opinion" and "authority" in interpretation.

30. See D. R. Kelley, "Budé and the First Historical School of Law," *AHR* 72 (1967): 807–34.

31. Cf. the analysis of *De Iudaeis,* pt. 2, chap. 6, par. 22 (infra. pp. 157–59). Cf. also *De Iudaeis,* pt. 3, chap. 1, passim (infra, pp. 125–48), and the analysis of pt. 2, chap. 6, par. 18 (infra, pp. 156–57), where de Susannis shows his own thorough grounding in classical literature and history.

32. Le Bras, *L'Age Classique,* p. 35; and Rambaud, *L'Age Classique,* pp. 169–86.

As Gratian himself had said: "Where they do not stand in the way of the Gospels and the canonical decrees, [the laws] are all deserving of reverence." [33] This idea was carried even further by Guillelmus Durandus in his *Speculum Iuris*. If for a given matter there exist both a canon and a law, and one of them is unclear, he declared, then the clear determination prevails. [34] The only stricture against such interchangeability was that no law may be introduced which contradicts a canon. As put most directly by the twelfth-century *Summa Coloniensis:*

> Here it must be noted that laws and canons alternate with each other, since laws rise up for canons, and, in turn, canons, in their defect, take laws for themselves, to such an extent that whatever is said in law is considered a canon, if it is not contradicted by a canon. [35]

After Cynus, however, legists rejected the notion that canons could supplement laws. [36] Nevertheless, the legists never went so far as to assert that the laws existed wholly apart from the canons. The opposite was true. The *Code* itself stated that the law condemns "all pragmatic sanctions which have been elicited contrary to ecclesiastical canons." And the medieval Gloss on this statement added: "The law succumbs to the canon where it [the law] is contrary to it [the canon]." [37] Lucas de Penna echoed this sentiment when he said: "The Holy Mother, Church, is not constrained by mundane laws." [38] In the sixteenth century, Stefano Federici, using

---

33. D. 10. d.p.c. 6.: "Ubi evangelicis atque canonicis decretis non obviaverint, [leges] omni reverentia dignae habeantur."

34. G. Durandus, *Speculum Iuris,* bk. 2, pt. 2, par. 5, n. 4, cited in Rambaud, *L'Age Classique,* p. 184.

35. S. Kuttner and G. Fransen, eds., *Summa 'Elegantius in iure divino' seu Coloniensis,* (New York, 1969), 1:63: "Hic advertendum est quod leges et canones mutuas sibi vices reponunt, quia et leges canonibus assurgunt et invicem canones in sui defectum leges assumunt, in tantum ut quicquid in lege dicitur, si a canone non contradicitur pro canone habeatur."

36. Rambaud, *L'Age Classique,* p. 184.

37. C. 1, 2, 12.: "Omnes pragmaticas sanctiones quae contra canones ecclesiasticos elicitae sunt." Glo: "Succumbit ergo lex canoni, ubi est ei contraria."

38. Ullmann, *Lucas de Penna,* p. 55, citing Lucas on C. 11, 18, 1, 14: "Mundanis legibus sancta mater ecclesia non constringitur."

the term *law* but surely referring to both laws and canons, propounded: "A law concerning sacred matters is always so understood that it limits a law concerning profane matters." [39]

While, then, legists would not use canons to support laws or to
supplement them, they certainly did admit, at least in theory, that
the canons took precedence over the laws. Furthermore, they surely
saw nothing wrong in the use of laws to supplement the canons. Thus
medieval lawyers conceived of an interdependence between the spiritual and temporal legal systems in the same way in which they
conceived of an overall interdependence between the spiritual and
temporal powers. Calasso goes so far as to call this interdependence
a *connubio*,[40] and he writes that it was the centrality of the bond
between both powers and both laws that gave rise to the institution of
utrumque ius.[41] Indeed, if medieval lawyers held basic the idea of
the unity of all law because it all derived from divine and natural
law, they had no choice but to view the canons and the laws as at
least theoretically complementary. Each reigned in its own sphere,
but between those spheres there could be no mechanical division.[42]
That de Susannis freely intermingled laws and canons, and that he
saw the two systems as complementary to each other, was the norm,
not the exception.

In addition, it must be noted in the light of the above discussion
that it would be unprofitable in any study of the Jews in medieval
law to question what their status would have been had they been
governed only by Roman law, only by the canons, or only by local
statutes. It is a question which medieval lawyers would have never
asked, for it corresponds to no situation that ever existed. What is
more, the Roman Jewry law itself was clearly influenced by the
theology of the Church, while the Jewry canons in turn, especially
those devolving from the letters of Pope Gregory the Great, rely heav-

---

39. Stefano Federici, *De Interpretatione Legum,* fol. 217ᵛ, cited in Piano-
Mortari, *Ricerche,* pp. 137–39: "Lex disponens de rebus sacris semper ita intel-
legenda est, ut potius deroget legi disponenti de rebus prophanis."

40. Calasso, *Medio Evo del diritto,* p. 407.

41. Ibid., p. 490.

42. Ibid., p. 407.

ily on the compilations of Roman law by Theodosian and Justinian for their wording and not infrequently for their content. It is thus only proper that the *De Iudaeis,* using both laws and canons together, seeks to define a harmonious and unified legal status for the Jews.

CHAPTER IV

PARS PRIMA: THE JEWS AND THE
CANON LAW

THE TEXT OF THE *De Iudaeis,* as with all medieval legal tracts, is difficult to follow. Far from a flowing essay, its style is choppy in the extreme. Sentences are often no more than phrases linking together the numerous legal citations (allegations) which de Susannis is attempting to harmonize and draw conclusions from. This difficulty, combined with the overall length of the tract, would make a translation bulky and doubtless confusing. Yet in examining the tract there is a need to convey its basic sense and internal arrangement, as well as to offer an exposition which is highly faithful to the original text. For this reason I have elected to present uninterrupted summaries, which are in fact nearly paraphrases, of the legal divisions of the tract, and to postpone all analysis until the summaries are completed. This method should also provide the reader with the opportunity to see the finer lines of de Susannis' arguments and conclusions for himself.

A. *Summary*

I, intro.   The *De Iudaeis,* states de Susannis, is intended to serve as a judges' handbook for matters pertaining to infidels, and especially to Jews.[1] It is a most apt project, because controversies have arisen about the matters it ventilates.[2]

---

1. *De Iudaeis,* pt. 1, intro. chap., intro. par. (Henceforth, all references to the *De Iudaeis* will be cited as follows: A Roman numeral to indicate part, and Arabic numerals to indicate chapter and paragraph, with no citation of the title. Thus, II,3,4–6 equals pt. 2, chap. 3, pars. 4 to 6.) Since these summary

Infidels are divided into three major groups: pagans (among whom are included Muslims), Jews, and heretics.[3] There is also a fourth group, the *Marani,* the *pessissimum genus hominum.* The prime concern of this book, however, is the Jews,[4] who are the off-spring of the tribe of Judah, the most excellent tribe, from which   I, 1 descended David and Christ.[5] But despite their origins, the modern Jews are blind, and they are no longer entitled to the name, Israel, which now belongs to the Christians.[6]

These modern Jews are religious enemies of Christianity. (They   I, 2 are not civil enemies.)[7] Nevertheless, the Church and Christianity receive them and sustain them out of piety and charity.[8] The Jews are sustained because their presence in a state of punishment reminds Christians of divine justice, and they may observe their rites because they prefigure both Christian rites and the truth of the faith. The Jews are the only infidels who have this privilege, for the rites of no other infidel group prefigure the truth. The protection given the Jews is in the tradition of Rome. They may not be molested in their lives

---

chapters are intended to present de Susannis' thought and conclusions, references to the canons and laws he cites will be made only when necessary. The reader is referred to the Index (Appendix 2) for citations of the laws, canons, and commentaries pertaining to the specific topics covered by de Susannis. N.B., since modern footnoting style had yet to be invented, the common practice of medieval lawyers (and I use this term for de Susannis, who by training and practice was a medieval lawyer) was to interrupt their sentences with citations of laws and commentaries. This practice destroys the flow of thought. To restore this flow, I have omitted these citations when quoting from the tract.

2. I,intro.,2–4.

3. I,intro.,1.

4. I,intro.,5.

5. I,1,2.

6. I,1,10–11.

7. By this de Susannis means that the Jews are not intrinsically guilty of civil or criminal delicts, and their status should in no way be predicated on the assumed imputation of such to them. Cf. also pp. 102f., infra, where this status of "civil friend" is the basis for de Susannis' decisions, and where the concept is applied with reference to the relationship of the Jews to *ius commune.*

8. I,2,1–3: "Et licet Iudaei sint inimici Crucis Christi Redemptoris nostri, et eiusdem nominis blasphemi, et ipsum esse iudaeum sit crimen et delictum habito respectu ad ipsum Deum et poenam aeternam, non autem quo ad iudicem et forum contentiosum. Ipsos tamen Iudaeos ex pietate sustinet Ecclesia et pietas Christiana receptat."

or in their property, and they may also have homes in Christian lands, unless they practice usury.[9]

I, 3   Because the Jews and their rites are tolerated, they may maintain old synagogues. But *ad favorem et decorem* of the Christian faith, they may not erect new ones.[10] Christians are prohibited from attacking synagogues, but in the event of their destruction, the problem of whether they may be rebuilt arises. Some hold that the land is the essence of a structure and that the reconstructed building is not a new synagogue. But the common, more true, and accepted opinion is that the structure itself is the essence, and that to rebuild is no different from erecting a new house of worship. Yet the pope may dispense in this matter, just as he may permit a new synagogue in a city recently settled by Jews.[11]

As a corollary to the toleration of rites, Jews may not be summoned to court on the Sabbath. This rule seems to impede Christians, and, to some, appears improper. But the legislation is made in favor of the holiday—the rite—and not the person.[12]

I, 4   So, too, none may violate Jewish cemeteries.[13]

The permission to dwell in Christian lands does not, however, extend to the uninhibited intermingling of Jews and Christians. To prevent the delicts which can result from such fraternization, the law requires Jews to wear a distinctive habit.[14] For similar reasons,

---

9. I,2,3–8: "Et ideo licite habent iudaei domos in terris Christianorum . . . nisi vellent in eis exercere usuram, quia tunc secus esset." This statement must be understood in the light of I,11,2–4. See n. 38 there.

10. I,3,1–2, 14–15.

11. I,3,8–15.

12. I,3,16–17: "Quia fuit inductum hoc in favorem festivitatis, et non iudaeorum."

13. I,3,18. It is worth noting that in Gratian's *Decretum,* D.1, c.27 and 28, *de cons.,* it is stated that a church may not be consecrated if infidels are buried on its grounds. Therefore, to permit consecration, their bodies may be exhumed. Most likely it was on the basis of these canons that Pius V ordered the bodies in the Jewish cemetery at Bologna to be exhumed in order to make way, in 1569, for a convent (*SRH,* 14:48–49). Cf. III,9,4, where de Susannis cites these canons and refers to the exhumation of infidels in order to make way for the erection of a church or convent.

14. 1,4,1–3. Cf. pp. 189, 191, infra, for examples of Christian princes in Italy permitting violations of this regulation. Because of its significance, I,4 is

Christians, especially *simplices,* are not to serve Jews in real servitude.[15] Nor may Jews and Christians sit at a common table.[16] However, Christians may work for Jews as day laborers, and Christians and Jews may attend schools together. Jews may also receive permission to employ Christian nurses outside, but never inside, their homes—if the life of the child would be otherwise endangered.[17] In addition, Christians may contract and trade with Saracens and Jews in legitimate business dealings.[18] But Jews may not sell Christians foodstuffs which they themselves would not purchase from Christians. Jews would thereby acquire superiority over Christians.[19] In time of war, moreover, trading with infidels must cease. Indeed, Christians may never trade with infidels in goods which directly or indirectly have a military value.[20]

I, 5 & 6

The question arises whether, despite the regular situation of toleration, Christian princes may, if they so will, expel Jews *absque causa . . . et ab eis auferre bona.* Some legists say that while no

I, 7

---

examined in detail in the analysis, infra, pp. 92–96. To avoid repetition, the summary has been abridged.

15. I,4,14.

16. I,4,20.

17. I,4,15–19. Cf. p. 191, infra, for violations of this rule in sixteenth-century Italy.

18. I,4,16 and I,5,1.

19. I,4,20.

20. I,5,2–6. Chap. six discusses when it is permissible for Christians to join in military alliances with infidels to fight other Christians, under what conditions truces can be made with Christians or with infidels, and the papal role in crusades. Though extraneous to the concerns of this book, the material in chap. six is surely of value to those studying the sixteenth-century treaties between the French and the Turks, as well as the military relations of Charles V with the Protestants. There are also data in this chapter which pertain to sixteenth-century papal theory. In addition, chap. six may be of value to those studying the case of David Reubeni, the Oriental Jew from the purported Jewish kingdom of Khaibar in northern Arabia, who appeared at the court of Clement VII in 1524, seeking an alliance between the forces of Christendom and the Jewish forces of Khaibar to attack the Turk with a pincers movement. See *SRH,* 13:109 ff.; and A. Z. Ascoli, *The Story of David Reubeni* (Hebrew), (Jerusalem, 1940), pp. 108–10 (Hebrew numbering), and esp. the letter of Clement VII, 172–75 (Arabic numerals) which states: ". . . cum quanquam hebreorum gens christiano nomini adversa sit, statuat tamen saepe Deus cum inimicis se vindicare de inimicis . . ." (Trans. in *SRH,* 13:111).

private person may do either, princes certainly may, for Jews are their *servi*. As a lord may sell his slaves, so too may he expel them and confiscate their goods.[21] Other legists assert that princes may indiscriminately expel and expropriate Jews on the grounds that the Jews are always a potential source of acts of malice against Christians.[22]

But if the Jews are expelled, how will the prophecies be fulfilled which speak of the saved remnant and which warn that this generation will not pass until all believe in Christ?[23] The contrary opinion, then, that without just cause Jews may not be expelled, is *verior et probabilior*. As many legists assert, the laws and canons indicate that princes may not expel Jews who dwell peacefully in their lands and who threaten no danger or scandal. For to expel Jews without cause violates the precept of *caritas*. Rather, Christians should tolerate infidels and win them for God.[24] If, however, the Jews threaten danger, scandal, machinations, or other enormous crimes, then they should under no circumstance be tolerated, but by the best law they should be expelled.[25]

Moreover, Jews, by law, are *de Populo Romano et de eodem corpore civitatis*. Therefore, one must have cause to expel them.[26]

There are, nevertheless, times when princes licitly may take property from Jews, such as the payment Jews make at imperial coronations.[27] But what about tribute, that is, taxes? Christians are forced to pay taxes because, as the subjects of princes, such is their obligation. Since Jews too are the subjects of princes, it seems that they are similarly obligated. However, the contrary is *verior*. The canons, especially *Sicut*,[28] prohibit the extraction of any forced

---

21. I,7,1.

22. I,7,2.

23. I,7,3: "Quod si expellerentur, deficeret in eis illud vaticinium Esaiae x.ibi, in veritate reliquiae convertentur . . . et Marci. xiii. non transibit generatio haec, donec omnia ista fiant."

24. I,7,4: "Debemus tolerare infideles et ipsos lucrifacere Deo."

25. I,7,4: "Nullatenus tollerandos, sed iure optimo expellendos." See the analysis of this statement, infra, p. 97.

26. I,7,5.

27. I,7,6.

28. X.5,6,9.

servitude not customarily given by Jews, and this prohibition is understood to disallow taxation. Yet in practice this prohibition is limited by other canons, which permit the leveling of fines in lieu of conversion, and by this means Jews in the Papal States are forced to make large payments. Still, these fines and "crown gold" are the only taxes a prince may level on Jews, no matter how anomalous it seems.[29]

Although Jews are received in Christian society out of Christian   I, 8
piety, and although Christian princes may not expel Jews without cause, Jews may not enjoy the immunities of the Church,[30] and they may not, specifically flee to a church for sanctuary. There is, however, a difference of opinion on the matter of immunities if it happens that a Jew seeking asylum in a church expresses the desire to convert. Some legists base their argument on an interpretation of canons, and they hold that the expressed intention to convert allows the Jew to take refuge. Yet the more common opinion, based on the literal wording of *l. Iudaei, Code, De his qui ad ecclesias confugiunt,*[31] denies asylum to Jews no matter what the circumstances. For, say those who hold this opinion, "Considering that there is an explicit text in the civil [Roman] law and no text in canon law which states the opposite [namely, that a Jew who expresses his intention of converting does receive asylum], it is impossible to 'correct' the civil law by the interpretations of the doctors and the glosses." This common opinion is correct.[32]

Similarly, no Jew may make the sign of the cross over himself   I, 9
to ward off the Devil. The success of this procedure depends on imagining Christ crucified during its performance. And if a man

---

29. I,7,6.

30. I,8,intro.

31. C.1,12.1.

32. I,8,1: "Considerans quod ex quo reperitur text. expressus de iure civili et nullus text. de iure canonico, qui dicat contrarium, videtur sibi (Io. de Anania) durum quod per Glos. et Docto. ius civile corrigatur." The law is C.1,12,1, and it states: "Iudaei, qui reatu aliquo vel debitis fatigati simulant se Christianae legi velle coniungi, ut ad ecclesias confugientes evitare possint crimina vel pondera debitorum, arceantur nec ante suscipiantur, quam debita universa reddiderint vel fuerint innocentia demonstrata purgati."

does so imagine when he signs himself, then the signing will benefit him, even if he is not a Christian, and even if he does not believe in Christ.[33] Therefore, although this procedure is a custom and is ordained by neither Scripture nor canon, it is prohibited to a Jew. For it would be unthinkable for an unbeliever to benefit from a privilege which rightly belongs only to believers.[34]

I, 10   In the same vein, it may seem improper to invoke the name of Christ in an act drawn for a Jew by a Christian notary, but Italian custom (although not law) establishes that the invocation is a required element in the substance of a valid act. In Italy, therefore, the invocation must be included, even in acts drawn for Jews. Elsewhere, the invocation is optional. It is, however, necessary to distinguish that it is the notary and not the Jew who makes the invocation, and thus it is the notary and not the Jew who benefits from the invocation.[35]

I, 11   Jews are allowed to live in Christian lands because of Christian piety. They should, then, not be ingrates, nor should they cause Christians to suffer losses; Christians should benefit from Jews. But it is the exact opposite of benefit which results when Jews ensnare Christians by various means and make the poor poorer, most especially through loans and usury.[36] As Aristotle wrote, moreover, usury is a sin against natural law. Usury also violates divine law as found in the Ten Commandments and in Deuteronomy 23, Exodus 22, and Leviticus 25.[37] All the legists and canonists inveigh against usury, both the civil (Roman) and Canon law prohibit it, and the restitution of exacted usuries can never be forbidden.[38]

---

33. I,9,1.
34. I,9,7.
35. I,10,1.
36. I,11,intro.
37. I,11,1–2.
38. I,11,2–4. It is worth noting that at this point de Susannis interjects *Sext.* 5,5,1, which states that anyone who has settled in any locality for the express purpose of usuring must be expelled. In practice this meant that no one was allowed to settle anywhere for the purpose of usuring. The commentators, de Susannis relates, held that this canon applied to Jews. Thus, it is likely that when Pius V listed usuries in *Hebraeorum gens* as one of the grounds for expulsion, he had this canon in mind.

Nor does Deuteronomy 23, which permits Jews to lend to aliens, make it possible for Jews to usure with Christians. Christians are not aliens to the Jews; they are *proximi,* worshipping the same God as the Jews and differing with them only on the question of whether the messiah has come. Deuteronomy 23 applied only to the Canaanites. And in the case of the Canaanites, the Jews were not usuring, but recuperating their goods, which the Canaanites had once expropriated. Similarly, the canon which permits usury as an act of war[39] must be understood as its Gloss interprets it, namely as a prohibition. All the commentators concur with this Gloss, and they add that usury is never permitted. The conclusion is thus *verissima:* usury is prohibited by all law.[40]

Nevertheless, some princes permit Jews to usure, claiming that usury benefits the common good. Some legists, moreover, defend the legality of this specific act even though they inveigh against usury in general. But to grant such permission is illegal, for usury is absolutely (*simpliciter*) prohibited by divine law, from which not even the emperor may dispense.[41] Even if princes could permit usury, it would be wrong for them to do so, for usury results not in the increase of public utility, but in the pauperization of Christians. Nor is there any necessity for the existence of usury. Even the poor can find alternate means of acquiring money, such as working.[42]

The pope, however, may permit usury. He may not simply dispense with the prohibition, for even he may not regularly dispense from divine law. Yet he may allow exceptions to divine law under special circumstances.[43] If, for instance, there is a danger that

---

39. C.14, q.4, c.12 *ab illo.*

40. I,11,5–6.

41. I,11,11. I,11,7–10 contains a discussion of whether secular or ecclesiastical courts have jurisdiction over Jewish usuring. De Susannis' conclusion is that ecclesiastical courts alone have cognizance in determining if a given act is usurious, but both courts can determine the question of fact: whether usury has been committed.

42. I,11,12.

43. I,11,13: "Possit papa ius divinum limitare ex causa." The question of the ability of the pope to make such dispensations was a hotly debated one. That de Susannis allows that the pope can so dispense places him squarely within the camp of the papal monarchists. Cf. M. Wilks, *The Problem of Sovereignty in the Later Middle Ages* (Cambridge, 1963), pp. 288–330, and esp. pp. 316 f.

without usury men will turn to crime, the pope may make a dispensation, permitting one evil to avoid a greater one. He may, however, grant this dispensation only to Jews, never to Christians.

But many legists object to this interpretation. First, these legists assert that while the Church sometimes tolerates evils to attain goods or to avoid greater evils, it may never expressly sanction an evil. More to the issue at hand, the canons prohibit infidels from acquiring any privilege whose performance could result not only in evildoing but also in opprobrium to the faith. Permitting infidels to usure would result in such opprobrium, because it would allow them to ignore the Gospel precept which prohibits usury. Second, these legists assert that the pope may never expressly permit acts which are prohibited in both the Old and the New Testaments.[44]

In response to these assertions, it may be said that the common opinion holds that the pope may dispense in the matter of usury. In this case, however, to cite the common opinion is no solution. The only way to justify dispensations permitting usury is to acknowledge that the pope is omnipotent in spiritual matters, and that this omnipotence enables him to permit Jews to publicly usure in the lands of Christian princes for the sake of the public good and in special circumstances. Even so, the pope may grant such permission only as long as the princes and their people consent.[45] Moreover, the pope himself may not wish to permit usury explicitly, and he may resort to a fiction (*dissimulatio*) and ordain that Jews should not be punished for usury. In this way he may avoid dispensing from what both Testaments forbid.[46]

If Jews are permitted to usure, it must be known that it is not

---

44. I,11,13–14.

45. I,11,14: "Ergo, quod summus Pontifex propter bonum publicum, ex causa . . . possit permittere Iudaeis, ut publice exerceant usuras in terris principum Christianorum, interveniente consensu Domini temporalis et populi sui." In I,11,14 de Susannis makes a remark which reveals his attitude about the pope as monarch. He says that when the pope makes this dispensation for usuring: "Facit ut Deus, non ut homo, cum sit in terris Dei Vicarius, nec habet superiorem, nec potest dici illi, cur ista facis . . . Et dicitur Deus vivens."

46. I,11,14. Cf. pp. 189 and 190, *infra*, on Jewish lending in sixteenth-century Italy without a papal permit.

a sin to receive at usury,[47] that one who receives at usury can spontaneously refuse to repay the usury, and that it remains sinful for Christians to lend at usury to Jews.[48] As for liabilities, the lender is responsible if through negligence he either loses a pledge or permits it to be damaged. If the pledge is a perishable, however, there can be no question of negligence. (These rulings also apply to Christians who make non-usurious loans.) If the pledge is a stolen item, and the lender was ignorant of the fact, then the owner must pay the lender the value of the item, if he wishes to retrieve it.[49]

The question arises whether there is greater sin in killing a   I, 12
Christian or an infidel. Some legists maintain that the graver sin is murdering an infidel, because killing a non-Christian destroys both a body and a soul. The soul of the Christian lives eternally, while the soul of the infidel perishes with his mortal body.[50] Other legists, following St. Thomas,[51] declare that it is a greater sin to kill a Christian because one is to love a Christian more than a non-Christian, because a Christian is more worthy (*dignus*), because the death of a Christian deprives the community of a greater good, and because killing a Christian is identical with despising God.[52] The majority of the doctors, however, accept the importance of the reasons advanced by both sides, and therefore they conclude that killing a Christian is a greater sin (*peccatum*), but that killing an infidel causes greater damage (*damnum*). They also make an important refinement on the grounds that there is still great hope for the conversion of an infidel child. They establish a greater penalty for killing an infidel child than for killing a Christian adult.[53]

Similarly, it is a graver sin for a Christian to have sexual rela-   I, 13

---

47. I,11,15.
48. I,11,6.
49. I,11,17–18.
50. I,12,1–2.
51. Thomas Aquinas, *Summa Theologica*, trans. Fathers of the English Dominican Province (New York, 1947), II,II,6,9,6. Thomas is the only non-legist cited by de Susannis in support of legal arguments. Future references to Thomas in "summary" chapters will indicate that de Susannis has cited this passage.
52. I,12,3–4.
53. I,12,4.

tions with a nun than to have sexual relations with a Jewess. Having sexual relations with a Jewess is indeed a serious crime, because Jews are enemies of the cross and blasphemers of the name of Christ, and to prevent this delict differences in dress were established.[54] Moreover, because this delict results in offense to God and injury to the sacrament of baptism, the civil law decrees capital punishment for knowingly having carnal relations with a Jewess, even if those relations occur within the figure of matrimony (*figura matrimonii*).[55] But the crime of carnal relations with a nun is a greater sin, because it results not only in insult to God and the faith, but also in sacrilege, debauchery (*stuprum*), the violation of a holy person, and, most of all, *lèse majesté* against God.[56]

I, 14   There are many who object to the wars of conquest in the New World.[57] They claim that there is no just cause for these wars, and that Spain is fighting the infidels in the New World on the illegal pretext that war against infidels is *ipso facto* permissible. They also claim that these wars have led to the forced conversion of many infidels, which is wholly improper, just as is the forced baptism of Jewish children without the consent of their parents.[58]

But these wars are licit. They are waged on the grounds that the infidels of the New World practice vices which violate the law of nature, namely the crimes of human sacrifice and idol worship. Divine law itself permits war to put an end to these crimes. Such a war is fought under papal leadership, because it is the

---

54. I,13,1.

55. I,13,2. See II,3, passim, for the case of Jews who have sexual relations with Christian women; II,3,17 for the case of a Christian unknowingly having sexual relations with a Jewess; and III,7–9 for a general discussion of marriage between Christians and infidels.

56. I,13,3–4. I,13,5–9 discusses the glories of virginity. De Susannis even speaks at length of the safeguards taken by the ancient Romans to protect their sacred virgins. This discussion is not surprising, since de Susannis wrote a tract entitled *De Celibatu*.

57. For a general treatment of the themes found in this chapter, themes which aroused great interest in de Susannis' day, see Willaert's discussion of the development of international law in the sixteenth century in L. Willaert, *La Restauration Catholique, 1563–1648* (Paris, 1960), pp. 434–48.

58. Cf. III,2,6–7 for de Susannis' full discussion of this problem.

right and duty of the pope to punish infidels who commit these sins.[59] These infidels, therefore, may legitimately be subjected to the Imperium of the Christians, not for the purpose of enslaving them or of expropriating their possessions, but in order to liberate them from their crimes.[60]

As for the additional objection which some advance, that infidels must be won by preaching alone, in the manner of Christ and the Apostles, it is an ideal and obtains only if infidels can be won in that way.[61]

In any case, these infidels were killing the missionaries who were sent to them, and it therefore became legal to employ force against them in order to enable the missionaries to preach. Nor are precedents lacking for such a course. Constantine forbade idolatry, and Gregory the Great commended Genadius, who compelled various peoples into submission in order to more easily lead them to Christianity.[62] Moreover, once preaching commenced, conversion was spontaneous. Indeed, the infidels thronged to the baptismal font.[63]

B. *Analysis*

The introduction and first chapter of the *De Iudaeis* set the tone for the entire work. The reader is alerted to search the book not only for solutions to legal queries, but also for answers to contemporary religious questions.[64] There also appears at this point the theological fundamental on which all the legal determinations are based. The Church, not the Jews, is now the True Israel. Whereas

I, intro,

I, 1

---

59. This is probably a reference to the "Donation of Alexander," through which Alexander VI, in 1494, divided the New World between Spain and Portugal, asserting that it was his right as pope to do so. For a discussion of this donation, especially in relation to the late-fifteenth-century revival of papal monarchism, see M. Maccarone, *Vicarius Christi* (Rome, 1952), pp. 270–75.

60. I,14,1: "Potuerunt ergo legitime Christianorum Imperio subiici, non ut servi fiant, aut eorum bonis priventur, sed ut a talibus fiagitiis liberentur."

61. I,14,1: "Si eo modo potuissent eos lucrari."

62. *Summa Theologica*, II,II, 10, 8.

63. I,14,1. "Agminatim ad baptismum convolasse."

64. Cf. p. 81, supra.

the Jews were once the favored people of God, they are now His enemies.

I, 2   It is the enemy status of the Jew which prompts the first question of the legal discussion. If the Jews are enemies, why can they live among God's faithful?[65] The assumption behind this question is that legally, as well as theologically, the Jews as religious enemies have no intrinsic right to live with Christians. The reply then stresses this rightlessness by indicating that the Jews live in Christian lands *only* because Christian piety tolerates them. In other words, Jews have no guaranteed rights, even their presence in Christian society is no more than a privilege. The repeated use of the phrases "although Jews are tolerated" and "because Jews are tolerated" to introduce additional privileges or restrictions demonstrates that the concept of toleration is fundamental. As a tolerated enemy, the Jew is, furthermore, dependent on Christian charity for all his privileges. Nor may any of his privileges alter that status. They must, rather, accentuate it. Jews are therefore allowed to observe their rites only because those rites glorify Christianity.[66] Similarly, the privilege of

I, 3   having synagogues is limited, because *ad favorem et decorem* of the Christian faith, no new synagogues may be erected.[67]

With this last proposition de Susannis delineates the first of two major corollaries to the basic principle of dependence. The dependent status of the Jew demands the subservience of Judaism to Christianity. It is, in fact, the inferiority of Judaism to Christianity, and the Jew's stubborn adherence to his religion, which creates the status of the Jew in the first place. Therefore Jews may freely observe their rites, but only if those rites neither insult Christianity nor detract from the honor and respect due her.

I, 4   The second major corollary is that as individuals, Jews must be inferior to Christians. The treatment de Susannis gives this issue is quite detailed, since it is most important for understanding the *De Iudaeis* as a whole. It makes the basic *rationes* on which all his

---

65. Cf. p. 81, supra.
66. Cf. p. 81, supra.
67. Cf. p. 82, supra.

arguments rest crystal clear. A close examination of this section is quite worthwhile.

The discussion opens with the statement, taken almost verbatim from the canons,[68] that to avoid the sexual delicts which often occur when Jews and Christians freely intermingle, Jews are required to wear distinctive clothing.[69] De Susannis then admits that the pope may dispense from this restriction.[70] But his sentiments clearly favor the requirement of special dress. He therefore offers[71] a number of arguments to explain why the canon *In nonnullis,*[72] which establishes the requirement, should be observed, at least when there is no papal dispensation to the contrary. First, distinctive habits are demanded by the Bible, as *In nonnullis* itself points out, referring to the *simbria,* ritual fringes, enjoined on the Jews in Numbers 15.[73] Second, there is nothing unusual in the idea that people of different status wear different habits, although for some the habit is a sign of honor, and for others a sign of ignominy.[74] Clerics, for instance, wear a special garb as a sign of honor. So, too, serving women and prostitutes wear clothing different from that of virgins and matrons. They do so as a sign of ignominy, in order to permit their easy recognition. Similarly, manumitted slaves at Rome wore the *pilleus* to distinguish them

---

68. X.5,6,15.

69. I,4,1–3.

70. I,4,4. He here cites: *Consilia . . . Raphaelis Cumani nempe et Raphaelis Fulgosii* (Venice, 1576), consilium 115, which the Jews of Ferrara had sollicited from Fulgosius. They had received a privilege from Martin V, *Quia imaginem,* Feb. 12, 1419 (Arch. Roma ITc or Raynaldus XVIII), which permitted them to dispense with the badge. A number of local Ferrara churchmen protested this privilege. The Jews then sought legal support. Fulgosius found this in the notion that local custom in Ferrara had never required a badge, and local custom, he declared, took precedence over written law. Thus the Jews did not even need the special dispensation. Fulgosius apparently won his case, and de Susannis felt a need to respond, claiming (see below) that the requirement of special dress was based on divine law, which superceded customary law. Fulgosius, consilium 115: "Consuetudo generalis legi scriptae contraria legi ipsi generaliter abroget, ff. de legi. et sen. consul., 1. de quibus, in fi."

71. I,4,5–7.

72. X,5,6,15.

73. See Friedberg, *Corpus Iuris,* for the full text of the papal letter printed together with X.5,6,15.

74. I,4,8–9.

from those still in bondage.[75] The same reasoning applies to
the habit of the Jews (*ut cognoscantur sicut Iudaei*). Once Jews
are recognized, Christians will avoid excessive familiarity with them
and also the danger of illicit sexual relations.[76]

As revealed in two other places in the *De Iudaeis,* however,
as well as by the canon *In nonnullis* itself, sexual relations between
Jews and Christians are forbidden not because they are a crime in
and of themselves, but on the grounds that such relations insult
Christianity.[77] Thus the special dress of the Jew ultimately prevents
insults to Christianity. In his discussion of the rules of synagogue
building, de Susannis showed that Judaism as a religion may not
insult Christianity. He has now shown that Christianity will also
not tolerate insult on the part of the individual Jew. That these two
topics are discussed back to back only serves to clarify and reinforce
the centrality of the prohibition of insult.

De Susannis also suggested another reason for dress regulations. Jews were to wear a distinctive habit as a sign of ignominy
which explicitly classed them with prostitutes and slaves in opposition to women of virtue and Christians. In other words, the special
habit designates the Jew as inferior to the Christian. As the Chris-

---

75. See C.7,6,1,5 (cited here by de Susannis), which speaks of the *pilleus.*
To support his contentions here, he cites *Pauli Castrensis, In Primam Codicis Partem Commentaria* (Venice, 1582), on C.1,4,4 *mimae:* "Per hanc legem patet quod
meretrices et iudaei possunt cogi ad portandum habitum distinctum ab aliis
mulieribus vel christianis secundum Doctores, ut cognoscantur. adde: tex. in c.
nonnullis." *l. mimae* itself prohibits female mimes, who display their bodies,
from wearing the habit of virgins.

76. I,4,14. To be precise, de Susannis states that Christians are to avoid
familiarity with Jews as Jews were to avoid fraternization with pagans, lest
the pagans seduce the Jews. The meaning remains the same as I have it in the
text.

77. I,13 and II,3. De Susannis explicitly connects I,13 and I,4 by noting in
I,13 that dress regulations were established to prevent sexual delicts; this in
the same breath with the statement that such delicts cause insult to the faith. Cf.
p.100, infra. The *c. in nonnullis* first orders the Jews to wear a special habit
to prevent sexual delicts. It then orders the Jews to remain indoors during Holy
Week, so that their actions do not bring contumely to the faith. Clearly, because
of the juxtaposition of topics, the canon sees sexual delicts also as potential
sources of contumely.

tian is free, the Jew is a slave, and the Jew's habit is a visible reminder of this theological and legal principle.

The prevention of overfamiliarity to avoid insults to Christianity and the necessary inferiority of the Jew to the Christian also
serve as the *rationes* for the regulations prohibiting Christians from
becoming the slaves of Jews and from eating at a Jew's table. So
de Susannis states explicitly: for the same reason (*ex hoc*) that Jews
wear a distinct habit, Christians may not become the slaves or servants of Jews. Such servitude would endanger the safety of their
souls as a result of continuous conversation and close familiarity
with Jews, and the Jews, moreover, would appear to be their superiors (*superiores*).[78]

At this point, to reinforce his arguments, de Susannis cites the
canons *Etsi*[79] and *Ad haec*.[80] The first states directly that servitude
to Jews results in Christian inferiority and thus in insults to the faith.
The second, originally a decree of the 1179 Third Lateran Council,
adds another dimension, which de Susannis also refers to, namely,
that through overfamiliarity and especially servitude the danger of
apostasy arises.[81] Realistic or not, the fear of apostasy, the greatest
of all possible insults, had persisted over the centuries.[82]

Thus de Susannis continues with a severe warning. There are
certain dealings which Jews and Christians may have with each
other. "What alone is forbidden is overfamiliarity." Nevertheless,
"it is safer to remain aloof from Jews, lest those who have deal-

---

78. I,4,14.

79. I,4,14. "Iudaei videantur superiores, si famulos habeant Christianos, et
ista ratio ponitur in c. etsi iudaeos. (X.5,6,13.)"

80. X.5,6,8 *ad haec* prohibits Jewish ownership of Christian slaves and warns
of the danger to the souls of such slaves.

81. X.5,6,8: "Ad suam superstitionem et perfidiam simplicium animas in-
clinarent" (*Ad haec*).

82. Thus de Susannis incorporates, with citation, the argument of the fifteenth-
century canonist Nicholas Tudeschis, *Lectura Super Libros V Decretalium* (Lyons,
1559), 4:96v, on X.5,6,8 *ad haec*. De Susannis also notes that Felynus Sandeus
(d. 1503), in his commentary on *ad haec,* both cited Nicholas Tudeschis and
agreed with him. F. Sandeus, *Commentaria in Decretales,* (Venice, 1574), 3:col.
961, on X.5,6,8. In both Tudeschis and Sandeus the terms *apostasy* and *danger
to the soul* are used interchangeably.

ings with Jews hear from him [Christ] on that day when he is about to judge them: 'Depart, I do not know you; you have communicated with those who crucified me.' And against those [who have dealings with Jews], see what Chrysostom says: 'You are a Christian? Why, then, do you molest the Church?' " [83] De Susannis has thus asserted that all relationships with Jews had best be avoided—not only overfamiliarity, which is prohibited— because relationships with Jews "molest the Church." They may even lead to apostasy.

To conclude this discussion, and to reiterate his points once more, de Susannis states that for the same reasons (*eisdem rationibus*) that continual conversation with Jews is forbidden, so too is eating and drinking at their table.[84] This prohibition was introduced out of detestation and odium of the Jewish depravity, and as the canon *Omnes* explicitly affirms,[85] we would appear to venerate the Jews and to be inferior to them if we ate at their table while they refuse to eat at ours.[86]

Now, *Omnes* also states that to dine at a Jew's table is sacrilege and a grave insult. Thus here again, as in the cases of servitude and dress regulations, both the canons and de Susannis explicitly link the issues of superiority and insult. Whenever the Jew becomes the Christian's superior, Christianity is insulted. In other words, the two principles presented in the discussion of these three cases are really the two sides of the basic principle de Susannis was intent on demonstrating: the necessary inferiority of the Jew to the Christian. Were it otherwise, the Jew would no longer be a tolerated enemy.

I, 5   The principles which de Susannis has now outlined underlie every other legal determination in the tract. Thus, Jews are normally allowed to have commercial relations with Christians, but

---

83. I,4,17: "Discedite, non novi vos, communicastis enim cum iis, qui me crucifixerunt."

84. I,4,20. C.28,q.1,c.13 *nullus,* and 14 *omnes.*

85. C.28,q.1,c.14: "Sacrilegium est eorum cibos a Christianis sumi . . . ac sic inferiores Christiani incipient esse quam Iudaei."

86. I,4,20: "Item hoc [c.omnes] fuit inductum in detestationem et odium iudaeicae pravitatis et caecitatis, ne videamur factum eorum venerari, vel ne videamur eis inferiores."

transactions through which Jews would become superior to Christians are prohibited.[87] Similarly, the inclusion of the restrictions on trade between Christians and Saracens [88] in the discussion of commercial relations between Jews and Christians implies that Jews may trade freely with Christians only because they are prepared to live peacefully with Christians as tolerated inferiors.

The principle that Jews reside in Christian lands only on the basis of a privilege raises the question of the limits of that privilege.[89] De Susannis' phrasing of this question is most significant. He does not ask whether Jews may be expelled, but whether Jews may be expelled without cause. There is no absolute prohibition against expulsion. Even the Jews' status as *cives* in the civil law[90] is no guarantee against expulsion, and their only real protection is that expulsion without cause would violate the precept of *caritas*. Their privilege of residence is, then, most precarious. Thus de Susannis asserts that if there is just cause, the Jews may be expelled *iure optimo,* and he offers not one law or canon to support his assertion. Undoubtedly, he assumed that his assertion was universally accepted as legal fact.

I, 7

Aside from these strictly legal determinations, it is significant that de Susannis gauges the propriety of expulsion on the basis of the effect of expulsion on conversion. Just how significant will eventually be seen.[91]

Appended to the discussion of expulsion is the conclusion that Jews cannot be forced to pay regular taxes.[92] This seems to grant them preferential treatment and to violate the principle of inferiority. But when de Susannis calls this conclusion an anomaly,

I, 7, 6

---

87. Cf. p. 83, supra.
88. I,5.2–6. X.5,6 *De Iudaeis et Sarracenis,* c.6 *ita quorundam,* c. 11 *significavit,* c. 12 *quod olim.* The fact that these restrictions appear in the same title of the *Decretals* as do the bulk of the canons on the Jews probably moved de Susannis to imply that these restrictions apply to Jews.
89. Cf. pp. 83f., supra.
90. Cf. II,1 on the relationship between the Jews' status as *cives* in Roman law and their status as assigned by the canons.
91. Cf. pp. 100f., infra, and the refs. cited there.
92. Cf. p. 84, supra.

he means only that it is a quirk of law that Jews do not pay regular taxes. For the taxes Jews do pay are construed as a payment in lieu of conversion, and Jews are thus taxed for the privilege of remaining Jews. While Christians pay taxes as a sign of loyalty and to enable the prince to maintain peace, Jews pay taxes simply for the privilege of existence. Since Jews are the only members of society who must pay for this privilege, their taxes are a sign of inferiority.

The resolutions of the problems of taxation and expulsion do, however, expose another basic principle of Jewry law, one which is central to the entire tract: the Jew is entitled to live under the protection of the law; he does not enjoy equal justice under the law, but he does enjoy justice.[93] Thus the Jew cannot be expelled without cause or taxed beyond legal limits.

The centrality of this principle is most evident when de Susannis' legal expressions are compared with his personal sentiments. Summarily put, he fears and despises Jews. He accuses them of inborn avarice [94] and of being taught to hate Christians before they are weaned.[95] He also appears to accept as true the dictum of John 8, that the Jews are sons of the Devil, for he declares in earnest that Jews are rarely bothered by demons, being their kinsmen.[96] Nor does he deny assertions that Jews are continually plotting against Christians, committing ritual murders, and poisoning wells.[97] He even offers a detailed description of the Trent blood libel, which he accepts as true.[98] Moreover, he praises the expulsion of the Jews from Udine (1556), because they had poisoned the wells and brought a plague to the city.[99]

93. Cf. p. 123, infra, for this idea specifically, and pp. 73-74, supra, for the medieval ideal of justice in general.

94. I,11,1.

95. III,1,65.

96. I,9,2.

97. II,7,2: which contains a list of crimes committed by Jews.

98. In the additions to the 1584 edition, III,11,5. (1558 ends at III,9,5.) On the Trent libel see H. Graetz, *History of the Jews* (Philadelphia, 1939), 4:298-99.

99. I,7,5. See Sonne, *Mi-Pavolo*, p. 188, on this expulsion, which he discusses as one of a number of minor expulsions during the later sixteenth century from the Veneto. See also the unpublished holograph of Pagano de Susannis referred

Undoubtedly de Susannis would have welcomed the expulsion of the Jews from all of Christendom. As a legist, however, such arbitrary action would have been unconscionable to him. Therefore, he rejects arguments in favor of arbitrary expulsion and sanctions the Udine expulsion only because he is convinced that in Udine cause for expulsion existed in fact. Indeed, at no point in the tract does de Susannis betray either his role as a legist or his intention of determining the just law for the Jews. This consistency is perhaps the best criterion for gauging both the quality of de Susannis as a legist and the value of the *De Iudaeis* as a key to the study of the Jews in medieval law.

The discussion of the unassailable right of Jews to justice concludes the presentation of the major determinants underlying Jewry law. The remainder of *Pars Prima* elaborates on these determinants. The basis of the prohibitions against Jews enjoying privileges which are reserved only for believers (Christians)[100] is that by availing themselves of these privileges, Jews would be denying the value of belief. They would be effectively making themselves the equals of Christians and thereby negating the principle of Jewish inferiority.   I, 8, 9, & 10

The principle of Jewish inferiority is again involved in the question of usury.[101] But the central problem here is that de Susannis   I, 11
has to find legal grounds on which usury may be permitted. For while usury is prohibited by all law, it is nevertheless practiced. In particular, *Cum nimis* does not forbid usury, but merely regulates it. And de Susannis does not want to contradict *Cum nimis*.[102] Thus he goes through an involved argument and concludes that the only

---

to above, p. 69, n. 24. Perhaps surprisingly, there is no real disagreement between these Latin sources and the Hebrew one cited by Sonne describing the event. All three agree that the Jews were expelled because they had brought on a plague by bringing an infected bed from Venice. There is some disagreement, however, about intentions.

100. Cf. pp. 85–86, supra. These privileges are: asylum, making the sign of the cross, and invoking Christ's name. The notion that certain laws and privileges pertain only to believers is discussed in some detail by de Susannis in II,5, under the heading of laws which are "aequae proportionabilis."

101. Cf. p. 86f., supra.

102. There is no way to prove this assertion, although de Susannis' dedication praising Paul IV's Jewry policy does support it.

legal way to allow usury is through a fiction in which the pope dis-
penses from the punishments for usuring. It is a conclusion which
reality forces de Susannis to draw. Ideally, as his cogent arguments
against usury demonstrate, he would never have drawn it.

    The discussion of usury also reinforces the concept that Jews
must be treated justly and not arbitrarily. It is the question of the
laws of negligence, not of the religion of the lender, which deter-

I, 12   mines liability for lost or damaged pledges. Similarly, in the deliber-
ations concerning the relative degree of sin incurred for murdering
a Jew or a Christian, there is no question that to murder a Jew is
a major sin.[103]

    This last issue, as well as that of having sexual relations with
a Jewess or a nun, also emphasizes the intrinsic superiority of the
Christian. In both cases it is established that the greater sin lies in
perpetrating a crime against a Christian, rather than against a
Jew. The essential purpose of the latter discussion, however, is to
specify that when Christian men have sexual relations with Jewish
women, they commit the same crime that is committed by having
relations with a nun, namely, that of insulting both baptism and
Christianity. Indeed, the sin of sexual relations between a Christian and a Jewess and the sin of sexual relations between a Christian and a nun are discussed together, as two sides of a single
problem, for the express purpose of emphasizing their common
nature.[104]

I, 14   Despite their *non sequitur* appearance, the arguments about
the wars in the New World are not out of place. By implication, de
Susannis' explicit conclusion, that the law permits the use of force
to predispose infidels to convert, also applies to Jews. In reaching
his conclusion de Susannis notes the principle that infidels may not
be forcibly converted. As an apparent afterthought he appends:

---

103. It is, of course, a violation of natural law. De Susannis never explicitly
mentions that Jews enjoy the benefits of natural law; the fact was obvious to his
audience.

104. Had de Susannis discussed the problem of mixed sexual relations
only in I,4, he would have obscured the fact that the sin was insult. He would have
also obscured the fact that the sin is caused irrespective of the religion of the male
sex partner. Thus he devoted I,12 entirely to this problem.

"Just as Jewish children may not be baptized against the will of their parents." [105] Within the specific context, however, the analogy to Jewish children seems superfluous. In fact, the analogy is the central issue of the chapter. De Susannis draws this explicit analogy in the matter of absolute force in order to prompt his readers to drawn an implicit analogy in the case of predisposing force.[106] While he may have wished to draw an explicit analogy, the lack of legal citations to support one limit him to the implicit. As for the force he has in mind to be applied to the Jews, it is not the force of arms but the pressure exerted on the Jew by his second-class status.[107] Thus, having defined the general legal status of the Jew in Christian society, and having shown that Jewry law rests on a small number of fundamental principles, de Susannis has now indicated that Jewry law, properly applied, can direct the Jew toward what Christian society sees as his proper end, namely, his conversion.[108]

---

105. Cf. III,2,6, p. 172, for a detailed discussion of this determination, with which de Susannis agrees.

106. Cf. p. 215, infra, where this analogy is made explicit by Fr. de Torres.

107. Cf. p. 145, infra, where these ideas are expressed directly, but in a non-legal context.

108. Cf. p. 84, supra, where this goal was first suggested.

CHAPTER V

PARS SECUNDA: THE JEWS AND THE IUS COMMUNE

A. Summary

II, 1   "WE HAVE SEEN ABOVE," says de Susannis, "by what right (*qualiter*)[1] Christian piety receives Jews to live with us. It follows that, once they are tolerated by the Church to dwell among us, and it happens that they make contracts, or are delinquent, or dispose of their goods, we should know to which laws they are subject."[2] As a general rule, Jews should live by *ius commune Romanorum*. As Bartolus and many others state: "Jews enjoy (*habent*) those things which pertain to Roman citizens." Whence, in matters outside the realm of their own rites and superstitions, they are subject to the *iuri communi*.[3]

---

1. See R. E. Latham, *Revised Medieval Latin Word List* (London, 1965), p. 386.

2. II,1, intro.: "Vidimus supra qualiter pietas Christiana recipit Iudaeos ad habitandum nobiscum, consequens est ut postquam inter nos per ecclesiam versari tolerantur, et contigit eos contrahere, delinquere et de rebus eorum disponere, sciamus etiam quibus legibus subiiciantur."

3. II,1,1: "Regulariter Iudaei ligantur iure communi et inter ipsos est servandum ius commune Romanorum, et eorum causae iudicantur secundum iura civilia . . . adeo licet illis praeserventur ritus et superstitiones ad eorum fidem spectantes, in ceteris tamen subiiciuntur iuri communi . . . et ideo Bartolus in d.l. iudaei (C.1,9,8): 'Iudaei habent ea quae sunt civium Romanorum.'" By *ius commune* de Susannis normally means Roman law as adapted and applied throughout Italy, although occasionally he uses the term to embrace both Roman law and local statutes. In II,1,13 de Susannis notes that unlike Jews, Saracens who dwell in Christian lands enjoy the benefits of neither *ius commune* nor local statutes.

102

Thus when Jews draw a will, they must follow the requirement of *ius commune* and have seven witnesses.[4] They must respect the restrictions of *ius commune* regulating loans made within families.[5] The immunities *ius commune* extends to the residents of a locality also extend to the Jews who dwell there. In cases of injury, a Jewish minor, like any other minor, receives full restitution. Because Jews do not go to war against Christians, they enjoy the benefits of the prohibition against seizure of shipwrecked goods—no other infidel group enjoys this right. A Jewish father may defend his son who has been charged with a capital crime, even with *lèse majesté,* with no fear of personal liability or penalty.[6] As is true of all heirs, the heirs of a Jew who has been condemned to die, even if he has been condemned for the crime of reverting to Judaism after baptism, do not forfeit their right to inherit his property.[7] Following the general rule, Jewish spouses may not make a donation to each other.[8] A Jewish father is bound by the regular obligation of raising his sons and dowring his daughters.[9] The wife of a Jew enjoys the right of tacit hypothecation in her dowry.[10] Jewish fathers, in the manner of Roman citizens, exercise complete power over their children.[11] And a Jew who is a member of a *societas* which has been granted

---

4. II,1,2.

5. II,1,4.

6. II,1,5.

7. II,1,6.

8. II,1,7. See Johannis Kahl, alias Calvini, *Magnum Lexicon Juridicum* (Coloniae Allobrogum, 1759), cols. 513–15, where he notes that *D. De donationibus inter viros et uxores, l.i.* simply prohibits such donations (which are defined as gifts, not legacies, etc.) on the grounds that they are detrimental to a marriage.

9. II,1,8.

10. II,1,9. See Calvini, *Lexicon,* col. 707, where he writes that a hypothec is a pledge which is retained by the owner and not given to the lender. A tacit hypothec is a hypothec which is established by law, not by volition. Thus the law establishes that a dowry is a pledge, but one which the wife retains in her possession. In other words, the husband may not appropriate the dowry for his own use. The establishment of the dowry as a tacit hypothec is made by C.8,17 *assiduis.*

11. II,1,10–11; cf. III,4,9–11.

certain exemptions (*securitas*) enjoys these exemptions along with the Christian members of the *societas*.[12]

II, 2   The Jews enjoy the above privileges because they are *de Populo Romano,* but they are also *de eodem corpore civitatis ubi degunt*. Therefore, they are bound by the statutes and the customary law of their place of residence.[13]

Besides being Roman citizens, and part of their local civic body, if Jews live peacefully among us, they may be called *fideles* of the Holy Roman Church, for they submit to its protection, and it, in turn, mercifully sustains them.[14] They are, assuredly, *fideles* of the militant, and not of the triumphant, Church. But as *fideles* of the militant Church, Jews may avail themselves of the rigor of *ius commune* and may even use prescription against individual Christians, as long as the prescription does not involve ecclesiastical property.[15]

Because Jews are governed by local statute law, they are entitled to the protection of the statute, found in all Italian civic law collections, which declares that female heirs are excluded from an inheritance if male heirs exist. There are those, however, who assert that this statute exists to preserve honor (*dignitas*) within a family, and that it does not apply to Jews since they are ineligible for honors.[16] But the common opinion determines that the main purpose of the statute is to preserve a family and its fortune, and that it therefore does apply to Jews. Moreover, not only is the protection of this statute not denied to Jews, but Mosaic law itself contains a similiar

---

12. II,1,12. See Calvini, *Lexicon,* col. 458, where he defines *securitas* as an exemption from certain payments, such as rent.

13. II,2,1: "Ligantur statutis locorum ubi degunt"; II,2,8: "Quod dictum est de statutis idem dicendum de consuetudine, eadem ratione." Cf. p. 84 supra, where de Susannis first identifies the Jews as *de populo romano*.

14. II,2,2: "Sed et Iudaei dicuntur, seu dici possunt fideles, et devoti sanctae Romanae Ecclesiae, si nobiscum pacifice versantur, et vivunt, quia eius protectioni se subiiciunt, et misericorditer ab ea sustinentur, et eis contumelias inhibet fieri."

15. II,2,3. See Calvini, *Lexicon,* col. 290, where *praescriptio* is defined as a time within which certain actions are prohibited. E.g., an inheritance may not be distributed until all heirs have been given a period within which to contest the will. See also Dynus de Mugillo, *Tract. de praescriptio, TUJ,* 17:fols. 50–52, where the various kinds of *praescriptio* are listed and explained.

16. II,2,4.

disposition. There is then no reason why Mosaic law should be rejected in this instance.[17]

In criminal matters also a Jew is punished according to local statutes. When a Jew commits adultery, he is punished according to the laws of the city in which he committed the crime and not according to either *ius commune* or Mosaic law.[18]

Since, then, it is established that *regulariter* Jews are bound   II, 3
by *ius commune*,[19] it is proper to examine the rules of punishment
for a Jew who has had carnal relations with a Christian woman. This
is an especially odious sin which occurs quite frequently[20] and which
both the canons and *ius commune* strictly forbid, irrespective of the
circumstances, for it causes insult to baptism and injury to the entire
Christian religion.[21] In order to punish the offenders properly, it is
necessary to distinguish and treat separately each of many variations
of the delict.

If this delict occurred with both parties aware of their different
religions and the woman was a prostitute, the penalty is left to the

---

17. II,2,5. By Mosaic law de Susannis means specifically the Old Testament. Here he cites Num. 26:(55), 27:(1–12), and 36:(1–12), all of which deal with inheritances. There is no doubt that the statute excluding female heirs was applied to Jews. It corresponds specifically to Jewish law, however, only to the extent that in the case of a man having sons and daughters, the sons alone inherit. Maimonides, *Mishneh Torah* (Jerusalem, 1964), *Nashim,* Personal Law, chap. 19, Halakhah 17, 60b. If, however, the son is dead, his heirs, whether male or female, inherit. Thus the rule is that the inheritance remains in the male line. Ibid., *Mishpatim,* Inheritances, chap. 1, Halakhah 3, 25a; J. Rabbinowitz, trans., *The Code of Maimonides* (New Haven, 1949), 2:260, par. 3. To this extent Jewish law is in harmony with the common law statute. De Susannis may have acquired his knowledge of the specifics of Jewish law from observing litigations between Jews at Udine, and perhaps even from participating in them as a jurisconsult if the case was aired before a Christian magistrate. Once in the tract, however, he cites the *Mishneh Torah* directly. Cf. p. 161, infra. That he does so raises the question of de Susannis' possible first-hand knowledge of Jewish law.

18. II,2,7: "Statutum loci in quo deliquit, non . . . prout esset de iure communi . . . nec etiam puniretur poena legis Mosis."

19. II,3, intro: "Supra conclusum est Iudaeos regulariter ligari iure communi tam in civilibus quam in criminalibus eorum causis."

20. II,3, intro.: "Quod saepe solet contingere."

21. II,3,1: "Et est odiosa talis commixtio, quia sit per eam iniuria baptismo et universae religioni Christianae."

discretion of the judge, because *ius commune* provides no penalty for this crime. While the "quality" of the person is normally considered in fixing penalties, in this case the fact that the offender is a Jew is not reason enough to demand a punishment of blood (mutilation, etc.), even though such a penalty is not prohibited. Indeed, there have been instances of its being exacted for this crime.[22]

If a Jew and a married prostitute have carnal relations, there is no question of punishment for adultery, because there can be no adultery with a prostitute. But the penalty is steeper than in the first case, because here the sacrament of marriage is violated.[23]

If a Jew has had sexual relations with a virtuous Christian woman, he is punished for his specific offense, such as adultery, debauchery, or rape. The penalty is determined by local statute, or by *ius commune* if there is no local statute.[24]

However, if a Jew has had sexual relations with any Christian woman with the intent of causing opprobrium to the faith, then he is guilty of *lèse majesté* against God, and he is punished by death and the confiscation of his property. Circumspect judges can easily discover if the Jew had this intention. They should be especially wary of a Jew who has had relations with a Christian prostitute, because it is quite probable that Jews have relations with prostitutes for the purpose of offending the faith. They believe the status of the woman will help them obscure their crime.[25]

Should a Jew knowingly marry a Christian woman, he is guilty of adultery and is punished capitally. He is, in fact, guilty of more than adultery, for his act brings injury to both baptism and the sacrament of marriage. In such a union all the values of

---

22. II,3,3–6.
23. II,3,7–9.
24. II,3,10–12.
25. II,3,13–14: "Advertendum est, quod ubi Iudaeus Christianam cognosceret carnaliter cuiuscunque conditionis esset mulier illa, et hoc faceret Iudaeus non per lasciviam et libidinis causa, sed in contemptum gloriosissimi domini nostri . . . tunc gravissime veniret castigandus; in meretrice confidentius posset cadere cum iudaeo contemptio fidei, et ipsae etiam meretrices sunt caractere baptismi sacri insignitae."

matrimony are lacking. In particular, the marriage of Christ to the Church is not symbolized.[26]

If a Jew and a Christian of either sex have carnal relations and there is no doubt that both were in complete ignorance of their crime, neither is punished for having sexual relations with an infidel. Yet they must be punished for the crime of fornication. But if a Christian ignorantly marries a Jewess, he is excused from all penalties, for his intention was to perform a legal act.[27]

While Jews are normally bound by *ius commune,* they should settle internal disputes according to Jewish law, especially if Jewish law contains specific provisions which apply to those disputes, and even if common law deals with those disputes in general (*in genere*).[28] Hence, for example, Jews should observe their own law in cases involving the prerogatives of primogeniture.[29] Nevertheless, on the grounds that Jews are regularly bound by *ius commune,* they do have the choice of electing to observe either common or Jewish law.[30] No tenet of Jewish law may be employed, moreover, if it is expressly reprobate (*reprobata*) in natural, canon, civil, statute, or customary law.

II, 4

There are legists who claim that Jews may not use their own law at all. Some of them argue that the *Code*[31] specifies that Jews

---

26. II,3,15: "Non est ibi perfecta significatio Christi ad ecclesiam."

27. II,3,16–17. II,3,18–23 contains a number of asides. Perhaps the most interesting is the statement that any infidel suffers the penalties described here for having sexual relations with a Christian. In turn, this statement is followed by the declaration that "Iudaeus transiens ad sectam sarracenorum non venit puniendus . . . cum secta sarracenorum sit minus mala quam iudaeorum . . . Mathe., xi, 'Tollerabilius erit sodomis in die iudicii quam vobis.' " Cf. III,1,42, with the reference by de Susannis there to C.1,q.1,c.37 *peiores,* which canon states that Jews are worse than Sodomites.

28. II,4,1–2: "[The rule which binds the Jews to common law] limitatur non habere locum in casibus in quibus lex Mosaica specialiter aliquid disponit quae non sit expresse reprobata per ius canonicum, civile, statuta, aut per consuetudinem . . . In illis casibus . . . inter iudaeos [lex Mosaica] servanda est, etiam si lex civilis in genere illud idem disponeret."

29. II,4,3: de Susannis cites Gen. 25 and Deut. 21 as the Mosaic law in question.

30. II,4,4.

31. C.1,9,8.

must use Roman common law. But this stipulation applies only when Roman law explicitly prohibits some article of Jewish law; otherwise, Jewish law is valid. Other legists would deny Jews the privilege of observing their own law on the basis of the accepted principle which grants legal validity to only those juridical principles of the Old Testament which have been approved by the New Testament. The common opinion and authority, however, dismisses this objection as irrelevant. There are also legists who take an intermediate position and assert that Jewish law should be "corrected" [32] by *ius commune*. They err in overstating their case. According to them, Jews may observe the Jewish law of succession in general, but they must also follow *ius commune* on succession in such matters as the statute which excludes female heirs. But there is no question of correcting Jewish law here, because in this instance Mosaic law does not differ from statute law. However, there are times when Jewish law must indeed be "corrected" by *ius commune*. Yet the unqualified claims that the Jews may never use Jewish law are all invalid, for the common opinion holds that in circumstances in which it is not reprobate, Jewish law is viable, even if the common law deals with the same situations. Moreover, the Jews' privilege of following their own law is established by long usage and custom.[33] Hence they marry according to Jewish law, even within the grades prohibited by Canon law, and they may also divorce.[34] On the other hand, according to Mosaic law, if there are two heirs, the elder divides the inheritance and the younger has the right to choose which portion he wants, in the manner of Abraham and Lot. But *ius commune* strictly forbids such prerogatives in the division of inheritances, and in this case, Jews must follow the common law and disregard their own.[35]

---

32. A technical term meaning: A law must be interpreted and limited in the light of another law whose interpretation is universally accepted. See Piano-Mortari, *Ricerche,* pp. 140–52.

33. II,4,5–8: "Inter Iudaeos esset consuetudo quod in successionibus eorum lex Mosaica deberet servari . . . est enim lex Mosis inter Iudaeos servanda, etiam si lex civilis in genere illud idem statueret."

34. II,4,9–10. Cf. the summary of II,8 to explain the apparent inconsistency between these marriage regulations and the general rule on the validity of Jewish law.

35. II,4,11–13. De Susannis cites Gen 8:[8–12]. He is possibly referring to

The use of Jewish law is not, however, the only limitation on the rule that the Jews are to live by common law. When the substance of a law is not equally proportionate (*aeque proportionabilis*) to Jews and Christians, that is, when the basic sense of a law (*lex loquens simpliciter*) neither includes Jews nor can be extended to include them, that law does not apply to them.[36] For instance, in our day a Jew cannot be a guardian because the oath a guardian must take obligates him to swear by Christ.[37] Nor can the law which prohibits church burial to usurers have any bearing on Jews, since Jews can never be buried in a church cemetery.[38] Similarly, the laws of excommunication do not apply to Jews, although a Jew can be indirectly excommunicated by forbidding him to have any contact (*communio*) with Christians.[39] In the same vein, Jews must live by the rigor of the law (*rigor iuris*) and may not enjoy the benefits of unwritten equity whose purpose is the salvation of souls.[40]

Since witnesses in cases involving Christians must swear an oath by Christ, there are those who declare that Jews may never testify against Christians, although they may testify against each other.[41] Yet this interpretation cannot be correct, because there are instances where Jews do testify against Christians. The difficulty of the oath is avoided by having the Jews swear by their own law.[42]

There are two additional, more cogent objections to accepting the testimony of Jews: first, that it is impossible to assume that Jews, who are unfaithful to God, can be trustworthy witnesses, faithful-

---

the Jewish law which states that if an inheritance is to be divided between heirs, some of whom are adults and others are minors, the court appoints guardians for the minors, and the guardians select for the minors "the fairest share." Maimonides, *Mishneh Torah, Mishpatim*, Inheritances, chap. 10, Halakhah 4, 34b; J. Rabbinowitz, trans. *Code of Maimonides*, 2:289, par. 4.

36. II,5,intro.

37. II,5,1: De Susannis notes that D.27,1,15,6, allowed Jews to be guardians, because the oath required of guardians in his day was not then in effect.

38. II,5,2.

39. II,5,3–4.

40. II,2,5–8; cf. pp. 149f., infra, for a discussion of the Jews in equity.

41. II,5,9.

42. II,5,10.

to men; second, that witnesses are supposed to be free men, while the Jews are the *servi Christianorum,* because of their crime against Christ.[43] Following the opinion of Baldus,[44] however, these objections are sufficient to disqualify Jewish witnesses only if enough qualified Christian witnesses can be found. Otherwise, the testimony of Jews is accepted, and the objections are disregarded.[45] Nevertheless, there is no question that normally Jews cannot testify against Christians. Similarly, Jews are not to be used as interpreters, nor should a court accept the translation of a single Jew to determine the meaning of a Hebrew document.[46]

There are also some who want to disqualify the testimony of a recent convert from Judaism. This is not correct. A convert is considered a "new man," and the fact that he was once a Jew is of no consequence after his conversion.[47] Recent converts are prohibited from testifying only if they have prevaricated in the faith, or if they are summoned to give testimony about an act which they witnessed prior to their conversion.[48]

As for Jews testifying against other Jews, there are no strictures. An exception is made to the general rule of using a Jewish witness only in cases of necessity, moreover, if the Christian against whom the Jew is called on to testify agrees to accept the testimony of the Jew, or if the Jew is called on to bear witness against a convert who is accused of relapse.[49] Finally, although one does not accept the oral plea (*viva vox*) of a Jewish moneylender, his loan books are incontrovertible when they are adduced in testimony.[50]

---

43. De Susannis does not directly oppose this objection. However, in II,2,6–7 he flatly denies that the servitude of the Jews is real slavery, and thus, in effect, rebuts this objection in the matter of testimony given by Jews.

44. Baldus, *Additiones in Speculum Iuris,* tit. de accusa., v. infamis (X.5,1).

45. II,5,11.

46. II,5,11.

47. Cf. III,6,1 (infra, p. 180) on other similar problems faced by converts and on the relationship between these problems and those which confronted converts in Spain.

48. II,5,12–13: "Cum ad fidem versus, incipiat esse novus homo."

49. II,5,14–15.

50. II,5,17.

Another limitation on the rule that Jews enjoy[51] *ius commune* is that while Christians may own slaves irrespective of their religion, both the civil law and the canons prohibit Jews from owning Christian slaves.[52] Likewise, *ius commune* prohibits Jewish communities (*collegium*), although not individual Jews, from receiving legacies from Christians.[53]

In addition (*etiam*), the portals of dignities are closed to the **II, 6**
Jews. They are restricted from all public offices and honors and may never preside over Christians or be in a position to cause Christians harm. Jews participate with Christians in human acts, not in divine acts, and never in any act of superiority.[54] This ruling exists because, as was prophesied,[55] that greatest and principal dignity, the *sacerdotium* and the *regnum spirituale,* was translated to Christ. When the Jews announced that we have no king but Caesar (John 19:15), they sentenced themselves and forfeited that dignity forever.[56] Their declaration brought about the fulfillment of the prophecies which warned of the destruction of the Temple and of Jerusalem and which foresaw a desolation lasting until the end of the world.[57]

The permanence of the desolation of the Jews is proved by the failure of the Jews to reestablish their republic in their war with

---

51. De Susannis has shifted from his usual phrase, "are bound by" *(ligantur),* to "enjoy" *(utitur).* The shift is significant.

52. II,5,18–19.

53. II,5,23–24.

54. II,6,1: "Clauduntur etiam Iudaeis portae dignitatum, et officiorum, sunt enim privati omnibus officiis publicis et dignitatibus. Nec est eis concedendum ut praesint Christianis; et non solum publicum officium est eis interdictum, sed etiam quodlibet officium seu commertium per quod Christianis possit aliquod gravamen inferri; quod Iudaei in humanis actibus nobiscum participant, non in divinis, neque in aliquo actu superioritatis, et in multis immunitatem habebant antequam Christus veniret in virginem, quae omnia perdiderunt." (Cf. the Index for the many allegations cited to support this statement.)

55. II,6,2; de Susannis explicitly refers here to Gen. 49:10. Cf. pp. 161–64, infra., on the polemics based on this verse.

56. II,6,5: "Nam et ipsimet Iudaei tulerunt sententiam contra se, circa regni ablationem in perpetuum, dum dixerunt, non habemus regem nisi Caesarem."

57. II,6,2–5; the prophecy is Dan. 9: "Erit talis ablatio usque ad consummationem saeculi."

Hadrian and by the ill fate of their attempt to rebuild the Temple in the time of Julian.[58] But what greater proof exists of the everlasting ruin of the Jews than their perpetual wretchedness since the death of Christ? All this misfortune was prophesied as their lot for killing Christ.[59] Indeed, once the priesthood was transferred to Christ, the Old Law was dead. Its subsequent observance would only be death-dealing (*mortifera*). Once Christ had come, moreover, the Jews' temporal scepter too was dead (*mortuum*).[60] For not only all spiritual power, but all temporal power, was transferred to Christ.[61]

Therefore, a Jew may not become emperor. The emperor must be "within the Church," for he could not perform many of his functions if he were not a Christian.[62] In addition, God ordains all power, and those who oppose the power of God oppose His ordinations also. It would therefore be absurd for the Jews, who are enemies of the son of God, to share in the power ordained by God.[63]

Not only, then, are Jews unworthy of the Imperium, but they are also unfit to possess any jurisdiction. Accordingly, the law establishes that no Jew may ever become a judge. A Jewish judge would be an insult to the faith. Besides, the Bible calls judges Gods (Exod. 22:7–8; Ps. 82:1), and Jews are sons of the Devil (John 8:44).[64] Moreover, Jews cannot be judges because to attain judgeships is to acquire dignities and honors, both of which Jews are forbidden to possess. Nevertheless, while a Jew is incapable

---

58. II,6,6.

59. II,6,7: "Cum Iudaeorum conditio a morte Christi citra, semper fuerit miserrima."

60. II,6,8–9: "Immo observantia legis Mosis eisdem iudaeis non solum est inutilis, sed etiam mortifera a resurrectione Christi citra . . . Nec non et sceptrum etiam eorum regale, temporale cum Christo mortuum fuit, et sicut sunt privati regno spirituali, ita etiam carent regno temporali."

61. II,6,10.

62. II,6,11: "Intra ecclesiam est."

63. II,6,12: "Item omnis potestas a Deo est ordinata, et qui resistit potestati, ordinationi Dei resistit. [Rom. 13:2] Absurdum esset ergo iudaeos inimicos filii Dei esse particeps dono Dei, quod est Imperium."

64. II,6,12–13.

of exercising jurisdiction, he may enjoy its fruit and product. He must, however, obtain them from others.[65]

Thus it is obvious that a Jew may never be a judge in cases which involve a Jew and a Christian. But Jews also may not be judges in suits in which the litigants are both Jews. Even in actions in which the dispute concerns nothing but ritual, Jews must approach Christian judges.[66] However, Jews may serve as arbiters, deciding litigations between Jews according to Jewish law. Still Jews are never required to resort to such arbiters. If they were, Jewish arbiters would belong to the class of "necessary arbiters" (*arbitri necessarii*). For Jews to be "necessary arbiters" is impermissible, because such arbiters possess jurisdiction.[67]

The Empire and judgeships are not the only offices from which Jews are excluded. According to the common opinion, a Jew may not receive a doctorate;[68] that too is a dignity. For the

II, 7

---

65. II,6,14: "Sed licet iudaeus sit incapax iurisdictionis, potest nihilominus emere fructus eius, et proventus, exigendos tamen per alium."

66. II,6,14–22. Cf. pp. 191, 192, infra, for examples of Jews possessing internal jurisdiction in sixteenth-century Italy. The complex problem of jurisdictional autonomy will be dealt with in a special chapter.

67. II,6,23–25. A "necessary arbiter" is a civil law category which refers to an arbiter whose services must be used; for example, in disputes between members of a family. Such arbiters possess true jurisdiction. Therefore, no Jew may function as such an arbiter. For a definition of this office, de Susannis refers to, among others: Bartolus, *Super Prima parte Codicis* (1610), on C.3,1,18. II,6,26 is an aside which deals with the question of whether any infidels ever legitimately exercise jurisdiction. De Susannis presents the arguments of the two major protagonists of this question, Innocent IV and Hostiensis (both commenting on X.3,34,8). Innocent IV held that infidels legitimately exercise jurisdiction in lands which never belonged to the Roman Emperor. Hostiensis concluded that despite *de facto* jurisdiction, no infidel ever exercises *de iure* jurisdiction, because all power was translated to Christ, and from Christ to his faithful. This, says de Susannis, is the common opinion, which he accepts.

68. The doctorate was awarded in law, medicine, and theology (see Calvini, *Lexicon,* cols. 504–06. One did not, however, need a doctorate to practice law or medicine. (See H. Friedenwald, *The Jews and Medicine* [Baltimore, 1944], I:225; and L. Martines, *Lawyers and Statecraft in Renaissance Florence* [Princeton, 1968], pp. 78–91, on this point with reference to lawyers, and esp. pp. 88–91 for a description of the examinations and ceremonies connected with the award of the doctoral degree.) Although no explicit law excluded Jews from the doctorate, the common opinion, extending the general prohibition on Jews possessing dignities,

same reason, a Jew may not be an advocate,[69] although he may be a procurator, because that office is a lowly one.[70] He may not, however, be the procurator, or even the cook, for a prince, because both those offices are dignities.[71] While the offices of notary and scribe are not dignities in fact, Jews are to be excluded from them also because they have a public character and can therefore appear to be dignities. Nevertheless, Jews may serve as scribes and notaries for other Jews.[72]

While there is no general ban on Jews becoming physicians, no Jew may become the physician of the pope or the Emperor, because those offices are dignities. The law also prohibits all Christians from employing Jewish physicians, although dispensations from this rule can be made either during a plague, when all physicians are needed, or if the Jew is the sole physician who knows how to cure an unusual disease.[73]

Finally, Jews may not serve as guardians for Christians. This office is not public, nor is it a dignity, but Jews may not hold it, lest the soul of the ward be endangered.[74]

II, 8   After examining how Jews are subject to *ius commune* and local statutes, it is now proper to examine how they are subject to Canon law as a system.[75] Jews are not subject to the canons that deal with spiritualities and sacraments.[76] Hence they are not subject

---

did exclude them, as did university statutes and a decree made by the unapproved Council of Basle in 1433 (Friedenwald, 1:263–67). It was, perhaps, this lack of an explicit law which accounts for the fact that Jews did indeed receive the doctorate in medicine (Friedenwald, 1:224–30, 257–67; see ibid., 1:221–40, for a review of Jews studying medicine in the universities, and 2:574–89, for Jewish physicians in sixteenth-century Italy, with special reference to papal appointments and doctorates. Cf. also p. 185, infra, on a Jewish professor of medicine at Rome in the sixteenth century).

    69. II,7,1–2.
    70. II,7,3–4.
    71. II,7,4, and 12.
    72. II,7,5–7.
    73. II,7,9–11. Cf. p. 190, infra, for examples of Jews as court physicians in sixteenth-century Italy, in violation of the general rule.
    74. II,7,13–14. De Susannis remarks that if a Jewish mother swears by the Jews' oath, she may be made the guardian of her own children.
    75. II,8, intro.: "Modo vero successive quaerendum est de legibus canonicis."
    76. II,8,1.

to spiritual penalties and ecclesiastical censure, although they can
be indirectly excommunicated. They are free from the canonical restrictions on marriage within prohibited grades. They may also
divorce; but they may do so only for good cause and in the presence
of a priest.[77] On the other hand, Jews may not make denunciations
about the religious behavior of Christians. Such denunciations are a
matter of equal proportion, for the proper form of denunciation requires the accuser to be a Christian.[78] The canons which require an
oath to guard against perjury also do not apply to Jews. This oath
was instituted to protect witnesses from damning their souls through
perjury. But the souls of Jews are damned anyway, and such protection is irrelevant to them. This same reasoning applies to a number of similar oaths established by the canons.[79] Nevertheless, the
Church can punish a Jew who has transgressed an oath, not for the
purpose of saving his soul, but to prevent a delict from going unpunished.[80] If a Jew swears an oath to a Christian, moreover, or for
some reason swears by Christ, the Church can force him to observe
his oath in order to prevent offense to both the Christian and the
faith.[81]

There are some canons to which Jews are subject.[82] For ex-   II, 9
ample, when Jews or infidels sin against the law of nature, or if
Jews transgress the moral precepts of the Old Testament, the
Church may judge and punish them.[83] Jews are also subject to
Church punishment if they are delinquent in opprobrium of the
Christian faith, if they blaspheme, if they prevent a Jew from con-
verting to Christianity, if they circumcise a Christian, or if they
secure a privilege from their prince which prohibits Christians

---

77. II,8,2–4: "Legitima tamen causa subsistente et interveniente praesentia
sacerdotis."
78. II,8,5.
79. II,8,6–9.
80. II,8,10.
81. II,8,11–13.
82. II,9,intro.
83. II,9,1–2; on this subject, see Y. Yerushalmi, "The Inquisition and the
Jews of France in the Time of Bernard Gui," *Harvard Theological Review* 63
(1970): 335–39, 346, 350–63.

from testifying against them.[84] In addition, the Church may inflict penalties on Jews who have committed ecclesiastical crimes. These include usury, sacrilege, heresy, simony, perjury, adultery, and fornication. In many of these actions, however, the pope, that is, the Church, often permits the secular courts to exercise jurisdiction.[85]

B. *Analysis*

II, 1   De Susannis' opening declaration is the key to comprehending all of *Pars Secunda*.

> We have seen above by what right Christian piety receives Jews to live with us; *it follows* [*consequens est*] that, once they are tolerated by the Church to dwell among us and it happens that they make contracts, or are delinquent, or dispose of their goods, we should know to which laws they are subject.

What is crucial here is the indication that the following discussion is predicated (*consequens est*) on the resolution of the fundamental question of the general status of the Jews. In other words, the status of the Jews in *ius commune* must complement their general status and be consistent with it. *Pars Secunda,* therefore, sets out not only to describe the status of the Jews in *ius commune,* but also to demonstrate how that status is compatible with the principles outlined in *Pars Prima.*

The correlation between the status of the Jews in *ius commune* and their general status was, in fact, hinted at in I,7,4. There it was seen that the designation of the Jews as *cives* in *ius commune* did not conflict with the notion that the Jews reside in Chris-

---

84. II,9,3.

85. II,9,4–8: This is an extremely complex jurisdictional problem, for despite de Susannis' unqualified assertion, the Church was not always prepared to relinquish jurisdiction, while secular authorities were often prepared to claim it. This problem thus became an aspect of the major dispute over jurisdictions carried on between secular and ecclesiastical courts throughout the Middle Ages. For a general sketch of some of the difficulties involved, esp. with reference to jurisdiction over Jews, see A. C. Jemolo, *Stato e Chiesa negli scrittori politici italiani del seicento e del settecento* (Turin, 1914), pp. 51–92.

tian lands only on the basis of privilege and not by right.[86] The fact that Jews are *cives* is an obstacle to expelling them; it does not, however, preclude their expulsion. In the same vein, II,1 does not say that the Jews live under *ius commune* and are therefore entitled to *all* the privileges of *cives*. Rather, II,6,1, which discusses offices and jurisdictions, indicates the precise opposite.[87] That Jews are subject to the same *ius commune* in criminal and civil affairs as Christians, does not moreover, make Jews the equals of Christians in violation of the principle of inferiority. In criminal and civil cases, at stake is not the matter of inferiority or the matter of insults to the faith, but the matter of the justice to which Jews are unequivocally entitled.[88]

Furthermore, the first question in *Pars Secunda* is not whether Jews may benefit from *ius commune* at their pleasure, but whether they are bound by *ius commune* in distinction to Mosaic law. In many of the twelve examples offered to prove that the Jews are so bound,[89] it is explicitly stated that in these cases the Jews may not resort to Mosaic law. Therefore, rather than privileging Jews, *ius commune* can function to restrict them.

Showing that the Jews' status in *ius commune* does not violate the principles and laws already discussed makes it possible to explain the paradox found in the first legal statement of the tract, namely, that Jews are religious but not civil enemies. If the Jews were to enjoy all the privileges of *cives* under *ius commune,* their treatment would not be that of religious enemies, because they would then no longer be inferiors. They would, for instance, be capable of holding offices and of presiding over Christians. If, on the other hand, Jews enjoyed none of the benefits of *ius commune*—specifically, the laws concerning civil and criminal litigations—their condition would not be that of civil friends, because their treatment would be unjust, and their Roman citizenship would thus be violated. Therefore, in order

---

86. Cf. the analysis of I,7,4 (supra, p. 97). On the Jews as *cives,* see the first essay in V. Colorni, *Legge ebraica e legge locale.*

87. Cf. p. 112, supra.

88. Cf. I,7,6; I,11,17–18; and II,6,14, where this concept is clearly enunciated. Cf. also p. 100, supra.

89. See p. 103f., supra.

to maintain Jews in their enemy-friend status, a compromise is affected. Jews enjoy *ius commune,* but only up to the point that *ius commune* grants them no privilege otherwise denied.[90] This solution is not original. It is the solution of Justinian's *Code* I,9. The tension between the Roman tradition of citizenship for the Jews and the desire of the early Church to repress the Jews and Judaism, which had been resolved in the *Code,* was still present and still identically resolved in the sixteenth century. One important change had occurred, however. By the sixteenth century, the lines of this resolution had been both elaborated and more precisely drawn. To show these distinct lines—that is, the complete and unified system of Jewry law—is one of the major reasons for de Susannis' compilation.

II, 2   That the status of the Jews in *ius commune* does not, indeed may not, contradict their general status is demonstrated conclusively by the brief aside that Jews living peacefully are considered *fideles* of the militant Church and may, therefore, use the rigor of *ius commune* against Christians.[91] This aside is taken verbatim from Baldus,[92] with the exception of the words "living peacefully," which de Susannis added. Now as defined by the *De Iudaeis,* in the case of the Jews, living peacefully means living passively and as tolerated enemies. Thus, because of the addition of "living peacefully," this aside makes it explicit that Jews receive the benefits they do under *ius commune* only when they accept their status as canonically prescribed.[93]

The topic of the Jews in local statute law needs little explanation.[94] Jews are bound by this law for the same reasons they are

---

90. Cf. esp. II,5–7 (supra, pp. 109–14).

91. See p. 104, supra.

92. Baldus de Ubaldis, *Consilia* (Venice, 1608), cons. 428, par. 5.

93. The *Archivio, Com. di Roma, Bolle . . . papali,* ITb, contains portions of a handwritten copy of an otherwise unavailable work of Cardinal D. Tuschi, *Practicarum conclusionum iuris in omne foro frequentiorum* (Rome, 1606). Pt. 4, p. 705 f., conclusion 371 cites the jurist Maranta. (*sic* and otherwise unidentified), *in prati. in tertia dist., no. 61,* where Maranta. states, with reference to the Jews and *immunitas* in particular and *ius commune* in general: "Si aliquid faciunt in contemptum religionis Cristiane omittunt tale privilegium." I cannot say if Maranta. preceded or succeeded de Susannis, but here is clearly set down the explicit form of what de Susannis is implying in his statement.

94. See pp. 104f., supra.

bound by *ius commune:* they are members of the corporate body which uses that law. As in the case of *ius commune,* moreover, living under local statutes is not an option, but a requirement (*Iudaei ligantur*).

In line with the precept that *ius commune* does not grant the Jews special privileges, Jewish adulterers are punished according to local statute and not according to *ius commune.*[95] This ruling refers to those instances when local statutes supplement or contradict *ius commune.* For the juridical norm was that local statutes take precedence over *ius commune.*[96] Thus the Jews are bound to local statutes in the same way that Christians are. They enjoy no exceptions. In addition, the almost universal local statute which excludes female in favor of male heirs is said to apply to Jews only because its intent is the preservation of families and not the preservation of dignities and offices.[97] This determination presupposes what will be made explicit further on, namely, that as the canons and as *ius commune,* so too local statutes prohibit the Jews from possessing jurisdictions.[98]

An additional aspect of the consistency of both canons and laws in assigning a status to the Jew is revealed in the discussion of the penalties inflicted on both Jews and Christians who commit the crime of having sexual intercourse with members of the opposite religion. Fixing these penalties is an involved and difficult process. The difficulty arises because the crime is essentially an ecclesiastical one, established by the canons. Yet these canons do not fix the penalties for the crime.[99] The solution given to this difficulty by the lawyers is most instructive. In cases where the crime of sexual relations between a Jew and a Christian is committed simultaneously with another crime, such as adultery, rape, or debauchery, the Jews are punished by the local statute or *ius commune* penalty for those

II, 3

---

95. See p. 105, supra.

96. Piano-Mortari, *Ricerche, pp.* 163–70; Calasso, *Medio Evo del diritto,* pp. 450–59.

97. See pp. 104f., supra.

98. See p. 122, infra.

99. The canons which forbid sexual relations between Jews and Christians are: X.5,6,13,14,15 and 16, and C.22,q.1,c.16. C.1,9,6 prohibits only marriage between Jews and Christians.

crimes. If the Jew has sexual relations with a married prostitute, the penalty is again fixed on the basis of the laws, although in this case, the canons prohibiting violations of the sacrament of marriage are invoked as the reason for inflicting a rather severe punishment. Most striking, the penalty for a Jew having sexual relations with a Christian prostitute is left to the discretion of the judge, because *ius commune* establishes no penalty for this crime.

In other words, the penalty for the essentially ecclesiastical crime of sexual relations between a Jew and a Christian is determined primarily on the basis of local statutes and *ius commune*. That such a situation existed means unquestionably that in the case of the Jews, at least, the laws were considered to function complementarily to the canons. In the case of sexual crimes between Jews and Christians, moreover, the lawyers had an explicit legal reason for complementing the canons by the laws. For C.1,9,11 (*l. Iudaeos*) prohibits Jews from insulting Christianity, and, as seen in I,4 and I,13,[100] the sin caused by such sexual crimes is insult to the faith. Indeed, de Susannis invokes *l. Iudaeos* when he asserts that a Jew who has had intercourse with a Christian woman for the explicit purpose of insulting the faith should be punished for the crime of *lèse majesté*. Thus, this discussion of sexual crimes suggests not only that the laws maintain the dependent status assigned to Jews by the canons, but that they do so for identical reasons. This generalization is substantiated by the subsequent four chapters (II,4–II,7). They reveal that the laws add to the canonical restrictions elaborations of their own.

II, 4   A prime example of the laws assigning the Jews to a status of dependence appears in the discussion of the right of the Jews to use their own law.[101] De Susannis has to explain the place of Jewish law in the balance of legal systems which together formed Jewry law as a whole.[102] For there is no question that there were times when Jews

---

100. See pp. 83 and 90 , supra.

101. See p. 107, supra.

102. There was nothing extraordinary in the fact that Jewry law as a whole was a composite of laws drawn from a number of legal systems. All medieval men lived under composite legal systems. And the harmonization of systems

might use their own law. The *Code,* the canons which permit the Jews to marry within the prohibited grades and also to divorce, and the bulk of authoritative opinion allow no other conclusion.[103] In addition, custom and usage establish this privilege for Jews. And customary law is considered valid, within certain limits.[104] The problem de Susannis faces is determining under what circumstances Jewish law may be used.

According to de Susannis and most other authorities, Jews are able to use their own law either when it does not contradict any other law, or when it adds specific provisions above and beyond that law (*in genere*).[105] This interpretation follows the interpretive method which determined either the meaning or the validity of a law on the basis of its being *praeter, secundum,* or *contra* the provisions of another law whose meaning or validity were beyond dispute.[106] De Susannis' interpretation also takes into account the interpretive method, which held that one law can be "corrected," that is, modified, by another law.[107] While both these methods were established to permit the harmonization of legal systems, the truth is that interpreted by these methods, one law is made dependent on another for both its existence and its meaning. This is precisely what happens to Jewish law. Allowed only when it agrees with or adds to other law, Jewish law becomes dependent on other law—that is, Canon and common law—for its applicability.[108] Thus, as the Jew's religion and his person are legally inferior and dependent, so too

---

was one of the major tasks of medieval legists. See Piano-Mortari, *Ricerche,* pp. 131–39, and Calasso, *Medio Evo del diritto,* pp. 371–75.

103. Cf. the Index on this subject. II,4 is, of course, filled with citations to this effect.

104. See Piano-Mortari, *Ricerche,* pp. 194–98 on the validity of customary law.

105. See pp. 107 and 108, supra.

106. For a discussion of this method, see Piano-Mortari, *Ricerche,* 163–83.

107. Ibid., pp. 140–52, on "corrective law."

108. An explicit statement of this principle is to be found in the bull of Martin V (Feb. 12, 1419) *Quia imaginem* (Raynaldus, *Annales* [Lucca, 1752], 8:503): Jews are permitted "omni impedimento cessante, leges iura consuetudines atque ordinamenta ipsorum ad bene tamen videndum, et non in vilipendium Catholice Fidei."

are his legal institutions. Most interestingly, it is the laws working
to complement and supplement the canons which create this institutional inferiority.

II, 5   The *ius commune* principle of "equal proportions," [109] too,
helps to bind Jews in their inferior status, although indirectly. By
excluding Jews from certain privileges which Christians enjoy, "equal
proportion" prevents Jews from enjoying all the privileges of citizenship.

Ius commune and local statutes also restrict the Jew's activities
directly. Jews are almost never accepted as valid witnesses, and
they are prohibited from owning Christian slaves. [110] In addition,
Jewish communities are banned from receiving legacies. [111] The gloss
on this ban (C.1,9,1), refers to *l. cum senatu* (D.34,5,20), which
prohibits non-approved *collegia* from receiving legacies. Quite
clearly, the gloss was attempting to explain the ban on the grounds
that the Jewish community was a "non-approved *collegium*." But a
non-approved *collegium* is one without corporate and, particularly,
jurisdictional rights. It was precisely this idea of the Jewish
community's lack of corporate rights which de Susannis wanted to
introduce at this point. [112] It serves as a transition to the discussion
in II,6 of the prohibitions against Jews acquiring offices, honors, and
jurisdictions.

II,6 is the climax of the *De Iudaeis.* All the themes which
have appeared and which will appear in the entire tract are brought
together in II,6, including the non-legal motifs of III,1. II,6 may
therefore be best understood only after these non-legal ideas have
been exposed and analyzed. But there are two points which may
be made immediately to illustrate how II,6 fits into the general context of the *De Iudaeis.*

---

109. See p. 109, supra.
110. See pp. 109–11, supra.
111. C.1,9,1. See p. 111, supra.
112. Cf. Bart. Saliceto, *Com. in Codicem* (1483), on C.1,9,1 (fol. e7vb),
where he shows that the prohibition on receiving legacies derives from the non-
approved status of Jewish *collegia.* Cf. also Bartolus, *Com. ad Digestum,* in
Opera Omnia (Venice, 1590), in D.34, 5,20 (vol. 4, fol. 101rb), where he shows
that a non-approved *collegium* is one without corporate or jurisdictional rights.

First, de Susannis supports his assertions that Jews are prohibited from holding offices and power not only by citing civil law,
but also by citing canons.[113] This juxtaposition of laws and canons
reinforces the concept that the laws and canons complement each
other in establishing the status of the Jew. The chapter opens, moreover, with the statement that Jews may not hold offices, because if
they did, they would preside over Christians, be their superiors, and
also be in a position to cause them harm. The *ratio* behind the *ius
commune* prohibitions on Jews attaining power is thus identical with
the *ratio* behind the canons which forbid Jews to hold Christian
slaves and which prohibit Christians from eating at a Jew's table,[114]
not to mention the *ratio* behind the canons which expressly prohibit
the Jews from acquiring superiority over Christians by holding
offices.[115]

The second point of importance is that II,6,14 is the locus
of the most explicit declaration in the tract that Jews must receive
justice. That this declaration is found here is no accident. Besides
reiterating the point that dependence and inferiority do not mean
license to treat Jews arbitrarily, it implies what never really needs
stating, namely, that the system of Jewry law created by the canons
and the laws is altogether a just system. In context and specifically,
however, it also implies that the combination of severe limitations
with consistently protected criminal and civil rights grants the Jew
justice.

The exposition of restrictions in II,6 and 7 concludes the dis-   II, 7
cussion of the relationship of the Jews to the system of *ius commune*.
The topic then shifts somewhat abruptly, but quite logically, to the
determination of the status of the Jews vis-à-vis the system of canon   II, 8 & 9
law. While the canons that restrict the Jews have been examined

---

113. The prime laws excluding Jews from jurisdictions are: C.1,9,8 and 17;
the canons, X.5,6,16 and 18. "Jurisdiction," as used here, refers to the ability of
Jews to function either as ordinary judges, irrespective of the religion of the
litigants, or as judges presiding over cases involving Jews alone.

114. See p. 83, supra.

115. In II,7 de Susannis continues the list of restrictions set out in chap. six.
It is in the specificity of these restrictions that the laws most clearly elaborate on
the canons.

at length, the relationship of the Jews to the canons as a body has not as yet been discussed. The main fact of the relationship of the Jews to the canons is that they pertain to Jews only when they restrict Jews. Otherwise Jews are excluded, or simply exempted, as in the case of the canons on marriage.[116] This relationship is precisely the reverse of the relationship of the Jews to *ius commune,* to which they are normally subject. Nevertheless, it is by making this very point that *Pars Secunda* has proved that both the canons and *ius commune* restrict the Jews in identical ways for the identical purpose, and that a continuum between the two legal systems does indeed exist. It is to reveal the existence of this continuum and the absence of contradictions between the status of the Jews in the two systems that de Susannis analyses the position of the Jews in the system of canon law at this point. It is now quite evident that the two systems complement each other in fixing the status of the Jew. Because the Jews are religious enemies, they are excluded from the benefits of most canons. For the same reason they are restricted by other canons. Likewise, the Jews are restricted by the laws when the laws touch on religious matters. But because the Jew is a civil friend, he is included in the laws in purely civil affairs. Thus de Susannis has shown that the canons and the laws, taken together, erect a harmonious and unified system of Jewry law.

---

116. See p. 115, supra.

CHAPTER VI

PARS TERTIA, CHAPTER ONE: THE SERMON, A POLEMIC

THIS CHAPTER DIFFERS RADICALLY from the rest of the tract. It is almost completely devoted to non-legal subjects, and the source material is drawn from the Bible, from various theologians, and from a large number of ancients.[1] Stylistically, too, this chapter differs significantly. In the legal sections there is rarely a sentence which is not broken into bits by legal citations, an effect caused in large part by the absence of modern footnoting style. In this chapter de Susannis waxes eloquent, almost poetic. For instance, there is the opening phrase of the chapter: "Nemo est tam rudis intellectus, aut hebetis, et obtusi ingennii . . . ." or the first line of paragraph thirty-one: "O quam suavis olim fuit verbi Evangelici praedicatio." Of course, de Susannis expected his audience to read this chapter, but its display of rhetoric and its passion of thought lead the reader to imagine de Susannis delivering a sermon.

---

1. The following is a list of the Fathers, medieval and Renaissance authors, ancients, and Jews cited in this chapter by de Susannis: Fathers: Ambrose, Augustine, Boethius, Cyprian, Cassiodorus, Chrysostom, Epiphanius, Eusebius, Gregory the Great, Isidore, Lactantius, Origen, Orosius, Rufinus of Aquileia, Socrates, Suetonius, Tertullian; medieval and Renaissance authors: Anselm, Alfonso de Espina, Bede, Bernard, Bonaventura, Erasmus, Hadrianus Finus, Iacobus Perez de Valencia, Isidore, Marsilio Ficino, Paul of Burgos, Thomas, Io. Turrecremata, Vincent of Beauvais; ancients: Aristotle, Augustus Caesar, Juvenal, Lampridius, Martial, the mythical Hermes Trismegistus, Ovid, Plato, Plotinus, Plautus, Pliny, Porphyry, Plutarch, Seneca, Strabo, Tacitus, and Virgil; Jews: Josephus, Maimonides, Neumia b. Haccarrae (a Christian Kabbalistic construct for Neḥuniah b. Haqqana, p. 143, n. 90, infra), the rabbis as a group, and the Muslim, Avicenna.

Its burden is that all haste must be made to convert the world's infidels. In de Susannis' own words of summation:

> It seemed necessary to me, about to treat the matter of the con-
> version of the infidels, to say something about their rites, so that
> by recounting them I could refute them, and, by these means, I
> could induce them to accept the sacrament of ·baptism, once they
> knew their error.[2]

This "sermon" is, then, a polemic. Not surprisingly it opens on an apologetic note. There is none, de Susannis says, who is so obtuse that he does not know that the ultimate end of man is to know God.[3] To attain this end man must practice *adoratio* and *amor* so that he may again unite (*copulemur*) with God.[4] Man must also recognize that Christ lived in poverty, and that he taught men to seek their treasure in heaven, to possess no gold, and to sell all their posses-sions and give them to the poor.[5]

Before Christ, however, the wise deceived themselves and others by involving themselves in philosophy.[6] But what can be learned from Aristotle, Averroes, and Plato?[7] Let him, therefore, who wishes to have true wisdom and to lead the happy life, rush to Christ[8] and adhere to the law of evangelical perfection. Through Christ all things are offered to men. Knowing this, martyrs followed the example of Christ's sacrifice and faced death with jubilation.[9]

---

2. III,1,81: "Nam tracturus de conversione infidelium, necessarium mihi visum est, aliquid de eorum ritibus recitare, et recitando refellere, et ipsos ad sacramentum baptismi, cognito eorum errore, his mediis invitare. . . ."

3. III,1,1: "Eius finis ultimus est ipsum Deum cognoscere."

4. III,1,2: "Cum Deo a quo sumus, iterum copulemur."

5. III,1,3: "Is enim in paupertate vivens, nos in coelo thesaurizare edocuit, nec possidere aurum . . . sed ut omnia venderentur et darentur pauperibus . . . ut in altum elevemur, videlicet ut de duobus aliis fidamus, eleemosyna scilicet et oratione."

6. III,1,4: "Qui se ipsos et alios per philosophiam involvendo et inanes fallacias deceperunt."

7. III,1,4: "Quid verae fidei ab impio Aristotele et perfido Averoe, aut ex Platonicorum superstitione."

8. III,1,5: "Quisquis ergo non vult vera sapientia et vita carere, sed veram sapientiam et beatam vitam agere, ad ipsum Iesum Christum properet."

9. III,1,6–8.

May, therefore, all who are aliens from the faith of Christ make haste, and may they rush to the son of God Himself. May they not delay. Then this city will not remain, but the future one will be sought out.[10]

In these opening paragraphs de Susannis has revealed his personal religious beliefs and emotions.[11] He has also advocated their universal acceptance, calling on all men, especially infidels (*alieni a fide Christi*), to believe in Christ.[12] The following statement, however—that when all men do believe in Christ, then this city will no longer remain—discloses an ulterior motive. What he is really advocating is conversionary activity on the part of his Christian audience, which in turn will hasten the advent of the eschaton. Why he favors such actions he only reveals further on.[13] In preparation for that revelation, he must first prove that Christ and the Gospel law are the true way to eternal life in order to substantiate his claim that universal belief in Christ will lead to the eschaton. Hence, he continues: "The excellence of this sacred law and faith can be most easily perceived by comparing them with the laws and faiths of other sects." [14]

For one, there are the horrendous falsehoods of idolatry as practiced by the ancient pagans. They served most destructive demons,[15] and their gods were in reality sinful humans.[16] They were

10. III,1,9: "Festinent igitur omnes a fide Christi alieni, et properent ad ipsum Dei filium . . . et non habemus hic civitatem manentem sed futuram inquirimus."

11. Cf. pp. 195–99, infra, where the relationship between de Susannis' religious ideals and sixteenth-century Catholic reform ideals is discussed at length.

12. Since de Susannis is addressing Christians, it is necessary to understand that his calls to non-Christians are in fact directives to his Christian audience to foster the conversion of the infidels by employing the methods he outlines as he develops his sermon.

13. Cf. pp. 130–33, infra.

14. III,1,11: "Cuius quidem sacrae legis et fidei excellentia ex caeterorum sectarum collatione facillime percipi poterit."

15. III,1,12: "Et in primis, si gentiles respiciamus solitos servire perditissimis demonibus, quos Deus in aeterna supplicia damnavit. . . ."

16. III,1,13. De Susannis cites, among others, Chrysostom, *Ad Titum Homilia V,* chap. 2, and Tertullian, *in lib. Adversus Gentes,* where descriptions of the sinful acts of these gods are recorded.

guilty of abominations, such as human sacrifice [17] and sexual pro-
miscuity in the name of sacrifice.[18] They were oblivious to the
divine retribution their idolatrous acts incurred.[19] The irrationality
of the pagans was beyond measure. They assigned the same name
to many gods, they called emperors gods, and they even venerated
natural phenomena. Worst of all, they worshipped beasts.[20] All
along they were blind to the wonders of God and to the help-
lessness of their multitude of deities.[21]

Thus, its evils and the resulting divine punishment prove the
falsity and vanity of idolatry. But so too does this punishment prove
the truth and the power of God. Indeed, Christ proved his divinity
by acting against idolatry.[22] "With his advent"—and this is the
crucial point for proving that Christ is the messiah—"the idols
ceased their responses." [23] Christ waged such a fierce war against
the tempter of the world that the Devil lost not only his power of
dominion, but even his power of speaking. On the day of the nati-
vity itself, "all the idols cried out (in mortal terror)." [24]

> And this should be all the more marveled at, because, although
> in the time of Moses and the prophets terrible wonders were per-
> formed by God in Egypt, with the greatest virtue, nevertheless,
> idolatry could not be extirpated from that people, Ismael [*sic*]. . . .
> This, however, was effected at the advent of Christ, so that it is
> clear that in him the prophecies concerning this event [namely,

---

17. III,1,16.
18. III,1,18.
19. III,1,14–15: For additional examples of the vanity of idolatry and for
examples of divine retribution, de Susannis cites Rufinus of Aquileia, *Historia
Ecclesiastica*, chap. 23 cum seq., Eusebius, *De Praeperatione Evangelica* (various
places), Alexander de Alessandro, *Geniales Dies* (various places), and Greg.
Giraldum, *Historia Deorum Gentilium*, passim (which de Susannis calls the most
important source for such material), Josephus, *Antiquities* XIII,9, and 2 Macc.
3:7 ff.
20. III,1,19–20.
21. III,1,21–22.
22. III,1,24: "Pariter etiam, D.N.I.C. de coelo missus a patre in hunc mun-
dum de ipsius idolatriae crimine vindictam sumpsit."
23. III,1,24: "Nam eo adveniente cessarunt Idola ab eorum responsis."
24. III,1,24: "Omnia Idola clamasse."

that with the coming of the messiah idolatry would cease] were fulfilled and that he is the true messiah.[25]

Indeed, with the advent of Christ, "the idols all turned their backs, and Christ, alone and dead, expelled an exceedingly great number of their gods, and transformed their cult to himself." [26]

In short, Christ and his Gospel are verified because with his advent not only was idolatry punished, but it also began to disappear.[27] Idolatry did not cease completely, however, with the appearance of Christ, but only with the work of his followers, the Apostles.[28] So Paul believed, when he said that in his day the Gospel had borne fruit in all creation (Col. 1:6). That Christ's followers, and not Christ himself, were intended to extirpate idolatry in full is indicated by Isaiah 66, where it is written: "Mittam ex eis qui salvati fuerint ad gentes in mare." [29]

The Gospel message did indeed spread.

---

25. III,1,24: "Et hoc magis admirandum est, quod licet tempore Mosis et prophetarum magnalia virtute Dei fierent terribilia in Aegypto . . . non tamen extirpari potuit ab ipso etiam populo Ismaelitico Idolatria . . . quod tamen effectum est adveniente Christo, ut in eo prophetiae de hoc impleretur et quod verus esset messias pateret." According to de Susannis, these prophecies are: Dan. 2, Isa. 2 and 31, Ezek. 6, Mic. 1, Hos. 2.

26. III,1,24: "Omnes eidem terga verterunt, et ipse solus et mortuus tot innumeros eorum Deos expulit et ad se cultum transtulit."

27. De Susannis cites, as the source for this proof, bk. 2, *De Vocatione Omnium gentium,* which he attributes to Ambrose. The work is in fact by Prosper of Aquitaine, but was attributed to Ambrose through the sixteenth century. See P. De Letter, trans., *The Call of All Nations of St. Prosper of Aquitaine* (London, 1952), p. 7; and p. 149, for the passage cited by De Susannis, bk. 2, chap. 35.

28. III,1,25: "Quod adimpletum est etiam per praedicationes Apostolorum."

29. III,1,25. At this point de Susannis introduces a long aside on the history of pagan temples which were consecrated as churches. He dwells particularly on the Cathedral and Patriarchate of Aquileia. Then he praises the contemporary patriarch, Joannis Grimani. Grimani was implicated in a charge of consorting with heretics. However, this charge probably had no bearing on de Susannis' panegyric. He wrote it most probably because he was in Grimani's employ from time to time (MS Joppi 1236—cf. p. 71, n. 37, supra—indicates as much), not to mention that Friuli was part of the Archdiocese of Aquileia, and de Susannis identified himself as an Aquileian (III,1,15). On Grimani, see *Enciclopedia Cattolica* (Vatican City, 1949), 6:col. 1168.

For by our day it seems that it can be said that the Gospel has now been preached in the entire world, . . . and, although its [idolatry's] remnant still exists in some corner of this world . . . a small bit is to be considered as nothing.[30]

Even if idolatry has raised its head again in some regions—

as we learn from the letters sent by members of the Order of Jesus, who obey the apostolic duty of preaching—the pious reader will perceive from these letters that the circumstances and conditions of the primitive church will return to those regions and also [will soon flourish in those regions] where the Gospel has not as yet been preached.[31]

But!

Since there are many barbarian nations which have not heard the word of Christ, especially in Africa, which is obvious from those who have been brought from those nations as captives, it is [rather] as Augustine says: "There are those who believe that what is said [in the verse:] 'The Gospel of the kingdom will be preached in the whole world,' was accomplished by the Apostles. But it was not so [accomplished], as is proved by certain documents." [32]

That is, idolatry has not completely disappeared. The Gospel did not bear fruit in all the nations in the time of the Apostles, or even afterward. The most certain proof that the Gospel message did not spread throughout the world in the time of the Apostles is the fact

30. III,1,28: "unde videtur posse dici iam fuisse praedicatum Evangelium in universo mundo . . . et licet eius reliquiae in aliquo terrae huius angulo superesset, . . . parum pro nihilo reputatur."

31. III,1,29: ". . . prout acceptum est ex literis missivis eorum qui sunt ex ordine Iesu, et munus apostolicum obeunt, ex quibus pius lector percipiet, redire in illas regiones tempora et status primitive ecclesiae, et ubi non adhuc denunciatum est evangelium."

32. III,1,29: "Sed quia sunt multae gentes Barbarae, quae non audiverunt Christi verbum, maxime in Aphrica, quod ex iis, qui ducuntur inde captivi, in promptu est, prout tradit Augustinus dicens, sunt qui putant hoc quod dicitur, praedicabitur Evangelium Regni in universo orbe per ipsos Apostolos factum esse, quod non ita esse certis documentis probatum est."

that the Spaniards have recently discovered lands which previously were completely unknown, and where it would have been impossible for the Gospel to penetrate.[33]

Clearly de Susannis has contradicted himself. This contradiction, however, is a rhetorical device. It serves to remind his reader that many infidels remain to be converted. But it also serves to introduce the point that since the discoveries, the New World infidels have been converting in droves—a fact of cosmic significance for de Susannis, and a fact which permits him at last to reveal why actions should be taken to hasten the approach of the eschaton.

Thus he says: *"But now, since we believe the end of the world to be near,* God has offered these nations the way of pursuing truth, and He has opened to them the way of His Gospel." [34] Indeed, if we were not near the end of the world, then why, in so brief a time, would the whole world have been filled with churches, and why would so many nations have come to the faith, abrogating their laws, customs, and ceremonies in the process?[35] It must therefore be said that although the mandate of preaching the Gospel was undertaken by the Apostles, pursued by their successors, and is still carried on today, it is not yet completed and finished.[36] Rather, Christ, who gave this mandate to preach the Gospel to all men, also told us when it would be fully carried out. Speaking of the things that would precede the end of the world and signal its imminent ruin, he declared that the Gospel of the kingdom will be

33. III,1,29: "Et nobis hoc tempore non est opus certioribus testimoniis quam eo . . . multas gentes reperiri . . . quibus nescio quomodo potuit Evangelium innotescere . . ."

34. III,1,29: "[. . . Innotescere,] at qui [read: *quibus*] nunc, cum iam prope credamus orbis excidium, praebuit illis Deus modum assequendae veritatis et viam aperuit suo Evangelio." (The citations in nn. 35, 36, and 37 are the next two sentences in the tract.)

35. III,1,29: "Quid sit in tam brevi tempore omnem sub sole terram tantis ecclesiis impleri, tantas gentes ad fidem transferri, populos persuaderi, ut patrias leges irritent, consuetudinem stabilitam revellant . . . et sacrificia abhorreant. . . ."

36. III,1,29: "Unde dicendum est fore, quod licet per Apostolos mandatum de Evangelii praedicatione fuerit ceptum, ac per eorum successores persecutum, et in dies procedat, completum tamen, et perfectum non possit dici . . ."

preached in the entire world in testimony to all nations, and then
the consummation will come.[37] Idolatry will be totally eliminated
only at the end of the world, when the Gospel has been universally
preached.[38]

At that time, it will be as Isaiah said: "Repleta est terra scientia Domini, sicut aqua maris operientis." So too will the prophecy
of Zechariah be verified: "Erit in die illa dicit Dominus exercituum
disperdam nomina Idolorum de terra, et non memorabuntur ultra."
And this verse, "Intelligatur de secundo Christi adventu." [39] In the
words of Isidore of Seville, moreover, at the time of the Second
Coming not only will all idols be removed, but even the Judaic
perfidy will be converted to Christ.[40] Thus, on the day of the Second
Coming "there will be one flock and one pastor." [41] On that day,
even the Muslim sect—if it survives—will conspire in the curse of
Antichrist and will be consumed.[42]

That day, however, as de Susannis has explicitly said, is upon
him, and the fulfillment of all the events he has just described is
imminent. Since at the heart of these events is the conversion of
all infidels, de Susannis will now prove himself most avid in advocating the immediate commencement of vigorous proselytizing ac-

37. III,1,29: ". . . nam qui mandatum dederat de Evangelio praedicando
omni creaturae, Christus, etiam tempus ex quo expleri et perfici deberet praedocuit, de mundi enim occasu praecedentibus et ipsius prope ruinam demonstrantibus
loquens subintulit, et praedicabitur Evangelium Regni in universo orbe in testimonium omnibus gentibus, et tunc veniret consummatio." (The verse is Matt.
24:14, and cf. Matt. 24, passim.)

38. III,1,29: "Eliminanda ergo erit Idolatria omnino ab universo orbe, cum
Evangelium Christi toti mundo propalatum fuerit in fine videlicet mundi."

39. III,1,30. De Susannis then cites verbatim the following from Augustine, given here in translation: M. Dods, trans., *The City of God* (New York,
1950), p. 762, bk. 20, chap. 30: "And in connection with that judgment the following events will come to pass, as we have learned: Elias the Tishbite shall
come; the Jews shall believe; Antichrist shall persecute; Christ shall judge; the
dead shall rise; the good and the wicked shall be separated; the world shall be
burned and renewed."

40. III,1,30. De Susannis cites Isidore, *De Sum. Bon.*, chaps. 25 and 26, and
Ethymologias.

41. III,1,30: "Et tunc fiet unum ovile et unus pastor" (John 10:16).

42. III,1,30: "Et tunc etiam maumetica secta (si supererit) estimatur in
Antichristi execrationem coire et consumari."

tivity. In particular, he assigns an important proselytizing role to the lawyers and judges to whom the *De Iudaeis* is directed. When he writes (III,I,30) that the conversion of the Jews is one of the events which will precede the consummation, he refers to a paragraph in the legal portion of the tract, II,6,28. This reference indicates that there is a link between proselytizing and Jewry law.[43] The precise nature of the link will be explained shortly.

Another important fact emerges when this eschatological material is examined in the context of the sermon as a whole. De Susannis started out to prove that Christ was the true messiah by demonstrating that with Christ's advent idolatry had begun to disappear. By speculating on the imminence of the Second Coming, he appeared to shift topics. But how much more positive would be the proof that Christ was the messiah if idolatry completely ceased at the eschaton, as Christ himself had prophesied. The two themes of the sermon are, then, in fact but one: the truth of Christ, of which the Second Coming will be the ultimate proof.

Confident, moreover, that his convictions are correct, de Susannis proceeds, "O faelices igitur nos Christicolae," and O how wretched and unhappy are the gentiles. We Christians possess the light of Christ; the infidels lie in darkness.[44] O how sweet it once was, when the Gospel word of Christ was preached among the nations.[45] As the faith of the preachers grew, so did the Church prosper, not because these preachers strove with arms, but because they fought with nothing but the example of their lives and the pious and humble message of the word of God, the true arms of the Church.[46] The Roman Church will never be destroyed. Who-

---

43. Cf. pp. 165f., infra, where this link is explained.

44. III,1,30.

45. III,1,31: "O quam suavis olim fuit verbi Evangelici praedicatio inter gentiles."

46. III,1,31: "Piae et humiles verbi Dei praedicationes et . . . mandatorum observatio." Cf. G. Contarini's similar expression of trust in preaching as the true arms of the Church, in G. Contarini, *Gegenreformatorische Schriften (1530–52)*, ed. F. Hünermann (Münster, 1923), p. 24. On the zeal for preaching in the sixteenth-century Church as a whole, and as manifest in such men as Philip Neri, see H. Daniel-Rops, *The Catholic Reformation* (New York, 1964), 2:16–18; L.

ever persecutes the Church, persecutes Christ himself.[47] Let the
persecutors of the Holy Roman Church beware, then. Let them
also consider how great is the crown of those who venerate the
Church. Whence, priests must be honored, since they were instituted by God.[48]

These paragraphs are intended both to warn and to reassure.
They warn the Protestants (the persecutors who, by implication, do
not venerate priests) that their rebellion will ultimately fail, and
they reassure the Catholics that their cause will ultimately triumph.
No matter how distressing the times are, Catholics should not lose
hope, because the final vindication of Christ and his Church is
imminent.

On this note de Susannis concludes what may be called the first
half of the sermon. The second half describes the steps that must
be taken in order to lead the infidels to Catholicism and thus to
make the Second Coming a reality.

De Susannis has, in fact, already described sufficiently the
missionary efforts in the New World and the East. The conversion
of the infidels in these lands presents no special problems, and no
more needs to be said on this subject. On the other hand, the missions to the Jews and the Muslims pose great difficulties. Of all
the nations that had heard the Gospel preached, these two alone
had not converted. De Susannis is therefore compelled to explain
why they have proved so recalcitrant and then to show how the
situation may be reversed.

"The preaching of the Gospel in the lands of the Muslims,"

Christiani, *L'Église à l'époque du Concile de Trente* (Paris, 1948), pp. 327–37;
and cf. infra, p. 196.

47. III,1,31: "Nunquam poterit sancta Romana Ecclesia destrui, funda-
menta enim ecclesiae in montibus sanctis, per montes insinuans prophetas, Apostolos, Evangelistas, atque praedicantes . . . licet eiusdem ecclesiae author per
principale fundamentum sit Christus. . . . et qui ecclesiam persequuntur, CHRISTUM,
ipsum persequuntur."

48. III,1,31: "Caveant ergo eiusdem Sanctae Romanae Ecclesiae persecutores
. . . et cogitent, quantum periculum eorum sit qui ecclesiam maerore afficiunt,
quanta corona eorum, qui ecclesiam venerantur; et agnoscant vocem Domini di-
centis, qui vos spernit, me spernit, unde sacerdotes merito sunt honorandi, cum
a Deo fuerint instituti."

he begins, "would bear the same fruit [i.e., conversion, as in the case of the other nations that heard the Gospel preached] if their most powerful emperor would permit the publication of the divine word." [49] For the Muslims would convert to Christ more easily than the ancients and more easily than other nations, if they heard the Gospel preached, because they are not idolators, but worship God. [50]

All that is needed is to preach to them. If preaching alone effects conversion among pagans, [51] how much more easily will preaching result in the conversion of those who already believe in God. [52]

The Muslims, moreover, believe that Jesus had miracle-working powers, and that he was born of Mary, who remained a virgin. [53] They are so close to the truth that we must seek their salvation daily. Indeed, if preachers were admitted to the Muslims' lands, they would quickly teach the Muslims that there are no prophecies about Muhammad, and that the Muslim conception of heaven is completely false. [54] Muhammad himself knew that the Muslims would recognize the errors of Islam and embrace Christianity if they heard the Gospel message. He therefore ordered his law to be defended only by the sword, so that what could not be protected by reason would be conserved through violence. [55] He did the precise opposite from Christ. Christ—and this little aside is in fact

---

49. III,1,32: "Eosdem fructus pareret praedicatio Evangelii in terris Maumetistarum si potentissimus eorum Imperator publicationem verbi eiusdem divini admitteret."

50. III,1,32: "Facilius quam antiqui et alii gentiles converterent . . . cum ipsi non sint idolatrae sed adorant Deum."

51. Cf. supra, p. 91 and p. 130.

52. Cf. pp. 196 and 199f., infra, on the value assigned to preaching, and esp. missionary preaching, by sixteenth-century Catholic thought.

53. III,1,33–35. Most of this material on the Muslims is taken almost directly from Ficino. Cf. M. Ficino, *Opera Omnia* (Basle, 1576), *De Christiana Religione*, pp. 17–18. Cf. N. Daniel, *Islam and the West* (Edinburgh, 1962), pp. 163–94, and esp. pp. 164–75 for a general discussion of medieval Christian conceptions of Muslim beliefs about Christ.

54. III,1,36–37.

55. III,1,37: "Et propterea caute providit Maumethes, non nisi gladio legem esse tuendam, ut quod ratione defendi non posset, id per violentiam fieret."

another proof of the excellence of Christ's law made from a comparison of that law with the laws of the other nations—defended
his law with miracles, not with force. He ordered it preached to all
men, for he had no fear. He knew that his law was the truth.

Thus, according to de Susannis, it was Muhammad's aware-
ness of the rational indefensibility of his law as well as his consequent
prohibition against Gospel preaching which was, and still is, the reason why Muslims have not converted. The difficulty is not to convince the Muslims; it is, rather, to convince the sultan to allow the
Gospel to be preached. Therefore, to persuade the sultan to admit
missionaries, de Susannis asserts that if the Muslims did convert, their
most powerful emperor, under the banner of Christ, would defeat and
completely rout the ferocious king of the Persians with the greatest
of ease.[56] Using no weapons at all, the prince of the Muslims would
bring the Persians, the northern infidels, and all other Orientals
under his yoke, and the entire Orient would turn to Christ. Never
again would troubles beset him or his empire, if only he placed all
his hope in Christ.[57] Let him, therefore, as well as all Muslims and
other infidels, confess Christ.[58]

It thus appears that de Susannis is claiming that the sultan
could be convinced to admit missionaries if he were promised military victories; he is, in fact, claiming much more. Immediately
after proclaiming the sultan's assured victory over the king of the
Persians, de Susannis states that in Daniel 10 it is written that the
kingdom of Persia withstood the Archangel Gabriel for twenty-one
days because of the power of its guardian angel. Both de Susannis
and Daniel 10 are somewhat obscure about the nature and purpose of this struggle. But when de Susannis adds that, according

---

56. III,1,39: "Eorundem potentissimus Imperator certus esset, Christi vexillo
insignitus posse facillime debellare, et penitus evertere ferocem illum Persarum
Regem."

57. III,1,39: "Et totus oriens ad Christum reverteretur, nec sibi et Imperio
suo quicquam sinistri contingeret, instans in Christo omnem spem suam." III,1,39–
41 contains a long aside. De Susannis relates how Christ always fights for his
faithful, but punishes Christians who are disloyal—a probable reference to the
Protestants. Also he raises the question: Why is it that loyal Christians are sometimes defeated? and he can only answer: Who can know the ways of God?

58. III,1,41.

to Daniel 10, Gabriel was protecting and fighting for Israel, his intentions become clear. He has allegorized the struggle in Daniel 10 to the war of the Muslims against the Persians, with Gabriel fighting on the side of the Muslims—if they convert and thus join the True Israel themselves. More important, since all wars in Daniel were interpreted to have eschatological importance, de Susannis is actually asserting that if the sultan converts, his war against the Persians will not be a mere military contest but a part of a great cosmic struggle, the ultimate war against Antichrist, in which weapons will be meaningless and the power of Christ alone determinant. What the sultan was to be promised, then, was not battlefield success, but the ultimate victory, the eschaton.[59]

In contrast to the optimism expressed in the introductory phrases on the conversion of the Muslims, the discourse on the Jews commences on a note of extreme anger, which betrays great despair. With what names or with what words, de Susannis says, can the Jews be aroused, except worthless, evil, and adulterous generation, or delinquent children?[60] God once loved the Jews more than any other nation, and He sent Christ first and foremost to them. But rather than recognize and accept Christ, they crucified him. The Jews are worse than the Sodomites.[61] The latter transgressed only natural law; the Jews had the written law, preachers, and miracles to guide them.

The magnitude of the Jews' sin is evident from the vengeance taken on them. Their cities and Temple were destroyed, they were slaughtered by Titus and Vespasian, they were beset by hunger and made captives, and even today they are wanderers and vaga-

---

59. It must be noted that there was an overall ambivalence in the sixteenth century about the fate of the Muslims. On the one hand, they were often identified with the forces of Antichrist (cf. pp. 252f., infra), and on the other, there was hope for their conversion (cf. Hoffmann, *Ursprung,* p. 90, where he notes that there are letters which indicate that Pius V thought he might be able to effect the conversion of the Turks after their defeat at Lepanto). Even de Susannis expresses this ambivalence. In par. 30 he spoke of the Muslim alliance with Antichrist, and now he is speaking of their conversion.

60. C.35,q.1,d.p.c.1, of which this sentence in III,1,41 is a paraphrase.

61. III,1,42. Cf. C.1,q.l,c.37 *nonne, glo.* in *v. peiores* for this idea *verbatim.* Cf. also *Summa Theologica,* II,II,10,6.

bonds. Their punishment, moreover, is proof that Christ was the messiah.[62] If he were not, why then did the Jews suffer their most severe castigation when they rejected him? The Jews surely know [63] that even now God has not calmed His burning anger. Since the time of Christ they have never experienced fire descending from heaven and consuming their sacrifices, nor have they had prophets or priests. Nor should anyone pay attention to the frivolous excuses they make. They attempt to conceal their perfidy by claiming that they have no power only because they are outside the promised land. But did not the prophets prophesy and the Apostles work miracles wherever they went?[64] The Jews see, moreover, how God has repulsed the perfidious synagogue and embraced the Church.[65] Today they do not worship idols, nor do they sacrifice their children, nor do they kill prophets, yet they dwell in perpetual calamity, and they have lived destitute of all divine aid for 1,555 years.[66]

Nevertheless, the Jews have persevered in following that false document of the scribes and the Pharisees, the Talmud, which corrupts the true meaning of the law and the prophets.[67]

62. III,1,43.

63. III,1,44: "Et certo sciunt . . ."

64. III,1,45: "Nec admittenda est frivola eorum excusatio dum criminantur peregrinationem suam, uti longe distantes a terra promissionis, et templo, ideo quod nihil authoritatis habent propter id, ut his modis obtegant eorum perfidiam." (The implication is that if God wanted the Jews to have power, they would have it anywhere.)

65. III,1,47: "Vident ergo quo modo deus reppulit perfidam Synagogam et Christi filii sui ecclesiam ex gentibus amplexatus est."

66. III,1,48: "Nunc vero cum non colant Idola, nec liberos mactent, nec prophetas occidant, in perpetua degunt calamitate, et vitam agunt ab annis 1555 citra omni auxilio Dei destitutam." Cf. Ficino, *Opera Omnia,* p. 32, for a similar statement. There, the number of years is 1,476.

67. III,1,48: "Qui tamen in duricie cordis eorum permanentes perseverant in sequendo falsa . . . documenta . . . et depravatione Talmudicae iniquitatis corrumpentis veram intelligentiam legis et prophetarum." In an aside he refers to the Talmud as the Deuterosis prohibited by Justinian in Novella 146. He claims that he is following the interpretation of Holoander (no allegation given). In fact, this interpretation of the meaning of that Novel must have been regular. Cf. de Torres, *De Sola Lectione,* pp. 50–100, where he stresses *ad infinitum* that Novella 146 prohibited the study of the Talmud.

Its deleriums prove the Jews' blindness and insanity.[68] Because they follow the Talmud, the Jews are no longer the people of God, the spiritual Israel, but they are carnal Idumeans, after that Mayr, whom they converted and instructed in their law with detestable ingeniousness.[69] Hence the Jews should not hope for liberation from their troubles. In the words of Daniel, they are living in a desolation which will last until the consummation.

Up to this point there is seemingly little to differentiate what de Susannis has written here from most other polemics.[70] Their common theme is the stubbornness of the Jews, despite the obvious truth of Christ and despite the severity of their punishments. In desperation, these polemics, as well as Church dogma, had accepted the theory found in Romans 11:25 that God had blinded the Jews to the truths of Christianity and that the Jews would convert only at the consummation.[71] These polemics contained no direct call to the Jews to embrace the faith, and were, in fact, not con-

68. III,1,48: "Quorum caecitas et insania probatur ex deliramentis quae scripta reperiuntur in eorum Talmut."

69. III,1,48: "Non sunt ideo amplius populus Dei, nec Israelitae, sed Idumei ab illo Mayr." De Susannis is not perfectly clear here. What he means is that Mayr composed the Talmud. For this idea, cf. I. Perez de Valencia, *Tractatus Adversus Iudaeos* (Lyons, 1514), fol. 467ᵛ. Perez de Valencia borrowed this idea, as perhaps did de Susannis also, from Paul of Burgos (see Ch. Merchavia, "The Talmud in the Additions of Paul of Burgos," *Journal of Jewish Studies* 16 [1965]: 117, n. 6), who based what he, a convert himself, knew to be a false claim on the fact that Mayr was in fact an Idumean convert. See ibid., p. 116, citing Paul's *Scrutinium Scripturarum* (1432–34): Paul tried to identify the Talmud "with Edom through 'Rabi Mayr, a cuius auctoritate dependet illa doctrina' seeing that R. Me'ir was of Idumean origin (principalis actor erat idumeus natione)"; see also G. D. Cohen, "Esau as Symbol," p. 31. See too Merchavia, *The Church versus Talmudic and Midrashic Literature*, p. 86, where he mentions an interpretative tradition, originating with Jerome, which identified certain Rabbis of the Mishnaic period, including R. Me'ir, as the Pharisees and Scribes spoken of in the Gospels. This tradition may have given Paul of Burgos the impetus for expounding his thesis. On the notion of the Jews as Idumeans (Edom, Esau), the carnal offspring of Abraham, as opposed to Israel (the Church), the spiritual offspring, a notion developed by the exegesis on Rom. 9:6–13 and employed as the cornerstone of Christian medieval attitudes toward Jews and Jewry legislation, see Cohen, "Esau," pp. 30–38.

70. For a discussion of some of these polemics, cf. pp. 243-46, infra.

71. See Browe, *Judenmission,* pp. 306–10, and cf. infra, pp. 242–48.

versionary tracts, but apologia.[72] However, while de Susannis too accepts the theory of Romans, he also believes that the consummation is at hand.[73] Therefore, when he speaks of the refusal of the Jews to convert, he adds the phrases "they see" and "they know" [74] that God is angry with them. In this way he indicates that God has finally removed the veil which blinded their eyes, and they are now able to accept the truths which their ancestors would not, indeed could not accept. That is, the time for their conversion has arrived.

Yet when he speaks of the Talmud and says that it perpetuates the Jews' blindness—adding that it was most proper to burn the Talmud publicly in 1553 [75]—he is warning that the ability of

72. Cf. B. Blumenkranz, *Juifs et Chrétiens dans le monde occidental* (Paris, 1960), pp. 68–84, esp. pp. 75 and 83, for a discussion of such polemics through the twelfth century. See also Blumenkranz, "Anti-Jewish Polemics and Legislation in the Middle Ages: Literary Fiction or Reality," *JJS* 16 (1965): 47–51, for further examples of apologetic polemics from the fourteenth century. Yet see Blumenkranz' edition of *Gisleberti Crispini Disputatio Iudei et Christiani* (Utrecht, 1956), about which he says: "Vera ergo controversia videtur fideliter relata esse . . ." (p. 8). R. Z. Werblowsky, however, in "Crispin's Disputation," *JJS* 11 (1960), takes issue with Blumenkranz and claims that there was no actual disputation. Rather, Crispin (1036–1117), abbot of Westminster and disciple of Anselm, had succeeded in converting a Jew after numerous conversations (p. 74) and later (1091–95) used these conversations as the basis for a scholastic defense of Christianity, in which the role of the Jewish interlocutor was to raise objections put into his mouth by Crispin himself (pp. 70–73). On polemics that were rational defenses of the faith, which had begun to appear in the late eleventh century, see A. Funkenstein, "Changes in the Patterns of Christian Anti-Jewish Polemics in the 12th Century," (Hebrew) *Zion* 33 (1968): 126 and 128–36. See also Funkenstein's conclusion (pp. 143–44) that from the twelfth century, Christian polemic turned essentially to attacking Judaism for self-defense. He does not indicate that the purpose behind these attacks was to foster conversion.

73. Cf. p. 131, supra.

74. Cf. p. 138, supra.

75. III,1,49: De Susannis notes that the burning of the Talmud in Venice accorded with the order of Paul IV. Most likely he is referring to the inquisitional order of 1553 (Stern, #100, p. 98). Cf. pp. 56–58, supra. At this point he also mentions a number of the *insania* which he claims are found in the Talmud. Many of these ideas are indeed found there. For instance, he speaks about a banquet ushering in the messianic age at which the body of the monster, Leviathan, is eaten (see L. Ginsberg, *The Legends of the Jews* [Philadelphia, 1968], 5:43–46). However, de Susannis does admit that his references to the Talmud come from a book of extracts from the Talmud compiled in Venice in 1553 by Benedict Valerio, Marcus Centani, and Franciscus Longum. On this

the Jews to see does not guarantee that they will see. Their vision only creates the opportunity for their conversion. It is now necessary to seize that opportunity and lead the Jews to the baptismal font. The first step is to break down the walls which the Jews themselves have erected, that is, to burn the Talmud. De Susannis does not explicitly state that this act will expedite their conversion. Since, however, every other action he has advocated has been conversionary, it is safe to assume that he viewed the burning of the Talmud too as a step leading to conversion.[76]

The next step is preaching, which can at last be effective. The modern Hebrews, he says, detailing just what should be preached, would do well to follow in the footsteps of their ancient fathers and patriarchs, who believed in Christ,[77] as may be seen from the prophets and from the law itself. The initials of the words "Iabo Siloch, velo" (Gen. 49:10), for example, render the name I(e)Su.[78] Moreover, all the prophecies concerning the messiah are fulfilled in Christ. He was born of a virgin (Isa. 7:14), he came from the seed of David (Isa. 11:1), and he offered himself as a lamb on the sacrificial altar (Isa. 49:6, 53:7). Herein, indeed, lies the great error of the Jews. They believe the prophets, but they refuse to believe in him whom the prophets predicted. And since

book see Stern, *Urkundliche Beiträge,* #104, p. 104. Its basis was probably the late-thirteenth-century *Pugio Fidei* of the Dominican Raymund Martini. On this work see the opinion of Y. F. Baer, *A History of the Jews in Christian Spain,* 1:167, 185, and 411, n. 54; and the opposing opinion of S. Lieberman, "Raymund Martini and His Alleged Forgeries," *Historia Judaica* 5 (1943): 87–102. Baer claims that Martini forged many of his texts, while Lieberman claims that they are all basically authentic.

76. It might be added that de Susannis did not need to make an explicit remark to this effect, for in the case of the Talmud, he was reflecting commonly held ideas, which it was unnecessary to repeat verbatim; the context here was sufficient. Cf. my remarks on the inquisitional order of 1553, supra., pp. 56–58, and esp. de Torres, *De Sola Lectione,* for the clearest expression of the idea that the Talmud should be burned to foster conversion, and also for the idea that Christians must play an active role in converting the Jews.

77. III,1,51: "Debuissent et deberent moderni hebraei sequi vestigia antiquissimorum patrum suorum et patriarcharum qui crediderunt in Christum."

78. III,1,52: "Quorum dictionum capita si asummantur, reddunt nomen Iesu." Cf. n. 90 infra.

every prophecy of the messiah has been fulfilled in Our Lord Jesus Christ—as the Jews see and know—they ought to believe in him.[79]

The elements too testified that Christ was the messiah. The sun hid its rays during the passion, and the earth trembled, as Pliny wrote.[80] But the Jews refuse to recognize the one whom it was least possible to ignore.[81]

Aside from these proofs, there is often value in using the arguments of the Gentiles themselves to quell their own vanity.[82] The Sybils in particular predicted many things which came true in Christ, even if, as servants of the Devil, they were unaware of the meaning of their prophecies. There are the words of the Persian Sybil, for instance: "The Lord will be born in the orb of the earth, and the bosom of a virgin will be the salvation of the nations." [83] Many other Gentile sources attest to the truth of Christ, such as Job, who says (19:25): "I know that my Lord, the redeemer, lives, and that in the end of days I will be resurrected from the earth." [84] Then there is the story of the Jew of Toledo who, in 1244, found a hollow rock in the river, which bore an inscription declaring that Christ was born of a virgin. As soon as the Jew read this inscription, he rushed to the baptismal font.[85] Similarly, in the time of Constantine, a man was found in a grave with a golden pendant resting on his breast. On this pendant was inscribed: "Christ, born of a virgin." [86]

---

79. III,1,54: "Postquam omnia et singula in Domino nostro Iesu Christo [Vaticinia] verificata sunt (prout vident et sciunt) in eundem credere deberent."

80. III,I,54: De Susannis cites Pliny, *Natu. Histo.* bk. 2, chap. 84.

81. III,1,55: "Dignoscere recusent quem ignorare minime possint."

82. De Susannis takes this idea from D.37, c.1,7, and 13.

83. III,1,56–59: "Et gignetur Dominus in orbem terrarum, et gremium virginis erit salus gentium." Cf. Ficino, *Opera,* pp. 25–30, for an almost identical presentation of Sybilline oracles. For the Greek text, see J. H. Friedlieb, ed., *Oracula Sibyllina* (Leipzig, 1852), p. 162, bk. 8, lines 457–59.

84. III,1,60: "Scio quod Dominus redemptor meus vivit, et in novissimo die resurrecturus sum de terra."

85. De Susannis gives no reference for this miracle story, nor have I been able to locate the source.

86. III,1,60. De Susannis cites Eutropius, *de Vita Imperatorum,* in Constanti, lib. 23.

The Jews err not only by ignoring the prophecies concerning the messiah, which were fulfilled in Christ, but also by believing that the messiah will be "temporal," [87] and that he will be potent with weapons. They think that he will lead them back to the promised land, which they will then rule, and that he will satiate them with material goods [88]—"ea est enim naturalis Iudaeorum cupido." Scripture did not speak of a temporal messiah, however, but only of a completely spiritual salvation.[89] The incorruptible kingdom of the messiah described by Daniel (chap. 7) is quite incompatible with a temporal kingdom. That the redemption brought by the messiah is spiritual is also the opinion of Rabbi Neumia b. Haccarrae (Neḥuniah ben Haqqana), whose authority is considerable among the Jews.[90] There were other ancient rabbis who held that

---

87. De Susannis is here deliberately ignoring the view of some medieval Jewish philosophers (cf. Maimonides, *Mishneh Torah*, "Teshubah," chaps. 8–10, 58a–60b) that the reward of the righteous was not messianic redemption and resurrection, but the incorporeal state of the soul in a world into which the souls of the righteous alone entered immediately after their deaths. On the appearance of this view, see G. D. Cohen, "The Soteriology of R. Abraham Maimuni," *Proceedings of the American Academy for Jewish Research* 36 (1968): 40–44, and the sources cited there.

88. III,1,61. Cf. Perez de Valencia, *Adversus Iudaeos*, fol. 468ᵛ, on these four errors of the Jews about the nature of the messiah.

89. III,1,61–62.

90. III,1,63: "Tradit eorundem Rabi Neumian filius Haccarrae, cuius magna est apud hebraeos authoritas." Neumia ben Haccarrae was a Christian spelling (cf. F. Secret, "Les Dominicains et la Kabbale Chrétienne à la Renaissance," *Archivum Fratrum Praedicatorum* 27 [1957]: 326 f., where he refers to the appearance of this name in Christian Kabbalistic texts), for the second-century rabbi, Neḥuniah ben Haqqana, to whose authorship later medieval Jewish Kabbalists attributed the *Sefer Bahir*, the earliest Kabbalistic text. See also G. Scholem, *Ursprung und Anfänge der Kabbala* [Berlin, 1962], pp. 34 and 45, where he notes that Christian Kabbalists relied basically on two Christian forgeries: the *'Iggeret Ha-Sodoth* of R. Neh. b. Haqqanah, and the *Gali'a Raz'a* of R. Judah Nasi, both the work of converts from the end of the fifteenth century. This reference to Neumia and the reading of the name I(e)su from the initials of "Iabo Siloch velo," which is an example of the Kabbalistic method of Notarikon, are the only two Kabbalistic references in the *De Iudaeis*. They are, however, sufficient to reveal that De Susannis, like many of his contemporaries, had been influenced by the Kabbalah. Cf. pp. 204f. infra, on Christian Kabbalah in the sixteenth century.

the reward of good works is not to be expected in this world.[91] But the Talmudists misunderstood them and claimed the opposite.[92] Finally, and most grievous, the Jews assert that the messiah is not God, but a man. Here again the texts prove them wrong.[93]

Hence, let the Jews discard their errors, open their eyes, and convert.[94] Their rejection of Christ has brought grave oppressions upon them. When they extend their hands in supplication, God turns His eyes from them. He has removed all ornament from their women. Instead of a sweet odor, they have a stench (*prout in veritate faetent*). They are oppressed and hated by all the nations of the world, and they have now suffered for 1,557 years.[95] Their condition is hopeless.[96] Their lot has been that of the enemies of God.[97]

---

91. III,1,63: De Susannis cites: "Bereshith raba i, in expositione libri Genesis, super illud Deuteronomii vii, scilicet, quae ego mando tibi hodie, ut facias, dicitur enim illi, hodie ut facias, non autem ut adhibeatur merces hodie, ubi omnes fere Talmudistae, per hodie praesens intelligunt seculum unde, et alibi asserunt merces bonorum operum in hoc seculo non est." Contrary to what might be expected, this interpretation does not appear in any of Raymund Martini's (*Pugio Fidei*, [Leipzig, 1687]) comments on *Bereshith Rabba* on Gen. 1. (For an index to Martini's citations from the *Bereshith Rabba* Midrashim, see S. Lieberman, *Shkiin* [Jerusalem, 1939], pp. 84–86.) The one reference to Deut. 7:11 in the *Pugio Fidei,* p. 787, interprets the verse to mean that *hodie* refers to the observance of the ceremonial law in the period before Christ, but not after Christ. De Susannis' source for his interpretation remains unknown.

92. III,1,63. III,1,64 is an aside. De Susannis declares that the messiah is supposed to be a pauper, as Christ himself was in his first advent. "Sed debuit esse pauper prout in primo eius adventu fuit D.N.I.C. [who taught his disciples] ut nolent possidere aurum . . . neque pecuniam in eorum zonis . . . neque calciamenta, et omnia venderentur. [He was born, lived, and died in poverty] . . . Et praemissa sint satis Iudaeis ut abstergant ab eorum animis maculas erroris abnegata paupertate messiae." In truth, de Susannis probably meant "Christianis" and not "Iudaeis" here, but did not want to say so explicitly. The question of apostolic poverty is extraneous to this work. De Susannis' reference to it is mentioned because of the interesting light it sheds on an old problem. But cf. infra, pp. 197f.

93. III,1,65.

94. III,1,65: "Recedant igitur Iudaeis a . . . gravissimis eorum erroribus . . . aperiant oculos et convertantur ad Iesum Christum."

95. Cf. p. 138, supra, where the number is 1,555 years. If the change is not a printer's error—and the difference remains in the 1584 edition—these dates aid in determining the period during which the tract was composed.

96. III,1,66.

If they wish to escape their afflictions, let them convert,[98] for God is most willing to save them. Although it is written in Jeremiah: "Do not inquire about that people, since I will not give you any heed" (Jer. 7:16, 11:14, 14:11), this verse does not mean that God wished Jeremiah to stop praying, but that God wished to terrify the people greatly. And the prophet, not ignorant of this matter, did not stop his entreaties. In the same way, God said through Jeremiah, "If you [the people] bathed in nitre and weighed yourselves down with cleanser, in My presence you would be sordid" (Jer. 2:22), not that the city should dwell in desperation, but that it should force itself to repent. Thus the cross of Christ pointed in all directions, offering salvation to the men of all nations. Let, therefore, the Jews and all other aliens from the faith of Christ approach the sacred baptismal font.[99]

The most outstanding feature of these paragraphs is that they are a direct summons. They are written in the third person, but the pleas of "Let the Jews convert" make it most clear that these words were intended to eventually reach the ears of the Jews. There is no indication, moreover, of a need to wait until the advent of the Second Coming at some future date before the Jews convert. The tone conveys the feeling that their conversion can be achieved imminently. There is also no question but that de Susannis believes the veil of blindness has been removed from their eyes. If he did

---

97. III,1,66: "Et quae patiuntur non sunt eorum qui Dei inimicos occidunt, sed qui Dei amicos interimunt."

98. III,1,66: "Qui si ab eorum captivitate, afflictionibus, et angustis cupiunt eximi, exuant vestes sordidas, induant Christum."

99. III,1,66: "Et licet scriptum sit per Hieremiam, ne roges pro populo isto, quoniam non te exaudiam, illud est. Non quod eum cessare vellet a precibus (quippe qui nostrae salutis cupientissimus est) sed quo eos magis terreret, cuius rei propheta non inscius praecari non destitit, sicut idem Hieremias alibi dixit, si laveris te nitro et aggregaveris tibi Borith, coram me sordida es, non ut eam civitatem in desperationem ageret, sed ut rescipiscere cogeret. Et propterea Crux Christi ad omnem partem extensa fuit. . . . Accedant igitur Iudaei . . . ad sacrum fontem baptismi." III,1,66–76 contains a long excursus on the value of baptism, especially with reference to circumcision, which, de Susannis states, is only a sign prefiguring the future sacrament of baptism.

not, he could never expect, as he does, that exposing the Jews' errors to them will result in their immediate mass conversion. The fact that he never explicitly states that they are no longer blind is unimportant. He has already said that he is living on the verge of the consummation. Since a corollary of that statement is that the Jews can now see the truth, it is unnecessary to say so explicitly. It is only necessary to remind the reader of this transformation with such phrases as "they see and know."

Besides exposing their errors, however, this appeal emphasized the Jews' inescapable sufferings. They must convert if they wish to escape their punishments. Their prayers for respite are useless. As long as they remain Jews, God will avert His eyes from them. With these statements the way is prepared for the last paragraph of this summons, in which Jeremiah is cited two times. Taken in context, these citations are unquestionably intended to apply analogously to the contemporary Jews. The threats contained in them are meant to refer to the punishments which the Jews had suffered for fifteen centuries, and the repentance, the result the threats were intended to produce, is meant, of course, to refer to conversion.

The meaning and significance of this analogy are best seen in the context of the entire method proposed for converting the Jews. The time for their conversion has arrived, for they can at last comprehend the truth. But the proper actions must be taken. First, the barrier the Jews themselves have erected, the Talmud, must be broken down. Second, the Jews must be instructed, to correct their misconceptions about Christ and the nature of the messiah. Finally, they must be made to see the causal relationship between their Jewishness and their afflictions. They must realize that their error of rejecting Christ has brought punishment upon them, and that as long as they remain Jews they will be punished and God will reject them. Punishment, de Susannis is thus saying, is a prime means, which God Himself has employed, to effect the conversion of the Jews. The punishments of the Jews are instituted by God—and this is the message of the analogy—not to destroy them, but to terrify them and to awaken them to the truth, so that they will approach the baptismal font.[100]

Hence he says, let Jews as well as Saracens, infidels of whatever other sect, and even all Christians awake to the fact that our felicity is found only in that life which is eternal and immortal.[101] No one was ever fully happy or untroubled in this world. Rather, all men must strive to find the way that leads to eternal beatitude, Christ. While there is time, let men cultivate the form of their souls to fashion them into worthy spouses of Christ.[102] This all men can do, for God is always prepared to indulge their sins. But let them not delay, lest God bring His anger against them. Men must cover themselves with the shield of faith and pursue, at the same time, good works.[103] They must not desire things of this world, for the world is only a place of pilgrimage, a hostile mansion.[104] Yet they must make haste, for the time of human life is too brief.[105] Before the Flood, man lived nine hundred years. Afterward, the time of life was shortened to six hundred years, although even that span was sufficiently long. But with Moses, life was shortened to one hundred and twenty years, and after David to seventy. Therefore, while there is time,[106] let men perform good works and adhere to Christ.[107]

With this final plea, the sermon is concluded by an artful return to its original theme. All men must seek salvation through

---

100. Cf. p. 166, infra, on the relationship between this concept and de Susannis' conception of the proper function of Jewry law.

101. III,1,77: "Animadvertunt ideo tam ipsi hebraei, quam sarraceni et cuiuscunque alterius sectae infideles, et etiam Christiani omnes, in hac vita mortali non esse finem aut faelicitatem nostram, sed in ea de qua supra diximus, aeterna et immortali."

102. III,1,77: "Et dum tempus est formam animae nostrae excolamus . . . ut efficiatur digna Christi sponsa."

103. III,1,78.

104. III,1,79: "mundus est enim locus peregrinationis nostrae, mansio hostilis."

105. III,1,81: "Tempus enim vitae humanis nimis breve est."

106. III,1,81: "Dum ergo tempus habemus . . ."

107. III,1,81: "Da quaesumus Dominae populo tuo Diabolica vitare contagia, et te solum Deum pura mente sectari per Dominum nostrum Iesum Christum."

Christ. But by now the reader knows that "all men" is no mere rhetorical device. He also knows why this plea is made, and he comprehends the meaning of the final clauses which warn of the brief life-span man has at his disposal. Time is short; the Second Coming is rapidly approaching. All men must devoutly embrace the true Catholic faith to insure their salvation. They must also make every effort to lead others to salvation. For only when the plenitude of nations enters into the faith of Christ will Christ himself return. At that time the truth of Christ and his law will be self-evident.

What, however, is the relationship between this eschatological sermon and the rest of the *De Iudaeis?* II,5,5–7 and II,6 supply the answer.

CHAPTER VII

PARS SECUNDA, CHAPTER SIX: CONVERSION THROUGH LEGAL RESTRICTION

PARS SECUNDA CHAPTER FIVE, paragraphs five to seven, contains a discussion of equity as it applies to the Jews. In the *mos italicus,* equity was the most important qualitative measure used in legal interpretation;[1] it was the criterion for determining whether a law conformed to the ideal of justice. In the words of Baldus, natural justice, reason, and equity were identical.[2] Theoretically, all human law derived from natural justice by way of equity, and to be considered just and rational, a law had to embody equity.[3]

Equity fell into two classes, written and unwritten. Written equity referred to a law which had been redacted because previous laws covering a specific situation were considered too strict and in violation of reason and justice.[4] Unwritten equity referred to the extra-legal reason, based on the requirements of justice, which a judge applied in making a decision. According to Bartolomeo Sali-

---

1. For a full discussion of equity, see Piano-Mortari, *Ricerche,* pp. 17–37, and N. Horn, *Aequitas in den Lehren des Baldus* (Cologne, 1968), passim.
2. Baldus on D.2,12,5,12: "Naturalis justitia et aequitas idem sunt," cited in Ullmann, *Lucas de Penna,* pp. 41–43.
3. Piano-Mortari, *Ricerche,* pp. 17, 19, 22, 24, and 30; Calasso, *Medio Evo del diritto,* p. 480.
4. See Calasso, *Medio Evo,* p. 480, who states, with no citation: "[Written equity is a] ius scriptum quod contra rigorem verborum iuris stricti regulariter est introductum"; and Piano-Mortari, *Ricerche,* p. 20, where he cites B. Saliceto on *C. De legibus et constitutionibus principum, 1. inter aequitatem:* written equity "est bono publico introducta, et sic ad praecepta redacta."

ceto, unwritten equity was "Pars sapientiae, quae a domino deo est." [5]

In theory, a judge could apply unwritten equity only in *casus omissi,* that is, where there was no written law pertaining to the case before him. Beyond that, only those with legislative powers were allowed to invoke unwritten equity if they believed that the existing laws were too rigorous and aborted justice. On the other hand, if a decision could be rendered on the basis of two laws, and one of them alone was *aequitas scripta,* the judge was bound to decide according to the equitable law.[6]

The practical purpose of invoking either form of equity was to safeguard against purely literal interpretations of law and to deprive strict law of its rigidity.[7] Both canonists and legists invoked it. But the canonists, following Hostiensis' definition of equity, "iustitia dulcore misericordiae temperata," found cause to apply unwritten equity more frequently than did the legists, especially as the basis for dispensations.[8]

The question de Susannis felt bound to answer in II,5,5–7 was how the rules of equity apply to Jews. In their case, he says, *rigor iuris,* and not *aequitas,* is observed. This point is established by the gloss on the words *iuris severitate* in the title "De Iudaeis:" [9] "Iuris severitas sive rigor servandus est (apud Iudaeis), sed hoc est in odium illorum Iudaeorum." Thus, he continues, Jason de Mayno holds that since it is equity which defers the requirement of taking an oath as a supplement to other forms of proof, the Jews, among whom equity should not be observed, should never be released from this oath.[10] Similarly, Hippolytus de Marsilius says that a Jew can-

---

5. Piano-Mortari, *Ricerche,* p. 20.

6. Ibid., pp. 24–27; Ullmann, *Lucas de Penna,* p. 43; Calasso, *Medio Evo,* pp. 481–83.

7. Ullmann, *Lucas de Penna,* p. 43.

8. Lefebvre, *L'Age Classique,* pp. 410, 417–20; Calasso, *Medio Evo,* p. 483.

9. Gloss on X.5,6,2.

10. *Iasonis Mayni, In primam Digesti Veteris partem . . . Commentaria* (Venice, 1589) 2:fol. 91ᵛ *in repeti., ff. 12,2 de iureiur., 1. 31 admonendi v. 36, istud sacramentum.* Normally, de Susannis simply refers to the location of a legal text without supplying its contents. Where the contents appear, I have supplied them.

not purge himself by a demurrer (*mora purgare*), because demurrers are established by equity.[11] This claim is supported by Jason de Mayno, who says: "Iudaeus nunquam potest moram purgare, quia iudaeo non est servanda aequitas, sed rigor, ut glo." in X.5,6,2.[12] Felynus Sandeus, too, notes that although there are arguments to the contrary, and although it is impossible to come to a definite conclusion, it is more probable that a Jew may not purge himself by a demurrer, because demurrers are established by equity.[13]

On the other hand, says de Susannis in rebuttal to the foregoing, if anyone injures a Jewish adult, the Jew receives full restitution,[14] and such restitution is established by equity. On the basis of C.1,9,8, which stipulates that Jews are to use common law, moreover, it does not seem that differences in law can be erected between Jews and Christians unless such differences are explicitly established by law. It is, after all, precisely C,1,9,8, which Sandeus cites as his reason for hesitating in the matter of demurrers.[15] Furthermore, if Jews may use the harsh measure of prescription against Christians, why may they not use the fair and just rules of equity? As for Jason de Mayno's stricture that equity is observed to avoid loss of salvation through judgments of guilt, and thus, according to the rule of "equal proportion," [16] does not apply to Jews,[17] he is incorrect. "Equal proportion" refers only to laws which "simply and absolutely" cannot apply to Jews, namely, laws governing *spiritualia*. But the matter of a demurrer can apply equally to both Christians and Jews.

Whence, de Susannis concludes, the matter should be solved as follows.[18] When it is a matter of written equity, the Jews should

---

11. *Singularium* 41, *Iudaeus,* in *Singula Doctorum* (1579), fol. 347ᵛ.

12. Jason de Mayno, *Commentaria* (Venice, 1598), 6:104⁴, on D.45, 1,84,10.

13. Felynus Sandeus, *Commentaria in Decretales* (Venice, 1574), 3:col. 952, on X.5,6,2, col. fi.: "Multi sunt causus in iure in quibus prorecitur de aequitate, qui non extendent ad Iudaeos, per istam glo."

14. De Susannis cites Philippus Corneus, *Consilia* (1572), consilium 260, *ad fin. lib.* 3.

15. Sandeus, *Commentaria,* 3:col. 980, on X.5,6,5.

16. Cf. p. 109, supra.

17. Jason de Mayno, *Commentaria,* 6:104 ⁴, on D.45,1,84,10.

18. II,5,7: "Unde putarem posse sic distingui."

enjoy equity, since their litigations are decided according to *ius commune*. This is the opinion of Franciscus Ripa, who says that the Jews may enjoy the benefits of law, even of law which derives from equity, provided that the contrary is not explicitly stated by law.[19] But when it is a matter of unwritten equity, then the Jews may not benefit from it.

Essentially, then, de Susannis' solution binds the Jews to the rigor of the law. He exceeds the stringently literal interpretation of rigor argued by Jason de Mayno only insofar as he extends the term *rigor* to include even laws that derive from equity. The importance of this solution resides in the fact that, practically speaking, equity is synonymous with justice. By defining the status of the Jews vis-à-vis equity, de Susannis has, in effect, defined the nature of the Jews' justice. It is rigid and precise: they receive the benefits of law, even of written equity, but at the same time they are strictly bound by the law. Conversely, they may not benefit from exemptions attained through decisions based on unwritten equity. This conception is the basis for the crucial interpretations in *Pars Secunda,* chapter six.

This chapter is unique. It is the only one in which law is discussed explicitly as a direct extension of theology. Because the Jews had rejected Christ, to whom all power had been translated, they had forfeited the right to hold public office and to possess jurisdictions.[20] Specifically, Jews could not be judges in cases involving only Christians, and no Jewish tribunal could sit in judgment over a case which involved Christians and Jews.[21]

On these restrictions all lawyers agreed. Opinions differed, however, on the question of Jews judging cases in which both litigants were Jews. The accepted opinion, de Susannis says, commencing an exhaustive summary of the ideas advanced by numer-

---

19. Francisci Ripae, *In primam et secudam ff. Novi* (Venice, 1636), fol. 77v nn. 9–11, on D.45,1,84: "Judaeis non sit servanda aequitas, quia verum in casibus expressis . . ."

20. Cf. the summary of II,6,11–13 (supra, p. 112).

21. II,6,14. It would be impossible to discuss here the whole question of Jewish jurisdiction. For a survey of this question, see Colorni, *Legge ebraica,* pp. 305–65.

ous legists on this issue, is that of Bartolus, who holds that Jews must litigate before Christian judges, as the wording of C.1,9,8 determines.[22] However, Ioannes de Anania cites Florianus de Sancto Petro, who says that cases among Jews should be determined by Jews and never by others. Florianus bases his argument on C.1,9,14, which stipulates that cases between Jews and Christians are to be terminated by ordinary judges. He says that the implied converse (*a contrario sensu*) is that cases among Jews should be handled only by Jewish judges.[23] However, the argument *a contrario sensu* creates a contradiction between laws (*connexio legum*), because C.1,9,8 explicitly permits Jews to be judged by non-Jews. Furthermore, Florianus' interpretation cannot stand, for, according to C.1,9,17, Jews are not to have any administrators. As for *l. generaliter* (D.50,2,3,3),[24] which says that Jews are supposed to hold honors, and which could in theory be used to argue that they may have judges, when it is interpreted by its gloss in terms of C.1,9,17, it is clear that it does not refer to judgeships. And this gloss is upheld by the common opinion of the doctors. Finally, if one tried to argue that Jews can judge themselves on the basis of C.1,9,8 itself, because that law allows Jews to use Jewish arbiters, it must be said that arbiters are not ordinary judges, for arbiters possess no true jurisdictional authority.[25]

---

22. Bartolus, *Super prima parte Codicis secundum primam et secundam lecturam* (Venice, 1590), 7:25, on C.1,9,8: "Judaei habent ea quae sunt civium Romanorum, ut coram iudicibus Christianis debent litigare." The full text of C.1,9,8 is: "Iudaei Romano communi iure viventes in his causis, quae tam ad superstitionem eorum quam ad forum et leges ac iura pertinent, adeant sollemni more iudicia omnesque Romanis legibus conferant et excipiant actiones. Si qui vero ex his communi pactione ad similitudinem arbitrorum apud Iudaeos in civili dumtaxat negotio putaverint litigandum, sortiri eorum iudicium iure publico non vetentur, tamquam ex sententia cognitoris arbitri fuerint attributi." Krueger-Mommsen, *Corpus Iuris Civilis* (Berlin, 1906, 1906, 1928).

23. Ioannis de Anania *Com. Super V Libro Decretalium* (1504), fol. qIʳ, on X.5,6,16 *cum sit nimis*. The work of Florianus de Sancto Petro was unavailable for reference.

24. The text of ff. de decurio; *l. generaliter*, par. fi. (D.50,2,3,3): "Eos qui Iudaicam superstitionem sequuntur divi Severus et Antoninus honores adipisci permiserunt, sed et necessitatem eis imposuerunt qua superstitionem non laederent" (Krueger-Mommsen text).

25. II,6,14.

De Susannis had no difficulty here. Yet he considered the matter of jurisdiction so vital that he was prepared to expend a good deal of energy to refute any contention that Jews may function as ordinary judges. He clearly believed it essential that the reality fully correspond to the theoretical ideal of exclusion from offices. The strength of this belief is evident from his solution to the question of Jewish jurisdiction in cases involving only Jewish ritual.

The weight of authority, he admits, argues that ritual cases are to be ventilated before Jewish elders. Among others, both Bartolus[26] and Baldus[27] affirm that in cases which principally regard the superstition and faith of the Jews, Jews take cognizance. By medieval standards of legal interpretation, which venerated authority, an opinion shared by both Bartolus and Baldus should have been considered unassailable.[28] But—and precisely here he exposes his strong determination to keep practice consistent with theory—de Susannis objects. C.1,9,8, he says, states that Jews are to approach ordinary (Christian) judges "in his causis quae *tam* ad superstitionem eorum *quam* ad forum et leges ac iura pertinent." The construction *tam . . . quam* permits no other conclusion except that even in ritual cases Jews must approach Christian judges. "So I have decided" (*hoc decidi*).[29]

De Susannis is aware, however, that he is going against the force of tradition. Accordingly, in support of his conclusion he cites the commentary of Innocent IV on the canon *quod super* (X.3,34,8), and the concurring exegesis of that canon by Ioannes Andreas and Hostiensis.[30] These commentaries, he notes, state that

26. Bartolus, *Com. ad . . . Codicem* (Venice, 1590), 7:25r, on C.1,9,7: ". . . in causis quae spectant principaliter ad superstitionem et fidem eorum, ipsimet cognoscunt. . . ."

27. Baldus, *Consilia* (Venice, 1608), vol. 5, fols. 113–14, consilium 428, *Inquisitio dicta.:* "Causae enim iudaeorum quae respiciunt eorum ritus . . . debent coram eorum iudicibus tractari."

28. See Engelmann, *Widergeburt,* p. 238.

29. II,6,15–16.

30. Innocent IV, *Apparatus Quinque Librorum Decretalium* (Argentinae, Eggesteyn, 1478), on X.3,34,8. Hostiensis, *Lectura in Decretales Gregorii IX* (1581), 3:128v.

when a Jew commits heresy against his own law and morals, thus violating the law of the Old Testament, he is to be punished by the Church. Similarly, he continues, Vincent of Beauvais asserts that the Church was acting within the limits of its authority when it ordered the Talmud burned because of the heresies it contained.[31] And Paul (Acts 23 and 24) went before a Roman judge when he was accused by the Jews in matters of Jewish law. As for Bartolus, who declares that the construction *tam . . . quam,* in C.1,9,8, must be understood to give non-Jewish judges the ability to determine matters of Jewish ritual only when these matters are incidental to a case which is essentially a dispute in common law—he is not interpreting, but merely guessing.[32] As for Baldus, who said in his consilium 428 that Jews can have jurisdiction in cases of Jewish ritual because, according to C.1,9,2,9,14 and 17, they do have *proceres, maiores, et seniores*[33]—none of the offices he cites in support of his claim are defined as judgeships, nor do they grant the power of judging to their possessors.

Finally, *l. generaliter*—contrary to some interpretations—cannot support the contention that Jews may have Jewish judges for ritual cases, because that law refers to curial offices. That *l. generaliter* does not permit the Jews to hold judgeships is proved by C.1,9,17, which the gloss on *l. generaliter* cites[34] in order to assert that *l. generaliter* does not allow Jews to hold public offices such as judgeships. This fact is also proved by the comments of the doc-

---

31. Vincent of Beauvais, *Speculum Historiale,* bk. 6, chap. 28.

32. II,6,17: "Hoc est divinare ad illud tex." Bartolus, *Com. ad . . . Codicem,* 7:25ʳ, on C.1,9,8: "Intellige tunc quia ea quae pertinent ad superstitionem eorum veniebant examinanda incidenter. . . ."

33. Baldus, *Consilia,* Consilium 428: "Habent enim eorum proceres et maiores et seniores ut 1. nemo exterus (9), 1. si qua (14), et 1. iudaeorum (17), et 1. ii, in pri. C. (C.1,9)" There Baldus states that he is following Bartolus. And the laws Baldus cites do indeed concede these offices to Jews.

34. I have used the medieval number of the law from the *Code,* 17. In modern editions it is two laws, 18 and 19. The law prohibits Jews from all *administrationes* and *dignitates.* The gloss on *l. generaliter* is as de Susannis states: it cites C.1,9,17 as opposing *l. generaliter* and concludes that neither law allows Jews honors such as judgeships. However, the gloss does add that Jews may possess internal offices.

tors on the canon *cum sit*[35] (which forbids public offices to Jews),
where they refer to *l. generaliter* as not permitting judgeships to
Jews. And this fact is further proved by the gloss on *l. omnes,*[36]
which indicates that *l. generaliter* refers purely to curial offices.

Despite his contentions to the contrary, however, *l. generaliter*
really is highly problematic for de Susannis. According to him, the
text of this law reads as follows:

> Eos qui Iudaicam superstitionem sequuntur, divi Severus et Anton-
> inus honores adipisci permiserunt, sed et necessitatem eis im-
> posuerunt qui superstitionem eorum laederent.[37]

Thus, he says, when the Romans enacted *l. generaliter,* they intended
Jews to acquire only onerous offices, which would cause offense to
their rites, and which would prevent them from observing the rites
of Mosaic law. Beyond that, *l. generaliter* was established by the
Romans in scorn of the Jewish superstition.[38] The deprecatory remarks of Tacitus, Seneca, and Martial reveal both the scorn which
the Romans had for Judaism and the unequivocal presence of this
intention.[39] *l. generaliter* must therefore be understood as having
a destructive purpose—to turn Jews away from their superstition
and away from their ceremonies.[40]

There are modern commentators too who understand that

---

35. X.5,6,16.

36. C.10,31 *De decurio,* 49 *omnes,* which states that: "Omnes, qui quolibet
curiae iure debentur, cuiuscunque superstitionis sint, ad implenda munia teneantur."
Gloss: "Superstitionis—ut Iudaei, ut 1. gen."

37. Cf. n. 24, supra, for the modern text and note that de Susannis' last
phrase differs in that he omits the word *non.* This omission is the source of the
problem now to be discussed.

38. II,6,18: "Sed qui [honores] eorum ritus offenderent . . . ut Iudaeos
ipsos distraherent ab observationibus rituum legis Mosaicae et hoc in spretum
superstitionis eorum.

39. II,6,19. De Susannis also cites the famous remark of Augustus: "Se
malle esse porcum herodis, quam filium," because Herod did not eat the meat of
pigs.

40. II,6,19: "Unde in opprobrium eorum concedebantur illis immo cogebantur
ut dicit ille tex. ad assumenda officia onerosa per quae distraherentur ab eorum
superstitionibus et ceremoniis Mosaicis et legis veteris.

l. generaliter does nothing less than burden the Jews. This is the opinion of Jason de Mayno in his commentary on D,1,1,rubric.[41] And there Jason cites Bartolus on *l. omnes,* where Bartolus writes: the decurionate is a dignity, and Jews are regularly excluded from dignities; but this law *(omnes)* explicitly includes Jews. Therefore,

> Dico quod in quantum decurionatis non habet de honore, bene competit Iudaeis, sed in quantum habet honorem, dico quod non cadit in Iudaeis.[42]

Bartolus' comment is, of course, intended by both Jason and de Susannis to apply to the decurionate, which *l. generaliter* in actuality did impose on the Jews under the name of *honores.*

All this has been adduced to prepare the way for a discussion of this law as interpreted by Andreas Alciatus. Alciatus claimed that *l. generaliter* refers not to Jews but to Christians; and to support this claim he asserted that the traditional dating of the law was incorrect, and that its text should read "Divi Verus et Antoninus," and not "Divi Severus et Antoninus," as it does.[43] De Susannis rejects this emendation. The historical details on both sides are irrelevant. What is relevant is that Alciatus decided on this variant because his text of *l. generaliter,* as de Susannis notes with some fluster, reads: "Quae superstitionem eorum *non* laederent." [44] Because of this reading, Alciatus was perplexed. He could not understand why the Romans took such care to exempt Jews from duties which created

---

41. Jason de Mayno, *Commentaria, 1,2ʳ⁻ᵛ, in rub. ff. de iusti. et iure,* col 2, *v. secundo et fortius* (D.1,1,rubric). The topic of D.1,1 is the invocation of the divine name. Jason raises the question of such invocations on notarial acts drawn for Jews, which leads him into a discussion of Jews and dignities. He says they may not have dignities and cites *l. generaliter* and also Bartolus on *l. omnes.*

42. Bartolus, *Com. ad . . . Codicem,* 8:18ʳ, on C.10,31,49.

43. *Andreae Alciati . . . Operum* (Basle, 1582), 4:cols. 213–14, *Dispunctionum, lib. 3, chap.* 8. In the marginalia to the Paris 1550 and Lyons 1612 editions of the *Corpus Iuris Civilis,* Alciatus' interpretation is accepted. Commenting on the word, *Iudaicam* in *l. gen.* the marginalia state: "v. Iudaicam: his verbis Christiani intelliguntur, ut Alciatus, dispunctio 5 ca. 8 [*sic*]." Cf. n. 24, supra, where the modern edition accepts de Susannis' reading of "Divi Severus," although it includes the word *non.*

44. II,6,21.

ritual difficulties for them[45] (i.e., he shares many of de Susannis' assumptions), and he therefore felt compelled to suggest emending the names of the edicting emperors, thereby making it chronologically possible to reinterpret the law to apply to Christians.

Now, *l. generaliter* created many difficulties for de Susannis, because it said that Jews are to assume *honores*. Seemingly, it would have been easiest for him to have accepted Alciatus' conclusions. Yet while he does not reject Alciatus' reading and interpretation outright,[46] he is unwilling to rely on it. Indeed, to establish his own reading as the correct one is, for de Susannis, crucial. To that end he prefaced his citation of the text of *l. generaliter* with the statement: "cuius haec sunt verba formalia secundum impressionem meam." Nevertheless, the fact is that many editions of Roman law— Paris 1550, Lyons 1604, and Lyons 1612—all included the word *non*. The 1550 and 1612 editions even contain a marginal note referring the reader to Alciatus' interpretation.[47] Moreover, because the thirteenth-century gloss found in all these editions works on the assumption that the word *non* is part of the text,[48] it cannot be said that these editions changed their texts to conform with Alciatus' version.[49] What version of Roman law de Susannis was using must remain a mystery.[50]

De Susannis did, however, have cogent reasons for not simply accepting Alciatus' interpretation and for insisting on his own version of the text. Thus, not only did he stress the fact that his text did

---

45. Alciatus, loc. cit.

46. II,6,22. De Susannis does explicitly reject the historical interpretation. Yet he indicates that if the law is read including the word *non*, then it may possibly be understood to apply to Christians. But he then proceeds to argue for his reading without *non*.

47. Cf. nn. 24 and 43, supra.

48. Gloss on *l. generaliter*: "Nam si laederentur non cogitur id agere."

49. Apparently, Alciatus had an old MS of the *Digest* with many variants from the text accepted in his day. However, in the case of *l. gen.*, at least with respect to the inclusion of the word *non*, his text did not vary. See G. Barni, "Notizie del Giurista e Umanista Andrea Alciato, su manoscritti non glossati delle Pandette," *Bibliothèque d'Humanisme et Renaissance* 20 (1958): 25–35.

50. Indeed, one wonders how he expected legists to accept an argument based on this most irregular text.

not contain the word *non,* but after he raised the point that Alciatus' text says "non laederentur," he continued his refutation by reiterating that the text should be read affirmatively, and by citing two other texts which he interpreted to support his reading.[51] The first of these texts is *l. iussio* (C.1,9,4), which rescinded the immunities the Jews once enjoyed from curial offices, and whose gloss refers to *l. generaliter.* The second is *l. spadonem, iam autem,* which orders Jews to serve as tutors of non-Jews. It also says: "Constitutiones enim in iis solis sine molestia eos esse iubent per quae cultus inquinari videtur."[52] According to de Susannis, *cultus* refers to Judaism, and his understanding of the clause is that the Jews were to assume burdens through which their cult would be contaminated. This interpretation argues strongly for de Susannis' text of *l. generaliter.* However, the gloss on *l. spadonem,* interprets *cultus* as Christianity.[53] Accordingly, the text means that Jews were prohibited from assuming any office which would put them in a position to harm Christianity. That de Susannis chose to ignore this gloss emphasizes all the more that his goal was to establish his text of *l. generaliter.*

This adamance becomes intelligible when de Susannis' text of *l. generaliter* is read in the light of his comments on the intention of the Romans when they issued the law. He wants his readers to be perfectly clear that the Romans not only prohibited Jews from acquiring honors, but that they also used the law to seduce the Jews away from Judaism. The inclusion of the word *non* in the text of the law would have precluded his interpretation. Why he wants

---

51. II,6,22: "Praeterea et hoc magis movet me, est advertendum quod non est dictio aliqua negativa in mea impressione quam esse supponit Alciatus, 'Quae superstitionem eorum non laederent,' cum illa dictione, 'non,' quae non est in libro meo, sed legitur affirmative, ut, 'Quae superstitionem eorum laederent,' Contra [Alciatum] etiam urget tex. in 1. spadonem. . . ."

52. *ff. de excusa. tuto. 1. spandonem, par. iam autem* (D.27,1,15,6): "Iam autem et Iudaei non Iudaeorum tutores erunt sicut et reliqua administrabunt. Constitutiones enim in iis solis sine molestia eos esse iubent, per quae cultus inquinari videtur."

53. Gloss on par. *iam autem:* ". . . Inquinaretur: id est pollueretur cultus, ut missam vel aliud officium christianorum exercere; illud non est eis permittendum; Eos: s. Iudaeos."

to convince his readers that this interpretation is the correct one will soon become apparent.

To establish his text, de Susannis had digressed from his original point, which was to show that *l. generaliter* may not be used to prove that Jews may exercise jurisdiction in cases involving their own ritual. Therefore, to return to his original point, he concludes his digression abruptly by saying that whether or not Alciatus' reading is accepted, his (de Susannis') opinion about Jews exercising jurisdiction over ritual matters still holds. Even Bartolus' interpretation of *l. generaliter,* which states that Jews can have *honores . . . inter suos,* does not change the matter.[54] For no matter what the objection, the text of C.1,9,8, which holds that Jews may not exercise jurisdiction over matters which "tam ad superstitionem eorum quam ad forum et leges ac iure pertinent," simply does not allow the Jews to function as judges, ever.[55]

Perhaps de Susannis ended his arguments on *l. generaliter* with a refutation of Bartolus because Bartolus' assertion that Jews may exercise jurisdiction over internal ritual matters was the strongest obstacle de Susannis faced in establishing his interpretation. The weight of both accepted practice and authority lay on Bartolus' side.[56] De Susannis' case, moreover, rests almost entirely on his reading of C.1,9,8. None of his proof texts and no other commentator explicitly states that Jews may not exercise jurisdiction over internal ritual disputes. Why, then, is de Susannis so bent on his own interpretation, so bent on it that he defies all previous exegesis and custom?

The answer to this question emerges from the structure of the chapter. It begins by asserting the theological ideal of the exclusion of Jews from all jurisdictions and proceeds by demonstrating that the

---

54. *Bartoli a Saxoferrato Omnium Iuris Interpretum . . . Commentaria* (Venice, 1590), 6:222ʳ, on *l. generaliter,* par. *fi.* He says that this paragraph seems to indicate that Jews can possess honors among Christians. "Sed hodie dic contrarium. . . . [Jews cannot possess] honores inter nos, sed inter suos sic."
55. II,6,22.
56. On Bartolus' authority, see Engelmann, *Widergeburt,* p. 238; on the Jews actually exercising jurisdiction in internal disputes, see Colorni, *Legge ebraica,* pp. 305–65.

laws and their interpretations actualize this ideal—that is, with the exception of the practice of allowing Jews to have jurisdiction over internal ritual disputes. But de Susannis sees no reason to dispense from the *ratio* behind these laws and interpretations and to make an exception on the basis of interpretation alone in the matter of internal ritual disputes. In fact, his strongest argument in favor of his interpretation is that it conforms to the *ratio,* while interpretations to the contrary violate it.

De Susannis' motive for adhering to an interpretation which unconditionally denies Jews any form of jurisdiction is, however, more than a simple desire to keep specific laws and interpretations in consonance with theory. In the paragraph immediately following the conclusion of the discussion of *l. generaliter,* this motive is revealed. He has discovered, de Susannis states, that Rabbi Moses Egyptius (Maimonides) claims[57] that the heads of the exile in Babylonia hold offices (*locum tenentes*), are capable of ruling (*possunt dominari*) in any other land, and can judge all Jews, whether the Jews wish it or not. As it is written: "Non auferretur sceptrum de Iuda" (Gen. 49:10).[58] But, replies de Susannis, the evidence proves that Maimonides' assertion is false. If by Babylonia he means Egypt, as Strabo calls that land, he is talking about a land which is desolate and uninhabitable. If he means Babylon on the Euphrates, he is talking about a city subject to Suleiman, the emperor of the Turks. No Jew could rule there, just as no Jew may rule in any Turkish city. If for some reason he means Nineveh, that is not in Babylonia. In fact, if Maimonides speaks any truth, it is when he says that they *locum tenent;* that is, in confusion and servitude, just as in the etymology of the word *Babylon.*[59] Besides,

57. II,6,22. De Susannis: "libro de iudicibus, in determinationibus suis de Canedrin, c. 4." Cf. A. Poznanski, *Schiloh* (Leipzig, 1804), pp. 111–12, for Maimonides' discussion of Gen. 49:10 (*Mishneh Torah,* Book of Judges, Hilkhot Sanhedrin, chap. 4, Halakhah 13, 7a: A. Hershman, trans., *The Code of Maimonides,* 3:15), and Poznanski, *passim,* for an examination of the exegetical tradition of this verse.

58. II,6,22.

59. II,6,22: "Sed aliter dixit Rabi Moses, vere dixit, qui ipsi locum tenent [*sic;* intended to be a pun] in Babylon, videlicet, in confusione, et servitute, prout sonat ethimologia illius vocabuli Babylon."

according to their rabbis it is not, nor was it ever, permissible for any Jew outside the promised land to pass criminal judgments which decree capital or physical punishments. Therefore, if they do exist in Babylon, the exilarchs may judge only minor crimes, and they certainly do not possess the scepter. They are mere municipal magistrates, inferiors, with but a modicum of power. In addition, the Hebrew exegetes of Hosea 4: "Dies multos sedebunt filii Israel sine rege, etc.," interpret this verse to apply to the state of the Jews in their present captivity.[60] Thus, to have judges in Babylon would be contrary to the truth of this prophecy.

De Susannis' point—that Jewish exercise of jurisdiction would violate not only Hosea 4, but especially Genesis 49:10: "The scepter will not depart from Judah until Shiloh comes"—is the key to the entire chapter. Genesis 49:10 was perhaps the most crucial biblical verse employed in medieval Judaeo-Christian polemic. It overshadowed all others in frequency of use, and more often than not it formed the basis of the core argument around which the minor disputes of a given polemic pivoted.[61] The verse was employed throughout the Middle Ages so regularly, by both Jews and Christians, that Poznanski was able to fill five hundred pages with examples of its use. Thus, de Susannis' citation of the verse as it is found in Maimonides' writings is merely paradigmatic. He is contending not against Maimonides alone, but against the whole tradition of Jewish polemic, which claimed that the Christian exegesis of Genesis 49:10 was incorrect. Christians claimed that the verse referred to Christ (= "Shiloh"), and that its full meaning was that upon Christ's advent, all power was translated to him and from him to his followers. Those who rejected Christ lost all power. The veracity of this interpretation is proved by the Jews' loss of their Temple and their city and by their enduring exile. On the other hand, the Jews continually tried to prove that there were

---

60. Cf. this interpretation in Kimchi (explicit), or Ibn Ezra (implicit), whose commentaries are printed in the standard rabbinical Bible (Hebrew: Hos. 3:4). Cf. also M. Ficino, *Opera*, p. 32, where he cites Gen. 49:10 and Hos. 4 together; and also de Torres, *De Sola Lectione*, p. 10, where he says that Gen. 49:10 is the most famous of controversial verses.

61. See nn. 57 and 60, supra.

places where they did possess true ruling power, thus precluding the Christological interpretation.[62]

De Susannis' reference to Maimonides is not, moreover, the only place where he is writing with these ideas in mind. II, 6, 1–10, which discuss the Jews' loss of all power, is really devoted to expounding the traditional Christian exegesis of Genesis 49:10. In fact, de Susannis opens the discussion: "Et maximam illam et principaliorem dignitatem amiserunt, scilicet, sacerdotium et regnum spiritualem, Gen. 49" (II,6,2). Therefore, when he subsequently insists on precisely correlating the laws excluding the Jews from jurisdictions with the theory found in the opening paragraphs, his motive is to insure the actualization of the prophecy of Genesis 49:10. He is insisting that the real mirrors the ideal, and his attack on Maimonides' assertion makes this point clear. For there he is explicit: the Jews' loss of jurisdiction is in fulfillment of the prophecies of Hosea 4 and Genesis 49:10.

There is a second, and more crucial, issue here too. By insuring the actualization of the prophecy of Genesis 49:10, the laws and interpretations found in II,6 also function in support of the polemic based on that verse. Through the rigid application of these laws, the Jews can be shown that the prophecy of the loss of jurisdiction has been absolutely fulfilled. This, however, takes on extreme significance in the light of de Susannis' claim that in his day the Jews can "now see." By proving to the Jews that Genesis 49:10 has been fulfilled according to its Christological interpretation, the strictly enforced laws prohibiting jurisdiction will persuade the Jews to approach the baptismal font. In short, de Susannis assigns to law a conversionary function. But this is the exact function which he claimed the ancient Romans assigned to *l. generaliter*. His reason for insisting on his text of *l. generaliter* should thus be clear. With his text, he was able to demonstrate that the Romans understood that law can function as a means to separate Jews from Judaism. This is precisely the concept he now wants Christians to grasp too.

---

62. See Poznanski, *Schiloh*, pp. 137–54, 206–66, 302–449, and Blumenkranz, *Juifs et Chrétiens*, pp. 227–37.

In specifics, law can perform a conversionary function in three ways. First, the absolute exclusion of Jews from jurisdictions concretizes the nebulous condition of Jewish desolation and servitude, which the theoretical polemic traditionally referred to in order to prove that Genesis 49:10 had been fulfilled. Second, the concrete fact of the loss of power precludes any claims to the contrary. Finally, and most important from the standpoint of its effect on the Jews, real exclusion from jurisdictions of every kind is a daily reminder to the Jews that the prophecy of that exclusion has been fulfilled, according to its Christian interpretation. These ends are achieved, however, only if Jewry law is interpreted and applied both consistently with the theological principles underlying it and also without exemptions which vitiate these principles. But this is precisely the reverse of what jurists had traditionally done by allowing the Jews even a grain of internal jurisdiction. De Susannis thus strategically introduced his discussion of jurisdiction with a discussion of equity. For there he concluded that Jews are entitled to justice, but a justice which conforms to the rigor of the law. That jurists adopt this conclusion was absolutely vital. Otherwise they would miss the entire point of the subsequent discussion. And if they did not apply the laws of jurisdiction without exception, then the conversionary function of those laws would be thoroughly obscured.

To emphasize his belief that the laws excluding Jews from jurisdictions perform a conversionary function, de Susannis closes this long chapter with the following statement:

> From what has been discussed here [*ex praemissis*], it is evident that, since the Jews may not have jurisdictions nor exercise them, they will never again reign temporally in this world, just as they did in ancient times. Nevertheless, they will convert near the end of the world, and, as converts, they will be able to reign eternally in beatified life.[63]

---

63. II,6,28: Ex praemissis patet quod Iudaei, cum non possent habere jurisdictiones, nec eas exercere, nunquam regnabunt amplius in hoc mundo temporaliter, sicut antiquis temporibus faciebant, convertentur tamen prope mundi finem et conversi regnare poterunt aeternaliter in vita beata.

He then offers a number of prophecies which predict this ultimate mass conversion, and he concludes: "Tunc erit unum ovile unus pastor" (John 10:16).[64] The words *ex praemissis* must refer to the entire chapter. De Susannis is therefore reaffirming that it is not only theology, but law too, which conveys the message of Genesis 49:10—the Jews are being punished for rejecting Christ; they will reign only when they finally convert.

Nevertheless, while de Susannis clearly implied that law has a conversionary function, he never stated as much explicitly. Nor could he have. To persuade jurists to apply Jewry law as he had interpreted it, de Susannis had to convince them that his conclusions were based on specific laws and sound interpretations. Even his innovation about ritual jurisdictions was directly based on an explicit text. There was, however, no law which stated that law was to perform a conversionary function, nor did any law permit arriving at this conclusion by interpretation. And there was certainly no interpretive precedent on which to lean. In the legal discussion, therefore, de Susannis had to confine himself to implications. But in the sermon-polemic of III,1 he was free to state that he was summoning the Jews to convert. It was there—although again only by hints—that he could make his ideas about the conversionary function of Jewry law clear.

In paragraph 30 of III,1, which is the location of his explicit affirmation that the Second Coming and the conversion of the nations is at hand, de Susannis inserts a cross-reference to the final paragraph (#28) of II,6; and in both paragraphs he cites John 10:16—"At that time there will be one flock and one pastor." For de Susannis' readers who shared his belief about the imminence of the consummation—and as will be seen, such men were not few in number in the sixteenth century—this cross-reference was probably superfluous. By III,1 they were most likely aware of his claim about law. For other readers, the cross-reference was required to make de Susannis' intention unmistakable. They would return to II,6 and, in the light of III,1,30, be compelled to add the brief phrase "and that is now" to the citation there of John 10:16. They would then

---

64. II,6,28.

read paragraph 28 in reverse order as follows: The time ordained for the conversion of the Jews is the present. Their blindness has thus been removed so that they can now accept Christian teaching, and, in particular, so they can grasp that the prophecy of Genesis 49:10 has been fulfilled. Furthermore, de Susannis informs his readers here (par. 28) that *ex praemissis* the fulfillment of this prophecy is declared. From the context he must mean that the law teaches of this fulfillment. And by common and long-standing assent, the Jews' recognition of this fulfillment will prove a major catalyst in convincing them of Christian truth. Therefore, de Susannis is telling his readers that law, when it is applied so that it actualizes the claims of this prophecy, can perform a most significant conversionary function.

In case, however, his readers do not comprehend precisely how law can promote conversion by actualizing Genesis 49:10, de Susannis provides a second clue, this time in III,1,66. Here, at the end of his discussion of the punishments which have befallen the Jews, he proposes, through an analogy, that God has instituted punishments to terrify the Jews, to awaken them to their error of rejecting Christ, and thus to lead them to convert. The punishments de Susannis speaks of fall into the category of desolations. He says that the Jews should realize that their punishments are the punishments of God's enemies, thereby implying that they should recognize the causal relationship between their afflictions and their Jewishness. At this point, however, he does not state how the Jews are to recognize that they are being punished as the enemies of God. He does not do so, for he has, in fact, already shown how this recognition is to be achieved. That was in II, 6. There he also spoke of punishments which desolated the Jews, namely those punishments which, in fulfillment of Genesis 49:10, were concretized in the laws of exclusion from jurisdiction. Now by III,1,66 de Susannis' reader is quite aware that law has a conversionary function. He therefore understands that when in III,1,66 de Susannis speaks of punishments which will terrify the Jews into repentance, he is referring to those punishments which are effected by law.

Thus, for de Susannis law was a major tool with which to secure the conversion of the Jews. To establish this principle was de Susannis' prime reason for writing the *De Iudaeis*. It is a tract addressed to jurists, and de Susannis wanted to impress upon them their role in the conversion of the Jews, an event which he believed was finally both imminent and possible. He wanted them to apply Jewry law as he had interpreted it, so that Jewry law would fulfill its conversionary function.

To establish the principle of the conversionary function of Jewry law, de Susannis concentrated on the conversionary effect of the laws prohibiting Jews from jurisdictions. However, the scope of the *De Iudaeis* is all Jewry law. And as presented by de Susannis, Jewry law established the just status of the Jew as that of a tolerated dependent enemy. But this status was a concretization of the basic theological principles applied by the Church to the Jews, especially as typified by the prophecies of Jewish servitude. Therefore, following the paradigm of the laws of exclusion from jurisdictions, all of Jewry law, applied according to de Susannis' interpretation, can perform a conversionary function. Surely de Susannis must have hoped that once his readers had understood the conversionary function of the laws of jurisdictions, they would also discover that the rest of Jewry law has the same potential.

It is now possible to comprehend how the *De Iudaeis* is a key to the understanding of the program of Paul IV. In *Cum nimis* Paul IV reedicted a number of the long-standing Jewry canons. He declared that he was reedicting these canons for the purpose of making the Jews realize that the prophecies of Jewish servitude had indeed been fulfilled. He further implied that once the Jews had come to this realization, they would convert.[65] This estimate of the poten-

---

65. Bromato, *Vita di Paolo IV* (Ravenna, 1748), 2:228, indeed seems to have sensed that Paul IV's goal was conversion. Thus, Bromato says: "E a se stesso (*Cum nimis*) avrebbe servito di lume per conoscere meglio nell'umiliazione i proprii errori, e capire a tante marche servili messegli addosso da Paolo IV, ch'Egli era nato collo spirito di servitù . . . tale umiliazione potendogli acquistare quella libertà colla quale Cristo ci ha liberati." See also A. Caraccioli, *De Vita Pauli Quarti* (Cologne, 1612), p. 116, at Paul IV's funeral: "O quanto sublimiori atque universo orbi christiano utiliora consilia atque instituta in animo habebat?

tial function of Jewry law was precisely the estimate which de Susannis arrived at. While *Cum nimis* merely asserted that Jewry law could promote conversion, however, the *De Iudaeis* demonstrated in detail why Jewry law could do so. There is, moreover, evidence which indicates a direct link between the two documents: the dedication to Paul IV, and the license Paul IV issued sanctioning the publication of the *De Iudaeis*.[66] Thus there is every reason to assume that de Susannis wrote his tract as a complement to both Paul IV's program and his bull.

However, with the exception of the dedication and the reference to Paul IV's Talmud edict, specifically, and his other constitutions to curb the Jews, in general,[67] there is no mention of Paul IV or of *Cum nimis* in the tract. There are, in addition, certain regulations in *Cum nimis* which do not explicitly appear in the *De Iudaeis*. But these facts do not negate the assertion that the *De Iudaeis* complements *Cum nimis*. While all papal bulls have the force of law, only those bulls included in officially promulgated canonical collections are considered law in the technical sense of the term.[68] In order to convince jurists to apply his version of Jewry law, de Susannis had to base his conclusions entirely on officially recognized law or on commonly accepted legal opinion. Resting on papal edicts, which might be questioned,[69] would have vitiated his case. In addition, Paul IV's decrees applied only to the Papal States, and de Susannis wanted his version of Jewry law applied wherever *ius commune* was observed. Only in 1566 did Pius V make the decrees of *Cum nimis* universally binding.[70]

Because, therefore, he could not support conclusions by citing papal edicts, de Susannis was unable to refer specifically to ghettoes. He undoubtedly indicated his support of their establishment when

---

Namque nihil ferme aliud, noctesque diesque iam postremo praecipue meditabatur, nisi ut a nostra religione alienos ad verum Dei cultum induceret."

66. Cf. pp. 64–65, supra.
67. These references are found in III,1,49 (cf. supra, p. 140).
68. See Rambaud, *L'Age Classique*, pp. 133 ff., and also the bull of approbation to the "Editio Romana" in Friedberg, *Corpus Iuris*, 1:lxxxvi.
69. Cf. the consilium of Fulgosius, p. 93, n.70, supra.
70. See the bull *Romanus Pontifex* (Apr. 19, 1566) in *B.R.*, 7:438.

he stated that Christians should avoid all contacts with Jews, lest the principle of inferiority be violated.[71] Indeed, Paul IV himself had defended his ghetto edict on the grounds that the absence of ghettoes endangered Christian superiority. But no canon or law had ever formally ordered ghettoes erected.[72] Hence, rather than put his entire legal methodology in question, de Susannis had to omit a specific reference to ghettoes.

Again de Susannis was limited by the absence of an explicit law when he omitted mention of the prohibition on honorific titles in *Cum Nimis.* It was, however, almost unnecessary to list this prohibition. Interpretive authority was quite vocal in extending the laws of exclusion from jurisdictions to include such honors as the doctorate.[73] The distinction between that and honorific titles of any kind is minimal. As for de Susannis' omission of the prohibition on ownership of real property, it is more apparent than real. He in fact carefully noted that accepted precedent confers upon princes the prerogative of forbidding Jews to own real property.[74] He could go no further; but he had unquestionably buttressed the prohibition in *Cum nimis.*

There is, furthermore, a significant point of contact between *Cum nimis* and the *De Iudaeis* which argues strongly for the interrelationship of the two. In *Cum nimis* Paul IV did not prohibit usury, but carefully regulated it. Conversely, de Susannis at first unequivocally asserted that the law demands the outright prohibition

---

71. Cf. pp. 95f., supra.

72. There were, however, ghettoes established by local statute. See S. Simonsohn, "Ha-Geto be-Italiah U-Mishtaro," in *Baer Jubilee Volume* (Jerusalem, 1960), pp. 270–86, and pp. esp. 270–72 for a short summary of the attempted and actual establishment of ghettoes from the ninth through the eighteenth century. Simonsohn, p. 270, writes that the Third Lateran Council considered ghettoes. However, the canon (26) of that council which states: "Excommunicentur [Christiani] autem qui cum eis praesumpserint habitare," refers, when it is read in context, only to Christian servants of Jews. Canon 26 is the sole canon from that council which deals with Jews. *Conciliorum Oecumenicorum Decreta,* ed. J. Aberigo et al. (Basle, 1962), p. 200.

73. II,7,1 (supra, p. 113); and see Bartolus on *l. generaliter,* where he notes that a Jew cannot be a doctor. He does so again in his commentary on C.1,9,17.

74. Cf. p. 174, infra.

of usury.[75] Nevertheless, he followed this flat assertion with a complex argument to prove that the pope has the prerogative of effectively permitting usury. It is, therefore, difficult not to believe that de Susannis arrived at this tenuous conclusion only to avoid a contradiction between the tract and the bull.

Thus, significant evidence points to the complementary nature of *Cum nimis* and the *De Iudaeis*. Furthermore, it seems reasonable to claim that by writing a *summa* of Jewry law based solely on official law and accepted interpretation, de Susannis was furnishing Paul IV with the foundation on which to support the edicts of *Cum nimis*. In that case, it also seems most reasonable to claim that the *De Iudaeis* may be used as a key with which to understand the shift in papal Jewry policy that began with Paul IV.

Whether Paul IV, like de Susannis, was eschatologically motivated to seek the conversion of the Jews—that is a question which will be answered shortly. At the moment, the concluding chapters of the *De Iudaeis* demand attention.

75. Cf. p. 87, supra.

CHAPTER VIII

PARS TERTIA, CHAPTERS TWO TO NINE: THE LAWS OF THE CONVERT

A. *Summary*

"JUST AS THE HOLY CHURCH of Christ receives all infidels and permits them to live among the faithful with their persons and property," de Susannis begins, "so too, she accepts all who are willing to flock to baptism. . . . Indeed, if she saves the bodies of those who flee to her, how much the more must she save their souls. . . ." [1] These souls, moreover, must be received benevolently and with all love, since it is always assumed that conversion follows divine inspiration.[2]

Nevertheless, no Jew may receive baptism the minute he expresses his desire for it. He must first wait forty days, so that his will is made perfectly clear and there is no doubt that he is converting from sincere devotion (*recta devotione*). At one time, a waiting period of eight months was observed. There was also a time when the interval was only eleven days, but many Jews whose wait was so brief returned to Judaism soon after their baptism. In the case of most infidels this interim is used to instruct them. Jews do not need as much instruction; but they are delayed as long as other infidels out of reverence for the faith.[3]

---

1. III,2,1: "Sicut sancta ecclesia Christi recipit omnes infideles ut habitare possint inter eius fideles, cum personis, et rebus suis, ita etiam aperto, sicut suscipit omnes volentes ad baptismum convolare, et neminem reiicit cum consulat potius animabus quam corporibus. Nam si salvat corpora ad se confugientium, multo fortius debet salvare et animas, cum sint praeciosiores corporibus, et debent benigne et cum omni caritate recipi. . . ."
2. III,2,2: ". . . quia convertentes se ad fidem praesumuntur Deo inspiratione . . . et hoc semper praesumitur."
3. III,2,3.

Since baptism frees a convert only from his sins against God, and since one must become free of all sins at baptism, a convert must make amends for his sins against men. Hence, a Jew must make restitution of all usurious gains before baptism.[4]

No one should ever be forcibly baptized, that is, by the use of absolute force (*coactio praecisa*) when the baptized is completely passive (*pati quam agere*). In this case, baptism does not effect its indelible imprint. But if force is used, and no objection is raised over a long period, then the baptism is considered valid.

On the employment of monetary inducements to inspire men to seek conversion, opinions differ, but it seems that this blandishment is permitted.[5]

Once a person has accepted baptism, moreover, he may never revert to his old faith. He may even be corporally compelled to be an observant Christian. As for those who simulate conversion, let them beware, lest they bring destruction on both themselves and those who remain Jews. Was not such the case in Lisbon in the year 1506, when the discovery of sham Christians led to the death of 1,930 Jews?[6]

There are those who hold that Jews, who are *servi,* do not have their children in their power.[7] Therefore, they argue, secular princes, who are the lords of the Jews, may baptize Jewish children irrespective of the wishes of the parents, unless the lords do so to force the parents themselves to embrace Christianity.[8] But the common opinion, following Nicholas Tudeschi,[9] holds that Jews, strictly speaking,

---

4. III,2,4, and 11.

5. III,2,5. In 1,7,6, also, de Susannis says that monetary incentives are licit, but there he makes a simple affirmation with no hesitations as here. Cf. p. 85, supra.

6. III,2,5. See Baron, *SRH,* 13:46, on this massacre. Baron gives the figure 2,000.

7. Cf. p. 103 supra, where de Susannis affirms that Jews do have their children in their power.

8. III,2,6: "Quod cum Iudaei sint servi non habeant filios in potestate, et quod propterea principes saeculares eorum domini possunt pueros etiam invitis parentibus facere baptizare, si hoc non faciunt propter compellendos eorum parentes ad fidem."

9. III,2,6: Cum Iudaei stricte et proprie non sint servi et ab eis non possint coacta servitia exigi, et quia [by forcible conversion of children] eorum parentes indirecte cogerentur ad fidem suscipiendam." Cf. Nicolaus Tudeschis, *Panormitani*

are not *servi* from whom forced service may be exacted, and their children may, therefore, not be forcibly baptized. In addition, such baptism would indirectly force their parents to accept the faith.[10] The gloss on C.28,q.1,c.11 *iudaeorum,* moreover, states that neither adults nor children may be forcibly baptized. If they were, the Jews would quickly disappear—and the prophecy of Jeremiah, that a remnant of Israel will be saved, would never be verified.[11]

If a child is forcibly baptized, however, he should not be returned to his parents, *propter favorem fidei Christianae.* If he should be returned, the chance is strong that he would revert to Judaism.[12] Despite the use of force, moreover, the baptism is valid in this instance, and the child may not claim that he is not a Christian when he reaches puberty. This is not a case of *coactio praecisa,* when a person is bound hand and foot and continually protests, but of *vis conditionata,* when the baptized at some point either assents, or at least does not object. *Vis conditionata* always results in valid baptism.[13] In addition, if one parent converts, it is his right to demand the baptism of his children, irrespective of the desires of his spouse.[14]

If a Jew demands baptism, arrives at the font, and then reneges, IIII, 3 he is to be forced to accept baptism, lest there be contumely to the faith.[15] At the other extreme, if a Jew desires baptism and nobody is present to give him the sacrament, he may not baptize himself. The canons require that the baptizer and the baptized be separate

---

in Quartum et Quintum Decretalium Commentaria (Lyons, 1559), on X.5,6,9 *sicut,* par. 3, where it becomes apparent that de Susannis is practically repeating Nicholas' argument verbatim, including the statement on the nature of Jewish servitude.

10. Cf. I,14,1, p. 90, supra, where de Susannis simply affirms that the forced baptism of children is prohibited.

11. III,2,6: "Si hoc fieret in brevi nullus esset Iudaeus et non posset verificari illud Hieremiae quod reliquiae Israel salvae fierent."

12. III,2,6.

13. III,2,7.

14. III,2,10. See A. Milano, "L'Impari lotta," *La Rassegna Mensile di Israel* 16 (1950): 355–68, and Ch. Dejob, "Documents . . . du Cardinal Sirleto," *REJ* 9 (1884): 82–84, 85–88, where such cases are discussed, showing that de Susannis here reflected practice, at least the practice of the Roman *domus.*

15. III,3,1.

persons.[16] In time of necessity, however, a pagan may baptize, if he observes the proper form of the sacrament.[17] Yet a non-Christian may not serve as a godfather at a baptism or at a christening, nor may he act as a procurator and give the baptismal responses for another.[18] Finally, if for some reason a Jew desired baptism during his life but was unable to secure it, he is deemed baptized, and at his death he flies to heaven (*moriens volat ad patriam*).[19]

The man who simulates his desire for baptism and receives the sacrament for ulterior motives is compelled to live as a Christian.[20]

A convert is never required to relinquish property which is lawfully his—despite the belief of many simpletons to the contrary.[21] Even Jews normally have dominion over their lawfully gained property, unless the prince of the locality legislates to the contrary. How much the more so, then, do Jews who convert, and whose status is supposed to improve, retain dominion over their property.[22] For the same reason,[23] converts do not lose their right to inherit their parents' estates. Above and beyond that, since natural birth and spiritual regeneration are equated with each other, a Jew or infidel who converts acquires full civil rights in the city in which his conversion took place, just as anyone acquires these rights by birthright.[24]

---

16. III,3,2–4.
17. III,3,5.
18. III,3,5 and 9.
19. III,3,7.
20. III,3,8.
21. III,2,11: "Non tamen tenetur relinquere alia licita quaesita, sicut multi simplices credunt."
22. III,2,11: "Mutant enim statum in melius et habent dominium rerum suarum, et etiam existentes iudaei licita habent rerum dominia . . . nisi aliter sit statutum per Dominos locorum ubi degunt." Cf. p. 84, supra, on the background of this problem, and p. 192, infra, on confiscations of converts' property in the sixteenth century, which indicate continued violations of this rule. X.5,4,5, which outlaws confiscation of a convert's property, is also the source of the principle of improved status: "Si qui . . . ad fidem converterint . . . , a possessionibus suis nullatenus excludantur, quum melioris conditionis ad fidem conversos esse oporteat, quam, antequam fidem susceperint, habebantur."
23. III,2,12: "Cum non debeant esse deterioris conditionis conversi ad fidem quam erunt in Iudaismo."
24. III,2,13: "Et nota quod Iudaeus vel infidelis suscipiens baptismum in aliqua civitate efficitur civis illius civitatis, sicut quis efficitur civis ex causa

When his children convert and they require support, a father   III, 4
is legally bound to support them. He must also provide a dowry for
a converted daughter. Moreover, although a widow is normally not
responsible for her daughter's dowry, the widowed mother of a converted daughter must supply a dowry.[25] On the other hand, a Christian son is bound to support his indigent Jewish father, even though
the father may not live with him. As Hostiensis says: Even animals
provide for the needs of their own; how much more, then, are humans required to do so.[26]

Despite these obligations, a baptized son is freed from the
power of his father,[27] lest his status be practically that of a Jew's

---

originis. Cum generatio naturalis et regeneratio spiritualis aequiparentur." Since
the burden of *Pars II* is that Jews are *cives*, but with limited rights, *civis* here must
refer to a citizen possessing full rights.

25. III,4,1–3.

26. Hostiensis, *Summa Aurea* (1537), 33r, on X.1,11 *De temporibus ordina-
tionum et qualitate ordinandorum*, par. *et cui*, col. 5. *v. septima*.

27. III,4,9–11. Although he has already made it clear (II,1,10–11 and III,2,6)
that Jewish children are legally bound by the power of their fathers, at this
point de Susannis adds that many dispute this point on the grounds that since
their children are *servi*, Jewish fathers fall into the category of fathers of
slaves, who have no power over their children. To this de Susannis replies that
Jews are not really slaves who are bought and sold, but are a special class
of slaves, whose slavery is instituted by the canons. In support of this last
claim he cites many opinions, including that of Hostiensis on X.2,20,21, and he
further claims that his conclusion reflects the common opinion. He also refers to
his previous arguments in support of this conclusion found in III,2,6. However,
de Susannis never denies, despite his clear statement about their "special servitude,"
that the Jews are the slaves of princes. He denies only that they are true slaves
in the strict sense of the term. So too, Thomas, in *Summa Theologica*, II,II,10,11
states explicitly that Jews are the slaves of princes. Thus it seems that medieval
lawyers, and probably theologians too, saw the servitude of the Jews both as
servitude to princes and as a special class of servitude established by the canons.
This notion of dual servitude must be fully examined if the concept of "Jewish
serfdom" is ever to be completely understood. Cf. S. W. Baron, "Plenitude of
Apostolic Powers and Medieval Jewish Serfdom" (Hebrew), in *Sefer Yovel
le-Yitzchak Baer* (Jerusalem, 1960); idem, "Medieval Nationalism and Jewish
Serfdom," in *Studies . . . A. A. Neumann*, pp. 19–48; G. Langmuir, " 'Iudei nostri'
and the Beginning of Capetian Legislation," *Traditio* 16 (1960): 201–40; and
idem, "The Jews and the Archives of Angevin England: Reflections on Medieval
Anti-Semitism," *Traditio* 19 (1963): 183–244.

slave. Beside, the son becomes a "new man" at baptism.[28] To free the converted son entirely from his father's power, however, would cause him to suffer loss under the commonly found local statute which orders the fisc to confiscate the property of a man who dies with no children in his power. Therefore, to preclude such disadvantages, a converted son is considered to be in the power of his father in the matter of legacies.[29]

III, 5   The privileges a convert gains are not, however, unlimited. He is not, as some would have it, freed from his responsibility to pay the penalty for crimes he committed before baptism. Baptism frees a man only from his sins against God, not from his sins against the republic. If baptism offered automatic exemption from penalties, moreover, many would convert simply to escape punishment.[30] For the same reasons, conversion offers no release from civil suits or from the obligation to return illicit gains.[31]

III, 6   Yet the convert is freed from the limitations imposed on Jews. He becomes eligible for the priesthood and for all public offices, including kingship, and he is free to serve as a witness at any time, unless he judaizes.[32] A woman convert benefits in all ways from the privilege of tacit hypothecation. As a Jew she enjoyed this privilege only in the case of her dowry.[33] A convert also acquires the unique privilege of receiving his inheritance while his father is still alive. This privilege runs counter to *ius commune,* which prohibits the acquisition of legacies from living persons.[34] And many believe that it is unlawful to place this burden on a Jewish father who enjoys

---

28. III,4,8: "Per baptismum quis efficitur novus homo . . . Ita in Iudaeo dicendum est, cum ad fidem convertitur et transit de terrenis ad celestia, et potitur dignitate sacerdotali et diademate regni."

29. III,4,12.

30. III,5,1.

31. III,5,6.

32. III,6,1, and III,4,8: "Ita in Iudaeo dicendum est, cum ad fidem convertitur et transit de terrenis ad celestia, et potitur dignitate sacerdotali et diademate regni." This statement on freedom from the limitations imposed on Jews suggests that converts in Italy were facing the same difficulties confronted by *conversos* in Spain. Cf. p. 180, infra.

33. III,6,2.

34. III,6,3. D.5,2,3,4.

the benefits of *ius commune*. But the canons[35] require that a convert's material status must improve. Therefore, it seems more true and safer (*tutior et verior*) to award this privilege to converts. In addition, this privilege is granted in favor of the Christian religion, for whose sake many concessions are made.[36]

In ancient times, when only one of two spouses converted, it   III, 7
was not overly optimistic to hope that the infidel spouse would soon convert himself. Such a couple was therefore permitted to live together, although they were not forced to do so. Yet contemporary infidels, especially Jews, rarely follow their spouses into Christianity. And although the old law has never been changed, today a couple with one converted spouse is not allowed to remain together. Such a marriage should, in fact, be dissolved, because cohabitation between its spouses invariably leads to contumely to the faith, blasphemy, and mortal sin.[37]

If the convert is the wife, the dissolution of such a marriage   III, 8
raises the significant question of whether she may regain her dowry and keep possession of it. Because the civil law permits a divorced Jewess to regain her dowry, and because the canons require that a convert may not be pauperized, as she would be if she left the marriage without her dowry, the common opinion answers this question affirmatively. The real difficulty, however, is not whether she may keep the dowry, but whether she may do so if the dowry was originally constituted from usuriously acquired property. Sentiment favors retention, and there are many attempts to explain away the predicament. Some say there is no reason to suspect that the dowry is a product of usury. Others maintain that irrespective of its origins, equity prescribes that the woman may hold onto the dowry to prevent her death from starvation. Still others claim that if the dowry came from usury which was practiced under a permit, then the usury, and hence the dowry, is not subject to restitution. Finally, there are those who say that if as a Jewess she could have a dowry

---

35. X.5,6,5.
36. III,6,3. This is an excellent example of the principle that secular laws are limited in the face of canons to the contrary. See supra, p. 77.
37. III,7,1.

constituted from usury, she should not lose this privilege if she converts.

But the true and common opinion is that she cannot retain such a dowry, because there are never exemptions from the rule which requires converts to make restitution of usury. Even the sustenance, inheritance, and dowry, which the law requires the parents of a converted daughter to furnish, must never be constituted from the products of usury.[38]

There is, nevertheless, a way for this woman to retain her dowry, or at least most of it. If she knows the persons who paid the usuries which constitute the dowry, she makes restitution to them. If not, she hands over the dowry—or what remains of it, if she knows some of the persons—to the bishop. At their discretion, bishops have the right to distribute such donations to unfortunate persons (*personae miserabiles*). But since this woman has given away her dowry, she herself has become a *persona miserabilis*.[39] Therefore, the bishop should distribute the dowry money to her.[40]

III, 9   A converted couple may remain together if they are related within the prohibited grades of consanguinity, provided that they are not related within the grades prohibited by divine law.[41] If a convert has more than one wife, however, he is forced to dissolve all but one marriage.[42] On the other hand, if a convert leaves his spouse for good reason, he may take another only with the approval of a bishop.[43]

"Finally I ask" (*quaero ultimo*), interjects de Susannis in a sweeping change of topic, how may the assertion that the Church receives all Jews and rejects none,[44] be reconciled with the laws which exclude Jews from church buildings? The answer is that the laws exclude Jews from churches only as long as they persist in their infidelity. Thus, when the divine office is celebrated, Jews are barred

---

38. III,8,1.

39. In his *Apparatus,* on X.5,6,5, Innocent IV notes that all converts are automatically considered *miserabiles personas.*

40. III,8,2.

41. III,9,1.

42. III,9,2.

43. III,9,3.

44. III,2,1.

The Laws of the Convert

from the Temple of God. Even the bodies in a Jewish cemetery must be exhumed (*iactari foras*) before a church may be erected on that spot.[45] But if a Jew wishes baptism, he is never ostracized. Indeed, Jews are to be invited into churches to hear the word of God preached. A bishop must never prevent them from entering a church for this purpose.[46]

Then de Susannis abruptly switches back to the principal subject of the chapter and, with one last interpretation, ends the tract. If a Jewess, he states, who lost her dowry when her husband converted and only later converted herself, seeks to rejoin her husband, and if, on his part, he wishes to take her back—provided there is no problem of consanguinity, and provided he has not remarried in the interim—then, with the marriage approved and ratified by the Church, she regains her dowry and all its attendant privileges.[47]

B. *Analysis*

Two conjoint principles determine the status of the convert. First, he is a new man,[48] whose past is erased and who is treated on a par with Christians, and second, his material status must improve.[49] For de Susannis these principles, and the laws which implement them, are as important for promoting conversion as the laws which apply to the Jew who has not converted. They serve as a balance to the laws which degrade the unconverted Jew, proving to him that his wretched state will continue only as long as he adheres to his faith. But, as de Susannis indicates, the application of the laws pertaining to converts, especially those ameliorating their condition, had been lax. Confiscation of a convert's property, for instance, was an old offense.[50] In addition, de Susannis' stress on the canon stating

---

45. D.21,c.1 states that infidels are to be kept from entering church buildings. C.24,q.2,c.1 and D.1,c.28, *de cons.* establish respectively that no infidel may be buried in church grounds and that the bodies of infidels must be exhumed before a church built over an infidel cemetery may be consecrated.

46. III,9,4.

47. III,9,5.

48. See p. 176, supra.

49. See p. 177, supra.

50. III,2,11–13, supra, p. 174.

that a convert becomes a "new man" and his repetition of the canon declaring converts eligible for the priesthood and the witness stand[51] suggest that some of the anti-*converso* spirit which had erupted in Spain had also appeared in Italy.[52] Both offenses negated the conversionary function of convert law. Hence, de Susannis discusses these laws after the polemic-sermon of III,1 in the hope that once it has aroused jurists to diligence in the proper application of Jewry law, it will also prepare them to grasp the importance of the laws of the convert and, accordingly, to apply them with equal zeal.

III, 2   III,2 opens with the declaration that as much as the Church is ready to protect those infidels who desire to live in Christian lands, it is more prepared to protect (i.e., save) their souls. This declaration affirms that the real interest of the Church in its policy toward infidels is the achievement of their sincere conversion. It also implies that the laws to follow reflect that interest.

Hence, with the exception of the principle of conversion through indirect force[53] and the requirement that any properly baptized per-

---

51. III,4,8 and III,6,1, supra pp. 176f.

52. On the anti-*converso* sentiment and the veritable war between Old and New Christian in mid-fifteenth-century Spain, see Y. F. Baer, *A History of the Jews in Christian Spain* (Philadelphia, 1966), 2:277–83, 300–309; and on the anti-*converso* regulations, including prohibitions on New Christians serving as witnesses against Christians, see ibid., 2:102, 125, and 379 f. See also A. A. Sicroff, *Les Controverses des Statuts de "Pureté de Sang" en Espagne de XVe au XVIIe Siècle* (Paris, 1960), pp. 41–55, on the *Defensorium Unitatis Christianae* (1449) of the jurist, bishop of Burgos, and son of the convert Paul of Burgos, Alonso de Cartagena, which became the defense manual of the conversos (p. 41). Of note is the argument (*Defensorium*, pp. 224–40) against one Marquillos of Toledo, who had attempted to support anti-*converso* legislation on the basis of C.17,q.4,c.31 ("iudei aut hi qui ex iudaeis sint officia publica nullatenus appetant . . ."), originally a product of the Fourth Toledan Council. Alonso retorted that the text refers only to those who practice Jewish rites, and he adduced the interpretation of c.31 by Guido de Baysio, which states that Jews are only those who, irrespective of descent, practice Jewish rites (Sicroff, pp. 54–55). The presence of anti-*converso* sentiment in Italy is suggested by Gregory XIII's bull *Antiqua* (cf. pp. 33f., supra), and by the fact that the controversy which erupted among the Jesuits about excluding those of *converso* descent from membership took place in Italy. See Baron, *SRH,* 14:10–17, and esp. p. 14, and Tacchi-Venturi, *Storia della Compagnia di Jesu,* II 1, pp. 99–100.

53. See p. 173, supra.

son must remain a Christian,[54] the law demands that only those who truly believe in Christ may be baptized.[55] Exceptions to the requirement of genuine belief are made only *ad favorem fidei.* This phrase is roughly equivalent to the phrase found in I,3, *ad honorem et decorem fidei,* which means that exceptions are allowed only to prevent the violation of the sacrosanct principle of the honor of the faith. This insistence on true willingness is explained in the discussion of the forced baptism of children.[56] The statement that such forced baptism would prevent the fulfillment of the prophecies of the saved remnant indicates that the goal of converting the Jews does not exist simply for the sake of eliminating them, but to hasten the advent of the consummation. Since that event is contingent on the true belief of all men in Christ, forced baptism is useless.[57]

Once a Jew has sincerely converted, his status must improve; III, 2,11-13 he must become *melioris conditionis.*[58] Not only may he lose none of the rights and privileges he had as a Jew, but he also gains those III, 4 & 6 which were explicitly denied to him.[59] So strong is this principle of *melior conditio* that it permits the violation of the law which prohibits sons from inheriting while their fathers are still alive.[60] In other words, the convert's status becomes the precise opposite of the status of the Jew.

Because they effect this radical change, these laws acquire a conversionary function and thus complement the laws which make the Jew a *servus.* Those laws prove to the Jew that his Jewishness is the cause of his afflictions. These laws prove to the Jew that once he quits Judaism, his afflictions cease; he becomes free. De Susannis makes no attempt to assert this conclusion. It is obvious to anyone

---

54. See p. 172, supra.

55. pp. 171f., supra.

56. Cf. p. 173, supra; and G. Kisch, *Zasius und Reuchlin* (Stuttgart, 1961), passim, for a full discussion of this problem.

57. Of course, these canons were edicted with no particular reference to the imminence of the consummation. Yet whether or not the consummation is imminent, the argument against forced baptism on the grounds that true conversion is required for the eventuality of the consummation still applies.

58. X.5,6,5.

59. See pp. 174–77, supra.

60. See p. 176, supra.

who has accepted his previous arguments about the conversionary function of law.

III, 5   Even so, the conversionary function of these laws is brought out in various ways, such as in the presentation of the laws which prohibit the cancellation of the criminal and civil liabilities a Jew may have incurred prior to his conversion.[61] As arbitrary treatment would prevent Jews from seeing that they are punished in accordance with the prophecies of punishment for those who reject Christ, so arbitrary treatment here (i.e., the granting of license) would prevent Jews from seeing that it is precisely from those same punishments that conversion will free them.

It is, in fact, to reiterate his postulate, that Jewry law can perform its conversionary function only through its rigorous but just application, that de Susannis dwells at length on the problem of allowing a converted Jewess to retain her usuriously constituted dowry and then accepts the solution of declaring her a *miserabilis persona.*[62] This solution permits her to keep the dowry without violating either the principle of *melior conditio* or the principle of restitution of usury at the time of conversion. Had de Susannis accepted a solution which violated either principle he would have completely destroyed his postulate about the nature and the method of application of Jewry law. Had he allowed an exception, all that had gone before would have been worthless.

III, 9   Thus the law of the convert operates on the same principles as does Jewry law for the Jew. In III,9 these principles are recapitulated. In the middle of a straightforward description of the laws which prescribe the steps which have to be taken to establish canonical marriages for converted infidels who, as infidels, had contracted uncanonical marriages, de Susannis suddenly interjects a different subject. This is the only such interjection in the entire tract, and de Susannis must have made it to get his readers' attention.

By asking how his statement that the Church receives all Jews may be reconciled with the laws which exclude Jews from church

---

61. See pp. 176f., supra.
62. See pp. 177–78, supra.

buildings,[63] de Susannis is challenging his entire thesis and asking whether it is really true that the function of Jewry law is to promote conversion. By replying that as infidels Jews are to be excluded from churches, but if they desire to convert or to hear the Gospel preached, the laws declare that they are not only to be admitted but must also never be excluded, his thesis is reaffirmed. The Jew who insists on remaining a Jew is to be restricted, but all the while the law beckons him to convert and to enter the church.

---

63. See pp. 178–79, supra.

CHAPTER IX

THE *DE IUDAEIS* AS AN IDEAL

UNDERLYING THE ANALYSIS OF the *De Iudaeis* has been the assumption that the tract was proposing an ideal system of Jewry law, one which conformed to the letter of the laws and the canons but which differed from Jewry law as applied in its day. Internal evidence has so far borne out this assumption. De Susannis is unique in arguing against Jewish jurisdiction in cases involving only Jewish ritual, and he states rather strongly that jurists were not following the principle of *melior conditio* in the case of converts. External evidence too validates this assumption, as will be seen momentarily. Proving that the system of Jewry law proposed by the *De Iudaeis* was an ideal is most important. Were it not an ideal, there would be no grounds for claiming that de Susannis' purpose in writing the tract was to urge jurists to apply Jewry law in a way in which it had not been applied, so that it could fulfill a conversionary function. There would also be no way of claiming that the tract is a key to understanding Paul IV's Jewry policy, which itself was based on the application of an ideal system of Jewry law.

Before 1555, even in the Papal States, there were violations of Jewry law as the *De Iudaeis* proposed it. In the late 1530s Cardinal Sadoleto complained loudly that the Jews in the French papal possessions had been given privileges which permitted them to dominate Christians.[1] The accuracy of this complaint should not be doubted. Earlier in the century, Alexander VI had given Bonetto de Lattes the

---

1. L. Erler, "Die Juden des Mittelalters," *AKKR,* 53 (1885): 39–41.

authority to hold court and to adjudicate legal disputes among Jews according to Jewish law,[2] and later on, Paul III appointed Jacob Mantino professor of medicine in the University of Rome.[3]

With the issuance of *Cum nimis* all this changed. The situation in Rome became, as it were, the model, and de Susannis hoped it would receive universal application through the princely establishment and judicial enforcement of those norms of the *De Iudaeis* which reproduced the decrees of *Cum nimis* through legal exegesis. By October 1555, barely three months after *Cum nimis* had appeared, nearly every one of its edicts had been put into effect. Even the walls of the Roman ghetto had been completed.[4] Various attempts were made by the Roman Jews over the next fifty years to have the enclosed area enlarged, but they met with only small success. Nor did any pope during this time ever waiver on the fundamental issue of the existence of the ghetto. By the start of the seventeenth century, Roman Jewry had become thoroughly convinced of its inexorable plight: to live tightly packed, thirty-five hundred people within an area of seven and one-half acres, inside a five-gated wall, which was locked from dusk to dawn.[5] Even during the day only certain Jews were given permits to do business outside the ghetto. Most were slowly strangled economically, so that, whereas in the early sixteenth century it was possible to speak of Jews ranging all along the economic scale, by the early seventeenth century there were no

---

2. Vogelstein, *Rome,* p. 243.

3. Ibid., p. 250; cf. p. 113, n. 68, supra, for additional information on Jews in universities with doctorates.

4. The following brief survey is based on materials drawn from the extensive study of Attilio Milano, *Il Ghetto di Roma* (Rome, 1964). Since the present study has no pretensions of being a complete political examination of the course of events in Italy in the later sixteenth century, only certain matters, which illustrate the point of the immediate discussion, have been chosen for presentation here. In any case, for a political history, Milano's work more than suffices. On the erection of the ghetto walls, see Milano, pp. 188 f; and pp. 74 ff. for the rapid institution of the edicts of *Cum nimis* in general.

5. On the size of the ghetto, see Milano, pp. 189–91; and on the generally tighter enforcement of regulations and the downhill slide of the Roman Jewish community, see pp. 85 ff.

upper-class but only a few middle-class and mostly lower-class Jews.[6] Economic weakness was further insured by the exorbitant taxation leveled by the papacy.[7] The prohibition on the ownership of private property even within the ghetto was also stringently enforced. Indeed, this property was itself initially liquidated in 1555 at a great loss to its owners, who received for it far less than its actual estimated worth.[8] This situation, along with all the other debilitating regulations and conditions, would pertain until the mid-nineteenth century (1858–70) and the destruction of the ghetto walls. In the papal possessions outside Rome, the simple facts of lower Jewish population density and the lessened official scrutiny of Jewish behavior allowed for some degree of evasion of the papal edicts. But these evasions were to be *ipso facto* halted in 1593, when Clement VIII once and for all restricted Jewish residence in the Papal States to Rome, Ancona, and Avignon (and then Ferrara, when it became a papal possession in 1597).

Culturally, too, the Jews of Rome were seriously weakened, first by the loss of the Talmud and other rabbinic literature, which, despite many dealings with the popes of the later sixteenth century, they never really did manage to recover, and second, by the reduction in the number of structures permitted for religious and educational use. Before 1555 there were nine congregations, each in its own building. Afterward, while the individual congregations remained, they were all compelled to occupy a single common structure.[9] Not surprisingly, there were but one or two rabbis of some true ability and knowledge in the course of the three-hundred-year existence of the ghetto. Apart from that, the general level of Judaic studies was quite low. Equally, the secular studies so avidly pursued

6. On communal wealth, see Milano, pp. 155–74, 177–83, and esp. p. 182 on the changes in wealth over the years; and see pp. 81–85 on the decline in Jewish banking.

7. For more details, see immediately infra, pp. 187f.

8. Milano, p. 188; see also pp. 199 f. on the *ius gazagà*, the law, allowed as a papal concession, which prohibited the new Christian owners of ghetto housing from raising rents and strangling the Jewish inhabitants, who would have had no recourse but to pay the increases.

9. On synagogues, see Milano, pp. 209–34, and esp. pp. 217–18.

prior to 1555 not only ceased for the most part afterward, but they were explicitly eschewed and denounced as pernicious to continued Jewish well-being.[10]

The Roman Jews were further pressed by three hundred years of continuous forced attendance at conversionary sermons[11] and by the financial exactions for the upkeep of the *Domus catechumenorum*. These exactions may themselves have been in large measure a prime cause of the economic erosion of the community, if not directly of conversions too. Nearly one-third of all taxes and payments made by the community to the Apostolic Camera and the Roman Civic Camera in the period 1555–1778 went specifically for the upkeep of the *domus* and its associated institutions. Roughly thirty percent of all payments for conversionary projects, moreover, were made between 1555 and 1604. Thus, it seems that the papacy of the later sixteenth century was literally trying to convince the Jews that it simply did not pay not to convert—a tactic which clearly met with some success.[12] Even after 1604, payments to the *domus* formed twenty percent of all communal expenses beyond those for debt service. Debt service itself formed two-thirds of communal expenses. Indeed, the communal debt mounted to the point that by 1717 the total debt equaled nearly twenty-eight times the average annual communal income.[13]

A more biting conversionary pressure was applied through the actions of the *domus*. From 1555 to 1600, only about twenty Jews on the average actually converted annually,[14] and afterward the figure fell to only ten. But whether the conversion came about by choice

---

10. On Jewish learning, see Milano, pp. 385–96, and esp. p. 389, where he speaks of the growing cultural sterility in all areas.

11. On these sermons, see Milano, pp. 269–82.

12. On finances in general, see Milano, pp. 129–54, and pp. 145–50 for complete tables of taxation and income. The figures cited here are found on pp. 148–49.

13. For these figures, see Milano, pp. 145 and 149.

14. This figure, as presented here, seems deceptively low. Multiplied out, it comes to eight hundred in forty years, out of an average population of thirty-five hundred—a sizable proportion. The question at issue here, however, is one of the immediate effects of individual conversions. Therefore, the deceptive figure of "only twenty a year" is more appropriate.

or by various pressures (to the exclusion of real force), the effects
of a conversion could be most threatening to the family and ac-
qaintances of the new convert. Any suggestion the convert made,
whether intentional or not, to the rectors of the *domus* that an ac-
quaintance had expressed a desire to convert would result immediately in the virtual arrest of that person. He would be taken into
the *domus,* and only with the greatest of efforts could he hope to
emerge still a Jew. The record of the legal battles of the Roman
Jewish community to extricate persons of all ages so ensnared is
both long and unsuccessful.[15] In addition, while the actual number
of converts, as just recorded, may appear low, given the small size
of the Roman Jewish community, as well as the fact that conversions
were indeed occurring with a constant regularity, the Jews, witness-
ing this trend, must have felt at once threatened and impelled themselves to go over to Christianity. If one is permitted to gauge by
opposites, then the satisfaction expressed by both Paul IV and Pius V
when they issued letters mandating the expansion of facilities for the
growing number of converts[16] may be taken as a measure of the
frustration and despair felt by the Jews.

In the territory under direct papal authority, then, the program
of Paul IV was put into effect, to stay in effect with hardly any mitiga-
tion for over three hundred years. Perhaps most interesting, when
looking at the practicalia of this program in the light of the *De
Iudaeis,* which was composed in the years immediately after its
inception, is the question of the jurisdictional authority of the Roman
community. Not only were the Jews denied all criminal and civil
jurisdiction, but even in those areas where rabbinic tribunals were
allowed to function, namely, family law and administrative matters
of the community, these tribunals by no means enjoyed actual juris-

---

15. On conversionary activities, and esp. on the struggle of the Jews with
the *domus,* see Milano, pp. 283–306.

16. *Copie delle Bolle, Cum sicut accepimus,* Paul IV, Nov. 18, 1556: "Nos
pro inde considerantes numerum cathecumenorum in Alma Urbe nostra divina
id efficiente gratia in dies magis, ac magis augeri, et propterea eorum necessitatibus
in aliquo subvenire . . ."; *Sacro. Cath. Eccl.,* Pius V, Nov. 29, 1566: We have
ever labored for conversion, "neque omnes irriti Dei benignitate labores nostri
fuerunt quando et satis multi" have converted, some even at our own hands.

diction. Rather, as voluntary arbiters without jurisdiction, the tribunals could act only if the defendants jointly agreed to approach them.[17] This is exactly the judicial structure which de Susannis uniquely argued for with such great efforts.

This structure, however, as well as the other restrictions just discussed, did not, to repeat, exist even in the Papal States prior to 1555. So too they did not exist elsewhere. Nor were they established elsewhere in the period shortly after the appearance of *Cum nimis*. At Florence, in 1555, Cosimo de Medici refused to implement a number of the restrictions found in *Cum nimis*. Although the bull technically affected only the Jews of the Papal States, Cosimo had apparently been pressured, unsuccessfully, to implement it in Tuscany. In particular, he did not require Tuscan Jews to wear any form of distinctive dress.[18] Only when he needed the help of Pius V in order to secure the ducal title did he capitulate to papal demands and institute restrictive laws.[19] At Milan the papacy had similar problems. The city put up a protracted resistance before it finally acceded to the inquisitional order to burn the Talmud.[20]

In many other cities there was considerable inconsistency in practice. Laws would be edicted in one year and rescinded in the next. Venice, in particular, based its Jewry regulations primarily on its own priorities.[21] In Urbino, in 1507, the establishment of the della Rovere as dukes meant the cancellation of old privileges, including, notably, those allowing the establishment of Jewish banks and the ownership of real estate.[22] By 1512, however, the municipal

---

17. Specifically on the issue of Jewish jurisdiction, see Milano, p. 87; and see also pp. 175–84, where it is shown that all administrative activities performed by Roman Jews were really carried out in such a manner as to make of the Jews no more than the agents of the papal vicar of Rome, who actually held all authority.

18. Cassuto, *Gli Ebrei a Firenze*, pp. 94–97.

19. Ibid., p. 98.

20. See the series of letters between Ghislieri, then the chief inquisitor, and the Senate of Milan, in Stern, *Urkundliche Beiträge*, #112–22, pp. 117–30.

21. Bouwsma, *Venice and the Defense of Republican Liberties*, pp. 296–305.

22. U. Cassuto, Jewish Encyclopedia, Xth ed., s.v. "Urbino."

council and the duke were again borrowing from the Jews.[23] In 1549, and even as late as 1624, the municipal statutes guaranteed the protection of Jewish *property* and privileges.[24] Moreover, in the midsixteenth century there were Jews at court and Jews functioning as communal physicians.[25] Then, in 1571, Duke Guidobaldo II, in response to the wishes of Pius V, expelled the Jews who had been living in Urbino for less than three years.[26] Nevertheless, by 1607 the number of Jewish loan banks in Urbino was greater than ever.[27] Similarly, in the small town of S. Daniele del Fruili, no less a figure than Giovanni Grimani, the patriarch of Aquileia, granted a Jew a five-year *condotta* in the 1540s to open a bank in that town. This *condotta* was subsequently renewed, until Grimani expelled the Jew in 1565. Still, in 1568 the same Jew's son was permitted to return and establish a new bank. He was also freed from the obligation of wearing a badge. Only in 1592 was he at last forced to give up all his real property.[28]

In Ferrara and Mantua Jews enjoyed an extremely large number of special privileges. In his exhaustive study of the Jews of Mantua, Simonsohn notes that the popes in the second half of the sixteenth century enjoyed much success in persuading local rulers to implement their most recent Jewry legislation. However, when, as late as 1576, Gregory XIII sent a legate through Italy to convince local rulers to apply the restrictions found in *Cum nimis,* Duke Guglielmo insisted on publishing the restrictions under his own name, and even so he published selectively.[29] In addition, although the duke did prohibit the ownership of real property, he considered it his prerogative—which he used, and which explains why he insisted

23. Ibid., and G. Luzzatto, *I Banchieri Ebrei in Urbino* (Verona, 1903), p. 42.

24. Luzzatto, p. 44.

25. Ibid., p. 43.

26. Ibid., p. 44.

27. Ibid., p. 41.

28. F. Luzzatto, *Cronache storiche della università degli Ebrei di San Daniele del Friuli (Rome, 1964),* pp. 12–38.

29. S. Simonsohn, *Toldoth ha-Yehudim be-Duksuth Mantovah* (Jerusalem, 1962–64), 1:18–20.

on publishing the restrictions under his own name—to make exceptions.[30] There was, moreover, an erosion of the enforcement of these restrictions, for by 1601 Clement VIII was complaining that the Jews in Mantua were dominating Christians.[31] As for the crucial matter of jurisdiction, in 1542 the Jewish community in Mantua was not only given the privilege of issuing a binding ban, but it was also empowered to request the aid of the duke if a Jew refused to submit to such a communally imposed decree. This privilege was renewed in 1596.[32]

The legal situation in Ferrara during most of the sixteenth century was extremely permissive. Most notably, civil disputes between Jews were normally resolved according to Jewish law by Jewish arbiters and by rabbinic tribunals.[33] Only in 1570 was the badge instituted. But this rule was not enforced, and it had to be reedicted in 1582. Even as late as 1602, after Ferrara had passed into papal hands (1597), the badge was dropped, not to be reinstituted until 1620.[34] Indeed, such long-standing canons as those prohibiting Jews from using Christian nurses and servants were not enforced until the late sixteenth century, and even then not consistently. The exception was also the rule in the matter of real property. As early as 1555 the council of Reggio, a city belonging to the Este dukes of Ferrara, prohibited Jews from owning such property, but exemptions were numerous.[35] However, once the papacy acquired control of Ferrara, most of the restrictive regulations edicted in the mid-sixteenth century were put into force.[36]

Aside from these specific examples, the following three general observations may be made. First, despite de Susannis' strictures that only the pope could license usury, agreements were continually being made, directly between individual Jews and individual cities, which granted these Jews the privilege of residence in return for

---

30. Ibid., 1:108–9.
31. Ibid., 1:78 f.
32. Ibid., 1:256–58.
33. A. Balletti, *Gli Ebrei e gli Estensi* (Modena, 1913), p. 91.
34. Ibid., pp. 134–36.
35. Ibid., pp. 143–52.
36. Ibid., pp. 128 f.

their establishment of loan banks.[37] Second, in violation of the principle of *melior conditio,* princes never ceased asserting their right
to confiscate converts' property.[38] The prevention of this practice
was one of the main reasons for the issuance of *Cupientes Iudaeos*
in 1543.[39] Third, Colorni devotes a good deal of space to describing the varying degrees of jurisdictional autonomy possessed by the
Jews in the different Italian cities, both before and after 1558.[40]
Perhaps more than anything else, de Susannis emphasized that the
law requires the exclusion of Jews from all jurisdictions. That Jews
were not so excluded argues most strongly, as indeed do all the examples just presented, that the system advocated by de Susannis in
1558 was not a reflection of the norm, but of the ideal.

These examples do, however, reveal that the later sixteenth century saw an increased stringency in the application of Jewry law.
What role the *De Iudaeis* played in this changed situation is impossible to estimate. But the chances are great that the diffusion of the
tract and the change in legal status proceeded concurrently.

---

37. M. Shulvass, *Jewish Life in Renaissance Italy* (Hebrew), pp. 102–20.
38. Cf. p. 174, supra.
39. Tacchi-Venturi, *Storia della Compagnia di Gesù in Italia,* II:2, pp. 152–54.
40. V. Colorni, *Legge Ebraica,* pp. 305–65. See also Shulvass, *Jewish Life,*
pp. 50–55, and Simonsohn, *Mantovah,* 1:256–58. For all the matters discussed
in this section, see Baron, *SRH,* 14:71-146.

PART THREE

The De Iudaeis as a Key to the Understanding of Contemporary Catholic Thought about the Jews

CHAPTER X

CONVERSION

In III, 1 de Susannis expressed beliefs which typify him as an exponent of the major tenets espoused by sixteenth-century Catholic reformers. To be sure, many of these tenets had also been embraced by earlier reformers and earlier reform movements. In line with reformers, both orthodox and heterodox, in all periods,[1] sixteenth-century reformers believed, for instance, that they were reviving the purity of the "Apostolic Church."[2] Still, a given reform movement and its exponents may be identified by isolating the particular aggregate of reforms that the movement as a whole, as well as its individual reformers, sought to effect.

Along with his contemporaries, de Susannis spoke of the restored "Apostolic Church," and his ideal Christian was the martyr of that early period.[3] He praised the activity of the Jesuits in the East because they were reestablishing the Apostolic Church[4] and were, in fact, doing so through the preaching of the Gospel word. For preaching was the true apostolic task.[5]

These ideals de Susannis shared with such men as Gasparo Contarini, who espoused "a new pastoral ideal and the Apostolate,"[6]

---

1. See H. Grundmann, *Religiöse Bewegungen im Mittelalter,* (Darmstadt, 1961), pp. 14–18.
2. See L. Christiani, *L'Église à l'époque du Concile de Trente* (Paris, 1948), pp. 252 ff.; A. Humbert, *Les Origines de la Théologie Moderne* (Paris, 1911), pp. 217–23; and L. Willaert, *La Restauration Catholique* (Paris, 1960), pp. 26, 67–68, 99–100.
3. III,1,8, and 31.
4. III,1,29.
5. III,1,25, and 31.
6. Jedin, *Council of Trent,* 1:419.

and Giles of Viterbo, whose most recent biographer asserts that he saw the revival of the purity of the primitive church as the true goal of reform.[7] This revival was also one of the major goals of both the reformed and the new religious orders of the early sixteenth century[8] —the Capuchins, the Somaschi, the Barnabites, the Jesuits, and the Theatines, founded in 1524 by, among others, Carafa himself. The Theatines called not only for new vigor in preaching, but they also sought to reestablish what they thought was the apostolic clergy, the clerks regular, who were priests living under monastic vows.[9]

Another characteristic of sixteenth-century reformers was their tendency to see piety as a personal and interior communion between the individual and God.[10] This tendency was the hallmark of the early reformers, whose gatherings for prayer and meditation were formalized into the Roman Oratory of Divine Love.[11] It also manifested itself in the asceticism of Pius V,[12] in the "methodical oratory" of the *Spiritual Exercises* of Ignatius of Loyola,[13] and in Cajetan of Thiene's desire for a perfect love of God.[14] So too de Susannis spoke of prayer as a means with which to achieve communion with God.[15] And he called on each man to seek union—indeed, a union pictured with sexual imagery—with God.[16]

De Susannis also asserted that righteous Christians must emu-

---

7. J. W. O'Malley, *Giles of Viterbo on Church and Reform* (Leiden, 1968), p. 142.

8. H. Daniel-Rops, *The Catholic Reformation,* trans. J. Warrington (New York, 1964), pp. 40–46.

9. Ibid., pp. 40–42; Christiani, *L'Église à l'époque du Concile de Trente,* pp. 252 ff.; Tacchi-Venturi, *Storia, della Compagnia di Gesù in Italia ,* I:1, 304–7; Kunkel, *The Theatines in the History of the Catholic Reformation,* pp. 78, 126–27.

10. Willaert, *La Restauration Catholique,* pp. 20–26, 99–100; Humbert, *Les Origines,* pp. 101–15.

11. Daniel-Rops, *Catholic Reformation,* pp. 16–25; Tacchi-Venturi, *Storia,* I:2, p. 25; Christiani, *L'Église à l'époque,* pp. 29 f.; and Kunkel, *The Theatines,* pp. 12 f.

12. Daniel-Rops, p. 156.

13. Christiani, *L'Église à l'époque,* pp. 252 ff.

14. Kunkel, *The Theatines,* p. 32.

15. III,1,3.

16. III,1,2.

late Christ through the practice of evangelical poverty,[17] and he called it an error to believe that Christ himself did not live as a pauper.[18] Although John XXII, in the 1322 bull *Cum inter nonnullos,*[19] had declared this belief heretical, in the sixteenth century the prohibition was apparently ignored. Not only were de Susannis' assertions about evangelical poverty not expunged from the reprintings of the *De Iudaeis,* but declarations of adherence to this belief and practice were made by numerous sixteenth-century churchmen. Cajetan of Thiene, who believed that the perfect manifestation of love for God was the life of poverty, declared: "I see Christ poor, and I am rich." The 1604 constitution of the Theatines made absolute poverty voluntary, but it also asserted that such poverty was a value, "That we might imitate the poverty of Christ." [20] And Carafa himself spoke of "Lo bello instituto della povertà evangelica." [21]

Sixteenth-century Catholic Reform thought was also marked by a return to the *fontes,* the Bible and the Patristics, both to discover in them the true faith and to verify through them the validity of the Catholic Church as the heir and representative of true Christianity.[22] The copious references to the Bible and the Fathers made by de Susannis in the sermon demonstrate his participation in this movement. His use of non-Christian sources, moreover, although

---

17. III,1,2. In his first call for evangelical poverty, de Susannis cited Matt. 19:21, which is used as an important gloss to the Franciscan *Regula Prima,* whose demand for absolute poverty is explicit. *Opuscoli del Serafico Patriarca S. Francesco d'Assisi* (Florence, 1880).

18. III,1,64.

19. Eubel, ed., *Bullarium Franciscanum* (Quarachi, 1898), 5:552–54.

20. Kunkel, *The Theatines,* pp. 32, 41–42, 88.

21. G. P. Carafa, "De Lutheranorum haeresia reprimenda et ecclesia reformanda, ad Clem. VII" (Oct. 4, 1532), V. Schweitzer, ed., *Concilii Tridentini Tractatuum* (Freiburg, 1930), 12:73: "Ma sopra tutto perchè a Sua ̲S.ta et alla republica Christiana importa più la vostra sola che molte altre sia per il gran numero come per lo bello instituto della povertà evangelica." Also cited by Bromato, *Storia di Paolo IV,* 1:215.

22. See Humbert, *Les Origines de la théologie moderne,* passim, and esp. pp. 97–115; P. Polman, *L'Élément historique dans la controverse religieuse du XVIe* siècle (Gembloux, 1932), passim, for the use of the Bible and the Patristics in polemics; Willaert, *La Restauration,* pp. 220–50, on the development of positive theology and its reliance on ancient texts.

legitimated by a citation from Gratian, was typical of sixteenth-century defenses of the faith.[23] Furthermore, in the sixteenth century a new type of polemic was developed which used non-dogmatic and non-scholastic sources to stress the historical veracity and consistency of Catholicism.[24] With its emphasis on historical moments as demonstrative of both the truth of Christ and the falsehood of other religions, the polemic-sermon of the *De Iudaeis* undoubtedly represents this development.

The same circles which relied heavily on the *fontes* for both theology and polemic also produced a reaction against scholasticism, and especially Aristotelianism.[25] De Susannis' attack on Aristotle and all philosophy is explicit.[26]

Finally, like all Catholic reformers of his time, de Susannis possessed an unshakable faith in the Church. No matter what perils threatened it, he was convinced that it would survive and grow stronger. Using a phrase found in the writings of many of his contemporaries, he proclaimed that the Church was a vessel which no storm could sink.[27] De Susannis was most assuredly, then, a representative of specifically sixteenth-century Catholic Reform thought. Hence the question must be asked: Was his desire to convert the Jews also a reflection of contemporary thought?

Missions were a hallmark of sixteenth-century Catholic activity. According to Caperan, a strong impulse was given to extra-

---

23. Cf. p. 142, n. 83, supra, on Ficino's use of testimony from the Sybilline oracles in the *De Christiana Religione* to prove that Christ was the true messiah; cf. also Domenico Maffei, *Alessandro d'Alessandro* (Milan, 1956), most of which is an analysis of the *Geniales Dies* of d'Alessandro, which contains a history of religion from paganism to Christianity, along with a proof of the truth of Christ that is based in large part on pagan sources.

24. For a comprehensive treatment and history of this development in polemics, see Polman, *L'Élément historique*, passim.

25. See esp. O'Malley, *Giles of Viterbo*, pp. 40–49, 108; also Humbert, *Les Origines*, pp. 105–178, 181, on the general reaction against scholasticism; and P. Kristeller, *The Philosophy of Marsilio Ficino*, trans. V. Conant (New York, 1943), pp. 12–13, 27.

26. III,1,4.

27. III,1,51. Cf., e.g., Giles of Viterbo: "Qua tempestate quibus fluctibus, qua scelerum procella non demersum Petri naviculum quis non miretur," cited in O'Malley, *Giles of Viterbo*, p. 108.

European missionary activity by the crisis in theology which the fifteenth-century discovery of the New World had produced. The necessity of missions was predicated on the degree to which the command to preach the Gospel universally had been carried out. Medieval theologians generally believed that they had obeyed this command in full and that salvation was available to all men. They had seen no pressing need for the establishment of missions. The discovery of the New World, however, revealed their error; there indeed was a need to send out missions.[28] Thus, in the late fifteenth century and throughout the sixteenth century, missions were organized on a large scale—to the New World, under the direction of the Franciscans and the Dominicans, and to the East, under the Jesuits.[29]

An excellent gauge of the significance of missions in the six-teenth century is the extent to which the papacy committed itself to them. Through the agency of the Congregation for the Propagation of the Faith, it gradually acquired direct control of all missions. The first attempt to establish such a congregation was made by Pius V in 1569, but it was doomed by political rivalries, as was a second attempt made by Clement VIII in 1595. Only in 1622 was this congregation firmly established. The year 1622 must be seen as a culmination, however, and not as a beginning.[30]

The discovery of the New World was not the only reason why missions became so important to the sixteenth-century Church. The Protestants had failed to organize extra-European missions, and this failure gave Catholic polemicists added cause to denounce Protestantism as false Christianity. The true Church is supposed to be universal and apostolic. Through their missions Catholics were able to claim to the Protestants that they alone were rightfully striving for the mantle of universality. So, too, missionary success was taken as proof not only of Catholic authenticity, but also of vitality and

28. L. Caperan, *Le Problème du salut des infidèles,* 2d ed. (Toulouse, 1934), pp. 216–18, 255–98.

29. For a general survey of sixteenth-century Catholic missions, see Daniel-Rops, *Catholic Reformation,* 2:16 ff.

30. For a brief history of the establishment of the congregation, see R. Song, *The Sacred Congregation for the Propagation of the Faith* (Washington, 1961), pp. 5–25.

regeneration; and this, in turn, also provided internal reassurance. In short, the existence of missions provided the Church with a powerful polemical and apologetical weapon.[31]

If, then, the sixteenth-century Church vigorously established extra-European missions, there is little reason to doubt that it also pursued an active missionary policy toward the nation that had already heard the Gospel message but had consistently rejected it, namely, the Jews. However, most historians who have studied sixteenth-century papal Jewry policy have overlooked the issue of missions, even though there was a great increase in the number of conversions from Judaism to Christianity at that time.[32] Only Browe and Hoffmann are aware of the importance of the missionary factor in Jewry policy,[33] but even they fail to note how central a factor it was. Yet as the *De Iudaeis* correctly indicates, and as it substantiated by additional evidence both theoretical and concrete, mission and conversion were indeed fundamental to that policy.

Paul IV not only issued the conversionary *Cum nimis,* but he also sent two converts, Sixtus of Siena and a Fra Filippo, to seek converts in the Romagna.[34] Of St. Philip Neri it was said that each time he encountered a Jew on the streets of Rome, he sought to convert him.[35] Nor were the *Domus catechumenorum* and forced preaching restricted to Rome. *Domus* were established in other cities, such as in Modena in 1631,[36] and sermons were delivered in various localities, as at Ferrara after it became a papal possession

---

31. See J. Schmidlin, "Reformation und Gegenreformation in ihrem Verhältniss zur Mission," *Zeitschrift für Missionwissenschaft* 7 (1917): 257–69. The above paragraph is a summary of this article.

32. Cf. Shulvass, *Jewish Life,* p. 8, and Sonne, *Mi-Pavolo,* p. 28. For actual figures, see n. 41, infra.

33. Cf. pp. 5f., supra.

34. Pastor, *History of the Popes,* 14:274; H. Graetz, *Dibre Yme Yisrael,* trans. S. P. Rabinowitz (Warsaw, 1908), 4:581; Roth, *History of the Jews in Italy,* p. 302. For general discussions of missionary activities and institutions promoted by the sixteenth-century Church to convert Jews, see Hoffmann, *Ursprung,* passim, and Browe, *Judenmission,* pp. 39–47, 155–59, 169–83, 247–49.

35. L. Erler, "Die Juden des Mittelalters," p. 39.

36. A. Balletti, *Gli Ebrei e gli Estensi,* pp. 176–94.

in 1597.[37] The many disputes between the rectors of the Roman *domus* and Jews over the right of the *domus* to retain certain people in its custody indicate the relentlessness of these efforts.[38] So too is great interest revealed by the growth of differences of opinion within the Christian community about the right means with which to foster conversion. An anonymous letter from a Christian to Pius V, for instance, admonishes the pope that leniency rather than severity will result in additional conversions.[39] Suggestions were also made to use the Kabbalah as a missionary device.[40]

These missionary activities were often successful, as it evidenced by the large number of conversions that took place in the second half of the sixteenth century.[41] To be sure, the goal of universal conversion was never attained. Nevertheless, the Church persisted in its efforts. As late as 1697 it was stated at a synod held at Reggio: "No matter how much we have tried, the Jews still will not convert." [42] Only in 1694, moreover, did Imbonati produce his *Bibliotheca Latino-Hebraica,* which itself concludes with a conversionary polemic.

The Church was prepared to exploit any opportunity for missionary purposes. In particular, it hoped to lure Jews to Christianity by the pomp displayed in the public baptismal ceremonies which were staged for converts. Such pomp was an old device,[43] but it was

---

37. Ibid., pp. 128–32.

38. See Milano, "L'Impari lotta," pp. 355–68, and Dejob, "Documents . . . du Cardinal Sirleto," pp. 82–88, for reports of such disputes.

39. Moise Schwab, "Une Supplique de la communauté de Rome à Pie V," *REJ* 25 (1892): 113–16.

40. See infra, pp. 204f., for a discussion of Christian Kabbalah and conversion.

41. Milano, "Battesimi di Ebrei dal Cinquecento all'Ottocento" in *Scritti in Memoria di Enzo Sereni* (Jerusalem, 1970), p. 140. He has no specific figures for the period 1554–1613. However, he states that the number of converts for 1634–1700 was 788, and for 1700–1790, 873. This figure, moreover, is only for Roman Jewry. He then points out (p. 148) that as a rule conversion was heavier in years in which the Jews experienced great distress and despair, such as 1616–20, 1801–5, and 1811–20. How much the more, then, must these factors have prompted conversion in the late sixteenth century?

42. Balletti, *Gli Ebrei e gli Estensi,* p. 133.

43. Browe, *Judenmission,* pp. 150–59.

used in especially noteworthy situations in the sixteenth century. Pius V himself served as godfather at the baptism of an Elias and then permitted the convert to assume his family name, Ghislieri.[44] According to Laderchio, this particular ceremony moved an additional three hundred Jews to convert.[45] A similar public baptism took place at Rome in 1541, under the aegis of Loyola,[46] and still another at Florence in 1551.[47] Most revealing, however, are the baptisms which occurred during the Council of Trent. In the thirteen quarto volumes which contain nearly every document pertinent to that council, including the minutes and acts of its session, there are but few references to contemporary Jews.[48] Nevertheless, two of the churchmen who attended the council saw fit to enter into their diaries elaborate descriptions of the baptismal ceremonies which were arranged for converts from Judaism. The Cardinal Burgensis, wrote Massarelli, presided at the conversion of two Jews which took place at a special mass in the presence of the pope.[49] Firmani too recorded that on three separate occasions, one in 1562 and two in 1563, Jews were converted at public ceremonies which were carried out with much splendor in the presence of the assembled prelates of the

44. Ibid., p. 159; Hoffmann, *Ursprung,* pp. 94–95; cf. Browe, p. 159, and Hoffmann, p. 25, where both refer to the frequency of such ceremonies in the sixteenth century.

45. G. Laderchio, *Annales Ecclesiastici* (Coloniae Agrippinae, 1733), 35:31. Laderchio also remarks (p. 31) of Pius V that he was bothered because the Jews were still causing trouble for Christians. He thus saw a need to reedict *Cum nimis.* However, he insisted on just treatment, for he wished the conversion of sinners, not their deaths. Indeed, because he administered discipline with justice and piety, many Jews converted. As for Pius V's missionary zeal in general, a number of letters printed in Fr. Goubau, *Apostolicarum Pii Quinti P.M. Epistolarum Libri Quinque* (Antwerp, 1640), reveal a considerable amount of such zeal. In 1568–69 he wrote praising the king of Portugal for the missions he had fostered (pp. 48, 248–50). In 1570 he wrote to the archbishop of Goano praising his missionary activity (p. 351). Indeed, Hoffmann, *Ursprung,* p. 90, notes that after Lepanto, Pius V thought that the time had arrived for the conversion of the Muslims. Thus, missions to *all* infidels were of great concern to this pope.

46. Tacchi-Venturi, *Storia,* II:2, p. 151.

47. Cassuto, *Gli Ebrei a Firenze,* p. 91.

48. *Concilium Tridentinum,* ed. G. Buschbell, S. Ehses, H. Jedin, S. Merkle, and V. Schweitzer (Freiburg, 1904–67).

49. *Concilii Tridentini, Diariorum,* ed. S. Merkle (Freiburg, 1911), 2:182.

council.[50] To the churchmen who made a record of them and to the churchman who witnessed them, these ceremonial baptisms must have been a symbol, as were all missionary achievements,[51] of both the vigor and the rejuvenation of the Church. In equal measure they also reflect the devotion of many sixteenth-century churchmen to the goal of the conversion of the Jews.

It is, however, the theoretical writings of a number of important sixteenth-century Catholic thinkers which indicate most distinctly the critical importance of Jewish conversion for the churchmen of that period.[52]

Although referring to Jews only incidentally, the following statement of Cardinal Gasparo Contarini[53] manifests his evident desire for their conversion. If Catholics wish to put an end to the Lutheran error and tumult, he said, they do not need to set forth against the Lutherans a body of books, Ciceronian orations, or subtle arguments, but the example of great probity of life and a humble soul, desiring naught but Christ and the love of their neighbors. With these arms the Lutherans, indeed (*imo*) the Turks and the Jews too, will be convinced (*convinceretur*) with no undue effort. To convince them is the task of Christian prelates.[54]

At the end of the century, Robert Bellarmine displayed his strong interest in the conversion of the Jews and in the methods of achieving that goal, when he wrote: "There is a greater possibility of urging the Jews [to convert] by the use of Hebrew writings than by the

---

50. Ibid., pp. 561–62.

51. Schmidlin, "Reformation und Gegenreformation in ihrem Verhältniss zur Mission," pp. 267–68.

52. Although the works of only a few men are here discussed, they may be considered representative of the period. The number of sixteenth-century Catholic polemics directed against Jews is voluminous. A complete list of polemics, from the earliest through the late seventeenth century, is available in Imbonati's *Bibliotheca Latino-Hebraica*. Browe, *Judenmission*, pp. 100–110, gives a selective, but perhaps more easily useful, chronological list.

53. Christiani, *L'Église à l'époque*, pp. 39 f.; Tacchi-Venturi, *Storia*, II:1 p. 106. Contarini was a Venetian noble and a close associate of such reformers as Ghiberti and Loyola.

54. G. Contarini, *Gegenreformatorische Schriften*, ed. Hünermann, pp. 22–24.

use of writings in Latin or Greek." [55] Accordingly he was deeply
involved in a project to censor Hebrew books in a way that would
make their supposed Christological references sharply stand out.[56]
That this sentiment was expressed by a Jesuit is not strange, for it
was Loyola himself who did much to foster the mission to the Jews.
According to his major biographer, Tacchi-Venturi, Loyola considered the conversion of the Jews a major duty of his apostolate. Indeed, the bulls *Cupientes Iudaeos* and *Illius qui* were his special
projects.[57]

The same concern was shared by many of those Jesuits who
were influenced by the Kabbalah.[58] As Renaissance scholars turned
to the study of ancient texts, their interest in Hebrew grew. In turn,
this interest led them to the Kabbalah.[59] Many of the Christians who
became its students—and Kabbalism was by no means limited to

55. R. Bellarmine, *Controversiae,* vol. 1. chap. 2, cited in A. Possevin
Bibliotheca Selecta (Cologne, 1607), p. 391: "E codicibus Hebraeis magis urgeri
posse iudaeo, quam ex Latinis et Graecis."

56. On Bellarmine's composition of a Hebrew grammar and his role in the
censorship of Hebrew books for conversionary purposes, see my article, "The
Burning of the Talmud in Italy in 1553," *Bibliothèque d'Humanisme et Renaissance* 34 (1972). 458.

57. Tacchi-Venturi, *Storia,* II:2, pp. 149–54.

58. F. Secret, "Les Jésuites et la Kabbalisme Chrétienne à la Renaissance,"
Bibliothèque d'Humanisme et Renaissance 20 (1958): 542–55. Among those
influenced by the Kabbalah, Secret mentions, perhaps, Bellarmine (p. 552), and,
clearly, Possevin (p. 548).

59. F. Secret, "Les Dominicains et la Kabbale Chrétienne à la Renaissance,"
Archivum Fratrum Praedicatorum 27 (1957): 321. On the origins of Christian
Kabbalistic studies, esp. those of Pico and Reuchlin, see J. Blau, *The Christian Interpretation of the Cabala in the Renaissance* (New York, 1944), pp. 17–30, 41–
64. On the revival of Hebrew studies in general, see Humbert, *Les Origines,* pp.
165–78. See E. Rodochanachi, *La Réforme en Italie* (Paris, 1920–21), 1: 56–70,
on the growth of interest in Hebrew studies for the purpose of converting the
Jews. A prime example of these studies, and one that is not Kabbalistically
oriented, is Agathius Guidacerius' *Ad Paulum III . . . in tres . . . Davidicos Psalmos
. . . (contra Mahometistas, Haereticos, Iudaeosque qui praesentibus malis, finem
accepturam Christi fidem falso expectant) summa, . . . secundum fontes Hebraeorum* (Paris, 1537). His goal is to prove the truth of Christ to infidels by an
exposition made directly from the Hebrew texts of Pss. 72, 88, and 132. On
Guidacerius, who was an Italian teaching at the College de France in the
1530s, and who also wrote a *Grammatica hebraicae linguae,* see H. Galliner,
"Agathius Guidacerius, 1477–1540," *Historia Judaica* 2 (1940): 85–110.

the Jesuits—convinced themselves that through Kabbalah the messianic nature of Christ could be proved.[60] Accordingly, they began to see the Kabbalah as a valuable missionary tool. In the words of Sixtus of Siena, "[With the books of the Kabbalah], Christians can stab Jews with their own weapons." [61] Indeed, when the Talmud was burned at Cremona in 1559, the same Sixtus insisted, successfully, that Kabbalistic tracts be spared. He argued that although the Inquisition had condemned the Kabbalah, what it had condemned was only the false rabbinic variety, and not the true Kabbalah.[62] The latter, he said on another occasion,

> is a more secret exposition of divine law, received by Moses from the mouth of God, and by the Fathers from the mouth of Moses in continuous succession, received not written, but orally. This Kabbalah returns us from the earthly to the heavenly.[63]

Another of the strong exponents of Kabbalistic learning was Giles of Viterbo, the general of the Augustinians in the early sixteenth century and a cardinal of the Church. His commitment stemmed from his belief that the correct study of Scripture required knowledge of both Hebrew and the Kabbalah. But he also concluded that the Kabbalah was the weapon which Christians had been searching for. It had the power to remove the veil of blindness from the eyes of the Jews.[64]

60. Secret, "Les Dominicains," pp. 321, 329–36; Blau *Christian Cabala,* pp. 24, 28, 53.

61. Sixtus Senensis, *Bibliotheca Sancta* (Venice, 1566), fol. 110b: ". . . Christiani Iudaeos suis telis confodiant." Sixtus was himself a convert (H. Graetz, *History of the Jews* [Philadelphia, 1939], 4:581). On other converts who hoped to use the Kabbalah for missionary purposes, see Blau, *Christian Cabala,* pp. 65–77.

62. Secret, "Les Dominicains," p. 328. According to Secret, the Inquisition had condemned "omnes libros ad cabalam pertinentes." Apparently, however, Sixtus of Siena's distinction was accepted. Indeed, as Secret notes, Kabbalism persevered among religious through the seventeenth century (pp. 330–36).

63. Sixtus Senensis, *Bibliotheca Sancta,* fol. 110b: "Est [autem Kabala] secretior divinae legis expositio, ex ore Dei a Moyse recepta, et ex ore Moysis a patribus per continuas successiones non quidem scripto, sed viva voce suscepta . . . quae rursum nos ducat a terrenis ad coelestia."

64. O'Malley, *Giles of Viterbo,* pp. 67–83.

This opinion seems to have had some validity, as may be seen from the writings of three sixteenth-century converts. Raffaele Aquilino devoted a large part of his *Ma'amar Ḥasidi,* dedicated to Pius V, to the praise of the Kabbalah's virtues in promoting conversion.[65] Joseph Schacki, an undisputedly sincere convert,[66] wrote an open letter declaring:

> The ancient Jews, the wise men and mystics [*Mkubalim*], whom the Jews call "the wise men of the truth," confess, as did R. Hai Gaon, "There are three lights: a preexisting light, a shining light, and an illuminating light; even so, it is but one God."

He proceeded to claim that the discussions of lights and spheres found in Maimonides and in ibn Giqatilia are but veiled acceptances of the Trinity on their parts.[67] In other words, one who reads the Kabbalah (and perhaps Jewish philosophy too) is apprised of Christian truth. Less clearly than Schacki, Ludovico Carrito too intimates that the Kabbalah has influenced him, for he cites ibn Giqatilia's *Sha'are 'Orah* on the subject of Jewish suffering until the appearance of the messiah.[68]

It is not surprising, then, that thoughts about the conversionary potential of the Kabbalah were echoed, but with anxiety, by Jews themselves. At the rabbinical synod of 1554 in Ferrara, it was argued that if Jews began to study the Kabbalah in place of the

---

65. R. Aquilino, *Ma'amar Ḥasidi* (Pesaro, 1571); cf. Sonne, *Mi-Pavolo,* p. 130.

66. *Paris, Bibl. Nat'le. Hebr.* MS 753/2 (Hebrew Univ. Film, #12058), "Lettre d'un nommé Jos. Schacki sur la réligion Chrétienne . . . L'auteur était un chretien converti"; (in Hebrew) "דברי אנגיאלו ייארני לפנים יוסף שאקי". On fol. 2ʳ he provides a picture of the feelings of the sincere convert: He writes, "ששכן בבטח, כבוד, ורווח באתינא י״ט שנה, מתאמץ בתוך עמנו ומתוכח בכל יום נגד הנוצרים... (אבל הכל ש) היה הפסד הממון, אם, ואחים, ירושה נפלאה, עזבתי לכבוש את נפשי תחת כנפי השכינה ... (כל שאיפתי היתה רק אחרי) הטוב המוחלט."

67. *Ibid.,* 5ʳˢᵛ: "היהודים הקדמונים החכמים המקובלים הנקראים אצל היהודים חכמי האמת יודו בזה כמו שאמר רבי האי גאון, שלושה אורות הם: אור קדמון, אור צח, ואור מצוחצח, ועם כל זה הכל אלוה אחד."

He then proceeds to speak of Maimonides and Giqatilia.

68. *Paris, B.N. Hebr.* 753/1, "Lettre de Louis Karrito, juif converti, contre un juif talmudiste" (in Hebrew).

proscribed Talmud, the Inquisition, following the advice of some Christian humanists, might approve the use of the Kabbalah for conversionary purposes. At the same time, the synod issued no ban on Kabbalistic studies, lest the Inquisition judge those who issued the ban guilty of preventing conversion.[69] Even so, fears of an opposite nature were also expressed. Might not the publication of Kabbalistic books result in their burning, just as the Talmud was burned?[70]

The rabbis must have been distressed by other convert writings too, which beside lauding the Kabbalah as a conversionary measure, also offered more general conversionary arguments. Among the more interesting of these, if not also the lengthiest, is the eight-hundred-page *Confusione dei Giudei* of Andrea del Monte, who converted in 1552. He composed the tract sometime between 1555 and 1559, but he did not make it public until the reign of Pius V, to whom it is dedicated. In the dedicatory epistle he states that he has written of the Christian faith for the edification of both Christians and Jews, and

> especially to confirm those who have recently come to the faith. And if the matters which are herein contained should be read by Jews and well considered and examined, I am certain that they will easily put aside the errors of Judaism and turn to Christian truth, now that they can clearly see that they have been persuaded and confused not only by the wisdom of Scripture and by Hebrew vanity, but also by the sayings and traditions of their Talmud teachers and rabbis, and similarly by the wicked and impious . . . reasoning which is contained in their Talmud, for which it has justly been condemned to the flames.[71]

Outlining the contents of the tract, however, he notes that he will

---

69. See Sonne, *Mi-Pavolo*, pp. 123–25, for documents pertaining to this synod.

70. See S. Assaf, *Texts and Studies in Jewish History* (Hebrew) (Jerusalem, 1946), pp. 238–46, and esp. pp. 241–46, for the letter of R. Jacob Israel Finzi arguing against publication. See also I. Barzilay, *Between Reason and Faith: Anti-Rationalism in Italian Jewish Thought 1250–1650* (Paris, 1967), pp. 64–65, and 177–78, on the publication of Kabbalistic works at Mantua, including the Zohar in 1558.

prove the truth of Christ and attack at length the Talmud and the rabbis, while at the same time relying on rabbinic literature as a source of Christian truth.[71] Del Monte also wrote the *Lettere di Pace,* which attempts to prove Christian truth as reflected in the verse Genesis 49:10.[72]

Beside the work of del Monte, there are, among others,[73] two dialogues between Christians and Jews. One, the Hebrew *Vikhuaḥ* of Alessandro Romano, tries to prove the truth of Christianity by using both rabbinic literature as a whole and also the Kabbalah.[74] The second, the Italian *Dialogo fra il Cathecumino e il Padre Cathechizante* of Fabiano Fioghi, also uses rabbinic literature. This work, however, has the distinction of being intended purely for use within the walls of the Roman *domus,* where Fioghi was a lector, to strengthen the Christian convictions of recent converts.[75] How important these convert writings actually were in influencing Jews to convert is at present a matter for speculation.

The full intensity of the Catholic fervor to convert the Jews appears in four documents. In 1565, at the first of the councils he convened, Charles Borromeo, the archbishop of Milan, issued a

71. *Vatican, Neofiti,* MS 38 (Hebr. Univ. Film, 18518), Andrea del Monte, *Confusione dei Giudei,* dedic.: ". . . massimamente per confirmatione di coloro i quali sono venuti novellamente alla . . . fede, e se le cose che qui si contengono, saranno lette da gli hebrei, e ben considerate e esaminate, mi tengo certissimo che facilmente lasciando gli errori della fede giudaica ritornaranno alla verità christiana adesso che possono chiaramente veder che essi restano convinti e confusi, non solamente per la sagia scrittura, e per l'hebraica vanità, ma etiandio per le dette e tradizione de lor maestri Talmudisti e Rabbini, similarmente per Ragioni . . . nefande e impie che nel lor Talmud si contenevano, per le quale degnamente è stato condannato al fuoco."

72. *Vat. Neof.,* 37 (Hebr. Univ. Film 18519), *Lettere di Pace, Iggereth Shalom.* In the 150 pages of this letter, del Monte essentially does little more than collect previous arguments based on the verse. Of note, however, is the format, one column in Hebrew faced by a second containing del Monte's own Italian translation.

73. This convert literature, largely unknown, is well worth researching.

74. *Vat. Ebr.* 267 (Hebr. Univ. Film, 324), A. Romano, *Vikuah.*

75. F. Fioghi, *Dialogo* (Rome, 1582). Of special interest is the dedicatory epistle, where he speaks of his obligation to aid his Jewish brothers of the flesh to enter the spiritual Israel.

number of decrees concerning the Jews. As a whole, these decrees reiterate the edicts of *Cum nimis,* including the edict instituting a ghetto, and they further order, in line with *Cupientes Iudaeos* and *Illius qui,* that provision be made for the establishment of a *domus* and for the material well-being of converts. But they also contain a new measure: henceforth missionary sermons are to be preached to the Jews, and attendance at the sermons is to be obligatory. According to Browe, this was the first time since the thirteenth century, with the exception of a somewhat enigmatic and short-lived order of Pope Nicholas V,[76] that a prelate had instituted forced preaching. The reason behind these decrees is provided by Borromeo himself:

> So that, as much as we are able, we remove from the Jews the opportunity of corrupting the behavior of Christians and of taking their possessions from them by fraud, *and desiring to guide them to the way of salvation,* from the decrees of the canons we edict the following . . .[77]

The similarity between this declaration and the proemium of *Cum nimis,* as well as the similarity between Borromeo's decrees and the edicts of the bull, is too striking to be coincidental. The bull and the decrees reflect on each other. Borromeo's intention in issuing his decrees was undeniably conversionary. Indeed, by instituting forced preaching, Borromeo was actually going beyond Paul IV and anticipating a refinement which would not enter papal Jewry policy until years later.

At the end of the sixteenth century, the Jesuit Antonius Possevin published his *Bibliotheca Selecta . . . ad salutem omnium gentium procurandum.*[78] Appropriately, the ninth book of the work is entitled: "De Iudaeis et Mahometanis et ceteris gentibus iuvan-

---

76. Browe, *Judenmission,* pp. 40–42. Cf. p. 20, n. 59, supra.

77. See J. D. Mansi, ed., *Noviss, et Ampliss. Collectio* (Paris, 1902), 34:cols. 96–97; or Hardouin, *Acta Conciliorum* (Paris, 1714), 10:724–25, for both the introduction and the decrees. ". . . ut quantum possumus, Judaeis corrumpendi Christianorum mores, et eis bona per fraudem auferendi occasionem adimamus, ipsosque ad viam salutis traducere studentes, ex sacrorum etiam canonum decretis edicimus . . ."

78. Antonius Possevin, *Bibliotheca Selecta . . .* (Cologne, 1607).

dis." The Jews require this help because they are guilty of many *damna,* principally the perversion of the sense of divine scripture and the daily blaspheming of the name of Christ.[79] The remedy Possevin suggests is not, however, to repress the Jews, but to preach to them.[80] These sermons should be delivered by converts who are specially trained for their task and should be based on material drawn from the whole range of polemical literature. (He lists approximately fifty polemics ranging chronologically from the *Dialogue* of Justin Martyr to the *De sola lectione* of Francisco de Torres.) The preachers should also draw on the Septaugint and on those rabbinical writings which attest to the truth of Christ.[81] And they must remind the Jews of the destruction of their Temple, of the Jewish rites which they are no longer able to observe, and of their overall wretched state.[82]

But, Possevin adds, "the other [procedures] which can help in this business [of conversion] must be summoned from the realm of the practical. Generally, such practical measures persuade more efficaciously than many others."[83] Under the heading of practical measures he enumerates nearly every piece of Jewry legislation which had appeared since 1543: *Cupientes Iudaeos* and *Illius qui* of Paul III, *Cum sicut nuper* of Julius III, *Cum nimis,* the *statuta optima adversus Iudaeos* of Paul IV, as well as his *Dudum postquam, Dudum a felicis* of Pius IV, *Hebraeorum gens* of Pius V, and *Caeca et obdurata* of Clement VIII. In addition, Possevin says, in order to facilitate this "business," it is possible to emulate the kings of Spain by expelling the Jews. All the major laws and canons which apply to the Jews should also be enforced.[84] Moreover, "Gregory XIII, as

---

79. Ibid., p. 388.
80. Ibid., p. 389.
81. Ibid., p. 390.
82. Ibid., p. 390.
83. Ibid., p. 391: "Iam quae reliqua iuvare hoc negotium possint, ex praxi accersenda sunt, quae fere efficacior est ad persuadendum quam pleraque alia." (By *negotium* he means conversion. Cf. n. 85, infra, where he speaks of the same *negotium,* but calls it the *negotium conversionis.* In addition the overall context argues that *negotium* means conversion.)
84. Ibid., p. 391. The laws and canons he cites are: C.28, q.1,c.10, et seq; X.5,6; Clem. 5,2; C.1,9 and 10.

he had entered into a calculation which was most suitable for leading souls to the faith, advanced this unfinished business of converting the Jews with a twofold benefit," namely, by edicting obligatory weekly sermons and by establishing seminaries to prepare catechumens to preach the Gospel to their former coreligionists.[85] All these measures must be applied wherever Jews live, especially in Germany and Poland. There is no better way to convince heretics and schismatics to return to the Church than by giving them the example of the conversion of the Jews.[86]

This section of the *Bibliotheca Selecta* thus provides sure confirmation that de Susannis' arguments do indeed reflect the goal of papal Jewry policy, as well as contemporary Catholic thought about the Jews. Possevin is explicit: the rigorous enforcement of both Jewry law and the edicts of recent papal Jewry policy are the most efficacious means to promote the *negotium conversionis*.

Two final documents conclusively establish the representative character of the *De Iudaeis*. These are the *De Sola Lectione* of Francisco de Torres, and the *Libellus ad Leonem Decem* of Quirini and Justiniani. In 1555 the Jesuit Francisco de Torres, who devoted most of his life to writing tracts defending the theological position of the Catholic Church and to making Latin translations from polemics written by the Greek Church Fathers,[87] and who was also a canonist of such note that he was appointed to be one of the *correctores* of the *Editio Romana* of the *Decretum*,[88] published the *De Sola Lectione Legis, et Prophetarum Iudaeis cum Mosaico Ritu, et Cultu Permittenda, et de Jesu in Synagogis Eorum ex Lege, ac Prophetis Ostendendo, et Annunciando. Ad Reverendissimos Inquisitores. Libri Duo* (Rome, 1555). This tract was written to urge the inquisitors to take the very actions that were soon to be man-

---

85. Ibid., p. 392: "At Gregorius XIII, ut eam rationem iniverat, quae commodissima erat alliciendis animis ad fidem, inchoatum hoc negotium de conversione Iudaeorum duplici beneficio promovit . . ."

86. Ibid., p. 392.

87. See Carlos Sommervogel, *Bibliothèque de la Compagnie de Jésus* (Strasbourg, 1898), 8:113–36, for a brief biography and a complete list of de Torres' works.

88. Friedberg, *Corpus Iuris,* 1:lxxvii.

dated by the sixteenth-century papal Jewry bulls. De Torres also explains why these actions should be taken, and therefore an exposition of certain portions of his tract is indispensable.

The first book of the *De Sola Lectione* demands of the inquisitors that they pursue to its conclusion the policy initiated by the burning of the Talmud. They should remove all rabbinic commentaries from the Jews. The inquisitors must not neglect, de Torres states,

> what is particularly necessary for the salvation of the Jews. Indeed, for the glory of Christ I will state boldly what I feel: if you do not interdict to the Jews all the remaining commentaries of the Jewish tradition, all of which . . . tend not only to make vanity of our cross and glory, but also both to hold the Jews back from embracing the faith and to lead them away from the observances of the Christians, I fear lest you will be charged with their blindness at the horrible judgment of the last day.[89]
>
> Once these books are removed, however, it will soon result that the more they are without that wisdom of their princes, that is, the rabbis, so much the more will they be prepared and disposed to receiving the faith and the wisdom of the word of God.[90]
>
> For when that wisdom—or rather the insanity of their traditions, of the Jewish fables, and of the commentaries—has been blotted from memory, they will easily understand the mysteries of Christ and the prophecies of his advent, as that of Jacob, the most famous of all: "Non auferretur sceptrum de Iuda, etc."[91]

---

89. De Torres, *De Sola Lectione*, pp. 6–7: ". . . quod tantopere ad eorum salutem necessarium est. Imo dicam pro Christi gloria audacter quod sentio, si iudaeis reliquos omnes commentarios traditionum Iudaeicarum non interdicitis, qui uno omnes sensu huc tendunt, ut tum crucem et gloriam nostram evacuent, tum iudaeos a fide capienda retrahunt, tum a consuetudine Christianorum eosdem abducant, vereor ne in horribili illius extremi diei iudicio caecitatis eorum rei futuri sitis."

90. Ibid., p. 9: "Ablatis libris, paulatim fiet, ut quo magis erunt sapientia ista principum suorum, idest Rabinorum per oblivionem vacui, eo sint ad fidem, et sapientiam verbi Dei capiendam magis idonei et faciles."

91. Ibid., p. 10: "Obliterata sapientia ista, vel potius insania traditionum et fabularum Iudaeicarum, et commentationum, facile iam de Christi mysteriis, et eius adventu prophetias intelligent, ut illam Iacob omnium alioqui clarissimam, 'Non auferetur sceptrum de Iuda, etc.' "

[Indeed, when they had the Talmud, the Jews used to claim:] That those wise men [the rabbis] should be considered the "Duces de femore Iudae."[92]

[Therefore,] How are you [the inquisitors] able to attend to saving their remnant if you do not remove that which brings them to grief? Are the Jews not insane enough by themselves, and are the Jews not blind enough, that you have to allow them that which teaches them insanity?[93]

Moreover, he continues, as for the Jews' argument that they need their books to observe their law, the truth is that when the Jews observe according to rabbinical interpretations, they are in fact observing corrupt laws. In an argument reminiscent of the thirteenth-century French attacks on the Talmud,[94] he asserts that the permission given to the Jews to observe their laws extends only to those laws which are not corrupt, namely, those laws which do not contradict the New Testament. Thus,

It is one thing for the Jews to profess the Law, another to corrupt the Law which they are permitted to profess. The Church permits the profession of the Law so that perhaps we may win them; the corruption of the Law it does not permit.[95]

The Catholic Church permits the Jews the ceremonies of the Law; ceremonies alien to the Law it does not permit. For these alien ceremonies never possessed any truth, nor do they possess any utility. Indeed, they provide many impediments to the salvation of the Jews and are also detrimental to our Catholic faith. Since, moreover, all legalities, as the Apostle has taught us, foreshadowed the future values of the Gospel of Christ, to mold other things

---

92. Ibid., p. 11: ". . . eosque sapientes habendos esse Duces de femore Iudae."

93. Ibid., p. 12: "Quomodo curare potestis ut eorum reliquiae salvae fiant, si quae eos impellant ad offendendum . . . non removetis? An non satis per se insaniunt, et caeci sunt Iudaei, nisi qui insaniam doceant, illis concedatis?"

94. See A. Funkenstein, "Changes in . . . Anti-Jewish Polemics," *Zion* 33 (1968): 137–41.

95. De Torres, *De Sola Lectione,* p. 35: "Sed alium est legem profiteri, aliud legem, quam profiteri permittuntur, corrumpere; illud permittit Ecclesia ut sic eos fortasse lucremur, hoc non permittit."

into legalities, which are not legalities, . . . is the same as accusing the Apostle of falsehood. . . . Wherefore, it pertains to the Catholic Church to provide lest the principle and the foreshadowings be depraved and corrupted, and lest, at the same time, the figure of heavenly affairs, that is, the constitution of both the evangelical life and the ecclesiastical form, be depraved.[96]

So indeed [he continues after a digression], the Church has not tolerated the Mosaic rites and the cult of the Old Law in the grace of honor, far be it from that, but rather, so that in the meantime, if it is possible, it can convert the Jews.[97]

The second book of the *De Sola Lectione* urges the establishment of obligatory weekly sermons to be held in the synagogues. De Torres introduces this book as follows:

I have written concerning the demonstration of Christ in the synagogues of the Jews only on the basis of the Law and the Prophets.[98]

. . . For who doubts that if the children of the Hebrews frequented the synagogues not to hear the rabbis, but him [who bespeaks Christ only from the Law and the Prophets,] many would convert.[99]

---

96. Ibid., pp. 38–39: "Cerimonias enim legis permitti Iudaeis ab Ecclesia catholica, cerimonias vero a lege alienas [i.e., rites of rabbinic rather than purely biblical origin] non permitti aiebam, quia non solum nihil veritatis umquam habuissent neque quicquam utilitatis haberent, sed potius afferent plurimum impedimenti ad salutem Iudaeorum, et non parvum detrimenti nostrae fidei catholicae. Cum nunc, omnia legalia, sicut nos Apostolus docuit umbra essent futurorum bonarum Evangelii Christi, fingere aliqua esse legalia, quae non sunt legalia . . . permitteret mendacium Apostoli imponi . . . Quare ad Ecclesiam catholicam pertinet providere, ne fundamentum et umbrae depraventur, et corrumpantur, ne simul depravetur imago rerum coelestium, idest, Evangelicae vitae et ecclesiasticae formae constitutio."

97. Ibid., p. 49: "Itaque, ritus Mosaicos, et cultum legis veteris non honoris gratia Ecclesia in Iudaeis tolerat, absit, sed magis ut Iudaeos interim, si possit, lucretur."

98. Ibid., p. 106: "Scribam de Iesu in synagogis Iudaeorum ex lege tantum ac prophetis ostendendo. Quae causa cum superioris libri causa de tollendis Rabinorum libris coniuncta est."

99. Ibid., p. 108: "Ecquis dubitat quin si pueri Hebraeorum synagogas quidem non ad audiendos Rabinos frequentarent, sed eum [who bespeaks Christ only from the law and the Prophets,] multi convertentur."

Above and beyond that, he adds, as long as there is no such preaching, the Jews will never convert.

> Give the Jews an option, therefore, either they depart or the synagogues of Satan are used only for the reading of the Law and Prophets.[100]

> Now I hear it cast about that perhaps the Jews will threaten that they prefer to betake themselves to the Turks rather than to permit these sermons.[101]

Why should that matter? For the Jews are useless except to blaspheme and usure. So let them depart if they prefer to do so rather than to hear the Gospel preached in the synagogues.[102] Furthermore, if force is used in the Indies to enable preachers to deliver their sermons, why should it be impermissible to force the Jews to listen to the Gospel in their synagogues?[103] Indeed, he demands of the inquisitors,

> Why do you not force them to hear the Word of God, since you have been given the power to do so? Why do you not compel them, either by expulsion, or by disproving [Judaism] in the synagogues on the basis of the Law itself, so that they wish to convert? [Did not indeed the Spanish expulsion compel many Jews to convert?] Therefore, either expel them from our cities, or if you do not wish to expel them altogether [at least compel them to attend sermons].[104]

---

100. Ibid., pp. 119–20: "Date ergo iudaeis optionem, ut aut recedant a nobis, aut dienceps Synagogis satanae ne utantur nisi ad lectionem legis et prophetarum."

101. Ibid., p. 138: "Sed ut iam a nonnullis iactari audio, minabuntur fortasse, malle se ad Turcas recedere, quam hoc [the sermons] pati. . . ."

102. Ibid., p. 141.

103. Ibid., p. 142: This statement supports my contention that de Susannis meant I,14 to apply to the Jews as well as the New World infidels.

104. Ibid., p. 159: "Hos ergo non cogetis verbo Dei et potestate vobis data? Hos non compelletis sive eiiciendo, sive ex lege in synagogis redarguendo ut intrare velint? [Did not, indeed, the Spanish expulsion compel many Jews to convert?] Ergo, vel eiicite eos ex urbibus nostris, vel si omnino eiicere non vultis [at least compel them to attend sermons]."

As for those who refuse to attend, imprison them, fine them, even
threaten them with expulsion.[105]

De Torres then concludes the tract on a belligerent note. He
sternly upbraids and admonishes the inquisitors:

> What is all this? You not only do not command that both sea and
> land be scoured so that you can bring over to the faith the Jews
> seized from the hands of the Turks and convinced by means of
> the Scriptures, but you do not even judge that you should trouble
> yourselves about those who are within our walls! You do not
> bring to them the salutary interpretation of the Law. What is
> worse, you permit them to live where they wish, to go without a
> distinguishing sign, to become rich, to be our physicians, and, by
> the grace of usuries, to be quite powerful in the association and
> society of Christians. That is, to be abundant, to be extended, and
> to be strengthened, so that they vehemently resist the Holy Spirit.
> They even believe that they have the favor of God, since they see
> that things go well with them. Permit them, rather, permit them to
> be destitute and to be consumed by hunger rather than to exact
> usuries and to be physicians. For you surely know that when they
> do begin to be in want or when, choked with hunger, they have
> desired to attack even husks, then, like the prodigal son, they will
> revert to God. [As Isaiah said:] "Vexation will give understanding
> to the sense of hearing. . . ." [106]

There can be no misgivings; this tract develops in full the premises

---

105. Ibid., p. 161.

106. Ibid., p. 172: "Quid igitur, vos, qui non solum non iubetis circuire
mare, et aridam, ut Iudaeos e medio Turcarum ereptos et scripturis revinctos ad
fidem transferetis, sed neque eos, qui intra moenia nostra sunt, curandos esse
iudicatis, quibus salutarem legis interpretationem non adhibetis, neque ad audien-
dum saltem cogitis, immo vero quod peius est, permittitur illis habitare ubi volunt,
non notari signis, fieri divites, esse nostros medicos, tum gratia, usuris, familiarita-
tibus Christianorum et societatibus multum posse, idest impingari, dilatari, et
incrassari, ut vehementius spiritui sancto resistant. Credunt enim habere Deum
propitium, cum suas res bene ire cernunt. Sinite potius, sinite egere, et fame
confici, quam usuras exigere, quam medicos esse, quid enim scitis, utrum cum
egere coeperint, cum fame enecti in siliquas suum invadere cupient, tunc cum
filio prodigo ad Deum revertantur. [As Isaiah said:] 'Dabit vexatio intellectum
auditui . . .' "

on which both the *De Iudaeis* and sixteenth-century papal Jewry policy rested.

The *De Sola Lectione* did, however, have a predecessor, the *Libellus ad Leonem Decem,* written in 1513 by two Camaldulese monks, Paulus Justiniani and Petrus Quirini. This tract, in all likelihood, served as the prototype, if not as the actual stimulus, for all the Jewry policy which subsequently developed in the sixteenth century. It outlines in precise detail the strategy which that policy eventually employed. Yet, according to Jedin, the basic concern of the *Libellus* is the proposal of a sweeping reform program for the Church as a whole. It calls for inner spiritual reform, administrative revamping, updating of the *Corpus Iuris Canonici,* reorganization of the religious, careful training of the clergy, unification of liturgy, and missionary efforts.[107] And while, Jedin adds, the Church was not prepared to implement this program at the time of its conception, it eventually did become the program of reform which "occupied the Church for a century."

Even so, of the six sections into which the tract is divided, four (2, 3, 4, and 6) deals with missions to the Jews, the Muslims, and other infidels. Of the remaining two sections, only one (5) handles the matter of internal reform, and the other (1) expounds on papal power. But even in this part, the topic of missions is prominent. Quirini and Justiniani praise Leo X (the tract is addressed to him in the second person), for he has, they say, made the conversion of non-Christians his foremost duty, as is fitting. It is a task which God has reserved for him.[108] They conclude the tract, moreover, with the admonition that the pope should devote his energies to converting the Jews and infidels, to leading the Muslims either to the faith or to their destruction, to subjecting all Christians to the power of the Roman Church, and to joining all Christians to the pope as their head.[109] In short, the conversion of the infidels is seen by the two

---

107. Jedin, *Council of Trent,* 1:128–30.

108. Quirini and Justiniani, *Libellus,* col. 631. The authors often employ the rhetorical device of telling Leo X that he has already done what they in fact are proposing that he should do.

109. Ibid., cols. 717–19.

authors as one of the most important elements, if not as the keystone element, in their reform program.

The problem of the Jews is discussed, interestingly enough, in the same portion of the *Libellus* (2) which treats the question of the infidels of the New World. In essence, the solution proposed to Leo X is twofold:

> Perhaps you will be able to make progress with the Jews if they are led to the faith by blandishments of the spirit and by all offices of humanity. However, if so led they have not wished to convert, on account of their stiff-necked perfidy, they should be handled with bitter and harsh measures: not because you wish to harm them, for no one should be forced to the faith; but, so that seeing those of them who have wished to convert to be treated caressingly, and the others, who have never had the repose to do this [convert], to be treated harshly, they will be more easily incited by these stimuli—as if by two spurs—to seize the way of truth and of life.[110]

Among the blandishments suggested are feeding and clothing the poor and permitting the wealthy to retain their justly acquired property. To support the poor, they add, is not the equivalent of buying their conversion. "To lead them [to convert] with these subsidies of life is not illicit." [111] Converts, moreover, should be allowed to attain both secular and ecclesiastical benefices.[112]

As for those Jews who do not respond to the blandishments, it is permissible to treat them harshly.

---

110. Ibid., col. 622: "Judaeis prodesse fortasse poteris, si ii animi blandimentiis, atque omnibus humanitatis officiis ad fidem alliciantur, inde vero si allecti converti noluerint, pro eorum cervicosa perfidia, acerbius, duriusque tractentur: non quod vis aliqua illis inferatur, ad fidem enim neminem cogendum esse, sacri canones definierunt; sed ut videntes illos, qui ex eis converti voluerunt foveri, illos vero, qui hoc facere nunquam acquieverunt, sperni atque durius haberi his stimulis, quasi duobus calcaribus, ad iter veritatis et vitae arripiendum facilius incitentur." N.B., the principle of promoting conversion by making those who have not converted aware of the improved status of the convert is the principle which underlies the laws of the convert as found in III,2–9.

111. Ibid., col. 623: ". . . his subsidiis allicere, non illicitum esse."

112. Ibid., col. 623.

> Not because it is equitable at any time for Christians to pursue them with odium, but so that with a certain great measure of paternal piety, those whom we were not able to soften with blandishments we can force, in a manner of speaking, with threats and pious lashes to return to the heart.[113]

Specifically, these "lashes" should include a prohibition on the practice of usury, a ban against engaging in commerce or in the arts, the establishment of higher tolls for Jews than for Christians, restrictions on the length of time Jews may reside in a given locality, a limit on the number of synagogues that may be erected, qualifications of the privilege to observe Jewish ritual, a prohibition against Jews dwelling among Christians or mingling socially with them, and the requirement that Jews wear a distinguishing badge, so that Christians may both recognize and avoid them.[114]

In addition to these "lashes," the pope should designate individuals:

> Who should incessantly administer to them the word of life, so that not from the reason of philosophers, not from the authority of our doctors, but from their own Scriptures they be convinced, and so that, their perfidy expelled, they be shown the light of truth and the doctrine of the sacred Gospel and of the Apostles.[115]

Furthermore, he should order prayers to be offered continually, beseeching the conversion of the Jews.[116]

> Nor, inasmuch as they seem quite pertinacious in their perfidy, should you give but little thought to their conversion, as if you

---

113. Ibid., col. 623: ". . . non quod odio illos prosequi ullo modo Christianis aequum sit, sed ut magna quadam paternae in eos pietatis norma, quos blanditiis emollire non potuimus, minis, piisque verberibus ad cor redire quoquo modo cogamus."

114. Ibid., col. 623.

115. Ibid., col. 624: ". . . Ut illis . . . verbum vitae incessanter administretur, ut non de Philosophorum rationibus, non de nostrorum Doctorum auctoritatibus, sed de suis propriis Scripturis convincantur, perfidiaque eorum expulsa eis veritatis lumen, et Sacri Evangelii, Apostolorumque doctrina ostendatur."

116. Ibid., col. 624.

have no hope of their salvation. . . . It is your office to be solicitous in all ways for the conversion of the Jews.[117]

If, however, he has tried everything and the Jews still prove recalcitrant, then:

> Last of all will be that you order them, as dead sheep, to be completely separated from the flocks of Christians, so that you do not permit them to remain in any place of Christian sovereignty, or even to journey through.[118]

On the basis of these arguments, Quirini and Justiniani conclude their discussion of the Jews with the recommendation that Leo X promulgate a law to implement their strategy. This law should establish a mission to the Jews which seeks their conversion first through blandishments and then, if necessary, through castigation. But the law should also stipulate that if the Jews have not converted after a reasonable number of years, then no Jews should be allowed "inter Christianos ullo modo reperiri." [119]

Leo X did not adopt this recommendation. But piece by piece, each of the popes between 1555 and 1593 did—as the bulls which were examined in chapter one indicate. Eventually, the program of the *Libellus* was also adopted by such men as Antonius Possevin, Francisco de Torres, and, of course, Marquardus de Susannis.

The *Libellus* program also seems to have been understood by at least one Jew, the physician David de Pomis. His *Enarratio Apologica* never mentions the *Libellus,* nor does it once explicitly mention conversion, except to label as foolish the fear of some Christians that Jews were clandestinely promoting conversion to Judaism, while in actuality the only conversion seen in his day, and that not infrequently, was of Jews who had been openly persuaded to become

---

117. Ibid., col. 624: "Neque in propterea quod aliquantulum in sua perfidia pertinaciores videntur, de eorum conversione, quasi tibi nulla spes salutis reliqua sit, minus cogitare debes . . . Officium [tuum] est, omnibus modis de Iudaeorum salute sollicitum esse. . . ."

118. Ibid., col. 625: "Postremum omnium erit, ut illos tanquam morbidas oves a Christianis gregibus ita omnino separari iubeas, ut in nullo Christianae potestatis loco permanere, aut per illum pertransire permittas."

119. Ibid., col. 625.

Christians.[120] Even so, viewed as a whole, the *Enarratio* emerges as an implicit denunciation of the *Libellus* program, in particular as it was embodied in the *De Iudaeis.*

As noted previously,[121] de Pomis more than once makes direct references to the *De Iudaeis.* At one point he cites the work to the effect that Jews are to be protected. De Susannis, he writes, declares that the Jews are our kin, to be treated kindly, not to be disturbed in their rites, nor to be molested, just as the Romans protected them.[122] In a second citation, de Pomis notes de Susannis' affirmation that Jews are Roman citizens, members of their local civic bodies, privileged to enjoy the rights of Roman law, and even considered faithful members of the Roman Church.[123] In other words, de Pomis refers to those sections of the *De Iudaeis* which form the basis of de Susannis' eventual claim that the Jews are entitled to equity and justice.

Explicitly, the *Enarratio* is a defense against the charges of Christian physicians that Jewish physicians purposefully do damage to their Christian patients.[124] The defense begins with a statement of the validity of Jewish law and its observance.[125] From there it proceeds to demonstrate the obligation of Jews to treat Christians as brothers,[126] as well as the obligation of Christians to do the same

---

120. *Enarratio,* p. 82; See p. 42, n. 156, supra, for the Latin text.

121. See p. 66, supra.

122. *Enarratio,* pp. 49 f.: "M. de Susannis in lib. *de Iud. c.*1 num. 3 ait: '[Jews are to be protected] . . . proximi nostri . . . diligendi . . . non sunt perturbandi in . . . cerimoniis, nec debet eis molestia inferri . . . et Romani sustinebant Iudaeos' . . . Haec ille plures adducens authoritates. . . ."

123. Ibid., pp. 59–60, where he cites II,1 in general and II,2,2 verbatim on the Jews as members of the militant Church.

124. Ibid., chaps. 1 and 2.

125. Ibid., chaps. 3–7.

126. Ibid., chap. 8. This chapter deals with the obligations of Jews toward Christians. The origin of this obligation, says de Pomis, is that the Christians are the descendants of Edom (Esau), whom Deut. 23 commands the Jews to love as brothers. De Pomis explicitly bases this ethnological datum on the theory propounded in the tenth-century, southern Italian *Yossipon* (ed. Hominer, Jerusalem, 1956), chaps. 1–2. The original, however, intended this theory to demonstrate the existence of eternal rivalry, not brotherhood, between Rome (Christians) and Israel. On this theory and its origins, cf. Cohen, "Esau," pp. 38–45.

for Jews.[127] Indeed, de Pomis states, Jesus himself ordered that Jews be dealt with kindly,[128] while Jews, on the other hand, are prohibited from causing injury to Christians. The charge that the Talmud calls on Jews to curse Jesus is simply not true.[129] Thus, contrary to what many think, there is no reason why Jews and Christians cannot live together in harmony. There is no basis for the fear that a Jewish physician will act maliciously toward a Christian.[130]

Furthermore, de Pomis adds, the just treatment Jews receive in Christendom prompts Jews to approach Christians with love, not with venom.[131] Christian princes should therefore treat Jews justly, and they should not impose on them heavy restrictions. They should rather embrace the tradition of previous emperors and kings who recognized the fidelity of their Jewish subjects.[132]

What stands out most in the entire tract is the call for justice. The actual question of the Jewish physician seems to be secondary. Princes are implored to spurn, and to condemn as a dog, anyone who drums up hatred for the Jew with false accusations, especially those concerning the crucifixion. They should recognize that religion should be defended by good deeds, not evil ones; whence they should enjoin all acts of violence directed against Jews.[133] Indeed, they should warn those who wish to emulate the ideals of Jesus that they must never act improperly toward other men.[134] In particular, such

127. Ibid., chap. 9, which is also the locus of the first citation of the *De Iudaeis* (p. 49).

128. Ibid., chap. 10, p. 51.

129. Ibid., chap. 11, pp. 62–65.

130. Ibid., chap. 11, p. 57 and 70. On p. 70 he claims that Jews would not hesitate in time of need to call a Christian physician, and he then adds that popes and cardinals have used Jewish physicians for hundreds of years.

131. Ibid., chap. 11, which is also (p. 60) the locus of the second citation from the *De Iudaeis*.

132. Ibid., chap. 12, p. 76.

133. Ibid., p. 80: ". . . nec inherendum ullo pacto est, persuasioni illi vulgari, fatuaeque dicente, est Iudaeus crucifige illum: Spernendus, negligendus, contemnendus, obiiciendus, canis nihilominus est. . . . At defendenda Religio omnis (Christiana praesertim) . . . non scelere, sed fide: necesseque est, bonum in Religionem versari, non malum . . . [and harm to the Jew] Princeps haud pati debet."

134. Ibid., p. 73: "Cavendum est igitur Christianis iis, qui Christianis moribus vivere student, Iesumque imitari optant, ne quid indigne . . . proferant."

acts as leveling restrictions on Jewish physicians and forcing Jews to wear a badge must be eschewed.[135]

In sum, de Pomis asserts, "It must be held that the height of justice is *aequitas* [equity] toward all and also toward the Jew." [136] Thus princes must realize that "justice totally rejects the absence of *aequitas*. And where all are not equal in justice, there is no *aequitas*." [137] For de Pomis, then, justice for the Jew consists of the Jews being freed from all repressive restrictions. Otherwise, they cannot be *pares in justitia*.

But this is precisely the opposite of de Susannis' concept of justice for the Jew, which consists of the right to the benefits of law but also of the obligation to live as second-class citizens. And de Pomis was undoubtedly aware of this opposition; for there can be no question but that he knew the *De Iudaeis* well. Because he cites de Susannis twice on the issue of justice and then proceeds to propound a diametrically opposed concept of justice, it seems quite certain that through his assertions, de Pomis is tacitly, but bluntly, denouncing de Susannis' ideas. The exigencies of the time,[138] however, prevented him from explicitly declaring his purpose. Beyond that, the probability is extremely great that de Pomis clearly understood why de Susannis wanted to have his ideas on justice implemented. By arguing against de Susannis' concept of justice, therefore, he was also arguing against its motive. Because, wrote de Pomis, religion is a matter of the will.[139] Indeed, there is nothing intrinsic in their nature as men to distinguish between a Jew and a Christian.[140]

Thus, as de Susannis was arguing that it is justice to push the Jew to convert, de Pomis was arguing that justice is the precise opposite. His arguments fell on deaf ears. Religious toleration and the

---

135. Ibid., p. 82.

136. Ibid., p. 80: "Habenda igitur, iustitiae summa ratio est, tum erga omnes, tum erga Iudaeus."

137. Ibid., p. 79: ". . . inequalitas . . . iustitia prorsus excludit . . . Ubi non sunt universi pares in iustitia, aequitas non est."

138. Cf. p. 38 f., supra, on censorship and the Inquisition at Bologna.

139. Ibid., p. 80: ". . . nihil profecto est tam voluntarium, quam religio."

140. Ibid., p. 54: "Consequens igitur est, ut Iudaeus, et Christianus, in uno et eodem subiecto, individuove, insimul esse possint."

equality of men were doctrines which began to emerge only during the Enlightenment, not during the Catholic Reformation. In sixteenth-century Italy, the doctrine which prevailed among Catholics was that of the *Libellus* and of Marquardus de Susannis. Indeed, one must suspect that de Pomis decided to challenge de Susannis precisely because the *De Iudaeis* was that work which, at least on the legal plane, was most representative of Catholic thought about the Jews.

CHAPTER XI

THE COMMUNITY OF
ESCHATOLOGICAL SPECULATION

DE SUSANNIS UNAMBIGUOUSLY PROFESSED his belief in the imminence of the consummation; and it was because of this belief that he
held that the mass conversion of the Jews was at last possible.[1] The
obvious question thus arises whether those of his contemporaries who
also strove for mass conversion—in particular the papacy—predicated their hopes on the same belief.

At first glance it would seem that a number of other reasons
may be advanced to explain why the papacy embarked on a new
Jewry policy in 1555, reasons which appear more substantial than
those resting on eschatological explanations, and which even elim-
inate the need to see the new policy as a conversionary one. Some
of these reasons have already been noted, but in a general discussion
of causes, it is worth looking at them again.

It would be convenient if one could elicit some straightforward
political, economic, or social explanation for Paul IV's actions; but in
this instance, the historian will not be able to extricate himself so
easily. Social explanations, such as repression, simply fail for their
inadequacy. Aside from the lack of proof for an argument based on
repression, such an all-encompassing claim cannot possibly explain
why in 1555 the papacy violated all its past standards of behavior
with the Jews. Nor is there any evidence to link the Jews to the
rivalries between the prominent families which at one time or another had representatives who assumed the papal throne, and to

---

1. Cf. III,1,29–30.

identify this as the source of their difficulties. The position of the Jews as middle men, seen by the lower classes as the agents of those in power, does not play a role here either. There is simply no record of a clamor by the Roman populace, or any other group within the Papal States for that matter, to have the Jews expelled or generally reduced in status.[2]

Isaiah Sonne has tried to find a political explanation in the quartermaster services provided by Jews to the Spanish armies during the war between Philip II and Paul IV. Sonne even tries to identify actual loyalties to the Hapsburgs on the part of some Jews.[3] But to accept this conclusion, which rests on sound facts, as the explanation for a policy which continued for a minimum of fifty years without the slightest interruption or deviation, and which had its origins sometime in the 1540s, at the latest, demands stretching the imagination. Sonne himself does not overwork it. Beyond that, the war did not commence until the fall of 1556; *Cum nimis* was issued over a year earlier. Even assuming that Paul IV enlarged in his imagination the activity of a handful of Jews into a demonstration of the intrinsic political disloyalty and treachery of all Jews within the Papal States, the simple fact remains that he had made his decision about Jewry policy long before he determined to go to war with Spain.

The Jews certainly in no way posed a threat to the papal economy. Aside from their activity in international trade at Ancona, the only area in which Jews played a role that might be called significant in the Italian economy was in loan banking. In the Papal States the role of the Jews had actually decreased from the middle of the fifteenth century, when, at the instigation of Franciscan preachers who railed against Jewish usury, a system of Monti di Pietà, banks offering interest-free (or nearly free) loans to the poor, was established.[4] These Franciscans had been even more concerned with what they saw as the effects of usury, namely, the subjugation

---

2. On these issues, see supra, pp. 3–5, and chap. 1, n. 36, and Pastor, 14:92–174.

3. Sonne, *Mi-Pavolo*, pp. 139–43.

4. Cf. infra., chap. 12, n. 3, on these Franciscans and their activities.

of Christians to Jews. Nevertheless, while it is true that *Cum nimis* does not neglect Jewish economic activity and its effects, the regulations in this sphere form but a small part of the bull's purview, and more, *Cum nimis* attempted merely to regulate the rate of usury, not to cut it off entirely. Apparently the Jewish economic function was a necessary one. There was to be no fundamental change here as in other areas.

As for Ancona, the lengthy discussion in chapter one has shown that not only was Anconitan Jewry an issue apart because of its members' status as former Marranos, but also that in terms of economics the papacy was literally standing on its head to keep the Jewish-run trade flourishing.[5] Still, it would be theoretically possible to make some kind of case on the grounds that the prime beneficiary of Ancona's commerce was not the papacy, but the sultan.[6] The Turks had realized the hard cash benefits of a favorable balance of trade and, accordingly, had fostered the growth of a quasi-enclave of Turkish subjects in Ancona. Apparently, the arrests of 1555 cost the sultan the sum of 400,000 ducats. Thus the arrest of the Marranos could be seen as a maneuver in the on-going war against the Turk. The boycott against Ancona proposed to the sultan by the ex-Marrano, Doña Gracia Mendes, irrespective of its ultimate failure because of the strong opposition to it displayed by Italian Jewry,[7] could then have been construed by the papacy as a sign of Jewish loyalty to the Turk, with the result being extreme sanctions placed upon the Jews. But here again the time factor will simply not permit such a conclusion. The arrests may have taken place more or less simultaneously with the issuance of *Cum nimis,* but the boycott, to

---

5. supra, pp. 28–34.

6. See H. Inalcik, "Capital Formation in the Ottoman Empire," *Journal of Economic History* 29 (1969): 97–140 and esp. 121–24, where he explains the role of merchants and merchants operating from foreign soil in Turkish economic considerations. They were seen as a prime instrument for the enrichment of the sultan's treasury. The Ancona Marranos, with their links to the Jews in Turkey, were a particularly fruitful source of revenue.

7. On the sum above and the boycott, see Inalcik, pp. 121–24, and C. Roth, *The House of Nasi: Doña Gracia* (Philadelphia, 1947), pp. 134–75, where he also portrays in depth the involved career of this most famous of Marrano women, who exercised great influence at the Turkish court.

whatever extent it succeeded, was conceived only afterward. Moreover, why would the papacy have issued such far-reaching sanctions
against Italian Jewry as a whole, if the issue were really economic-
political and not intrinsically one concerning the Jews? Why too
would Paul IV have carried the case against the Marranos to the
extreme of burnings? Finally, why would subsequent popes reverse Paul IV's approach to Ancona by going back to the old policy
of privilege for the Anconitans?[8] In short, there is nothing of substance through which to connect the policy toward Ancona and the
policy toward the rest of Italian Jewry. Indeed, as shown above, the
documents of the period offer solid evidence that in the mind of the
papacy the two policies were entirely separate ones.

One final matter that may be labeled as an explanation resting
on general economic, social, or political causes is the renewed and
vigorous application of the canons. Paul IV, it could be claimed,
was merely reasserting and applying canons pertaining to the Jews
which had long fallen into desuetude; he was seeking to make the
papal state function according to its proper constitution. But on
closer inspection, this claim is seen to be inaccurate in its facts.
Apart from the changes in legal formulation, the clauses of *Cum
nimis* establishing ghettoes and prohibiting private property and titles
are, at root, canonical innovations, in the sense that they interpret
the Jewry canons in a completely novel way. More important, this
claim, as indeed all those just examined, would have to ignore the
substantial information which has been elicited to show a scope and
purpose to papal policy far exceeding the simple application of law.
To accept any of the above hypotheses, every bit of evidence regard-
ing conversion would have to be laid aside, evidence which is too
firm, too weighty, and too direct to be impeachable; and in its place
evidence which is at best inferential would have to be accepted.

Perhaps a more reasonable explanation may be found by
examining possible religious motivations underlying the papal
actions. Yet it would be glib to attempt to label the new Jewry
policy as a typical manifestation of the Catholic Reformation

---

8. See supra, pp. 30–32.

Church seeking to control and remove from its midst all dissidence.[9] Not that such an explanation would be inaccurate. It is
rather insufficient, elucidating none of the specifics and in the end
explaining nothing. It also contains the element of the cynical,
implying that sixteenth-century churchmen erected a whole conversionary program as nothing but a ruse to exploit in ridding
themselves of the Jewish pest. If, furthermore, anything definite
can be said about Paul IV, it is that every one of his actions was
deeply rooted in a religious fervor and conviction that bordered
on fanaticism.[10] There is no reason to see an exception in the case
of his actions toward the Jews. The same criticism must apply to
any attempt to interpret later-sixteenth-century Jewry policy as
an economic, social, or political policy camouflaged, or actually
colored, by religious motives. Only a small segment of the policy
could be so explained, although without any real hard evidence,
while the major aspect, conversion, would be left begging for an
interpretation.

The issue of conversion was, however, a factor in the expulsion of the Jews from Spain in 1492, at least in the sense that numbers of Jews converted rather than leave. Is it possible, then, that
the papacy of 1555 was acting in imitation of what it thought to have
been the policy of the Spanish king of 1492? Indeed, Francisco de
Torres had counseled that expulsion, following the model of Spain,
was an excellent device to promote conversions, thereby giving the
impression that the Spanish expulsion was devised solely as a conversionary device.[11] It matters little whether de Torres correctly understood what had happened sixty-five years before he wrote. The
issue is his perception of that event and the degree to which his
perception had become a common one. Nevertheless, in the context
of the entire *De Sola Lectione* expulsion was, even for de Torres,
only a last means to be used when other methods failed.[12] In this he
mirrored perfectly, if he did not actually influence, the papacy in its

---

9. See supra, pp. 4–5.
10. See infra, pp. 262–64.
11. See supra, pp. 215.
12. See supra, pp. 216.

approach toward expulsion. If the papacy conceived of the Spanish
expulsion as a spontaneous action, a self-contained conversionary
program, it certainly did not opt to take that action, but resorted to
expulsion only after fifteen years of other tactics. Moreover, comparing the actual dimensions of the papal, as opposed to the Spanish,
expulsion, what first stands out is that Pius V, and later Clement
VIII, did not resort to wholesale expulsions.[13] Apparently, unlike the
Spanish, at no time did the papacy feel that the presence of Jews and
the lack of total religious conformity presented a critical danger to
society, or that there was a necessity to order an expulsion for its own
sake. Paul IV and all the other popes, rather than feeling compelled
to imitate Spain and rid themselves of the Jews, actually restated the
traditional principle that Catholic society tolerates Jews in its midst.[14]

Going further, trying to discern whether there is some connection between the real historical causes of the Spanish expulsion and
the sixteenth-century papal Jewry policy, a prime difficulty arises,
namely, the absolute lack of consensus on the part of historians about
the nature of those causes. Yitzhak Baer and Haim Beinart have
discerned a planned program on the part of hostile forces, chiefly
the Inquisition, stretching over forty years and devoted to the eventual elimination of Jews from Spanish society.[15] The concern was
not so much to acquire new converts, but to protect earlier ones from
contamination and relapse into their old beliefs. This thesis receives
support from both the Decree of Expulsion itself and the various
records of the Inquisition.[16] Beinart, in particular, has pointed to the
mid-fifteenth-century *Fortalitium Fidei* of Alfonso de Espina as a
carefully drawn schema for the repression and eventual expulsion
of the Jews which was assiduously followed by the Inquisition.[17]
Recently, Stephen Haliczer has tried to upset this picture by sug-

---

13. See supra, p. 26 n. 83 and p. 34 n. 122.

14. See the promeia of all the bulls cited in chap. 1.

15. Y. Baer, *A History of the Jews in Christian Spain* (Philadelphia, 1966),
and H. Beinart, *Conversos on Trial before the Inquisition* (Hebrew) (Tel-Aviv,
1965).

16. See Baer, *History*, vol. 2, chap. 15.

17. See Beinart, *Conversos*, chap. 1, for a thorough discussion of the *Fortalitium* and its importance.

gesting that the expulsion was unplanned and uncontemplated until the very last minute, but was forced upon the Spanish monarchs by none other than the *Conversos* themselves, who had been struggling for decades to free themselves of the stigma of being New Christians. To end all questions about their Catholic loyalty, they forced Ferdinand and Isabella to issue the expulsion decree in return for the services they provided the monarchy as members of the local Spanish city councils, which consistently voted monies for the prosecution of the war against Granada.[18] A more encompassing explanation is offered by Gabriel Jackson, who sees in fifteenth-century Spain the failure of the one medieval attempt to create a poly-ethnic state. The Jews had to go because there was simply no room for them, a minority of some importance, in the newly united Spanish state.[19] This view dovetails with the earlier opinions which sought out nascent nationalism or simple religious fanaticism for religious purity to explain the events of 1492.[20]

This is, of course, not the place to evaluate these conclusions. What is pertinent here is that little or no connection may be drawn between these conclusions and the situation in sixteenth-century Italy. Nationalism and poly-ethnicism were assuredly not burning issues then in Italy; and even if they were, they could have effected the Jews only through a total expulsion from all of Italy, and not merely from the Papal States and a few other localities.[21] Anti-Semitism and religious fanaticism have been ruled out repeatedly. Perhaps there was a *Converso* conspiracy in Spain, but the conditions which would have produced it were so special that they could hardly be expected to reproduce themselves elsewhere. As for a long-term plan by an Inquisition or Inquisition-like organization, intended to end in the elimination of Jews from the Papal States, this

---

18. S. Haliczer, "The Castilian Urban Patriciate and the Jewish Expulsions," *American Historical Review* 78 (1973): 35–58.

19. G. Jackson, *The Making of Medieval Spain* (New York, 1972), pp. 181–97.

20. See Baron, *SRH*, 11:232–49; and Haliczer, "Urban Patriciate," pp. 35–36, where he discusses earlier opinions.

21. Sonne, *Mi-Pavolo*, pp. 183–203, discusses, with documents, the scattered local expulsions in Italy in the later sixteenth century.

too did not exist. The only organization of this type, the Papal Inquisition, seems to have had only an occasional and tangential role to play in the case of the Jews.[22] The papacy itself concentrated principally on conversion, and it issued but one bull during the entire period under review, *Antiqua Iudaeorum improbitas* (July 1, 1581),[23] linking the Jews with the type of activity—the enticement of converts to relapse to Judaism—that the Spanish Inquisition devoted so much of its energy to. And actual elimination, as has been stated repeatedly, was simply not considered by the papacy. In short, there is no link between the Jewry policy of later-fifteenth-century Spain on the one hand and that of later-sixteenth-century Italy on the other.

Still, it may be argued that the sixteenth-century papacy was not reacting to any specific action or program undertaken in fifteenth-century Spain, but to the simple fact that so many conversions had occurred in Spain during that period. In effect, conversion could now be conceived of as a real possibility which ought to be pursued, doctrinal traditions about the time of Jewish conversion notwithstanding, for such pursuit would be assuredly efficacious. But this line of reasoning, while tantalizing because of its simplicity, is ultimately impressionistic and must be put aside, not so much for the lack of hard evidence which might support it, but for the presense of severe objections which militate against it. The most severe of these is the issue of timing.

The logical moment for the papacy to adopt a conversionist policy for the reason just suggested would have been around 1415, immediately after the massive conversions of 1391 and 1412–15.[24] But whereas Benedict XIII, whose activities will be examined in some depth in the next chapter of this study, had in fact engaged in conversionary activity, his immediate successor, Martin V, did nothing along this line. It appears that from the start of his pontifi-

---

22. Cf. Dejob, "Documents . . . du Cardinal Sirleto," passim; Milano, "Battesimi," pp. 133–46; and Perugini, "L'Inquisition Romaine," pp. 94–108.

23. Cf. supra, chap. 1.

24. On the riots of 1391, and on the conversionary activity of 1412–15 and the Debate at Tortosa, see Baer, *History,* vol. 2, chaps. 10 and 11, passim.

cate in 1417 he actually oversaw the dismantling of any conversionary programs that Benedict XIII had established.[25] Nor did any
of Martin V's successors reverse his stand. Outside the papacy,
there equally seems to have been no organized or persistent push
for converts.[26] Even in Spain, among the Franciscans and Dominicans, who had engaged in conversionary activity in the thirteenth
and late fourteenth century, the concern was with the pernicious
effects of the New Christians and not with augmenting their numbers.[27] If the sixteenth-century popes, then, or for that matter,
others within the Church who became interested in the conversion
of the Jews, were reacting to the unadorned fact of conversions,
the question must be raised: What stimulus did they have, which
no one else within the Church seems to have had since 1415, to make
them conscious of this fact and of the ensuing possibilities? Further,
why did the sixteenth-century popes become so convinced of their
conversionary powers that they erected and then maintained machinery toward that end on so elaborate a scale? They were perhaps acting knowingly in imitation of Benedict XIII; yet to say
this raises anew the question of the hiatus between Benedict XIII
and Paul IV. This possibility also, as will be seen, raises questions
about the motivations of Benedict XIII himself. In other words,
the invitingly uncomplicated solution of sheer momentum must
also be passed over.

Determining the effect, or lack of effect, of the Protestant
Reformation on Catholic Jewry policy will not prove such a clear-
cut issue. The problem is compounded by the haziness and am-

---

25. On the direct opposition of Martin V to the conversionary activities of
Benedict XIII, see Simonsohn, *Judengesetzgebung,* chap. 3, passim.

26. For the lack of conversionary activity in the fifteenth century, see Browe,
Judenmission, pp. 27–28 and 86, for Spain, and pp. 31–38, 68–71, for other
countries in Europe. The point of interest in these pages is the little evidence
Browe can muster for activities in this period, in opposition to the greater quantity
of material he has discovered for other periods. Of special note is his statement
that the activities of the Franciscans in fifteenth-century Italy were so destructive
that they actually worked against conversion.

27. On activities directed against New Christians, see Baer, *History,* 2:chaps.
12–14, passim.

biguities inherent in the Protestant teachings concerning the Jews.[28] Leaving aside Calvin, whose statements about the Jews have little reference to contemporary Jewry,[29] a review of the writings of Luther, who was quite immersed in the question of the proper policy to be adopted toward the Jews, will reveal that his posture was inconsistent at best. The case normally presented is that Luther at first believed that there was a possibility of converting the Jews by means of preaching, on the one hand, and treating them with kindness, on the other. Preaching and convincing the Jews of the truth of Jesus as messiah was now possible because the Jews would finally hear the true interpretation, that is, the Lutheran interpretation, of the New Testament, previously obscured by Catholic distortions. The approach of kindness, in distinction to the repressive Catholic canons, would convince the Jews of Protestant good will and thus predispose them to accept the preaching.[30] These views were ostensibly expressed in the 1523 "That Jesus Was Born a Jew." By 1542, however, seeing the stubborn refusal of the Jews to accept his rational and reasonable approach, Luther radically altered his stance, and in "Concerning the Jews and Their Lies," he advocated repression more severe and purposeful than could ever have occurred through the most rigorous application of the canons. Together with this, he accused the Jews of the basest plots and crimes against Christians and Christianity.[31] So violent were his sallies that Martin Bucer, himself an advocate of strong measures to control the Jews, strongly condemned the contents of Luther's book.

In truth, Luther's attitudes are by no means so clear-cut or so facilely divided into two. For example, in 1537 he wrote to Yosel of Rosheim, refusing to aid in securing privileges for the perverse Jews

---

28. See Baron, *SRH*, 13:205–96, for an overview of these teachings in their formative period.

29. Ibid., pp. 279–91.

30. Martin Luther, "That Jesus Christ Was Born a Jew," trans. W. I. Brandt, in *Luther's Works* (henceforth *LW*) (Philadelphia, 1971), 45:195–229. Cf. Baron, *SRH*, 13:205 ff., and M. H. Bertram's remarks in *LW*, 47:125 f.

31. Martin Luther, "Concerning the Jews and Their Lies" (1542), trans. M. H. Bertram *LW*, 47:121–306.

but at the same time renewing his claim that kind treatment would lead some Jews to convert.[32] Luther had apparently moved from his position of 1523, but he had not yet abandoned it either. Exactly what happened between 1537 and 1542 to cause Luther to advocate repression remains to be discovered. It does, however, seem unlikely that he came to a sudden conclusion that the Jews were unalterably stubborn and therefore changed his course. He seems to have realized this much by 1537. Moreover, there appears to be some question whether any of the views of 1542 were a product solely of the later Luther. William Maurer has suggested that by as early as 1514 Luther was advocating the basic themes on which "The Jews and Their Lies" is built.[33] On the other hand, there is some doubt that the tract of 1523 really anticipated a massive conversion of Jews, doubt that Luther truly thought that he could bring huge numbers to the baptismal font. Thus Luther states explicitly: if we "deal with them gently and instruct them from Scripture; then *some* of them may come along." [34] Nowhere does he claim any more than this. To be sure, the context suggests that by "some" Luther meant a not insignificant number, but his very caution in expressing himself and in his terminology implies that he fundamentally anticipated no overwhelming response.

The Catholic documents examined in the last chapter have none of this hesitancy and speak without qualification. The Jews, as a whole, are to be proselytized until success is achieved. And there is not the slightest quiver of hesitation that such success will be achieved. Even the expulsion bulls of 1569 and 1593 refuse to openly admit failure, but speak of new ways to attain the conversionary goal.[35] When twenty years had passed and Luther had not activated a large Jewish movement toward Christianity, however, he openly spoke of the tremendous and insurmountable problems

---

32. For text and comments, see *LW*, 47:62: ". . . I would have interceded . . . but your people so shamefully misuse this service of mine. . . . My opinion was and still is that one should treat the Jews in a kindly manner, that God may perhaps . . . bring them to their Messiah. . . ." see also n. 36, infra.

33. See *LW*, 47:126.

34. *LW*, 45:229 and similarly 200.

35. Cf. supra, pp. 24–27.

faced in gaining converts; [36] he repeatedly invoked as justification the traditional doctrine of Jewish blindness [37]—the very theological blindness whose cure and elimination de Susannis and others in the Catholic camp now undeniably ascribed to; and he even went so far as to declare in one instance that the conversion of the Jews was simply impossible.[38]

A greater contrast between Luther and the Catholics is the fully articulated conversionary programs of the latter as opposed to the complete lack of such programs among the Protestants. Beyond his statements about preaching and kindness, Luther never even entered upon a methodological discussion for achieving conversions.[39] A careful inspection of "That Jesus Christ Was Born a Jew" reveals that the first half of the pamphlet discusses problems associated with Mariology, while the second offers a rather standard exegesis of Genesis 49:10 and Daniel 9.[40] The Jews and their possible conversion are dealt with but briefly in only two places, where Luther does no more than make his broad assertions about preaching and kindness.[41] One begins to wonder

36. In the opening paragraphs of the 1538 "Against the Sabbatarians," trans. and intro. M. H. Bertram, *LW*, 47:65–66, Luther recounts the difficulties which he feels have prevented conversion, in particular, stubborn adherence to the rabbis and perverse comprehension of Scripture.

37. See *LW*, 47:155, 171, 213.

38. *LW*, 47:137: "Much less do I propose to convert the Jews, for that is impossible.

39. See A. K. Helmio, *The Lutheran Reformation and the Jews* (Hancock, Mich., 1949). Despite the subtitle of this book, *The Birth of the Protestant Jewish Missions*, Helmio admits that in the case of Luther there was "no systematic converting of Jews" (p. 90), and he furthermore brings no evidence to indicate active implementation of missions on the part of any other early Protestant figure.

40. *LW*, 45:199–213, and 213–229.

41. *LW*, 45:199–201 and 229; cf. p. 235, supra. In the course of his Mariology discussion it often appears that Luther is arguing explicitly against Jewish exegesis and so arguing to Jews. Yet Luther opens his case by announcing (p. 199) that he is about to refute charges made about *his* Mariology. Whence the assertion about Jewish exegetical errors may be a purely stylistic device and one that Luther borrowed from polemics, which frequently were cast in the form of a fictitious dialogue between a Christian and a Jew for the sole purpose of demonstrating Christian truths. On this, see Funkenstein, "Changes . . . in . . . Polemics," pp. 125–44.

whether the contemporary Jews and their fate are in fact the intended focus of the pamphlet! Thus, even in the early period Luther's missionizing activities—and according to Helmio,[42] the student of early Protestant missions to the Jews, Luther was the only one of the Protestants who seriously got involved in such— appear quite limited. They simply do not compare with the activity of the Catholics in this field.

In this light, it is possible to suggest that Luther's 1542 reversals had nothing to do with missions, but reflect his opinions of 1538 as they are found in his tract "Against the Sabbatarians."[43] There he pictures the Jews as fomenters of Christian heresy—specifically, the heresy of the Sabbatarians. This was one of a number of splinter sects which had appeared in early sixteenth-century Germany[44] and had adopted such Biblical practices as the observance of the Sabbath.[45] While it is highly improbable that Jews had anything directly to do with the appearance of these sects,[46] Luther believed they did.[47] Accordingly, in "Against the Sabbatarians," but especially in "Concerning the Jews and Their Lies," he spoke at length about bottling up the Jewish threat, and he warned against the snares of the devilish Jews.[48] So aroused was he that he called for the burning down of

---

42. Helmio, *Lutheran Reformation*, p. 92.

43. M. H. Bertram, trans. and intro., *LW*, 47:57–98.

44. On these sects, see G. H. Williams, *The Radical Reformation* (Philadelphia, 1962).

45. Ibid., pp. 252, 686, 731, 739, 834–35, for examples.

46. See Baron, *SRH*, 13:247–67. One reason Luther may have believed Jews were behind these sects was the numerous rather free disputes going on in Germany at that time between Jews and Christian humanists. On these debates, see H. H. Ben-Sasson, "Jewish-Christian Disputation in the Setting of Humanism and Reformation in the German Empire," *Harvard Theological Review* 59 (1966): 369–90.

47. *LW*, 4:65: "You informed me that the Jews are making inroads at various places throughout the country with their venom and their doctrine, and that they have already induced some Christians to let themselves be circumcised and to believe that the Messiah or Christ has not yet appeared, that the law of the Jews must prevail forever, that it must also be adopted by all the Gentiles, etc."

48. *LW*, 47:137: "I have published this little book, so that I might be found

Jewish houses and the eventual expulsion of the Jews from all of Germany,[49] to bring an end to their multifarious crimes and plots.

All this is a far cry from the Catholic position. Any references to Jewish crimes and subversion, whether in the *De Iudaeis* or in other Catholic writings, were tangential and always subordinated to the prime issue of conversion. Just the opposite, Luther made Jewish crimes central, and he wrote within the context of the impossibility of conversion.[50]

The absence of any specific conversionary purpose or program is also the case in Martin Bucer's tract on the Jews.[51] His 1538 *Judenratschlag* (*Opinion*) propounds a novel thesis in which the Protestants are the Chosen People, Israel, and the Jews the "strangers" spoken of in the Ten Commandments, by which Bucer understands "foreign residents." [52] These Jewish strangers, in conformity to the dictates of the commandment to observe the Sabbath, should abide by the customs of the land in which they live, that is, Christianity.[53] But because of the hope of their ultimate conversion,[54] the

---

among those . . . who warned the Christians to be on their guard against them"; and p. 140: "We are not talking with the Jews, but about the Jews and their dealings, so that our Germans too, might be informed." Indeed (*LW*, 47:268): ". . . we dare not tolerate their [Jews'] conduct. . . . if we do, we become sharers in their lies, cursing and blasphemy . . ."; (*LW*, 47:285): "Accordingly, it must and dare not be considered a trifling matter but a most serious one to seek counsel against this and to save our souls from the Jews, that is, from the devil and from eternal death. . . . If we permit Jewish blasphemy of Jesus, we together with the Jews and on their account will lose God the Father and his dear Son, who purchased us at such cost . . . and we will be eternally lost . . ."

49. *LW*, 47:139–75, 255–68, and 269–306, respectively.

50. Cf. *LW*, 47:137 and esp. 140.

51. All the documents concerning this opinion and the debate which engendered it have been conveniently gathered together in R. Stupperich, ed., *Martin Bucers Deutsche Schriften*, vol. 7, *Schriften der Jahre* 1538–39 (Gütersloh, 1964). The three documents used in the following brief discussion of Bucer are: (1) "Ratschlag, ob christlicher oberkeit gebüren müge, das sye die Juden undter den Christen zu wonen gedulden, und wa sye zu gedulden, wölcher gstalt und mass" (1538), pp. 342–61 (*Judenratschlag*); (2) "Bucers Brief an einen güten Freund" (May 10, 1539), pp. 362–76; and (3) "Philipps Brief und die Räte vom 23 Dezember 1538," pp. 380–82.

52. Ibid., p. 344, lines 15–21.

53. Ibid., p. 355: "Also habenn alle weisen, die ye von rechter Policey ges-

Jews are excused from this obligation, providing they adhere to the strict regulations placed upon them.[55]

To Landgrave Philip of Hesse, for whom the *Opinion* was composed, and who later wrote to Bucer that Jews should be treated kindly, in accordance with the writings of Paul,[56] Bucer responded that Paul's admonition to love Jews meant to tolerate them, but not to permit their excesses.[57] As for conversion, that is for the future.[58] Indeed, Bucer has no trust in those Jews who do convert, for conversion does not seem to halt their accustomed usuring and oppression of Christians.[59] Here again Protestant and Catholic opinion on the Jews is seen to be completely divergent.

Despite all that has been said, the possibility does remain that Catholic policy was erected as a reaction against either the actions or the theory of the Protestants. As for the actions, beyond the restrictions which both Catholics and Protestants placed upon the Jews, the one place in which there is a fairly clear line of demarcation between the two groups is, interestingly enough, in the general Protestant eschewal, as opposed to the heavy Catholic espousal, of missions. But to explain the Catholic missions as merely a pragmatic response to their absence among the Protestants is to be superficial. The question is why missions; for given the history of the lack of such activity on a significant scale throughout the Middle Ages, there is no *a priori* reason to assume that a lack of missions on the part of one of two contending parties would automatically stimulate the establishment of missions on the part of the other.

The Protestants, especially Luther, did, however, make some claims about the meaning and implication of conversion which the

chriebenn, das erkennet, das alle, die / jn einem volckh ader Stadt seindt sich der Religion desselbigen volcks halten . . ."

54. Ibid., p. 345 and p. 360.

55. Ibid., pp. 345–50.

56. *Philipps Brief,* ibid., p. 380: "Wir konnen aber bey uns nitt finden . . . das man die Juden eben also hart und gantz enge halten sollte, als der gelerharten Ratschlag ausweiset. . . . So spricht auch St. Paulus zun Romern am xi Cap. . . ."

57. *Bucer's Brief,* ibid., p. 374, lines 21–34.

58. Ibid. pp. 369–71.

59. *Opinion,* p. 355, lines 9–13.

Catholics, were they aware of them, could not have ignored. In 1523 Luther wrote that he would suggest some method and appropriate passages for those who wish to work with the Jews:

> For many, even of the sophists [scholastic theologians], have attempted this; but insofar as they have set about it in their own name, nothing has come of it. For they were trying to cast out the devil by means of the devil, and not by the finger of God.[60]

The clear implication is that the Catholic missions to the Jews have failed because the Catholics promote the message of the Devil and not the truth of Christianity, which is expounded solely by the Protestants. Conversely, the Protestant successes, which Luther may have expected at this point, would substantiate his assumptions about the truth of Protestantism and the falsity of Catholicism.

Now as discussed earlier, de Susannis had argued that the conversion of infidels, pagans, and Jews, which was so manifest in his day, was reaffirming Christian truth.[61] By Christian, of course, he meant Catholic, and it was not by coincidence that he chose to warn the Protestants of their error just at this point.[62] Furthermore, de Susannis was but one of many Catholics who advanced this particular argument.[63] On first inspection, therefore, one might assume that Protestant arguments about conversion were stimulating Catholic counter-arguments (or, of course, vice versa) and thus Catholic policy as well. In truth, little if any evidence can be adduced to support this thesis. Indeed, Luther himself did not persevere with his claims about Protestant conversionary potential.[64] Nor did others, such as John Knox, who had made statements similar to that of Luther.[65] The purpose behind such statements appears to have been only rhetorical, another way in which to deprecate Catholi-

---

60. *LW*, 45:213, and cf. there pp. 200 and 229.
61. III,1,29–31.
62. III,1,31.
63. Cf. supra, chap. 10, n. 30.
64. See esp. *LW*, 47:176–91, and see also Helmio, Lutheran Reformation, p. 92.
65. Cited in Helmio, *Protestant Reformation,* 90.

cism. In short, there was hardly any Protestant argument to which the Catholics might have been responding.[66]

Just the opposite, Catholics repeatedly and frequently pilloried the Protestants because the latter failed to seriously consider missions to any group, pagan or Jew, let alone to actively engage in them.[67] In addition, as discussed in the previous chapter, Catholics saw in the lack of Protestant missions a sure proof of Protestant error. On this level, then, Catholic missions may be seen as a response to the Protestants. Nevertheless, Catholic missions had been in existence since the fifteenth century. The lack of Protestant missions afforded Catholics an opportunity to deride Protestantism; this was not the positive reason which motivated their establishment by the Catholics. The same judgment must apply to the establishment of missions to the Jews. There has to be some specific positive reason which originated in the Catholic camp and militated toward an actively conversionary Jewry policy. Nor is it sufficient to see the Jewish missions as merely an extension of the general missions. Inertia, a feeling that if the pagans are to be proselytized why not the Jews also, will not account for the reversal of the Jewry policy of passive expectancy rooted in tradition and time.

The only area of possible cause left unexplored is that difficult and amorphous one of societal upheaval. In reaction to Protestantism, that is, to the disruption of the old world order, and thus in a general and overwhelming and not a particular or specific sense, Catholicism had to prove itself anew—to itself. One possible proof could come from the affirmation of Catholicism by the one group, the Jews, that had been so unyielding since the foundation of Christianity in its will to reject Christianity as truth. Indeed, there exists a literary motif which extends back to at least the ninth century in which Christian truth is particularly reaffirmed through the conversion of a Jew. Thus, in his tract *De Corpore et Sanguine Domini*,

---

66. Cf. immed., infra, on the ninth-century origins (if not earlier) of the notion that Jewish conversion confirmed Christian truth. Thus, the reappearance of this notion among sixteenth-century Catholics does not need to be attributed to the necessity to respond to a novel Protestant argument.

67. Cf. supra, chap. 10, n. 30.

an essay on the efficacy of the Eucharist, Paschasius Radabertus recounts the episodes of two Jews who first planned to mock the Eucharist, but then, through miraculous intercessions in which the wafer cleaved to the roof of the mouth of one and turned to real flesh in the mouth of the other, recognized and accepted Christian truth and baptism.[68] However, there is a vast difference between narrations, legendary at that, concerning the acts of individual Jews, and the actual conversion, and pursuit of conversion, of the Jews *en masse.* Something has to explain directly why the Church might have felt that it could reverse its centuries-old tradition and policy, so that it could obtain reaffirmation through the collective movement of the Jews to the baptismal font. The explanations suggested to now have all proved wanting.

Logically, then, an examination of the traditional teaching on the conversion of the Jews, and of the attitudes of sixteenth-century Catholics to that teaching, is now in order. According to tradition, the conversion of the Jews would occur simultaneously with the entrance into Christianity of the "plenitude of nations," that is, all the nations that had remained outside the Christian world. That event would take place at the time of the Last Judgment.[69] Put most directly and succinctly by St. Augustine:

And in connection with that judgment the following events will come to pass, as we have learned: Elias the Tishbite shall come; the Jew shall believe; Antichrist shall persecute; Christ shall judge; the dead shall rise; the good and the wicked shall be separated; the world shall be burned and renewed.[70]

With the publication of the *Catechism of the Council of Trent* at the command of Pius V, moreover, this tradition became dogma.[71] The

68. On this tale, see Blumenkranz, *Auteurs,* pp. 191–95, and p. 260, for a similar story in which Wazo, bishop of Liège, is proved worthy because of his ability to defeat a Jew in a religious dispute.
69. Matt. 24:14, Rom. 11:25. See Browe, *Judenmission,* pp. 306–10, for a discussion of this subject.
70. *City of God,* trans. M. Dods, bk. 20, chap. 30, p. 762.
71. *The Catechism of the Council of Trent: Published by the Command of Pope Pius the Fifth,* trans. J. Donovan (New York, 1929), p. 64.

origin of this tradition is to be found in Romans 11:25, "Caecitas ex parte cecidit in Israel, donec plenitudo gentium intraret; et sic [v. 26] omnis Israel salvus fieret." And Romans 11:25 was universally taken to refer to the end of the world. Accordingly, in his commentary on Psalm 58:7, "Convertentur ad vesperam . . . ," Robert Bellarmine[72] explains that this verse speaks "De conversione iudaeorum circa finem mundi, [as in] Rom. 11:25, caecitas, etc." [73] In short, tradition, dogma, and exegesis were all in agreement: the Jews would not convert as a group until the consummation. Now this, of course, was de Susannis' view too; except that he believed the consummation was nearly at hand. Whence it does not seem unreasonable to hypothesize that those who supported the papal policy of immediate mass conversion must have done so because, like de Susannis, they too believed in the imminence of the consummation.

A brief examination of some fifteenth-century and early-sixteenth-century polemics will begin to support this hypothesis. Between 1440 and 1459 St. Antoninus, the archbishop of Florence, wrote his *Historiarum Domini*.[74] Attached to the end of the second part of this history is the "Epistola Rabbi Samuelis missa Rabbi Isaac," purportedly written in the year 1000. According to Antoninus, the letter was originally written in Arabic and was then translated into Latin in 1339 by a Dominican, Alfonso de Bonihominis.[75] Bonihominis, who taught in Paris, not only translated the letter, but in fact he trumped it up, reworking an anti-Jewish tract written in 1163 by a Jewish convert to Islam, Samual ibn Abbas.[76] Whatever

---

72. Bellarmine's exegesis is cited to show that the traditional interpretation of the verse continued through the sixteenth century.

73. R. Bellarmine, *Opera Omnia*, ed. J. Feure (Paris, 1874), 10:382.

74. Antonini Archipresulis Florenti, *Historiarum Domini* (Lyons, 1517).

75. "Epistola Rabbi Samuelis missa Rabbi Isaac sub anno domini Millesimo, Translata de Arabico in Latinum per fratrem Alphonsum bonihominis, Ordinis Praedicatorum, sub anno domini MCCCXXXIX," is the title given by Antoninus to this letter, which is printed as an appendix, divided into its own chapters, to the *Historiarum Domini*.

76. See B. Blumenkranz, "Anti-Jewish Polemics," *Journal of Jewish Studies* 15 (1964): 133; and N. Daniels, *Islam and the West*, p. 189. The tract of Ibn Abbas (al-Maghribi), which Blumenkranz leaves unnamed, was probably the *Ifḥam al-Yahud*. See "Samau'al al-Maghribi Ifḥam al-Yahud (Silencing the Jews),"

its real provenance, the letter represents Antoninus' opinions. In essence it conveys Rabbi Samuel's conviction that the Jews are in error, a conviction he elucidates through such statements as: "I fear, my lord, that we became renegades from God at the first advent," and therefore merited punishment has fallen on the Jews,[77] or "What are we waiting for? Do we not see that [God] has dispersed us?" [78]

But Rabbi Samuel also writes in many of the chapters, almost as a refrain:

> I fear, my lord, that what God said through the mouth of Isaiah has been fulfilled in us: Blindness has fallen on Israel until that time when all the nations convert,[79] . . . [and] therefore, we are either blind or the deceivers of the simple [if we do not see] that our captivity will not end until the end of the world.[80]

In other words, Antoninus is convinced that the Jews will remain in their error until the consummation. The letter nowhere indicates that the Jews will soon convert, nor does it call for efforts to be made to seek their conversion.

In 1484 Iacob Perez de Valencia, the bishop of Christopolis, wrote a commentary on the Psalms. To this he attached a *Tractatus Contra Iudaeos*,[81] whose purpose is to explain the errors of the Jews concerning the messiah. Four things, Perez de Valencia says,

ed. and trans. Moshe Perlmann, *Proceedings of the American Academy for Jewish Research* 32 (1964). Interestingly, the so-called "Letter of Rabbi Samuel" was printed in the sixteenth century as: Samuel Abu Nasr Ibn Abbas, *Tractatus Rabbi Samuelis, errorem Iudaeorum indicans* (Venice, 1514). See the *Short Title Catalog of Books Printed in Italy . . . 1501–1600 . . .* (Boston, 1970), 1:1, which indicates that this edition can be found at the Hebrew Union College, Cincinnati.

77. "Epistola Rabbi Samuelis," chap. 25.

78. Ibid., chap. 15.

79. Ibid., chap. 14: "Timeo domine mi quod sit completum in nobis quod dixit Deus per Esaiam: cecidit cecitas super Israel quousque intraverit gentium plenitudo."

80. Ibid., chap. 4: "Ergo vel sumus ceci vel deceptores simplicium, [if we do not see] . . . ista captivitate . . . non habet finem nisi in fine mundi."

81. *Centum ac Quinquaginta Psalmi Davidi, Cum . . . Expositione Reverendi in Christo Patris Domini Iacobi Perez de Valencia . . . Accessit ad Haec Tractatus Contra Iudaeos* (Lyons, 1514).

hold the Jews in their obstinacy and blindness: they believe the literal observance of their law is sufficient to win salvation; they see the reward promised them as a temporal reward; they see the messiah as a human; and they call the Gospels false.[82] Even those Spanish Jews who have converted have not necessarily seen the truth. For of those who convert today, there are many who are brought to baptism through force, as the result of riots, and they often revert to Judaism. Many others convert with no conviction, but only for the purpose of their business dealings, and they become sincere converts only in the third generation. It is but the remaining few out of this large number who really do see the truth, whence we are forced to conclude that

> The Jews will remain blind in their obstinacy until the second advent of Christ, until Elijah comes to preach to them and to declare to them the truth of the Law of Moses and the Prophets. And then they will recognize that they have been deluded and deceived; and thus they will convert.[83]

Quite clearly, then, Perez de Valencia, like St. Antoninus, believes that true conversion, let alone sincere mass conversion, will occur only at the time of the Second Coming.

What both men were in fact doing when they wrote about the Jews is well illustrated by the *De Christiana Religione* (1476) of Marsilio Ficino.[84] At both the beginning and end of this work Ficino states that his arguments have proved the truth of Christianity. He commences with an array of proofs drawn from the Old[85] and New Testaments[86] and from the Sybilline oracles,[87] and he concludes with a review of "rabbinic learning" which attests to the messianic nature

---

82. Ibid., fol. 467[r].

83. Ibid., fol. 467[v]: "Et sic manent Iudaei caeci in sua obstinatione usque ad secundum adventum Christi: antequam veniet Helyas ad praedicandum eis et declarandum eis veritatem legis moysi et prophetarum. Et tunc cognoscent se esse delusos et deceptos: et sic convertent. . . ."

84. M. Ficino, *Opera Omnia* (Basle, 1576), I[i], pp. 1–77.

85. Ibid., pp. 30–52.

86. Ibid., pp. 1–25.

87. Ibid., pp. 25–30.

of Christ.[88] In the course of the tract he refers to the "desolate condition" of the Jews. Their wretchedness, he says, refutes their interpretations of Genesis 49:10; those who believe that the Jews still possess
any *regnum* are delirious. After 1,476 years, they have no hope
of restoration.[89] Using a rhetorical direct address, he asks the Jews
why they maintain their observance of the Law and why they do
not recognize that they have been punished for killing Christ.[90] But
Ficino has no hope of converting the Jews, at least not for the present. At the end of the tract he says that the Jews insist on remaining in their error because of their inability to grasp the truth about
Christ, and because of their love of greed and their inborn hatred of
Christians.[91]

Thus the *De Christiana Religione* is precisely what Ficino
says it is, an apologetic. It discusses the Jews only for the purpose
of demonstrating the truth of Christianity, both by expounding on
the fate of those who have rejected Christ, and also by showing that
the Jewish texts themselves indicate that Christ was the messiah.
Essentially, St. Antoninus and Perez de Valencia had the same
apologetic goal as Ficino. It is quite understandable, therefore, that
in each of the three apologies an attempt was made to explain away
the failure of the Jews to convert, as well as to explain why such
conversion was not to be expected in the near future. God, all three
concurred, had decided that the Jews would see the truth only in the
distant future, at the time of the Second Coming. Thus, those who
did not believe in the imminence of the consummation produced
apologetic polemics. But as was seen in the previous chapter,
polemics calling for immediate conversionary activity began to ap-

---

88. Ibid., pp. 52–71.
89. Ibid., p. 32.
90. Ibid., pp. 51–53.
91. Ibid., p. 77: "Quaeritur igitur, quae nam causa sit, quae Iudaeos adhuc
multos in perfidia detinet? Propheticorum, Christianorumque mysteriorum divina
profunditas, et quia divina, ideo humana intelligentia non penetrabilis, atque e
converso. Rursus ingenium mercenariorum, miserabiliumque iudaeorum incultum
prorsus et pertinax. Avaritia tum eius quod suum est servandi, tum faciendi foe-
noris inexplebilis naturalis suorum amor, innatum odium Christianorum."

pear in the sixteenth century. This suggests a reverse of position on the issue of the imminence of the Second Coming.[92]

That men did predicate the feasibility of missions to the Jews on the basis of the belief that the consummation and the conversion of the Jews would occur simultaneously is readily demonstrable. In his *De Convocando Concilia,* Aleander expressed his hope that the Christians who had left the Church could still be easily brought back to it. These Christians, he said, differ from the non-Christian nations, for only God knows when the latter will return to the right faith.

> They are now so confirmed in their errors that they seem unrecallable by human labor or counsel. Therefore, they should be left to the justice and will of the highest God, just as the case of the Jews should be committed to the one God. And if He does not alter His determination, *in that final age* all will return to the Christian flock, when, with the end of all force and the rendering of peace to miserable mortals, "there will be one flock and one shepherd."[93]

Quite clearly, Aleander sees no purpose in establishing missions to the Jews. He is convinced that their conversion will be the result of an act of God which will occur only *illa postrema etate.*

This point of view is seen most clearly in de Torres' *De Sola Lectione.* There are some, he notes, who question why efforts should be made to convert the Jews, since the Jews are blind and will not

---

92. Cf. Blumenkranz, *Juifs et Chrétiens,* pp. 68–83, esp. pp. 75 and 83, where he discusses apologetical polemics in the early Middle Ages. What he concludes about the polemic of the early Middle Ages applies equally to the polemic of the end of the Middle Ages, namely, that much polemic was written not for the purpose of winning converts but as apologia for internal consumption. Cf. the discussion of this subject, p. 243f., supra.

93. Hieronymo Aleander, "De Convocando Concilio Sententia" (1537), in V. Schweitzer, ed., *Concilii Tridentini Tractatum,* 12:121: "Adeo iam sunt confirmati in suis illis erroribus, ut videantur nulla humana opereque consilio revocare posse. Relinquendi sunt igitur iustitie atque arbitrio summi Dei veluti Iudaeorum etiam cura uno Deo committenda est, et si constat, illa postrema etate omnes ad ovile christianum perventuros, quando, cessante omni vi paceque reddita miseris mortalibus, fiet unum ovile et unus pastor."

convert until the entrance of the plenitude of nations. At first, de Torres combats this objection by proposing that the Jews have been blinded not only by God, but also by their own actions, and that this self-imposed blindness can be removed.[94] Further on, he expands on this theme by stipulating that there are two kinds of power which effect conversions. The first is the power of the Gospel word, which is ever efficacious. The second is the power "compellendi virtute, ac potestate puniendi, non ad destruendam, sed ad aedificanda data,"[95] and this is to be used only at the end of days.[96] However, he then adds,

> You see, reverend fathers, the situation, the time, and the reason [for using] this holy compulsion. [For in our cities all except the Jews believe in Christ.] Therefore, why do you not force them with the power that has been given to you to hear the word of God.[97]

In other words, de Torres personally does believe that he is living in the end of days. It is this conviction which provides the true basis for his missionary ardor. Yet he finds it more expedient not to speak of the consummation. Rather, he claimed that the Jews have blinded themselves, for he recognized that to encourage conversionary efforts he had to dissipate the opposition to such efforts based on the claim that the consummation was not at hand. It was apparently easier to accomplish this by finding an entirely different basis for missions than by convincing men that the consummation was imminent. The accepted teaching that the conversion of the Jews would occur only *ad vesperam* was thus, beyond a doubt, a decisive factor in inhibiting missions to the Jews. The appearance of such missions in the sixteenth century argues strongly that the impetus behind their creation was the growth of eschatological speculation.

The studies of Delio Cantimori and G. H. Williams have demonstrated the existence of considerable eschatology among the

---

94. De Torres, *De Sola Lectione,* p. 143.
95. Ibid., p. 158.
96. Ibid., p. 158.
97. Ibid., p. 159: "Videtis Rev. patres sanctae huius compulsionis genus, tempus, et rationem. . . . Hos ergo non cogetis verbo Dei, et potestate vobis data?"

Evangelicals and heretics.[98] Cantimori, for example, describes how many heretics were persuaded that in the immediate future there would be a revival of the Apostolic Church, and that following this renewal, there would occur the mass conversion of the infidels and the Last Judgment.[99] Williams points to a number of eschatological references in the sermons of the Evangelicals, and adds that the Erastians often colored their hopes for the revival of the primitive Church with eschatological overtones. The later Italian Anabaptists, too, intimately associated their hope for Church renewal with a belief in the nearness of the eschaton.[100]

Such theorizing was not limited to heretical or marginally orthodox circles. In their studies of Giles of Viterbo and Geronimo de Mendieta, O'Malley and Phelan, respectively, note that the age was filled with apocalyptic speculation.[101] Humbert refers to apocalyptic ferment in 1476 and again in 1500.[102] And Chastel, discussing the eschatology of men of various shades of orthodoxy in his article on Antichrist in the Renaissance, adverts to the anticipation of an imminent Golden Age,[103] to the predictions of astrologers, and to the prophecies of many wandering preachers.[104] One of these preachers, Francesco da Meleto, reported a conversation he had with a rabbi at Constantinople. The rabbi had told him that if the messiah did not arrive by 1484, all Jews would embrace Christianity.[105] Meleto, to be sure, was already independently con-

---

98. Delio Cantimori, *Eretici Italiani del cinquecento* (Florence, 1939); idem, *Prospettive di storia ereticale italiana del cinquecento* (Bari, 1960); G. H. Williams, *The Radical Reformation* (Philadelphia, 1962). Cf. Eva-Marie Jung, "On the Nature of Evangelism in Sixteenth Century Italy," *Journal of the History of Ideas* 14 (1953): 511–27, for a description of the Evangelicals.

99. Cantimori, *Eretici Italiani*, pp. 13–17.

100. Williams, *Radical Reformation*, pp. 1–18, 560–61.

101. J. W. O'Malley, *Giles of Viterbo*, p. 109; J. L. Phelan, *The Millennial Kingdom of the Franciscans in the New World: A Study of the Writings of Geronimo de Mendieta (1525–1604)* (Berkeley, 1956), pp. 19–27.

102. Humbert, *Les Origines*, p. 112.

103. Andre Chastel, "L'Antichrist à la Renaissance," in *L'Umanesimo e il Demoniaco nell'arte*, ed. Enrico Castelli (Milan, 1952), p. 177.

104. Ibid., p. 178.

105. Ibid., p. 179.

vinced that the early sixteenth century would be a time of conversion. The Jews would convert by 1517, the Muslims would follow by 1536, and in the 1530s a true unity of all Christians would be achieved.[106] Paul of Middleburg engaged in explicitly eschatological astrology which convinced him that the period between 1450 and 1520 would be a revolutionary one, in which Antichrist would appear and the Jews would convert.[107] In 1496 Giovanni Nesi, one of Ficino's pupils, wrote the poem "Oraculum de novo saeculo," which speaks of the reform of the Church, millennial catastrophes, and the ultimate triumph of the Church, all of which are at hand.[108] In addition, Chastel feels that the works of da Vinci, Signorelli, and Duhrer depicting apocalyptic catastrophes provide strong evidence for the existence of eschatological speculation.[109] Eschatological speculation also materialized in 1588, based on the astrological predictions of Regiomontanus.[110] Nor was such speculation confined to Christians. Messianic ferment developed in Sephardic Jewish circles,[111] especially in the writings of Abravanel and Ibn Yaḥya,[112] around the figure of Solomon Molcho,[113] and perhaps in the 1538 Ordination Controversy in Safed.[114] It also seems to have played a role in the 1558 drive

106. Ibid., p. 184.
107. Ibid., p. 180.
108. Ibid., p. 183.
109. Ibid., p. 185.
110. Garrett Mattingly, *The Armada* (Boston, 1962), pp. 175–86.
111. Confirmation of this ferment is found in the warnings of Azariah de Rossi, *Sefer Me'or 'Eynayim*, ed. D. Cassel and Z. H. Yafe (Warsaw, 1899), chap. 43. See also H. H. Ben-Sasson, "Jewish-Christian Disputation in the Setting of Humanism and Reformation in the German Empire," *Harvard Theological Review* 59 (1966), p. 383.
112. Abravanel's messianic speculation is contained in his trilogy: *Ma'ayenai ha-Yeshu'ah* (Ferrara, 1551), *Mashmi'a Yeshu'ah* (Salonika, 1526), and *Yeshu'ot Meshiḥo* (Koenigsburg, 1861). Ibn Yaḥya, *Shalshelet ha-Qabbalah*, pp. 105–9, although with a great deal of obfuscation, states his belief that 1598 will be the messianic year.
113. See Baron, *SRH*, 13:112–15.
114. See J. Katz, "The Controversy on the Semikha (Ordination) between Rabbi Yacob Bei-Rav and the Ralbaḥ" (Hebrew), *Zion* 16 (1951): 38 ff. In opposition to Katz, who attributes the controversy to messianic ferment, see H. Dimitrovsky, "Rabbi Yaakov Berab's Academy" (Hebrew), *Sefunot* 7 (1963): 57.

which culminated in the publication of the Zohar at Mantua.[115]

It thus appears that eschatological speculation was not at all unusual in the sixteenth century. Indeed, the amount of speculation was so great that in 1590 the Jesuit Jose de Acosta wrote a tract attacking it. He condemned, however, only attempts to fix the precise date of the consummation, but made no attempt to deny that men were living in the last days.[116]

This particular stance may have had its origin in the decree on preaching issued in 1516 at the Fifth Lateran Council, which ordered that only those clerics who had been approved for preaching by their bishops could deliver sermons. Approval, however, did not grant license. Preachers were to adhere to traditional interpretations of Scripture and not introduce their own opinions. Specifically,

> They should in no way presume to preach or bring the news of the exact time of future evils, Antichrist's advent, or the precise day of Judgment, since the truth says that it is not ours to know the times or the moments which the Father has placed in His power. . . . Nevertheless, if the Lord shall have revealed to certain [preachers], by a special inspiration, particular future events, we do not at all wish to impede these men.[117]

---

115. In his introduction to this edition, Isa. Lattes is specific: „גילוי סתרי תורה על ידי האל הוא ישועה. והנה כמעט ועבר „השליש הששי" ומתי נדע דעת ה'. באלף השביעי, כשכבר נחרב העולם?
[In order to lead Israel from exile, the people need to know all that is secret—הנסתר] וכל שכן עתה שקרובה הישועה להגלות . . . זכות העיון בספר הזהר מספיק להסיר שבותנו ולהעביר גלותנו . . . ובשר הזהר שבדור שעתיד המשיח להתגלות, בו יותן הרשות להתגלות ספרו וחבורו."
In short, the Zohar should be published as part of the preparation for the imminent appearance of the messiah.

116. Phelan, *Mendieta,* pp. 25–27. (Jose de Acosta, *De Temporibus Novissimis* [Rome, 1590].)

117. *Conciliorum Oecumenicorum Decreta,* ed. J. Alberigo et al. (Basle, 1962), pp. 613, 1–31; or Hardouin, *Acta,* 9:1808: "Tempus quoque praefixum futurorum malorum, vel Antichristi adventum, aut certum diem iudicii praedicare vel afferre nequaquam praesumant: cum veritas dicat, non esse nostrum nosse tempora vel momenta, quae pater posuit in sua potestate. . . . Ceterum si quibusdam eorum Dominus futura quaedam in Dei ecclesia inspiratione quapiam revelaverit, hos . . . impediri minime volumus."

Like de Acosta's tract, this decree specifically opposes precise cal-
culations. On the other hand, it also seems to suggest that the news
of the imminence of the consummation was expected at any moment.

All this speculation must have been stimulated by three events
that were seen as the defection from the faith, the coming of Antichrist, and the conversion of the nations, which both tradition and
doctrine had established as preconditions of the consummation.[118]
The outbreak of Protestantism and the threat of engulfment by the
Turks were interpreted as the defection and as Antichrist. Salvatore
Meucci, for instance, identified the Turk with Antichrist, and he
feared that the Turk and the Emperor were about to join in a league
of destruction.[119] Giles of Viterbo, too, claimed that the Turk was
Antichrist, who was soon to scourge the nations in recompense for
their worldliness.[120] Accordingly, Braudel writes that many saw the
Turk as the scourge of God, the Assyria and the Babylonia of the
Church, who was sent to punish it for its sinful state.[121] Similarly,
Jedin states that the advance of the Turk after 1453 put men into
an apocalyptic mood.[122] Luther too was seen as Antichrist, or as
his forerunner.[123] Nowhere is this identification more evident than
in the tract, *Il Modello de Lutero,* written in 1554 by Jacobus Moronessa, who eventually became the vicar general of the Celestines.[124]

The third event stimulating eschatological speculation was the
discovery of the New World; for many began to interpret this discovery to mean that God had finally made possible the universal
preaching of His Word, and hence the conversion of the nations.[125]
The success of the missions which had followed the discoveries,

---

118. Donovan, *Catechism of Trent,* p. 64.

119. M. Reeves, "Joachimist Expectations in the Order of Augustinian
Hermits," *Recherches de Théologie ancienne et médiévale* 25 (1958): 133–34.

120. O'Malley, *Giles of Viterbo,* pp. 106, 110, 113.

121. F. Braudel, *La Mediterranée et le monde mediterranéen a l'époque de
Philippe II* (Paris, 1963).

122. Jedin, *Council of Trent,* 1:44–45.

123. Chastel, "L'Anticrist," p. 185; Phelan, *Mendieta,* p. 25.

124. For a description of this tract, see F. Lauchert, *Die Italienischen literarischer Gegner Luthers* (Freiburg, 1912), pp. 633–69.

125. Phelan, *Mendieta,* pp. 66–74.

moreover, was taken as a confirmation of this interpretation. The Franciscan missionary Geronimo de Mendieta is perhaps the most outstanding example of a man who was convinced of the eschatological meaning of the discoveries.[126] Mendieta spent his life working for the conversion of the New World Indians, believing that the second advent was contingent on the regeneration of the primitive Church, which in his mind was identical with the Indian Church.[127] This conviction Mendieta propagandized in his *Historia Indiana Ecclesiastica,*[128] which was apparently well received by Spanish Franciscans.[129]

Thus the general missionary impulse of the sixteenth century was in part a product of eschatological hopes.[130] It is only logical therefore, especially in the light of Romans 11:25, to assume that the same speculation was also responsible for the establishment of missions to the Jews. What is more, Romans 11:25 had linked the conversion of the Jews not only with the consummation, but also with the conversion of the nations. Thus, whatever impulses eschatological speculation gave toward the establishment of missions to the Jews, these could only be strengthened beyond measure by the fact of the missionary successes which were being recorded daily among the infidels. These points are borne out by the *De Iudaeis.* The factor which convinced de Susannis of the imminence of the consummation was the discovery of the New World and the ensuing large-scale conversions. It was this conviction which, in turn, prompted him to call for the conversion of both Muslim and Jew.[131]

De Susannis was not the only one who thought this way. Others did too, particularly Giles of Viterbo, whose eschatological hopes are explicit.[132] In his famous speech before the Fifth Lateran

---

126. Ibid., pp. 12, 17 ff.

127. Ibid., pp. 49 ff., 66–74.

128. Ibid., p. 56. Still (p. 102), the book was not published until 1870, but only because of its criticisms of Spanish New World policies.

129. Ibid., pp. 17 f., 42–45, 104.

130. The Jesuits too were probably stimulated in their missionary activities by the application of Joachitic prophecies to them. See infra, pp. 254–57.

131. III,1,29.

132. O'Malley, *Giles of Viterbo,* passim. Also on Giles, see M. Reeves,

Council in 1512, he said that after twenty years of preaching about
the wonders of the apocalypse, he was certain that he was about
to experience their fulfillment.[133] Underlying this certainty was
Giles' theory that the world was destined to pass through ten increasingly imperfect ages, which were comparable to the Ten Sefi-
roth of the Kabbalah. The ninth age had begun with the death of
Celestine V and had ended with the death of Julius II. It had ended,
however, with hopeful signs—the discoveries in the New World,
the building of St. Peter's in Rome, and the renewal of Biblical
studies.[134] These signs portended the events of the tenth age, in
which Giles believed that he was living.[135] During this age, the true
goal of reform, the consummation, would be achieved, through the
unity of all men within the Church.[136] It is not surprising, then, that
Giles saw the discovery of the New World as both the herald of unity
and also the signal that the time for the conversion of the infidels,
including the Jews, had arrived.[137]

Eschatological speculation in the sixteenth century was also
promoted by the revival of Joachimism. As Marjorie Reeves has
demonstrated, Joachitic thought penetrated both the Jesuits and the
Augustinian Hermits.[138] Through the writings of Salvatore Meucci,

---

Prophecy in the Later Middle Ages (Oxford, 1969), pp. 270, 364–67; this book
contains a wealth of material pertinent to the whole question of eschatology
in the sixteenth century, esp. pp. 359–92, 429–503.

133. Mansi, 32:col. 669; or Hardouin, *Acta,* 9:1567–81; 1576: "Joaniis
Apolcalypsim de successu ecclesiae, universae ferme Italiae enarraverim; ac saepe
numero affirmaverim, eos qui tunc audiebant, ingentes ecclesiae aliquando con-
specturos, et agitationes et clades visuros. Illius emendationem nunc par esse
visum est, ut qui haec dixerat ventura, idem venisse testatur." Cf. the comments
on this address in Reeves, "Joachimist Expectations," pp. 135–40.

134. O'Malley, *Giles of Viterbo,* pp. 100–08.

135. Ibid., pp. 108–09.

136. Ibid., p. 110.

137. Ibid., pp. 113–15. Cf. supra, p. 205, on Giles' Kabbalism and infra,
p. 255, on his Joachimism, both of which encouraged his eschatological speculations and his efforts to convert the Jews.

138. Reeves, "Joachimist Expectations," pp. 111–41, idem, "The Abbot
Joachim and the Society of Jesus," *Medieval and Renaissance Studies* 5 (1961):
163–81, and also idem, *Prophecy,* pp. 251–90. The early chapters of Reeves'
work provide an excellent study of Joachim's thought and its subsequent influence.

a number of Augustinian Hermits began to see themselves as the *ordo heremitarum,* one of two orders which Joachim had claimed would arise to prepare the way for the third *status.* Significantly, one of those who was influenced by Meucci was Giles of Viterbo.[139] The Jesuits, according to Reeves, did not regularly apply Joachitic terminology to themselves, but they were nevertheless highly flattered when others referred to them as the second of the two orders foreseen by Joachim, the *ordo monachorum.*[140] Many Jesuits, she furthermore notes, probably did consider themselves to be in fact the spiritual men of Joachim, who among other things were the agents appointed to fulfill the missionary prophecies of Vincent Ferrer, who was himself highly influenced by Joachim.[141] Joachimism flourished among certain groups of Franciscans too. Phelan claims that after the reforms of Cardinal Cisneros in the late fifteenth century, no Spanish Franciscan was without Joachitic influence, including, of course, Mendieta.[142] Not surprisingly, Joachimism also penetrated the Celestines, in the person of Moronessa, the author of *Il Modello de Lutero.*[143] Of interest is the fact that Moronessa dedicated this work, which identifies Luther with Antichrist, to Scipio Rebiba, who was made a cardinal by Paul IV and was one of that pope's few confidants.[144] Thus, directly and by association, Joachimism and its eschatology appeared among groups and individuals who, as seen

Phelan, *Mendieta,* p. 24, notes that in the early sixteenth century the Venetian publishers were busy republishing both authentic and pseudo-Joachimist tracts.

139. Reeves, "Joachimist Expectations," pp. 128–35. Reeves claims that Giles was clearly interested in the work of Meucci's circle. O'Malley, *Giles of Viterbo,* pp. 61–62, however, is only prepared to admit that many of Giles' ideas are compatible with those of Joachim. He makes this stricture because, he says, Giles stated that he rejected Joachimism. But then O'Malley admits that the full extent of Gile's Joachimism remains to be measured.

140. Reeves, "The Abbot Joachim," passim; she notes especially that some Jesuits were describing Loyola in explicitly Joachimist terms (p. 170).

141. Ibid., pp. 167–68; she notes there that Ferrer's prophecies enjoyed much popularity in the sixteenth century.

142. Phelan, *Mendieta,* pp. 15, 43; Reeves, *Prophecy,* p. 446, where she especially notes Cisneros' expectation of the imminence of the Last Things.

143. Lauchert, *Literarischen Gegner Luthers,* p. 637.

144. Ibid., p. 633. On Rebiba, see R. Ancel, "L'Activité réformatrice de Paul IV," *Revue des Questiones Historiques* 86 (1907): 72 f.

here and in the previous chapter too, were deeply involved in the promotion of missions to both the infidels and the Jews.

The relationship between Jochimism and missions is explained by Joachim's own tract, *Adversus Iudaeos*.[145] Not an apologetic, this tract avows as its explicit purpose to teach the Jews the validity of Christian truth and thereby to affect their conversion. It is not surprising, therefore, that early in the tract Joachim states that he feels compelled to write: "Because I feel that the time of having pity on the Jews has arrived, the time of their consolation and conversion." [146] Ostensibly the "time" Joachim refers to is the consummation, because he further declares: "Cum plenitudo gentium intraverit tunc omnis Israel salvus fierit." [147] However, he distinguishes two stages in the conversion of the Jews. First, near the end of the world, a substantial number of Jews will convert. But an equal number, at least, will join forces with Antichrist and will convert only after Antichrist's defeat.[148] Thus the time of the Jews' "consolation" is not only the consummation, but also the period immediately preceding it. Accordingly, Joachim, who believes that he is living at the time fixed for the first stage in the conversion of the Jews, says:

> Desiring some of you, at least, even before this general time, by virtue of the propinquity of the kingdom of light, to break out of the darkness, we have labored over this work in order to lead you, O Jewish men, into the benedictions of sweetness.[149]

---

145. Arsenio Frugoni, ed., *Adversus Judaeos di Gioacchino da Fiore* (Rome, 1957).

146. Ibid., p. 3: ". . . verum etiam quia adesse sentio tempus miserandi eis, tempus consolationis et conversionis eorum." Also, p. 85: ". . . Annuntio Vobis adesse tempus consolationis vestrae tantum ut afflicti pro peccatis vestris agnoscitis et confiteamini iniquitates vestras, scientes et intelligentes quod non absque causa abstulerit vobis Deus sacerdotium et regnum . . ."

147. Ibid., p. 92.

148. Ibid., p. 48: "Inde est quod effectus caecus, secundum maiorem sui partem, recepturus est Antichristum." There p. (48) Frugoni cites the parallel in the *Tractatus super Quattuor Evangelia:* "Et verum est quod Iudaeorum populus circa finem mundi convertetur ad Deum, et verum est quod suscipiet Antichristum, quia et plenitudo quidem eorum convertetur ad Deum, et pars non modica adherebit Antichristo, deseviens in persecutione eorum qui convertentur ad Deum."

149. Ibid., p. 95: "Sed cupientes aliquos vestrum etiam ante tempus illud

This statement, the heart of the *Adversus Iudaeos,* propounds the necessity of making immediate efforts to convert the Jews. Those sixteenth-century men who were influenced by Joachimism and who were also fostering conversion certainly could have found no incompatibility between their views on the Jews and those of Joachim himself. On the contrary, in those views they probably found encouragement. There can, furthermore, be little doubt that their ideas about conversion, like Joachim's, were predicated on the "propinquity of the kingdom of light." [150]

Thus a pervasive eschatological climate undeniably stimulated efforts to convert the Jews. But while the relationship between this climate and such efforts may be discussed in terms of Joachimism, Protestantism, and New World discoveries, most indicative of the effect this climate exerted on the issue of missions to the Jews was the use almost as a slogan of the phrase, "Et fiet unum ovile et unus pastor" (John 10:16), to express eschatological hopes. Indeed, the use of this phrase is also most indicative of the very existence of this climate. Nicholas of Lyra's *Expositiones* on the *Glossa Ordinaria* interpret this phrase as follows: "et fiet: una ecclesia ex iudaeis et gentibus collecta; unus pastor: s. Christus." [151] In the context of the whole verse: "And other sheep I have which are not of this fold; them also I must bring, and they shall hear my voice; and there shall be one flock and one shepherd," Lyra's interpretation invests the phrase with eschatological significance: it rings of Matthew 24:14, "intraverit gentium plenitudo," as well as of Romans 11:25. Lyra's interpretations were also in general use.[152]

Paradoxically, the citation of John 10:16 that shows most

---

generale saltim pro ipsa vicinitate lucis de regno eripere tenebrarum, dedimus operam in hoc opusculo prevenire vos, O viri Iudaei, in benedictionibus."

150. Cf. Reeves, *Prophecy,* pp. 235–37, where she speaks of the Franciscan Petrus Galatinus, who combined a belief in the imminence of the consummation with Joachimism and Kabbalistic studies, and who, of course, expected the imminent conversion of the Jews.

151. *Bibliorum Sacrorum cum glossa ordinaria et N. Lyrani expositionibus* (Lyons, 1545), 6:fol. 216ᵛ.

152. B. Smalley, *The Study of the Bible in the Middle Ages* (Notre Dame, 1964), pp. 274, 367.

clearly that Lyra's interpretation was standard comes from Aleander, who did not believe in the imminence of the consummation.
Discussing the conversion of the nations, he wrote that he had little
hope for their conversion. That would only occur *"illa postrema
etate* [when] fiet unum ovile et unus pastor." [153] The difference between Aleander and those who did believe in the imminence of the
consummation was that the latter used a phrase like "When X happens" rather than "illa postrema etate" before their citations of "Et
fiet . . . ." And the X they had in mind was an event which they expected would soon occur. De Susannis, for example, said that when
the Jews are converted, then "fiet unum ovile et unus pastor." [154]
Concerning Giles of Viterbo, O'Malley reports that as a result of
the discovery of the New World, his "expectations were high for the
final accomplishment of the Johanine prophecy, 'So there shall be
one flock and one shepherd.' " [155] Interestingly, Giles pictured a
succession of first a temporal and then a spiritual pastor. The temporal pastor was Charles V, whose 1527 sack of Rome Giles called
a needed purgation, and whose next task was to defeat the Turk.
At that point the flock would become a spiritual flock, and its pastor
would be the pope. [156] Similarly, Cardinal Cisneros dreamed that
after a final Crusade led by Spain, there would be one flock and one
pastor, a *renovatio mundi,* and he himself would celebrate Mass
before the Holy Sepulchre. [157] John 10:16 also found its way into
the writings of Mendieta. Like Giles, Mendieta conceived of a temporal pastor followed by a spiritual one. His temporal pastor, however, was Philip II. [158]

Of great significance is the fact that John 10:16 was used
publicly. In his speech before the Fifth Lateran Council, Balthazar
del Rio called on Ferdinand of Aragon and Leo X to organize a

153. See supra, p. 247, n. 93, for the full citation.
154. III,1,29: "Sed etiam Iudaica perfidia ad Christum convertetur ['prope
mundi finem' (II,6,28), which is cited at this point in III,1,29; and he has just
said that he is now 'prope excidium mundi'] . . . et tunc fiet. . . ."
155. O'Malley, *Giles of Viterbo,* p. 115.
156. Ibid., pp. 170–78; and Reeves, *Prophecy,* pp. 364–67, 441–45.
157. Reeves, *Prophecy,* p. 446.
158. Phelan, *Mendieta,* pp. 11–14, 103.

Crusade against the Turk, with Ferdinand as field general and Leo
as commander-in-chief. No ordinary war, however, this Crusade
was to serve eschatological ends. Hence, del Rio says to Ferdinand: "We hope that the supreme judge will come again by virtue
of your conquest of Jerusalem." [159] Indeed, there is a prophecy that
the sect of Islam will endure only to the fifteen hundredth year.[160]
And if Christians are not lazy or negligent, this prophecy will soon
be fulfilled. All that they must do is unite in a Crusade.

Yet despite Ferdinand's crucial role, the real leader of this
Crusade must be the pope.[161] Addressing Leo X, del Rio says that
God has entrusted this Crusade to him because, as the possessor
of both swords, it is his task: "Alias oves quas habes, quae non
sunt de hoc ovili, ad tuum ovile reduceres, alliceres, et revoc-
ares." [162] Indeed, the pope is the one the synod calls on, in the
words of the prophecy:

> "Tu es qui restitues hereditatem meum mihi," to strive so that
> under his leadership, who is first and the head of the Christian
> Republic, sit una fides, una baptisma; denique ut es unus pastor
> et sit unum ovile.[163]

John 10:16 was also cited two times at the Council of Trent.[164]

---

159. Mansi, 32:col. 821; or Hardouin, *Acta*, 9:1701: ". . . quo ipsum rursus
supremum iudicem venturum speramus, pro acquirenda tua Jerusalem . . ."
160. Mansi, 32:823; or Hardouin, 9:1703: ". . . esse apud Mahumatanos
hostes indubiam prophetiam, cuius praetextu ad annum millesimum quingentesi-
mum a Christo ortu duraturam eorum sectam . . ."
161. Mansi, 32:825; or Hardouin, 9:1704.
162. Mansi, 32:826; or Hardouin, 9:1705. (This clause is the first half of
John 10:16.)
163. Mansi, 32:827; or Hardouin, 9:1705: " 'Tu es qui restitues hereditatem
meam mihi,' . . . nitere ut te duce, qui . . . Christianae rei publicae primus et
caput es, sit una fides, una baptisma: denique ut es unus pastor, sit unum ovile
. . ."
164. Actually, three times. On Nov. 5, 1562, Iustino Politanus delivered an
oration on the need for the unity of the episcopacy under the pope. In support
of his case he cited John 10:16, declaring that such unity would result in one
flock under one pastor. The use of the verse in this instance, however, is clearly
publicistic, and likely metaphorical. Episcopal obedience and unity are being
figuratively equated with the preconditions for the consummation. The purpose

In his speech of August 29, 1562 on the question of giving the chalice to laymen at communion, the archbishop of Surrentini expressed his desire that all of Germany and every other nation would accept the decision of the council: "For if they did so, we could hope that *nostra aetate* there would be but one flock under one pastor." [165] The phrase *nostra aetate* makes it clear that Surrentini has in mind much more than just the unity of the Church. He intends John 10:16 to be understood in its eschatological sense.

The eschatological resolve behind the use of John 10:16 by Hieronymo Rogazono Veneto, bishop of Nazaianzeno, is indubitable. At the end of an oration he delivered at the council on December 3, 1563, he declared:

> O Fathers, how great is the merit of your actions. O that happy day of rebuilding. O God, act so, that the seed we planted in the divine field bears fruit, and let that, which you promised would someday be, occur in our time, so that there should be one flock and one pastor.[166]

Perhaps the most significant use of John 10:16 occurs in the *De Emendanda Ecclesia,*[167] the secret reform proposal which was prepared in 1537, at the request of Paul III, by a commission which included Carafa, and possibly Contarini. Its use in this document suggests what will very soon be made explicit: that in the later sixteenth century, even the papacy was not immune from eschatological speculation. The bulk of the *De Emendanda* is a list of practical reforms, which includes the reform of clergy, the regulation of the use and abuse of papal power, and the prohibition of suspect books. The last sentence of the document, however, declares that if the pope follows the program the *De Emendanda* outlines, then "oves

---

of mentioning this oration is to show that even in figurative usages, John 10:16 always retained its eschatological sense. S. Ehses, ed., *Concilii Tridentini Actorum,* 9:126.

165. Ibid., 8:802: "Nam si sic agerent, nostra aetate, unum fieri sub uno tantum pastore ovile, sperandum esset."

166. Ibid., 9:103: ". . . atque id, quod fore aliquando pollicitus est, fiat temporibus nostris, ut unum sit omnium ovile et unus pastor."

167. Printed in V. Schweitzer, *Concilii Tridentini Tractatuum,* 12:144 f.

Christi in unum ovile reducas." The specifics of the document are, then, not the only goal of the proposed reform—there is a more comprehensive goal, and appropriately its clearest expression comes in the statement made to the commission by Paul III when he charged it to draw up a reform program. He used the same phrase which the commission used to designate its goal, but with an addition: He directed it

> To restore in our hearts and acts the name of Christ, which has now been forgotten by the nations and by our clerics; to heal the despairing; *to lead back the lambs of Christ into one flock;* and to remove from us the ire of God and that vengeance which we deserve, which is now prepared and imminent.[168]

The phrase "oves Christi . . . reducas" is not precisely "Fiet unum . . . ," but the context suggests that it was John 10:16 which Paul III had in mind.

Quite clearly, then, John 10:16 had become a byword in sixteenth-century reforming circles for expressing the hope, which was also an expectation, that the implementation of certain reforms would of a certainty hasten the advent of the consummation. But the traditional interpretation of John 10:16 spoke of a union of all men, including infidels and Jews, within one Church. Because of this exegesis, every citation of the verse was a reminder that the consummation would occur only when all Jews and infidels had converted. That a verse which contains such a message came to be the byword for expressing eschatological hopes is perhaps the strongest confirmation that sixteenth-century eschatological speculation was firmly bound up with the question of the conversion of the Jews. Above and beyond all else, therefore, it is this point which makes absolutely inescapable the conclusion that the conversionary atti-

---

168. Cited in C. Cantù, *Les Hérètiques d'Italie, trans.* A. Digard and E. Martin (Paris, 1869), 2:203: "Te speramus electum, ut nomen Christi, iam oblitum a gentibus et a nobis clericis, restituas in cordibus et in operibus nostris; aegritudines sanes; oves Christi in unum ovile reducas; amoveasque a nobis iram Dei et ultionem eam quam meremur, iam paratam, iam cervicibus nostris imminentem."

tudes expressed in the *De Iudaeis* represented a community of eschatological thought.

Most appropriately, the man directly responsible for the establishment of the papacy's conversionary Jewry policy, Paul IV, was thoroughly convinced of the imminence of the consummation.[169] This side of Paul IV has gone unnoticed. He has on the one hand been associated with inquisitorial bigotry and on the other with staunch reform, but never with eschatological speculation.

The standard picture drawn of this pope, both by his contemporaries and also in retrospect, has been that of a man completely devoted to repression. Paul IV was undeniably free, perhaps excessive, in his use of the Inquisition to inhibit all dissidence. Buschbell claims that the Inquisition became a truly suppressive agency only after Carafa became chief inquisitor.[170] According to Pastor, the Inquisition was the only court Paul IV trusted, for he saw in it the one effective remedy for the plague of heresy which had erupted.[171] These assertions are supported by a number of critiques of the Inquisition which were written around 1542 and which accused Carafa of seeing heresy everywhere, even where it did not exist.[172] Nor did such criticisms stop after Carafa had be-

---

169. It is beyond the scope of the present discussion to trace the eschatological orientation of the other popes of the later sixteenth century. Moreover, my real interest is to demonstrate that the *De Iudaeis* reflects the policy shift which took place under Paul IV. However, it is worthwhile to present some evidence of Pius V's eschatological tendencies, if only to show that it is more likely than not that the other sixteenth-century popes shared Paul IV's beliefs. Pius V evinced great interest in missions and expressed great joy over their success (cf. supra, p. 202, n. 45). In addition, it seems as though Pius V believed that Antichrist was gathering his forces for the final battle. In a 1570 letter to the king of France (printed in F. Goubau, *Pii Quinti Espistolarum*, p. 294), urging him to join the war against the Turk, he wrote that the state of the Christian Republic was *perturbatissimum,* and that the Catholic faith was in the *extremum discrimen.* He feared that: "Impletum temporibus nostris Regii Prophetae videmus oraculum, atque adversus Omnipotentem Deum et Christum Redemptorem nostrum, sanctissimamque illius Ecclesiam, omnes qui sunt haereticos, schismaticos atque infideles convenisse cernimus."

170. G. Buschbell, *Reformation und Inquisition* (Paderborn, 1910), p. 222.

171. Pastor, *History of the Popes,* 14:259 f.

172. See Bromato, *Storia di Paolo IV,* pp. 55–69.

come Paul IV. Cardinal Seripando, the general of the Augustinians, called the acts of the Inquisition inhuman.[173] Cardinal Morone, against whom Paul IV directed one of the most controversial accusations of heresy, charged that Paul IV had so distorted matters that he used the Inquisition to silence any opposition to his policies. The pope, he said, considered such opposition equal to affronting God.[174] Similarly, Navagero, the Venetian ambassador, reported that Paul IV displayed as much zeal for the prosecution of a single heretic as he did for the defense of Rome during his war with Philip II. In fact, Paul IV never missed a session of the Inquisition, even when his infirmities caused him to curtail his other duties.[175] Most notable, even those who actually favored Paul IV's use of the Inquisition expose his severity. At Paul IV's funeral, Ghislieri, the future Pius V, praised him because he had established the standards of severity which were necessary to reestablish the Church and its discipline.[176]

The view of Paul IV as a repressive, almost tyrannical ruler is strengthened by the fact that his estimates of the monarchical power of the pope exceeded any of those which were in vogue in the late fifteenth century and the sixteenth century.[177] He de-

---

173. Pastor, *History,* 14:260.

174. Ibid., p. 69.

175. E. Alberi, *Relazione degli Ambasciatori Veneti al Senato,* ser. 2, tom. 3 (vol. 9), (Florence, 1846). B. Navagero, "Relazione di Roma," pp. 380–82.

176. Cited in A. Caraccioli, *De Vita Pauli Quarti* (Coloniae Ubiorum, 1612), pp. 103–4; cf. also the oration of J. P. Flavius, ibid., pp. 116–24.

177. For the strongest formal assertion of these powers, see the bull *Cum ex apostolatus officio* (Feb. 15, 1559), in C. Mirbt, *Quellen zur Geschichte des Papsttums und des Romischen Katholizimus,* 3d ed. (Tubingen, 1911), #355, p. 208: "Romanus pontifex, qui Dei et . . . Christi vices gerit in terris et super gentis et regna plenitudinem obtinet potestatis omnesque iudicat a nemine in hoc saeculo iudicandus . . . [judges that] duces, reges, et imperatores . . . aut in haeresim incidisse seu schisma incurrisse . . . , vel convicti fuerint . . . regnis et imperio penitus et in totum perpetuo privati [sunt] . . . etc." Cf. L. Christiani, *L'Église à l'époque du Trente,* pp. 149–50; Braudel, *Le Mediterranée,* pp. 255 f.; Daniel-Rops, *Catholic Reformation,* I:127 f. All agree that Paul IV would have been more comfortable as pope in the thirteenth century. Cf. M. Maccarone, *Vicarius Christi,* pp. 267–301, for a history of the recrudescence of, and opposition to, papal monarchism in the late fifteenth century and the sixteenth century.

manded total acquiescence to the command of the pope in all matters.[178] Should princes ever compromise the papal dignity, the pope would have no choice but to wage war against them. Paul IV thus justified his war against Spain by asserting that Philip II had to be punished, because his father, Charles V, had oppressed the papacy by permitting heresy to exist in Germany, and because Philip II himself had tried to make the Vicar of Christ into his servant.[179]

This zeal for discipline and mastery was matched only by Paul IV's zeal for reform. His efforts in this direction were noted as early as 1515 by none other than Erasmus.[180] The Venetian ambassador, Mocenigo, reported that despite the hatred which many felt for Paul IV's inquisitorial passion, no one could deny his integrity, personal piety, and reforming ardor.[181] The funeral orations delivered at Paul IV's death all stress his piety and his efforts for reform.[182]

This side of Paul IV's personality has not been neglected by modern researchers. Dom Ancel, in particular, has emphasized his devotion to the rehabilitation of the Church. He has shown, for example, how Paul IV eschewed all political factors in his

---

178. Alberi, *Relazione* (1857), 10:48: Luigi Mocenigo, "Relazione di Roma, 1560."

179. Bromato, *Storia di Paolo IV*, 2:262–63; Navagero, in Alberi, *Relazione,* 9:388; Caraccioli, *Vita Pauli Quarti, p.* 164, where he cites Card. Ant. Carafa, Paul IV's nephew, "De Pauli IV vita, ad Senatum Venetum, notae apologeticae," who stated that the pope's sole motive for war was "zeal for divine honor and for safeguarding the pontifical dignity." During the period of hostilities, Paul IV referred to Philip II and Spain as "enemies of God, renegade moriscos [or *marani,* depending on the version], spawn of Jews [*seme di giudei*]" (B. Navagero, in Rawdon-Brown, *Calendar of State Papers,* Venetian, 6, #674, p. 732 [Oct. 23, 1556], #546, p. 520 [July 13, 1556], and #798, pp. 922–23 [Jan. 22, 1557]). In I,intro., de Susannis called *marani* the "pessimum genus hominum." It was probably this sentiment which Paul IV wanted most to convey, although there is enough truth in the remark to permit the conclusion that in part Paul IV meant the remark to be taken literally.

180. Kerker, "Die Kirchliche Reform in Italien unmittelbar vor dem Tridentinum," *Theologische Quartalschrift* 41 (1859): 10.

181. Mocenigo, in Alberi, *Relazione,* 10:47.

182. E.g., the oration of Sirleto, in which he called Paul IV "Christianae pietatis assertor atque restaurator," in Caraccioli, *Vita Pauli Quarti, p.* 95.

choice of cardinals, thus beginning the depoliticization of the curia which was completed during the pontificate of Sixtus V.[183] As for his personal aspirations, Jedin remarks that Carafa identified himself with Contarini and with the latter's "new pastoral ideal and the Apostolate." [184]

What element made possible this combination in one personality of the tyrant and the reformer? The answer to this question is to be found in the extensive documentation which appears in the two biographies of Carafa written by Caraccioli and Bromato. Bromato even includes a large number of lengthy citations from the letters which Carafa wrote to his sister, Maria.[185] These are an invaluable source, for as personal letters they contain an unimpeachable expression of his deepest beliefs. They reveal, in particular, that he believed in the imminence of the consummation. It is this belief which explains his other activities and opinions.

Even without these biographies, it should be evident from at least two items already discussed that Paul IV was convinced of the approach of the consummation. He established a Jewry policy whose goal was conversion. And he licensed the *De Iudaeis*, which not only spoke explicitly of the swiftly-approaching consummation, but also declared in its dedication to Paul IV:

> At this time, by those who are obeying the Apostolic duty, and to whom you have been the *magister* of sincere piety and religion, the borders of the Christian Republic have been extended into previously unknown regions of the world so that, while you are presiding over the world, that prophecy seems to be fulfilled: "in omnem terram exivit sonus eorum." And now, at last, what the Apostle said has come true: "Evangelium fructificare in omni creatura." [186]

---

183. See esp. Ancel, "L'Activité réformatice de Paul IV," passim, and Jedin, *Council of Trent,* 2:130.

184. Ibid., 1:419; see also Kunkel, *Theatines,* p. 41.

185. Bromato refers to F. M. Maggio (C.R., 1612–86), *Vita di Suor Maria.*

186. *De Iudaeis,* dedication: ". . . nunc ab iis quibus fuisti sincerae pietatis et religionis magister, Apostolicum munus obeuntibus in ignotis prius orbis regionibus Christianae Reipublicae fines ita propagantur, ut te orbi praesidente vaticinium

Another eschatological tract, the Joachitic *Il Modello de Lutero* of Jacobus Moronessa, was dedicated to Paul IV's confidant, Scipio Rebiba. The possibility is therefore raised that Rebiba himself had Joachitic tendencies, and that he imparted them to Carafa, or at least influenced him along Joachitic lines.

Carafa's own words, however, furnish the best criteria for ascertaining his involvement with eschatological speculation. In the 1520s he wrote to his sister of his conviction that the wars between Spain and France were inspired by the Devil. He saw demoniac influence everywhere, and he despaired of any major reforms. All he wanted to do was to withdraw from the world in order to become a monk and save his own soul.[187] In the same vein he addressed a letter to Charles V in 1535, admonishing the Emperor that if he did not achieve peace, then that band of Lucifer, the Turk, would continue its advance.[188] So, too, when Paul IV fought a war with Spain, he confided in Navagero, the Venetian ambassador, his trust that he would win the war through divine intervention. How could God forsake him in a war which had been instigated by the Devil to halt his reforms? [189] When he lost the war, he began to call it a fitting punishment wrought by God in recompense for the sins of the Church.[190]

This predisposition to seeing divine or demoniac intervention everywhere must have made Paul IV susceptible to the belief that he could imminently expect the ultimate interventions, that of Antichrist at Armageddon and that of Christ at the Last Judgment. For this reason, when he wrote of a demoniac intervention in his 1532 tract on the reform of the heresies he had found among the Franciscans at Venice, he expounded that a single group can pose a danger so great that its heresy can bring ruin to the world. These friars, he said, were "the wolves in the fold." [191] This appella-

---

illud adimpletum videatur, in omnem terram exivit sonus eorum. Et nunc demum verum sit (quod ait Apostolus), Evangelium fructificare in omni creatura . . ."
187. Bromato, *Storia,* 1:91–95.
188. Ibid., 2:22 f.
189. See Pastor, *History of the Popes,* 14:125 f. and 199.
190. Ibid., p. 206.
191. G. P. Carafa, "De Lutheranorum haeresi reprimenda et ecclesia re-

tion, taken from 2 Timothy 3, refers to the minions of Antichrist, who will deceptively corrupt the souls of men at the end of days.[192] And Paul IV's use of it implies that he associated the outbreak of heresy in his day with the approach of Antichrist.

That Paul IV connected the eruption of heresy with the appearance of Antichrist suggests that his eschatological tendencies are also to be sought in his pursuit of discipline. If he conceived of heresy as the growth of the forces of Antichrist, then he surely saw the discipline with which he fought heresy as the weapon which would defeat those forces and therefore hasten the advent of the consummation.

The link between discipline and eschatology in Carafa's thought is best perceived from his 1532 reform *Memorial* to Clement VII. Here he wrote that the state of the clergy in his day was crucial:

> The importance is that it is on the state of the religious [the clergy] that the salvation or the ruin of the world depends: the salvation, if their state were sound, in its pristine order; the ruin, because that state is now collapsed and deformed.[193]

Carafa was not alone in voicing an opinion on the "collapsed and deformed" state of the clergy, void of all discipline, as a danger to the Catholic body. But in the context of some of his other opinions, as just seen, it is difficult not to take him literally when he speaks of "ruin," suggesting the general situation which, by tradition, would obtain right before the consummation. This interpretation is sup-

---

formanda ad Clem. VII" (Oct. 4, 1532), in V. Schweitzer, ed., *Concilii Tridentini Tractatuum,* 12:75; See Tacchi-Venturi, *Storia,* I:1, pp. 73–75, for a description of this tract.

192. On the allegorizing of 2 Tim. 3 to apply to contemporary events and figures, see esp. Wm. de St. Amour, "De Periculis Novissimorum Temporum" (1255), in *Magistri Guillelmi de Sancto Amore Opera Omnia* (Constance, 1632). See also the letters of Agobard of Lyons.

193. *BAV, Barb. Lat.* 5697, fols. 1–10, esp. fol. 6, as here; published by G. M. Monti, *Richerche su Papa Paolo IV Carafa* (Benevento, 1923), pp. 57–77, esp. pp. 67–70, as here: "Questa importanza è del stato delle religioni dal qual dipende la salute o la ruina del mondo, la salute, se 'l detto stato fosse integro nel suo primo instituto, la ruina, perchè è già collapso et deformato. . . . La cosa è tanto sporcha che spanda hormai la puzza sua per tutto."

ported by noting the vitriolic terms he employed in continuing his discussion of clerical heresy: it was *sporcha*—filth, and a *puzza*— a stench. More directly, in two letters written between 1530 and 1544, Carafa pursued his description of his times, shedding light on what he meant when he spoke of "ruin."

> The world has been placed in a cancerous situation. . . . and in the cancerousness of the age . . . in the great tempest of religion, and in the great distress of affairs . . . most particularly through so many dangerous and pernicious infirmities and through so many seditious and turbulent acts, we see today the Church afflicted and vexed according to the merit of our sins.[194]

> [Accordingly,] I have desired to save the wretched just from such *extreme tribulations:* [that is, specifically,] the malice and the idolatry of the supposed servants of God, the soiled petty nuns and the dreadful pigs of monks, who exhale a sulphurous stench. All of this is heading for a *contagiose ruine*. . . .[195]

The words may be descriptive of clerical corruption in specifics, but the overall impression conveyed is much broader. Clerical error must be halted; for in this way alone will the Church emerge victorious in its great battle against world chaos and ruin—that is, in the cosmic battle which is to occur immediately preceding the End of Days.

This explicit linkage of conceptions of "world ruin" with an indictment of clerical behavior is also, perhaps, a clue to understanding Giles of Viterbo, whose eschatological speculations were explicit, but whose reforms were limited solely to clerical disci-

---

194. *Barb. Lat.* 5697, 132ʳ: ". . . mundus in maligno positus est . . . temporum malignitate . . . tanta rerum perturbatione tantaque religionis tempestate . . . quum praesertim tot pernitiosis periculosisque languoribus, tot seditiosis turbulentisque moribus, quibus hodie ecclesiam peccatorum nostrorum merito vexatam afflictamque videmus . . ." This letter, and the one cited next, lack both specific dates and addresses. This letter is, however, known to be in Paul IV's own hand.

195. Ibid., 136ʳ: ". . . ho desiderato . . . a sublevare il recto misere da si extremi flagitii: malitia idolatriaque [of the supposed servants of God], contaminate meschine monache et lutuosi porci [of monks].

pline.[196] Carafa is expressing here what Giles left unsaid: namely, the reason why such discipline was of such crucial importance. In turn, this parallel with Giles provides all the more reason why Carafa's statements about ruin should be taken in an eschatological sense.

The connection between the 1532 *Memorial* and the 1537 *De Emendanda* must also be considered in the present context. Carafa was one of the nine cardinals who drafted the 1537 document, and perhaps its prime author. There may, in any case, be no doubt of the general correspondence between the contents of the two documents.[197] Thus, on the one hand, in the light of what has just been said about the *Memorial,* the suggestions above about the possible eschatological indications in the *De Emendanda* must be considered even more seriously, while, on the other hand, the *De Emendanda*'s ideas must be seen as explaining those of the 1532 *Memorial.* In other words, taken together, the two documents provide much evidence in favor of the hypothesis of Paul IV's eschatological leanings.

The strongest argument for asserting that Carafa believed that he would witness the consummation comes from three statements whose implications border on, if they do not actually constitute, a direct affirmation. In 1543 he wrote an emotional letter to Bernardino Ochino, the general of the Capuchins, who had just defected to the Protestants. He first implored Ochino to tell him why he, Ochino, was now preaching Antichrist in place of Christ, and why he had exchanged the role of pastor for the role of wolf.[198] He then pleaded with Ochino to return to Catholicism, lest he be cut down as a rebel. For cut down he must be, said Carafa in summation; that is the duty of Christian princes. But the return of rebels, or their extirpation, was not all that Carafa desired. Thus, he concluded this letter by declaiming:

---

196. See O'Malley, *Giles of Viterbo,* pp. 138–60. Interestingly, O'Malley was perplexed by the seeming inconsistency between Giles' speculations and his limited disciplinary reforms.

197. Monti, *Ricerche,* pp. 41–47.

198. Cited in Bromato, 2:74: ". . . qui Antichristum pro Christo praedicaveris . . . pastorem in lupum conversum . . . Christi praeconem diabolum effectum."

Let there be one faith, and there will be one peace; Let there be one confession in the Church, and one path of brotherhood. Remove the golden calves; remove the haughty; let there not be Rehoboam and Jeroboam, Jerusalem and Samaria; let there be one flock and one pastor.[199]

Four years later Carafa wrote to his sister. In a mood of great despair he told her to read the ninth chapter of Daniel.

Read it if you wish to see the despair of our times. One cannot read it without tears; of it one can say it describes so clearly our state. But if the great mercy of God does not aid us, then we ourselves must be expeditious. Indeed, the clemency of that great *Signor* who said, "From the time of John the Baptist, the kingdom of heaven submits to force, and the violent may seize it," is the sole reason I do not despair completely, because such great strength has been conceded me that I am capable of making that violence on heaven.[200]

Daniel 9 describes the coming of an Antichrist-like figure and the time of extreme despair and tribulation which precedes his coming.[201] Hence Carafa has implied that he expects Antichrist momentarily. What is more, he has also implied that he himself has been selected to hasten the consummation.

Finally, in a letter to Maria of August 24, 1549,[202] Carafa

---

199. Ibid., 2:74: "Sit una fides, et erit una pax; sit una Ecclesie confessio, et una amicitiae ratio. Tolle vitulos aureos, tolle excelsa; non sint Roboam et Hieroboam; Hierusalem et Samaria; sit unum ovile et unus pastor." To be sure, Paul IV is referring here to a union of Protestants and Catholics. Yet he clearly expects reunion to bring something additional in its wake, namely, the consummation.

200. Cited from Maggio, ibid., 2:136.

201. The standard Christian interpretation of this chapter explains it as a prophecy of the first advent. However, as far back as the early centuries of the Church, a second interpretation declared that the chapter also refers to the coming of Antichrist (see *S. Hieronymi Presbyteri Opera, Commentariorum in Danielem Libri III [IV]* [Turnhoult, 1964], pp. 878–80, where Jerome cites Hippolytus and Appolinaris of Laodicea as holding this view). In the fourteenth century, Nicholas of Lyra simply asserted that the events of Dan. 9 will be repeated in the days of Antichrist (*Bibliorum Sacrorum cum glossa ordinaria et N. Lyrani Expositionibus*, IV, 314v, on Dan. 9, v. "In primo anno . . .").

202. See for text, Monti, *Ricerche*, pp. 243–44, or Maggio, *Vita*, pp. 274–76; orig. *Vat. Lat.* 10652, f. 91.

abandons hints and implications, and he expresses himself openly. The practical end of this letter is to lament the awful state of the clergy, "the preachers who should be the consolation of souls, and the salvation of the world [who] have now become, for the most part, the perdition and the contamination of the miserable Christian people." This, as previously noted, was a constant theme in Carafa's reformist writings. But to such imputed perversions of priestly functions he also attached the sensation of feeling the world in a state of ruin and chaos. This sensation was interpreted as reflecting a probable belief on Carafa's part in the approaching end of the world. In the present letter, probability becomes explicit certainty.

The practical aspect of clerical degeneracy appears only in the last sentence of the letter. Its bulk is devoted to expressing a perception of the state of the world. This perception certainly resulted from Carafa's estimation of clerical degeneracy, but its forceful exposition here reveals that in his grasp of his world, Carafa had left details and immediate problems behind. He had arrived at a point where he could see his surroundings only in terms of eschatological prophecies—which, he distinctly indicates, were being realized in his own day. Thus he writes:

> I am now aged, but I may never permit myself an hour of repose, in addition to the infinite sorrows which I perceive at every minute, to see in this unhappy time the ruin of the World and the subversion of the faith, and to hear from every side the bad news, in the way that the messengers of Job kept arriving without one waiting for the next. Worse, with all this huge blaze, there is no one who, for the zeal of God, has the desire to toss on it one glass of water; but there are many indeed who ceaselessly toss on it sulphur and wood. *We have surely arrived at that calamitous moment* about which my . . . most holy father [Peter] in his second epistle prophesied, saying, "In the End of Days false, deceiving men will appear, acting according to their own willfulness; and for you they will be false teachers, who will introduce the sects of perdition; and many will go in the way of their viciousness, and through them the way of truth will be blasphemed; and in avarice, through false words, they will make commerce of you." And that

great doctor of the nations [Paul], in his first epistle to his dear
disciple, Timothy, said: "The Spirit speaks manifestly, whereby
in the End of Days there will be a split from the faith, men await-
ing the spirits of error and the doctrine of the Devil." And in his
second epistle to the same, in the third chapter, see the frightful
things which he predicts. *These things we see taking place before
our very eyes.* And note that the whole long series of evils commences with the traitor, love of one's self. *Behold, that is right
where we are now! How indeed do we see fulfilled the prophecies
of our holy fathers,* that which my master said, "With the coming
of the Son of Man, you would think he would find faith in the
world," but he *does not know* to whom to turn, nor in whom to
trust, who has the concern and cure of souls. All things have
become contaminated, everything is corrupt, the whole body is
sick, "from the soul of the foot, to the crown of the head, nothing
is sound." . . .[203]

That is, the son of man is indeed *now* coming—if in fact he has not

---

203. Ibid. ". . . senza che io mai mi possa permetter pur un'hora quieta, ultra
l'infiniti dolori che ad ogn'hora si senteno, per veder, in questo infelice tenpo
[*sic*], la roina del mondo, e la sovversion de la fede, e per sentir d'ogni banda
le male novelle, che como li nuncii di Job, senza aspettar l'un l'altro ne sopprav-
vengono, e peggio è che in tanto incendio non v'è chi per zelo di dio, ci voglia
gittar un bicchier d'acqua, ma ben molti che non cessano di gettarci del solfo e
de le legna: ben siamo giunti a quel calamitoso tempo, che il sopradetto mio sanc-
tissimo padre nella seconda epistola sua ne prophetiza, dicendo, 'que venient in
novissimis diebus viri illusores iuxta proprias concupiscentias ambulantes; et in
vobis, inquit, erunt magistri mendaces, qui introducent sectas perditionis; et multi
sequentur eorum luxurias, per quos via veritatis blasphemabitur: et in avaritia
fictis verbis de vobis negociabuntur:' e quel gran dottore de le genti, nella prima
epistola sua al suo caro discepolo Timotheo dice: 'Spiritus autem manifeste
dicit, quare in novissimis temporibus discedetur quidam a fide, attendentes spiriti-
bus erroris, et doctrinis demonorium,' e nella seconda epistola, al medesimo, nel 3
cap. vedete le spaventose cose che lui predice, e noi le vedemo in effetto, e notate
che tutta quella lunga serie di male incomincia dal traditor amor di sè stesso:
ecco dove noi siamo, e como vedemo adimpite le prophetie di nostri sancti patri.
e questo è quel 'l mio signor diceva, 'Filius hominis veniens, putas inveniet fidem
in terra'; non sa più dove revoltarsi, nè di chi fidarsi, chi ha qualche peso e cura
d'anime, ogni cosa adulterata, ogni stato corrotto, tutto 'l corpo infermo, 'a planta
pedis, usque ad verticem, non est in eo sanitas': li predicatori, che solevano esser
la consolation de le anime e la salute del mondo son fatti hora in gran parte la
perditione e la contaminatione del misero popolo christiano. . . ."

already arrived. The consummation is nearly upon the world. Accordingly, in his belief that he had been selected to hasten the advent of the consummation, Carafa set out to reform the Church, cut off the heretic, and lead the infidel into the Christian fold.

But why, it must be asked, did eschatological speculation arise in the sixteenth century? To be sure, it is possible to respond that the discoveries in the New World, followed by mass conversions, and the threat posed to Christian society by the advance of the Turk and the eruption of Protestantism created a situation which was identified as the conjuncture of events that, according to Christian tradition, would herald the consummation. But despite its accuracy, this answer is premised on the assumption that men were predisposed to interpret contemporary events in eschatological terms. To understand the growth of eschatological speculation in the sixteenth century, therefore, this predisposition must be explained. This in turn creates the delicate problem of delving into the recesses of minds. Even so, a plausible explanation may still be advanced.

The key which may provide this explanation is the obsession with discipline manifested by Paul IV, Giles of Viterbo, and Marquardus de Susannis. Discipline is a device which fosters unity and certainty. And both unity and certainty were major desiderata of the sixteenth-century Church. Why this was so has been suggested by Braudel and also by Bouwsma. Braudel sees a turning-inward on the part of Mediterranean civilization for the sake of preserving itself through the establishment of internal unity.[204] Bouwsma describes the collective actions of the Church as a pursuit of certainties for the purpose of curing itself of the disease of insecurity.[205]

Applying these generalizations to the particular, it must first be noted that Paul IV, Giles of Viterbo, and Marquardus de Susannis were insecure men. They were members, indeed leaders, of an establishment which saw its world failing, and which reacted to this

---

204. Braudel, *La Mediteranée*, pp. 150–52.
205. Bouwsma, *Venice*, p. 296.

sight with ever greater anxiety about the validity of its truths and the continued stability of its world order. Anxiety led to such statements as "the Church will never be shipwrecked";[206] and to the trepidation that the Devil was ever present.

At least one of these men, moreover, Paul IV, was chronically depressed. He continually thought about withdrawing from the world in times of stress. As a response to the Franco-Spanish wars of the 1520s and to the failure of reform movements within the Church, he wanted to retire to the cloister.[207] When Ghiberti and Contarini begged him to accept a nomination to the College of Cardinals in 1537, he acceded only after persistent entreaties.[208] He furthermore often wrote to his sister complaining of the bitterness of his life and of his constant despair.[209] This context confers great credibility on his deathbed statement. He told Mocenigo that he had never wished to be pope; it must have been divine election which thrust the office upon him.[210] Because he made a similar statement about divine election when he became a cardinal, it appears that his sense of being a divine instrument was a crucial factor in motivating him to act.

Most indicative of Paul IV's mental state are two letters composed in 1534 to his sister, both in response to her expressions of disaffection for a life so full of frustration.[211] Her appeals functioned as catalysts, inducing Carafa to reveal his profoundest dissatisfaction with himself and with his accomplishments. In the manner of the classically depressed, he views all his actions as futile and valueless. He has become so self-derisive that he prefers death to life, a death whose approach he would himself hasten, were it within his power to do so.

> Oh how I hate this life and call on death, except that death is so
> deaf to those who call upon her. She is only ready to make herself

---

206. III,1,51; O'Malley, *Giles of Viterbo*, p. 108.
207. Bromato, *Storia*, 2:91–95.
208. Ibid., 2:287; also Caraccioli, *Vita*, p. 40.
209. Bromato, *Storia*, e.g., pp. 40–42. Other examples, passim.
210. Mocenigo, "Relazione," in Alberi, *Relazione*, 10:48.
211. For the texts see Maggio, *Vita*, pp. 169–70, 174–75.

felt importunely to those who do not expect her. But what is there that is capable of keeping me willingly in this life, especially since I have been involved in the intrigues of this troubled place? . . .

I can only wonder at the years poorly spent, and at the infinite miseries, and the fatigues I tolerated in vain, and that which is worse, at the grave number of my sins. With inward sadness I am constrained to say with that Saint: "I have had empty months, and I have counted for myself laborious nights, and my days have passed more quickly than cloth is sewn by the weaver; and they have been consumed without any hope . . ." And so it is written: "The day of death is better than that of birth."

And having already consumed my years in bitterness [he writes in the second letter], and having found this mortal life full of that which I would have wished for less, I have grown a callous to miseries and to worries. . . . To say it with the sacred words: "My life has tired me, whence I have ceased, and my heart has renounced to labor further under the sun." So, I have not written, nor spoken, nor done anything which has pleased me: I have acted only according to the occasion, and the worst duties have dragged at me, so that I have been pulled to pieces from every side. With pious tears and hot breath, beseech for me the grave, to be liberated from this inferno of life.[212]

212. Ibid., pp. 169–70: "Come io posso odiar questa vita, e chiamar la morte, bench'ella sia si sorda a chi la chiama, come pronta a ingerirsi importunamente, dove altri non l'aspetta. Ma che cosa è quella, che mi possa ritener volentieri in questa vita, massimamente dopo che fui messo in questi'ntrighi di questo travagliato luogo? . . . voglio mirare a gli anni male spesi, e alle infinite miserie, e fatiche tollerate indarno, e quel ch'è peggio, alla grave soma de'miei peccati; con intimo dolore farò costretto a dire con quel Santo: 'Ego habui menses vacuos, et noctes laboriosas enumeravi mihi, et dies mei velocius transierunt, quam a texente tela succiditur, et consumpti sunt absque ulla spe' . . . ma pur'è scritto: '. . . melior est dies mortis, die nativitatis.' And pp. 170–75: ". . . E havendo omai [sic] consumato gli anni miei in amaritudine, e trovata questa mortal vita sempre piena di quel, ch'io meno havrei voluto, ho fatto il callo alle miserie, e a gli affanni . . . E per dirvelo con le parole sacre: 'Taeduit me vitae meae; unde cessavi, renunciavitque cor meum ultra laborare sub sole.' E così non iscrivo, nè parlo, nè fa cosa che mi piaccia: ma secondo che le occasioni, e le pessime occupazioni mi tirano, cosi mi lascio stracciare da ogni banda . . . E con pietose lagrime e caldi sospiri impetratemi la grazia di esser liberato da questo inferno di vivi, per potere sperar di fuggire ancora quell'altro."

Whether Giles of Viterbo shared Paul IV's depression I cannot say, although his theory of declining ages seems to indicate that he did. That de Susannis was at least mildly depressed seems likely. If he were not, why did he conclude his polemic sermon with the declaration that there is no happiness in this hostile mansion of a world, and that man had best hurry to repent while he still has time?

There is, however, a defense which permits escape from such a state of anxiety and depression. It is to turn inward and to fantasize that there is a perfect order of things, whose observance of itself will set the world on its proper course and obviate all problems.[213] It was to establish just such an order that Paul IV, Giles of Viterbo, and de Susannis insisted on the rigid observance of discipline. Once discipline had achieved order, the world would no longer be falling apart; or so they thought. In truth, of course, such thinking made it unnecessary to face the real problems of a disintegrating world order. Thus Paul IV was furious when Contarini refused to take a precise Catholic stance at the Colloquium of Regensburg.[214] And Giles of Viterbo thought that he could effect a *renovatio* within the Augustinian Order if he could force the brothers to observe the Order's constitution down to the last detail.[215] The best example of this defense mechanism is, however, the *De Iudaeis*. Its thesis that the strict application of Jewry law will make the Jews realize the truth of Christianity is fantastic. Granted that de Susannis was calling for a greater rigor and consistency than had ever before been followed, and granted that he believed that in his day the Jews were open to persuasion, nevertheless, his applications were not so different from the norm that they would accomplish what centuries of practice had failed to accomplish, and what men had never even considered that Jewry law could accomplish.

This same judgment applies to *Cum nimis* and, as has been indicated above, to Paul IV's inquisitorial ardor. Like de Susannis,

---

213. Cf. A. Freud, *The Ego and the Mechanisms of Defense* (New York, 1946), "Denial in Phantasy," pp. 73–88, and esp. 78–84.

214. Bromato, *Storia*, 2:42 f.

215. O'Malley, *Giles of Viterbo*, p. 166.

Paul IV used the order imposed through discipline to substitute for realistic solutions in the face of problems he found insoluble. Indeed, for Paul IV solving problems by the imposition of order was a necessity. In so many of his letters to his sister, he complained of the ineffectiveness of his actions and of his resulting desire to withdraw. But once he became chief inquisitor he thought his actions had become effective. The semblance of unity, which he believed he was achieving in reality through his work as inquisitor, defended him from the truth that he remained as ineffective as before. Thus it was the imposition of order which alone enabled him to function outside a monk's cell.

The conversion of the Jews would also establish order. But this order would possess a special virtue. With it would come an end to all anxiety about the validity of Catholic truth and the stability of the Catholic world. For the order which their conversion would establish was the millennium. The attempt to convert the Jews thus suggests that the desire for order as a solution predisposed men to seek the ultimate order, when "fiet unum ovile et unus pastor." Naturally, the way to achieve this state was through the prime instrument of order, discipline. Accordingly, de Susannis indicated in III,1 that the real testimony to the truth of Christ and his Church was the millennium. And he then proceeded to show that the way to hasten the advent of the millennium was through discipline. Those who already were Christians must adhere to Church discipline; those who were not yet Christians must be made Christians by means of discipline.

The belief in the imminence of the millennium and the accompanying belief that discipline can hasten its approach were, therefore, the reactions of men of the establishment to the fact that their world was falling apart. These two beliefs sprang from the desperate attempts of these men to put that world back together and to prove the validity of its truths, if only in their minds. In the coming of the millennium they saw the establishment of perfect unity and order, two goals which in their day were at worst the fomenters of repression, and at best a dream.

CHAPTER XII

THE PRECEDENT

ONE QUESTION REMAINS: WHAT was the origin of the ideas which motivated sixteenth-century papal Jewry policy and which received their expression in the *De Iudaeis?* In chapter one, the claim was made that this policy was innovative in both concept and practice, and it was confirmed by a sketch of the bulls issued between 1200 and 1500. In truth, a conversionary policy was edicted once before by the papacy—but *not* by the Roman papacy. The period of this mandate was the Spanish-Avignonese pontificate of Pedro de Luna, Benedict XIII. With his demise, however, the mandate disappeared. While some echoes of it were heard at the Council of Basle,[1] by the mid-fifteenth century de Luna's policy was dead. It did not survive even as a memory in the important Spanish polemics of de Espina and Perez de Valencia.[2] Nor did any of the concepts underlying that

---

1. For the decrees of Basle pertaining to Jews, see *Conciliorum Oecumenicorum Decreta,* pp. 459–61; or Hardouin, *Acta,* 8:1190–93. At the nineteenth session of the non-papally-approved Council of Basle (Sept. 7, 1434), Jews were ordered to attend conversionary sermons on pain of indirect excommunication. In addition, past canonical Jewry law was ordered reedicted, and the Jews were ordered to be confined in special quarters. M. Simonsohn, *Die Kirchliche Judengesetzgebung in Zeitalter der Reform Konzilien* (Breslau, 1912), pp. 25–50, claims that the impulse for this legislation, especially for the conversion-oriented decrees, came from the Spanish bishops at the council. Simonsohn also sees Spanish influence in the legislation of Martin V and Eugenius IV (cf. chap. 1). However, although in the 1425 bull, *Sedes Apostolica pietatis,* Martin V had stated that the Church tolerates Jews "sub spe conversionis eorumdem," in 1418, as Simonsohn notes, Alfonso V of Aragon convinced Martin V to cancel Benedict XIII's bull. Thus the papacy severed itself from Benedict XIII's policy only three years (see infra, p. 283) after its inception.

2. See supra, p. 244f., for Perez de Valencia. A summary of de Espina's *Fortalitium Fidei* is found in Y. Baer, *A History of the Jews in Christian Spain* (Philadelphia, 1966), 2:282–92.

policy make their way into the polemics of the fifteenth-century Italian Franciscans, Siena, Capistrano, Feltre, and Busti.[3] Ideas similar to those of Benedict XIII reappeared only in the *Libellus ad Leonem Decem*. But it remained for *Cum nimis* and the *De Iudaeis* to reproduce Benedict XIII's program in precise detail.

Indeed, it is because of the nearly complete correspondence between the programs of Benedict XIII and Paul IV that discussion of Benedict XIII's activities has been reserved for this final chapter. Standing out so vividly, the various components of Benedect XIII's indisputably conversionist policy[4] reveal at once that Paul's IV's policy must be described in identical terms. Beyond that and truly crucial, this single previous attempt at large-scale conversion was also motivated by eschatological drives, as will soon be seen. The correspondence between the programs of Benedict XIII and Paul IV is, then, not solely one of substance but of underlying motivation as well. In brief, the following discussion of Benedict XIII's activities provides excellent corroboration for the case which has been argued in the foregoing chapters of this study.

Even the circumstances which initially evoked Benedict XIII's actions were most similar to those prevailing at the time of Paul IV. Thus, while most likely not intentional, the correspondence between the programs of the two popes may not have been mere coincidence. Benedict XIII faced a severe challenge to his authority. Not only did he have to confront the Great Schism within the Church, but as an outgrowth of that schism, he had to defend his very right to occupy the papal throne.[5] As a means of self-preser-

---

3. See H. Elie, "Contribution à l'étude du statut des Juifs en Italie aux XVe siècles; L'opinion de Bernardin de Busti," *Revue de l'Histoire des Religions* 142 (1952): 67–96, for a summary of Busti's thinking about the Jews, esp. as found in Busti's *Rosarium sermonum praedicabilium* (1495). Busti was the last in a chain of teacher-pupil relationships: Bern. da Siena, Juan Capistrano, Bern. da Feltre, and Busti. See also Browe, *Judenmission,* pp. 37 f., where he stresses that the major efforts of these Franciscans were directed toward repression, with little or no effort directed toward conversion.

4. See here Simonsohn, *Judengesetzgebung,* chap. 1, passim, and Browe, *Judenmission,* pp. 25–28, 79–86, and esp. 25–26.

5. Simonsohn, *Judengesetzgebung,* pp. 3–5, claims that Benedict XIII embarked on a conversionary policy to prove to the Council of Constance that

vation at a time of acute stress, he adopted a radical conversionary program. Had it succeeded, all opposition to him would quite probably have faded away.[6] Paul IV, of course, found himself in an exceedingly similar, if not identical, predicament.

The history of Benedict XIII's policy begins in 1412 when, at the instigation of Vincent Ferrer, the regents for Juan II of Castile promulgated the decrees which Baer has named the laws of Valladolid.[7] The ideological origin of these laws, as well as of Benedict XIII's policy, however, must perhaps be sought in the mid-fourteenth-century *Mostrador de Justicia* of the convert Abner of Burgos. Baer has provided a full discussion of this tract,[8] whose theme is Jewish obstinancy, along with ample citations; there is no need to repeat him at length. Yet two of Abner's thoughts, as presented by Baer, are worth reviewing in the present context.

According to R. Simlai (Sanhedrin 98a), says Abner,

> "The son of David will not come until all judges and officers disappear from Israel." By that he meant their rabbis and communal leaders who prolong their exile by keeping alive their foolish faith and vain hope. R. Hama b. Hanina said (Sanhedrin, 98a):

---

he was the true pope. Cf. p. 285, infra, the proemium of *Etsi doctoris,* where Benedict implies that he has initiated his Jewry policy in the light of the schism.

6. The number of converts certainly was unusually high during both pontificates. Cf. p. 201, n. 41, supra, for figures for the sixteenth century. B. Netanyahu, *The Marranos of Spain* (New York, 1966), p. 240, asserts that the Spanish Marranos numbered in the hundreds of thousands, approximately 200,000 of whom converted voluntarily between 1412 and 1415. (Netanyahu, pp. 235–45, discusses both contemporary figures and those arrived at by modern researchers.) G. Cohen, "Review Article: B. Netanyahu, *The Marranos of Spain,*" *Jewish Social Studies* 29 (1966–67): 182, calls Netanyahu's figures extremely doubtful. Baer, *History,* 2:246, puts the figure in the tens of thousands. To be sure, the need to expel Jews in 1492 proves that Benedict XIII's policy did not totally succeed. On a more subtle level—but also a more crucial one for determining the success of the policy, considering that both Benedict XIII and Paul IV were seeking sincere conversion (cf. p. 289, infra)—Netanyahu, *Marranos,* pp. 1–4, claims that the Marranos became true Christians. Cohen, however, raises doubts about Netanyahu's methodology (loc. cit., pp. 180–82), and Baer's opinion, *History,* 2:246, is the precise opposite of that held by Netanyahu.

7. Baer, *History,* 2:166–69.

8. Cf. ibid., 1:331–54. The *Mostrador* remains unpublished and is found only in a MS at Parma. See Baer's notes on this MS.

> "The son of David will not come until even petty authority ceases in Israel," that is, until the Jews possess no authority, not even such petty authority as is exercised over them by their rabbis and communal wardens, those coarse creatures who lord it over the people like kings. They hold out vain promises to them in order to keep them under their constant control. Only with the elimination of these dignitaries and judges and officers will salvation come to the masses.[9]

Later on Abner adds:

> R. Nehemiah said (Sanhedrin 97a), "In the generation of the messiah's coming, shamelessness will increase and prices will rise"; meaning that high prices will cause impoverishment . . . and the pain of impoverishment will lead to an increase of shamelessness among them, that is, they will no longer be ashamed to profess the truth openly and convert to Christianity.[10]

It is precisely this thinking, as will be seen momentarily, which is reflected in the laws of Valladolid ānd in the subsequent activity of Benedict XIII.

According to the provisions of the laws of Valladolid, Jews were to be segregated in special residential quarters and to wear a distinctive habit. They were also never to be addressed as *Don,* to be admitted to positions at court, or to be employed as tax farmers. Jewish merchants were prohibited from selling foodstuffs to Christians, and while allowed to own land, Jews were banned from employing Christians to cultivate it. Jews were not, however, prevented from taking interest.[11] But of exceeding importance, they were deprived of jurisdictional authority, and were henceforth to be judged only by Christian *alcaldes.*[12]

---

9. Baer, *History,* 1:350, citing the Parma MS, fol. 58.

10. Ibid., pp. 353–54, citing the Parma MS, fol. 59.

11. Baer, ibid., claims that the taking of interest was *probably* forbidden by special legislation. However, the fact that *Cum nimis* only regulated usury, and did not prohibit it, suggests that in the case of the laws of Valladolid, too, there was never a complete prohibition of usury.

12. For the actual texts of these laws, see Baer, *Die Juden im Christlichen Spanien* (Berlin, 1936), #275–77, and idem, *History,* 2:166–69 for a summary.

The purpose behind these laws is made explicit in the introduction to the version which was issued at Guadalajara on October 4, 1412. It is here that they can be seen to reflect the thinking of Abner of Burgos. Jews who convert, the introduction states, are not to be prosecuted for violations of these laws before their conversion, because "the said ordinances have been made for one sole end: that they [the Jews] should come to leave their error in recognition of the truth [Christianity]."[13] In other words, the laws of Valladolid mark the beginning of a conversionary policy. Of greatest significance, however, is the supposition on which this policy rested. It is through the means of legal restriction that Jews are to be induced to approach the baptismal font. This, of course, particularly in the light of the specifics of the laws, is but a paraphrase of Abner of Burgos' notion of impoverishment and its conversionary function. To point out the identity of these ideas with those expressed by Paul IV, Marquardus de Susannis, and Francisco de Torres would, at this time, only be superfluous.

Irrespective of ideological origins, however, were it not for Vincent Ferrer, these ideas would never have been implemented. Hence it was not coincidence that this man, who fashioned the laws of Valladolid, was itinerating through Castile in 1412 and forcing Jews to listen to his sermons.[14]

This conversionary policy was furthered by the Disputation at

---

13. Baer, *Juden,* #277: ". . . las dichas ordenancas pues fueron fechas a este solo fin, que ellos dexando su heror viniesen en conoscienmento de la verdat." In *History,* 2:168, Baer says that the intention of the legislators was to convert Jews to Christianity by means of servitude and oppression. Then (p. 169) he says that there is hardly a trace of uniform purpose or definite goal in these laws. He is probably bothered by the preamble to the version of the laws issued in January 1412 (*Juden,* #275), which states that the laws have been issued to put an end to the influence of New Christians on Old Christians. Baer claims that the logical end of such measures is banishment. Therefore the laws seem to have two self-contradictory purposes. However, as seen above, banishment and conversion are not necessarily separate matters. Cf. esp. de Torres, p. 289, who claimed that the Spanish expulsion was propitious to conversionarv efforts.

14. Baer, *History,* 2:166. See also F. Vendrell, "La actividad proselitista de San Vincente Ferrer durante el reinado de Fernando I de Aragon," *Sefarad* 13 (1953): 87–104, which deals with the scope and intensity and also relates various incidents in the course of Ferrer's missionary work.

Tortosa (1413–14), and it was culminated in May of 1415, with the issuance by Benedict XIII of the bull *Etsi doctoris gentium*,[15] whose decrees, as will be seen momentarily, closely follow the lines of the Valladolid laws.

There is ample reason to assume that Benedict XIII himself, who had also summoned the Tortosa disputants, was anxious to promote conversion. He had not infrequently expressed a desire to do so, and as a cardinal he had disputed with Shemtob b. Isaac Shaprut.[16] His personal library, moreover, included the *Pugio Fidei* and the *Mostrador de Justicia*.[17] There is also the issue of self-preservation, noted above, which should be taken into account. Not surprisingly, however, the man actually behind *Etsi doctoris* was none other than Vincent Ferrer,[18] the man who had once declared that the way to bring Jews to convert was through preaching, forcing them to live in full isolation from Christians, and the leveling upon them of stiff economic sanctions.[19]

---

15. Published by I. Döllinger in *Beiträge zur politischen, kirchlichen, und Kultur-Geschichte* (Regensburg, 1863), 2:393–403. (All citations from this bull come from Döllinger.)

16. De Rossi, *Bibliotheca Judaica Antichristiana* (Parma, 1800), p. 105, #147, refers to: R. Scem Tov ibn. Jos. ben Palkira, *Vikhuah*, seu *Disputatio cum Petro de Luna cardinali in Aragonia habita*. MS publ. Paris. V Catal. MSS bibl. reg. Paris. T. 1 p. 13 cod. 144 n. 4; et Catal. bibl. Colbert n. 5452.

17. See Baer, *History*, 2:171–72.

18. Cf. Baer, *Juden*, p. 270, where he calls *Etsi doctoris* the culmination of the legislation begun in 1412, and adds that V. Ferrer was the guiding force behind all this legislation. In *History*, 2:231, Baer indicates that Ferrer influenced Benedict XIII through 1416. M. Simonsohn, *Judengesetzgebung*, pp. 3–5, also sees the influence of Ferrer, and possibly of Paul of Burgos too, behind *Etsi doctoris*.

19. See José Millas, "San Vincente Ferrer y el antisemitismo," *Sefarad* 10 (1950): 182–84; and Browe, *Judenmission*, p. 26. Browe, with no reference, claims that as part of his conversionary drive, Ferrer was promoting the issuance of laws ordering the separation of Jews and Christians. This would apparently refer jointly to the laws of Valladolid, *Etsi doctoris*, and the confirmation of Ferdinand I. Further, Vendrell, in "La actividad proselitista" (cf. n. 14 supra), repeatedly speaks of Ferrer's promotion for conversionary reasons of the separation of Jews from Christians, and esp. from *Conversos*. It is with this background that the following statement, cited by Vendrell in "San Vincente," p. 184, must be understood: "Los Senyors temporals deuen convertir los seus infels moros e juheus, pero sens forca injuriosa, be juridica, que aquell avalot que's feu ara d'aquests anys, dels juheus, molt deplague a Deu, mas [cal convertirlos] ab bones amonestacions e fent los

To complete this picture, Ferdinand I of Aragon, who had previously given extremely active support to Vincent Ferrer's preaching, the Tortosa debate, and conversionary projects in general,[20] formally ratified *Etsi doctoris* on July 23, 1415, thereby creating a legal situation in Aragon closely parallel, if not identical, to that in Castile.[21] Thus Church and State in all of Spain were now, at least in theory, united in a program of rigorous conversionary activity.

In the proemium of *Etsi doctoris* Benedict XIII states the following:

> The Apostle teaches us that that branch of the Jews, [now broken off, but originating as the offspring of the patriarchs and prophets and rightfully a limb of the tree of Christ] will at some time be grafted on [to its proper root]. Moreover, the Apostle said they did not so offend that they should perish; on account of their delict, salvation has been made possible for the nations. Indeed, blindness has touched Israel in part, but only until the plenitude of nations enters, and then all Israel will be saved. Not only do we read these things, but we see them daily with our very eyes. In diverse parts of the world, the Church—made fecund by the birth of new offspring, [that is] by the conversion of Jews—

estar a depart e no lexar los negociar lo dichmenge palesament, no haver juheus familiars ne tractadors de matrimonis. Axi'ls convertiran."

20. See F. Vendrell, "La politica proselitista del rey D. Fernando I de Aragon," *Sefarad* 10 (1950): 349–66, where she cites, in particular, projects of Ferdinand to convert members of the Cabaleria and Abulafia families, as well as to procure for them after conversion freedom from obligations to the Jewish *aljamas* and Church benefices too. Vendrell also notes that Ferdinand freed a number of other converts from debts, and that in 1413 he devoted nearly all his attention to Tortosa.

21. See F. Vendrell de Millas, "En torno a la confirmacion real, en Aragon, de la Pragmatica de Benedicto XIII," *Sefarad* 20 (1960): 319–51. In an appendix Vendrell gives a full text of this confirmation (it is called a *Confirmatio*), which repeats in Catalonian the clauses of *Etsi doctoris*, but also makes their conversionary intent crystal clear. Of additional note, on p. 322 Vendrell reports a petition from a group of Jews complaining that they were literally starving as a result of the overly rigid application of these regulations. Ferdinand apparently stopped this extreme; but it is worth recalling here, for it obviously smacks of the phrase of de Torres 125 years later, that when the Jews were forced to seek sustenance from husks, they would then convert.

delights that those, whom it formerly held as enemies, have converted to be sons in peace. Hence, while we have been most occupied [trying to achieve unity and end the schism], we have done as much as we can, with the aid of God, to foster this work of grafting. [For two years now we have devoted our energies to a great altercation (Tortosa) which has resulted in the sincere conversion of a very great number of Jews.][22]

Indeed, these efforts have convinced three thousand, and a copious multitude is expected to follow their example.

However, since it is manifest . . . that the prime cause of the Jewish blindness . . . is a certain perverse doctrine, which was formulated after Christ and which the Jews call Talmud, . . . we have had this Talmud most carefully examined. As a result, because we desire to remove the whole veil from their eyes . . . , we have edicted that no one . . . should presume to hear, read, or teach that doctrine.[23]

---

22. Dollinger, p. 393: "Etsi doctoris gentium instruamur notissimo documento, nihil ad nos de his qui foris sunt pertinere, ipso tamen apostolo edocente ramos illos ex Judaeorum populo propter incredulitatem suam si quidem fractos ea radice tamen sancta patriarcharum et prophetarum progenie ortos, si in sua incredulitate non permanserint, propriae olivae salvatori nostro Jesu Christo, qui ex tribu Juda in sacratissimo Virginis utero pro humani generis redemptione tanquam oliva fructifera carnem sumpsit, aliquando fore legimus inserendos, nec enim, inquit apostolus, sic offenderunt, ut caderent, sed illorum delicto salus gentibus facta est. Sic profecto caecitas in Israel contigit ex parte, donec plenitudo gentium intraret et sic omnis Israel salvus fieret. Haec si quidem nedum in codicibus legimus, sed etiam corporeis oculis quotidie intuemur, dum in diversis mundi partibus ex conversione Judaeorum, foetu novae prolis ecclesia foecundata illos, quos inimicos prius habuerat, in pacis filios laetatur esse conversos. Nos itaque . . . his impacatis temporibus . . . quam plurimum occupati, quantum tamen in nos fuit, Domino cooperante, huic insertione dedimus operam efficacem. A biennio namque, citra quo circa inserendos ramos huius modi efficacius intendere coepimus, . . . assiduis altercationibus . . . ut Deo inspirante eorum quam plurimi sacrum baptisma puro corde reciperent. . . ."

23. Ibid., p. 394: ". . . verum quia prout manifesta percepimus . . . occasio Judaicae caecitatis . . . quaedam perversa doctrina potissima est, quae post Jesu Christi . . . confecta et apud Judaeos Talmud vocata . . . examinari fecimus studiose. Nos itaque omne velamen ab eorum oculis evellere cupientes . . . statuimus, ut nemo . . . doctrinam ipsam audire, legere, aut docere praesumat. . . ."

In addition, although the civil law forbids the Jews to function as judges, word has come to our apostolate that, in certain regions subject to Catholic princes, the Jews have not feared to establish judges among themselves, pretending—with the boldest temerity— that they have been armed with the privilege to do so by the kings or by other secular lords. However, since it is most disagreeable and contrary to the Christian religion that those, whom the death of Christ handed over into servitude to the worshippers of Christ, should exalt themselves with privileges, [kings and princes ought not to permit the Jews to possess such privileges.] And so that these Jews should recognize all the more easily that he, who had to be sent, has indeed already come, . . . they should perceive through experience that no scepter of prerogative or excellence remains among them . . . We [therefore] discern and order that, in the future, no Jew, no matter what the privileges he has secured, shall dare in any way, in whatever causes, criminal, civil, or others, or even in those causes against those whom they call *malsini* [informers], to be a judge or to practice the office of judging. To preclude opportunities of defrauding this constitution, we statute and mandate that they should not presume to function as arbiters [either] among themselves or . . . among any other persons. . . . And we declare null and void any privilege obtained contrary to this pronouncement.[24]

---

24. Ibid., p. 396: "Insuper licet Judaeis officium iudicandi lex civilis etiam interdicat, ad apostolatus nostri tamen saepe pervenit auditum, quod in quibusdam partibus catholicis subjectis principibus Judaei privilegiis regum seu aliorum dominorum saecularium se praetendentes munitos ausu temerario judices inter se constituere non verentur. Cum autem valde sit absonum et religioni contrarium christianae, ut, quos mors Jesu Christi tradidit servituti colentium Christum privilegia sic exaltent. . . . Et ut tanto facilius illum, qui mittendus erat, Judaei ipsi iam venisse cognoscant, quantum per effectum operis nullum sceptrum praerogativae aut excellentiae inter se perceperint remanisse, praesentium tenore decernimus et jubemus, ut nullus Judaeus de cetero, quibuscunque privilegiis fuerit communitus, in aliquibus causis criminalibus, civilibus, aut aliis quibuscunque etiam contra illos, quos ipsi Malsini appellant, vel quocunque alio exquisito colore judex existere aut iudicandi officium etiam inter Judaeos quomodo libet audeat exercere. Et ne huiusmodi constitutione fraudandi occasio relinquatur, statuimus et mandamus, ut nec arbitrium in se suscipere aut per viam compromissi seu arbitramenti quomodocunque aut inter quascunque personas pronuntiare praesumant, decernentes irritum et inane quidquid contra praemissa fuerit attentatum."

Benedict XIII then decrees the observance of the traditional restrictions which prohibit Jews from using Christian servants and
nurses, bar them from mingling freely with Christians, and require them to wear a distinctive habit. He also restricts to one the
number of synagogues allowed in a community, and he further demands that princes "assign the Jews certain districts, outside of
which they may not live." [25] Next he addresses the problem of Jews
who have been reluctant to convert because of their fear that upon
conversion they will forfeit their property. Any such fear, he propounds, must be removed.

In case anyone has missed the fact that the subject of this
entire bull is the promotion of conversion, Benedict XIII then declares:

> It remains for us, who have attempted by the tenor of the present
> constitution to restrain the fraudulent cunning of the Jews and to
> turn the dark cloud of blindness from their gaze, to rise up with
> all our strength so that we may impress upon them the clarity of
> the true light.[26]

This statement is also an introduction to the following edict, in
which the pope orders that suitable men must be chosen, whose
task will be "to deliver public sermons, three times a year . . . in
the presence of all the Jews," [27] so that the Jews will recognize
their errors. The preachers must discourse on the truth of Christ,
on the evils of the Talmud, which blinds the Jews from this truth,
and on the perpetual servitude of the Jews, which commenced
with the destruction of their Temple. If the Jews fail to attend

---

25. Ibid., p. 398: ". . . certos [Iudaeis] assignent limites, extra quos eis
non liceat habitare. . . ."

26. Ibid., p. 401: ". . . inserere nobis, qui Judaeorum fraudulentas astutias
cohibere caliginosamque nebulam caecitatis ab eorum obtutibus tergere praesentium
constitutionum tenore conamur, restat, ut ad imprimendum in eis veri luminis
claritatem totis viribus insurgamus."

27. Ibid., p. 401: ". . . fiant sermones publici ter in anno . . . praesentibus
omnibus Judaeis. . . ."

these sermons, "We order that they be indirectly excommunicated." [28]

Finally, Benedict XIII says that in order to convert the Jews, "it is necessary to treat them more with blandishments than with asperities, lest inhuman asperity casts into complete ruin those whom Christian kindness has perhaps called back to the way of right." [29] In the light of the rest of the bull, this statement seems contradictory. But what Benedict XIII means by "blandishments" is justice, rigorous justice. Thus he concludes:

> Therefore, we order Catholic princes, ecclesiastical prelates and faithful Christians . . . to compel the Jews to observe the present constitution. . . . Nevertheless, the princes must never again permit the Jews to be *burdened beyond the limits* of the present constitution, to be molested, to be offended in their persons or to have their goods seized, or to be otherwise vexed in any way without rational cause. Indeed they should treat the Jews humanely and with clemency, and insure that they are so treated by others, so that . . . they can be preserved from injurious disturbances. For the troubled spirit is believed to offer a sacrific acceptable to God on the altar of the heart, when that sacrifice is offered voluntarily and not through coercion. And according to the sanctions of the holy canons, it is more advisable that the faithful lead the Jews to the recognition of truth . . . through *pious admonitions* and through preaching than through violence.[30]

---

28. Ibid., p. 401: ". . . procedi volumus . . . per subtractionem communionis Christianorum."

29. Ibid., p. 402: ". . . plus enim blandimentis quam asperitatibus erga eos agendum est, ne quos christiana benignitas ad viam rectam forsitan revocaret, pellat procul inhumana asperitas in ruinam."

30. Ibid., p. 402: ". . . [in ruinam.] Universos igitur Catholicos principes obnixe rogamus et hortamur attente et nihilominus omnibus ecclesiarum praelatis ac ceteris Christi fidelibus in virtute sanctae obedientiae districte praecipiendo mandamus, quatenus sic Juadeos ipsos ad observantiam praesentium constitutionum, quantum in eis fuerit et ad cuiuslibet eorum officium pertinent, non omittant compellere, quod tamen ipsos ultra ea quae in praedictis constitutionibus continentur, gravari, molestari seu in eorum personis offendi aut bona eorum diripi seu alias quoquo modo absque rationabili causa vexari ulterius non permittant, quin immo eos tractent humaniter et clementer ac per alios etiam . . . iaciant sic tractari, ita quod tali mediante suffragio ab injuriosis inquietationibus valeant

Etsi doctoris confirms everything that has been said about *Cum nimis* and the *De Iudaeis,* especially when it is read in the context of the laws of Valladolid and the activity of Vincent Ferrer. Its explicitly declared purpose is to foster conversion, and the method it proposes to achieve that end is the rigorous application of Jewry law. It even contains de Susannis' thesis that the Jews can be predisposed to convert by abrogating their jurisdictional autonomy. That it also orders the confiscation of the Talmud and the establishment of forced preaching as aids to conversion is an added dividend.

Above and beyond all this, the bull opened with the traditional statement that the Jews will not convert until the "plenitude of nations enters." Yet in the very next sentence Benedict XIII exulted: while on the one hand he reads of this ultimate conversion, he in fact sees the Church rejoicing daily because of conversions. Accordingly he is making every effort to increase their number. He thus tacitly, but purposefully, identifies the time of the Jews' ultimate conversion with the present. What is more, in the proemium Benedict repeated the prophecy that the Jews would remain blind until the consummation. Later on he announced that in publishing this bull his intention was "to turn the dark cloud of blindness from their gaze." The impetus which led Benedict XIII to erect a conversionary policy was, then, a belief in the imminence of the consummation. Even if Benedict did not so believe, the man truly responsible for *Etsi doctoris,* Vincent Ferrer, certainly did.[31]

---

praeservari. Tunc enim in cordis ara sacrificium Deo acceptum tribulatus spiritus vere creditur immolari, cum inspectori cordium illud offertur voluntarie non coacte, nam secundum Sanctorum canonum sanctiones consultius agitur, si ad Veritatis cognitionem et divini cultus amorem piis monitis informando et praedicando, quam violentiam inferendo a fidelibus inducantur."

31. On V. Ferrer's eschatology, see M. Reeves, "The Abbot Joachim and the Society of Jesus," pp. 167–68, and esp. the article by M. M. Gorce on Vincent Ferrer in *Dictionnaire de Théologie Catholique* (Paris, 1920), 15:col. 3037. Both articles state that Ferrer was under the influence of Joachimism. This fact, in the light of Joachim's *Adversus Judaeos,* may explain the idea found in *Etsi doctoris* of trying "to turn the dark cloud of blindness from their gaze." The idea may well refer to Joachim's belief that "by virtue of the propinquity of the kingdom of light," it was possible to bring many Jews to see the true light of Christianity.

TEXT AND TRANSLATION OF *CUM NIMIS*

THE COMPLETE TEXT AND TRANSLATION of *Cum nimis* of Paul IV. The text is taken from the *Bullarium Romanum* . . . *Editio Taurensis* (Turin, 1857), 6:498–500.

Leges et ordinationes a iudaeis in Statu Ecclesiastico degentibus observandae

Paulus episcopus servus servorum Dei,
ad futuram rei memoriam.

Cum nimis absurdum et inconveniens existat ut iudaei, quos propria culpa perpetuae servituti submisit, sub praetextu quod pietas christiana illos receptet et eorum cohabitationem sustineat, christianis adeo sint ingrati, ut, eis pro gratia, contumeliam reddant, et in eos, pro servitute, quam illis debent, dominatum vendicare procurent; nos, ad quorum notitiam nuper devenit eosdem iudæos in alma Urbe nostra et nonnullis S. R. E. civitatibus, terris et locis, in id insolentiae prorupisse, ut non solum mixtim cum christianis et prope eorum ecclasias, nulla intercedente habitus distinctione, cohabitare, verum etiam domos in nobilioribus civitatum, terrarum et locorum, in quibus degunt, vicis et plateis conducere, et bona stabilia comparare et possidere, ac nutrices et ancillas aliosque servientes christianos mercenarios habere, et diversa alia in ignominiam et contemptum christiani nominis perpetrare praesumant, considerantes Ecclesiam Romanam eosdem iudæos tolerare in testimonium verae fidei christianae et ad hoc, ut ipsi, Sedis Apostolicae pietate et benignitate allecti, errores suos tandem recognoscant, et ad verum catholicae fidei lumen pervenire satagant, et propterea convenire ut quamdiu in eorum erroribus persistunt, effectu operis recognoscant se servos, christianos vero liberos per Iesum Christum Deum et Dominum nostrum effectos fuisse, iniquumque existere ut filii liberae filiis famulentur ancillae.

§ 1. Volentes in præmissis, quantum cum Deo possumus, salubriter providere, hac nostra perpetuo valitura constitutione sancimus quod de cetero perpetuis futuris temporibus, tam in Urbe quam in quibusvis aliis ipsius Romanae Ecclesiae civitatibus, terris et locis, iudaei omnes in uno et eodem, ac si ille capax non fuerit, in duobus aut tribus vel tot quot satis sint, contiguis et ab habitationibus christianorum penitus seiunctis, per nos in Urbe et per magistratus nostros in aliis civitatibus, terris et locis praedictis designandis vicis, ad quos unicus tantum ingressus pateat, et quibus solum unicus exitus detur, omnino habitent.

§ 2. Et in singulis civitatibus, terris et locis in quibus habitaverint, unicam tantum synagogam in loco solito habeant, nec aliam de novo construere, aut bona immobilia possidere possint. Quinimmo omnes eorum synagogas, praeter unam tantum, demoliri et devastare. Ac bona immobilia, quae ad praesens possident, infra tempus eis per ipsos magistratus praesignandum, christianis vendere.

§ 3. Et ad hoc ut pro iudaeis ubique dignoscantur, masculi biretum, foeminae vero aliud signum patens, ita ut nullo modo celari aut abscondi possint, glauci coloris, palam deferre teneantur et adstricti sint; nec super non delatione bireti aut alterius signi huiusmodi, praetextu cuiusvis eorum gradus vel præeminentiae seu tolerantiae excusari, aut per eiusdem Ecclesiae camerarium vel Camerae Apostolicae clericos, seu alias illi praesidentes personas, aut Sedis Apostolicae legatos vel eorum vicelegatos quovis modo dispensari aut absolvi possint.

§ 4. Nutrices quoque seu ancillas aut alias utriusque sexus servientes christianos habere, vel eorum infantes per mulieres christianas lactari aut nutriri facere.

§ 5. Seu dominicis vel aliis de praecepto Ecclesiae festis diebus in publico laborare aut laborari facere.

§ 6. Seu christianos quoquo modo gravare, aut contractus fictos vel simulatos celebrare.

§ 7. Seu cum ipsis christianis ludere aut comedere vel familiaritatem seu conversationem habere nullatenus praesumant.

§ 8. Nec in libris rationum et computorum, quae cum christianis pro tempore habebunt, aliis, quam latinis literis et alio quam vulgari italico sermone, uti possint, et si utantur, libri huiusmodi contra christianos nullam fidem faciant.

§ 9. Iudaei quoque praefati sola arte strazzariae, seu cenciariae (ut vulgo dicitur) contenti, aliquam mercaturam frumenti vel hordei, aut aliarum rerum usui humano necessariarum facere.

§ 10. Et qui ex eis medici fuerint, etiam vocati et rogati, ad curam christianorum accedere aut illi interesse nequeant.

§ 11. Nec se a pauperibus christianis dominos vocari patiantur.

§ 12. Et menses in eorum rationibus et computis ex triginta diebus completis omnino conficiant, et dies, qui ad numerum triginta non ascenderint, non pro mensibus integris, sed solum pro tot diebus quot in effectu fuerint, computentur, et iuxta ipsorum dierum numerum et non ad rationem integri mensis eorum credita exigant. Ac pignora, eis pro cautione pecuniarum suarum pro tempore consignata, nisi transactis prius a die, quo illa eis data fuerint, decem et octo integris mensibus, vendere nequeant, et postquam menses praedicti effluxerint, si ipsi iudaei pignora huiusmodi vendiderint, omnem pecuniam, quae eorum credito superfuerit, domino pignorum consignare.

§ 13. Et statuta civitatum, terrarum et locorum, in quibus pro tempore habitaverint, favorem christianorum concernentia, inviolabiliter observata etiam teneantur.

§ 14. Et si circa praemissa in aliquo quomodolibet defecerint, iuxta qualitatem delicti, in Urbe per nos seu vicarium nostrum, aut alios a nobis deputandos, ac in civitatibus, terris et locis praedictis per eosdem magistratus, etiam tamquam rebelles et criminis lesae maiestatis rei, ac toto populo christiano diffidati, nostro et ipsorum vicarii, ac deputandorum et magistratuum arbitrio puniri possint.

§ 15. Non obstantibus constitutionibus et ordinationibus apostolicis, ac quibusvis tolerantiis seu privilegiis et indultis apostolicis eisdem iudaeis per quoscumque Romanos Pontifices praedecessores nostros ac Sedem praedictam aut illius legatos, vel ipsius Romanae Ecclesiae camerarios et Camerae Apostolicae clericos, seu alios illius praesidentes, sub quibuscumque tenoribus et formis, ac cum quibusvis, etiam derogatoriarum derogatoriis, aliisque efficacioribus et insolitis clausulis, necnon irritantibus et aliis decretis, etiam motu proprio et ex certa scientia ac de apostolicae potestatis plenitudine concessis, ac etiam iteratis vicibus approbatis et innovatis, quibus omnibus, etiamsi, pro illorum sufficienti derogatione, de eis eorumque totis tenoribus specialis, specifica, expressa et individua ac de verbo ad verbum, non autem per clausulas generales idem importantes, mentio, seu quaevis alia expressio habenda, aut aliqua exquisita forma servanda esset, tenores huiusmodi, ac si de verbo ad verbum, nihil penitus omisso, et forma in illis tradita observata inserti forent, præsentibus pro sufficienter expressis habentes, illis alias in suo robore permansuris, hac vice dumtaxat specialiter et expresse derogamus, ceterisque contrariis quibuscumque.

Nulli ergo *etc.*
Si quis autem *etc.*
Datum Romae apud S. Marcum, anno Incarnationis dominicae millesimo quingentesimo quinquagesimo quinto, pridie idus iulii, pontificatus nostri anno I.
Dat. die 14 iulii 1555, pontif. anno I.

Since it is absurd and improper that Jews—whose own guilt has consigned them to perpetual servitude—under the pretext that Christian piety receives them and tolerates their presence should be ingrates to Christians, so that they attempt to exchange the servitude they owe to Christians for dominion over them; we—to whose notice it has lately come that these Jews, in our dear city and in some other cities, holdings, and territories of the Holy Roman Church, have erupted into insolence: they presume not only to dwell side by side with Christians and near their churches, with no distinct habit to separate them, but even to erect homes in the more noble sections and streets of the cities, holdings, and territories where they dwell, and to buy and possess fixed property, and to have nurses, house-maids, and other hired Christian servants, and to perpetrate many other things in ignominy and contempt of the Christian name—considering that the Roman Church tolerates the Jews in testimony of the true Christian faith and to the end [*ad hoc, ut*] that they, led by the piety and kindness of the Apostolic See, should at length recognize their errors, and make all haste to arrive at the true light of the Catholic faith, and thereby [*propterea*] to agree that, as long as they persist in their errors, they should recognize through experience that they have been made slaves while Christians have been made free through Jesus Christ, God and our Lord, and that it is iniquitous that the children of the free woman should serve the children of the maid-servant—

1. Desiring to make sound provisions as best we can, with the help of God, in the above matter, we sanction by this our perpetually valid constitution that, among other things, in all future times in this city, as in all other cities, holdings, and territories belonging to the Roman Church, all Jews should live solely in one and the same location, or if that is not possible, in two or three or as many as are necessary, which are to be contiguous and separated completely from the dwellings of Christians. These places are to be designated by us in our city and by our magistrates in the other cities, holdings, and territories. And they should have one entry alone, and so too one exit.

2. And in the individual cities, holdings, and territories where they dwell, they [the Jews] should have one synagogue alone in its customary location, and they may construct no new synagogue. Nor may they possess any real property. Accordingly, they must demolish and destroy all their [other] synagogues except for this one alone. The real property which they now possess, they must sell to Christians within a period of time designated by the local magistrates.

3. And so that they be identified everywhere as Jews, men and women are respectively required and bound to wear in full view a hat or some obvious marking, both to be blue in color, in such a way that they may not be concealed or hidden. Nor may

they be excused from wearing the hat or marking on the pretext of rank, eminence, or privilege; nor may they acquire an absolution or dispensation through the ecclesiastical chamberlain, clerics of the Apostolic Camera and other persons presiding there, or through legates and vice-legates of the Apostolic See.

4. [And they shall not] have nurses or serving women or any other Christians serving them, of whatever sex. Nor shall they have their children wet-nursed or reared by Christian women.

5. Nor may they themselves or anyone in their employ labor in public on Sundays or other feast days declared by the Church.

6. Nor may they oppress Christians in any manner, [especially by] drawing up fictitious or simulated contracts [of debt].

7. Nor should they be so presumptuous as to entertain or dine with Christians or to develop close relations and friendships with them.

8. Nor may they use in the ledgers and account books which they have with Christians, [stipulating] the duration [of loans, etc.], any other alphabet than the Latin one or any other language than everyday Italian. If they do otherwise, these books will have no value [when brought as testimony in court] against Christians [who have defaulted on repayment].

9. Additionally, these Jews may carry on no business as purveyors of grain, barley, or other items necessary for human sustenance, but must be limited [in this sphere] to dealing only in second-hand clothing, the *arte cenciariae* (as it is commonly called).

10. As for those among them [the Jews] who are physicians, even if they are summoned and requested, they may not come forth and attend to the care of Christians.

11. Nor may they permit the Christian poor [or any other Christian for that matter] to address them as Master.

12. And in their computations and accounting, months must be composed of thirty fully completed days, and days that do not add up to the number thirty must be computed not as full months, but only as the actual number of days that have elapsed—and they [the Jews] may demand repayment only according to the number of days, not according to the rate for completed months. Pledges temporarily

given them as collateral for their money, they may not sell for eighteen months, unless [otherwise] agreed upon prior to the day on which the pledges were actually given. After eighteen months have passed, if the Jews sell these pledges, all receipts over and above the value of the original loan must be made over to the owner of the pledge [i.e., the original borrower].

13. They will be held to observe without exception all statutes of the cities, holdings, and territories in which they dwell that give advantage to [lit. concern the favor of] Christians [over Jews].

14. And if they transgress the above in any way, either by us, or by our vicar, or by others deputized by us in the city, or by those same magistrates [noted above] in the other cities, holdings, and territories, they should be punished according to the nature of the transgression, either as rebels or perpetrators of the crime of *lèse majesté*, and as those who have renounced their allegiance to the entire Christian people, in accordance with the determination made by us or the vicars, deputies, and magistrates.

15. Notwithstanding the apostolic constitutions and ordinations and whatever apostolic tolerations, privileges, or indults conceded to those Jews through any of our predecessors, the Roman pontiffs, or legates of that See, or chamberlains of this Roman Church, or clerics of the Apostolic Camera or others presiding there, under whatever decree or edict and with whatever limitations —even limitations of limitations—and other more valid and unusual clauses, and equally with other decrees and invalidations, indeed, by our own action and from our clear knowledge and by the plenitude of apostolic power, and even by approbations, and so too by changes which have been renewed and approved repeatedly—with respect to all the foregoing, as well as with respect to anything whatsoever contrary [to this letter], even if in place of a general abrogation concerning them and all their stipulations a special, specific, express, and individual mention or whatever other expression has had to be made or some carefully chosen form has had to be retained, for each and every word and not only for the general clauses themselves important, we, in this place, both specifically and expressly, abrogate decrees of this kind, even if word

for word, with nothing at all omitted, and the traditional form preserved in them they have been inserted [into this present letter], having expressed clearly in this letter that these decrees should otherwise remain in force.

No one [may act against this letter], etc.

If anyone [so dares, he will call upon himself Apostolic censure], etc.

Given at Rome at St. Mark's, in the year of the Incarnation of the Lord one thousand five hundred fifty-five, on the day before the Ides of July, in the first year of our pontificate.

INDEX OF LAWS, CANONS, AND COMMENTARIES PERTAINING TO THE JEWS

The following is an index of the laws, canons, and commentaries cited in the *De Iudaeis*. It also includes additional entries which de Susannis himself did not cite, but which come from the works of the various legists and canonists he relied on in composing his own body of sources. In addition, the index lists the laws and canons from the Justinianic Corpus and the Corpus of Canon Law which refer to Jews, but to which de Susannis did not refer.

The index is divided into three parts. Part I lists the laws and canons which apply to the Jews and also has cross-references to Part III. Part II, also cross-referenced with Part III, lists the commentators (on both Roman and Canon law) who commented on legal questions involving Jews and Jewry law. Part III lists the basic themes found in Jewry law and in the commentaries on it. The index is so arranged that it will be possible to approach the study of medieval Roman and Canon law as it applies to the Jews either by choosing a law and studying the development of the interpretation on that law (Part I cross-referencing with Part III), by studying as a whole the legal theorizing on the Jews produced by individual lawyers (Part II), or by studying at once all the laws and interpretations applying to a given theme of Roman and Canon Jewry law (Part III).

The laws cited in Part I are provided with cross-references to the *De Iudaeis* to enable the reader to see which laws underlie de Susannis' specific arguments. These references have been omitted from Parts II and III. Such references would have no value, for as a rule de Susannis merely cites the locus, and not the content, of a jurist's commentary. Thus, cross-references to the *De Iudaeis* in

Parts II and III would be redundant. The reader would find there no more information than is already provided in the index. In fact, he would find less if he did not understand the medieval system of abbreviations employed by de Susannis. The true function of Parts II and III, moreover, is not to furnish an index to the *De Iudaeis* but to provide the basis for future studies of Jewry law and its attendant commentaries.

KEY TO ROMAN AND CANON LAW REFERENCES

Canon law—edited by E. Friedberg, *Corpus Iuris Canonici*—will be cited, as will be Roman law also, by the traditional abbreviations.—For example,
Gratian's *Decretum:*

    Part 1:   D.1,c.1 (Distinctio 1, canon 1)

    Part 2:   C.1,q.1,c.1 (Causa 1, quaestio 1, canon 1) Causa 33, q.3 is known as *De Penitentia.* It is divided into distinctions and canons.
              D.1,c.1, *de pen.*

    Part 3:   D.1, c.1, *de cons.* (Dist. 1, can. 1, *De Consecratione*)

Decretales of Gregory IX (*Liber Extra*): X.1,1,1 (*Lib. Extra,* Book 1, title, 1, canon 1)

Liber Sextus of Boniface VIII: *Sext.* 1,1,1 (same as *Decretales*)

Constitutiones of Clement V: *Clem.* 1,1,1 (same as *Decretales*)

Roman law—edited by Krueger-Mommsen, *Corpus Iuris Civilis*—
    Inst. 1,1 (*Institutes,* book 1, title 1)
    D. 1,1,1 (*Digest,* book 1, title 1, law 1) (ff.=D. in medieval citations)
    C. 1,1,1 (*Code,* and same as Digest)
    Nov. 1 (Novels, #1)

N.B., the editions of both Roman and Canon law are arranged according to the above system, and texts may be located by means of it.

Part I

The Laws and Canons Comprising Jewry Law

Laws [1]	Themes [2]	Location in *De Iudaeis*
Roman Laws	(The topics dealt with in each law or canon; to be used for cross-ref. with Part III)	
Inst.2,1	Jewish observance of Jewish law, synagogue building	I,3,8
D.27,1,15,6(G)	Exclusion from jurisdictions	II,6,21
D.48,8,34	Jewish observance of Jewish law, ritual	I,2,3; II,9,3
D.50,2,3,3	Exclusion from jurisdiction, loss of immunities	II,6,19
C.1,1,1(G)	Status of Jews, enemies	II,6,14
C.1,3,54,8–10	Exclusion from jurisdictions, prohibition of Jewish ownership of Christian slaves	II,5,19
C.1,4,15(I)	Exclusion from jurisdictions	II,7,3
C.1,5,12,4–14	Exclusion from jurisdictions [3]	

---

1. The following list includes laws and canons which deal with Jews. A (G) following the citation indicates pertinent materials in the gloss. An (I) indicates that the subject matter of the law pertains indirectly to Jews: e.g., D.32,c.6, which limits ordination only to Christians, thus implying that Jews may not ordain. An (I) also indicates laws which specify infidels in general but which clearly pertain to Jews. However, in each case with an (I) de Susannis has cited the law as applying to Jews. In addition, frequently in citations marked with both a (G) and an (I), the law is indirect, but the gloss is direct.

2. All the laws and canons comprising Jewry law have been divided into thirteen basic themes (and a number of subthemes), and constitute the major headings of Part III of the index. These themes have also been noted in Parts I and II, both for the convenience of the reader and also to make cross-references between parts of the index possible.

3. Omission of a reference indicates that the law or canon does not appear in the tract.

Laws [1]	Themes [2]	Location in *De Iudaeis*
C.1,5,12,18–22	Conversion, improved status of converts	
C.1,5,18(I)	Conversion, problems involving children	
C.1,5,19(I)	Conversion, problems involving children	III,4,1
C.1,5,21(G)	Restrictions on Jewish witnesses	II,5,9&14
C.1,9,1(G)	Exclusion from jurisdictions	II,6,14
C.1,9,4	Jewish observance of Jewish law, synagogue rebuilding	I,3,1
C.19,5(G)	Exclusion from jurisdictions, loss of immunities	II,6,21
C.1,9,6(G)	Restrictions on social intercourse, marriage	I,13,2; II,3,5
C.1,9,7	Jews bound to follow Roman law	II,1,1
C.1,9,8(G)	Jews as *cives;* Jews bound to Roman law	II,1,1; II,2,1; II,6,14
C.1,9,9	Jews bound to follow Roman law	
C.1,9,11	Jews forbidden to insult Christianity	I,9,4&7; II,3,13
C.1,9,13	Jewish observance of Jewish law ritual	I,2,3; I,3,16
C.1,9,14	Right of Jews to justice; Jews forbidden to insult Christianity	I,2,3
C.1,9,15	Exclusion from jurisdictions	II,6,14

Laws [1]	Themes [2]	Location in *De Iudaeis*
C.1,9,16	Conversion, Jews prohibited from accepting proselytes	II,3,23; II,9,3
C.1,9,17	Exclusion from jurisdictions	I,7,3
C.1,9,18–19	Exclusions from jurisdictions; Jews forbidden to insult Christianity	II,6,1&14
C.1,9,19	Jewish observance of Jewish law, synagogue rebuilding	I,3,1
C.1,10,1	Exclusions from jurisdictions, prohibition of Jewish ownership of Christian slaves	II,5,19
C.1,11,6	Right of Jews to justice	I,2,4
C.1,12,1	Conversion, conditions for	I,8,1
C.2,6,8(G) (I)	Exclusion from jurisdictions	II,7,3
C.3,28,11	Restrictions on Jewish witnesses	II,5,14
C.10,31,49(G)	Exclusion from jurisdiction, loss of immunities	II,6,19
C.10,76(I) (G)	Jews bound to follow Roman law	I,7,5
Nov. 37	Jews forbidden to insult Christianity; exclusion from jurisdictions, prohibition on Jewish ownership of Christian slaves	
Nov. 45	Restrictions on Jewish witnesses; Jews bound to follow Roman law	
Nov. 131	Jews forbidden to insult Christianity; Jewish observance of Jewish law, synagogue rebuilding	

Laws [1]	Themes [2]	Location in *De Iudaeis*
Nov. 146	Jewish observance of Jewish law, ritual restrictions	III,1,48
Canons		
D.21,c.1(I)	Jews forbidden to insult Christianity	III,9,4
D.25,c.1(I)	Jews forbidden to insult Christianity	III,9,4
D.26,c.3(I)	Jewish observance of Jewish law, marital	II,1,17
D.26,c.4(I)	Conversion, improved status of converts	III,9,1
D.26,d.p.c.4.(I)	Conversion, improved status of converts	II,1,17
D.30,c.1(G)	Right of Jews to justice, to fair treatment in general	III,4,5
D.32,c.6(I)	Exclusion from jurisdictions, spiritual	II,6,4
D.37,c.13(I)	Conversion, methods	III,1,56
D.42,c.2(I)	Right of Jews to justice, to fair treatment in general	I,5,7
D.45,c.3(G)	Jewish observance of Jewish law, ritual; conversion, methods	III,8,2
D.45,c.5(G)	Conversion, methods	I,7,6; I,14,1; III,2,5&8; III,6,1
D.48,c.1	Conversion, improved status of convert	III,5,8

		Location in *De Iudaeis*
Laws [1]	Themes [2]	
D.50,c.40	Right of Jews to justice; conversion, methods	II,2,8
D.54,d.p.c.12	Exclusion from jurisdictions, prohibition on Jewish ownership of Christian slaves	III,2,8
D.54,c.13(G)	Exclusion from jurisdictions, prohibition on Jewish ownership of Christian slaves	III,5,10
D.54,c.14	Jews forbidden to insult Christianity; exclusion from jurisdictions, offices; conversions, Jews prohibited from accepting proselytes	II,6,1; II,9,3; III,5,7
D.54,c.15	Exclusion from jurisdictions, prohibition on Jewish ownership of Christian slaves	
D.54,c.16	Exclusion from jurisdictions, prohibition on Jewish ownership of Christian slaves	
D.54,c.17	Exclusion from jurisdictions, prohibition on Jewish ownership of Christian slaves	
D.54,c.18(I)	Exclusion from jurisdictions, prohibition on Jewish ownership of Christian slaves	
D.86,c.14(G) (I)	Right of Jews to justice, to fair treatment in general	I,5,7; III,4,7
D.86,c.21(I)	Right of Jews to justice, to fair treatment in general	II,7,11
C.1,q.1,c.35(G)	Jews forbidden to insult Christianity	III,3,8

Laws [1]	Themes [2]	Location in *De Iudaeis*
C.1,q.1,c.37(G)	Status of Jews, enemies	III,1,42
C.1,q.4,c.7(G)	Conversion, prevarication	II,1,6; II,9,3
C.2,q.1,c.18	Social intercourse, prohibition on overfamiliarity	II,5,4
C.2,q.6,c.32(I)	Exclusion from jurisdictions	II,6,27
C.2,q.7,c.24	Restrictions on Jewish witnesses	II,5,11; III,6,1
C.2,q.7,c.25	Restrictions on Jewish witnesses	I,1,18; II,5,9
C.2,q.7,c.26 Palea(I)	Restrictions on Jewish witnesses	II,5,7
C.6,q.1,c.6	Restrictions on Jewish witnesses	II,5,12
C.14,q.4,c.12(G)	Usury	I,11,3&6
C.17,q.4,c.31(G)	Exclusion from jurisdictions, offices; Church jurisdiction over Jews, direct	II,6,1; II,7,3; II,9,3; III,5,7
C.22,q.1,c.16	Restrictions on Jewish witnesses, Jew's oath	II,5,10
C.23,q.4,c.53(G) (I)	Conversion, methods	III,8,2
C.23,q.5,c.33(G)	Conversion, methods	I,14,1; III,2,5
C.23,q.6,c.4(G) (I)	Conversion, methods	I,7,6
C.23,q.8,c.11	Status of Jews, toleration	III,4,9

Laws [1]	Themes [2]	Location in *De Iudaeis*
C.23,q.8,c.21 rubr.	Exclusion from jurisdictions, offices	II,6,11
C.24,q.2,c.1(I)	Jews in relation to canons as a whole, exclusion from Christian ritual	III,9,4
C.28,q.1,c.2(G)	Conversion, problems involving marriage	III,3,16; III,7,1
C.28,q.1,c.7(G)	Conversion, problems involving marriage	III,7,1
C.28,q.1,c.10(G)	Conversion, problems involving marriage, problems involving children	III,2,10; III,8,1 II,2,6;
C.28,q.1,c.11(G)	Conversion, problems involving children	III,4,8&12
C.28,q.1,c.12	Conversion, prevention of overfamiliarity between converts and Jews; Church jurisdiction over Jews, direct	III,2,6
C.28,q.1,c.13	Social intercourse, forbidden in general	I,4,20; II,7,10; III,5,10
C.28,q.1,c.14	Social intercourse, prohibition on dining	I,4,20
C.28,q.1,c.15(G)	Social intercourse, prohibition on intermarriage	I,13,2; II,3,1; II,3,5
C.28,q.1,c.16(I)	Social intercourse, prohibition on intermarriage	
C.28,q.1,c.17	Social intercourse, prohibition on intermarriage	

Laws [1]	Themes [2]	Location in *De Iudaeis*
D.1,c.7 de pen. (G) (I)	Exclusion from jurisdictions, offices	I,2,3; I,5,7
D.1,c.27 de cons. (I)	Jews in relation to canons as a whole, exclusion from Christian ritual	I,3,17
D.1,c.67 de cons.	Conversion, desire for	III,9,4
D.4,c.24 de cons. (G)	Conversion, methods	III,3,5
D.4,c.93 de cons. (G)	Conversion, methods, conditions for, desire for	III,2,3,4 &11
D.4,c.94 de cons. (G)	Conversion, prevarication, Jews prohibited from accepting proselytes	II,5,13; II,9,3; III,2,5; III,5,8; III,6,1
D.4,c.98 de cons. (G)	Conversion, methods	III,2,3
X.1,3,7 (G)	Conversion, improved status of converts	III,5,7
X.2,20,2(G)	Restrictions on Jewish witnesses; status of Jews, toleration	I,2,3; III,6,1
X.2,20,23	Restrictions on Jewish witnesses; status of Jews, enemies	I,2,1; I,13,1; II,6,12
X.3,30,16(G)	Church jurisdiction over Jews, indirect excommunication	II,5,4
X.3,32,20(G)	Conversion, problems involving marriage	III,9,5

Laws [1]	Themes [2]	Location in *De Iudaeis*
X.3,33,2(G)	Conversion, problems involving children	III,2,2 &10; III,3,1; III,4,11; III,8,1
X.3,42,3(G) (I)	Conversion, methods	I,14,1; III,2,7; III,3,1
X.3,42,4(G)	Conversion, methods	III,3,1&2
X.4,14,4(G)	Conversion, problems involving marriage; Jewish observance of Jewish law, general, marital; Jews in relation to canons as a whole	II,4,9; II,8,1&3; III,4,9
X.4,7,15(G)	Conversion, problems involving marriage; Jewish observance of Jewish law, general	II,4,9
X.4,19,7(G)	Conversion, problems involving marriage	II,3,16; III,7,2
X.4,19,8(G) (I)	Conversion, marital problems; Jewish observance of Jewish law, marital	I,4,9; II,1,7; III,4,9; III,9,1
X.4,19,9(G)	Conversion, problems involving marriage; Jewish observance of Jewish law, general; Jews in relation to canons as a whole	II,4,9 II,8,1
X.5,6,1(G)	Exclusion from jurisdictions, prohibition on Jewish ownership of Christian slaves	II,5,19; II,6,1; III,5,9

Laws [1]	Themes [2]	Location in *De Iudaeis*
X.5,6,2(G)	Exclusion from jurisdictions, prohibition on Jewish ownership of Christian slaves; right of Jews to justice	II,5,9,19& 21
X.5,6,3(G)	Jewish observance of Jewish law, ritual	I,2,3; I,3,1
X.5,6,4(G)	Jews forbidden to insult Christianity; social intercourse, Holy Week restrictions	I,7,2
X.5,6,5(G)	Exclusion from jurisdictions, prohibition on Jews having Christian servants; conversion, improved status of converts	III,2,2
X.5,6,7(G)	Jewish observance of Jewish law, ritual	I,2,7; I,3,1
X.5,6,8(G)	Exclusion from jurisdictions, prohibition on Jewish ownership of Christian slaves; social intercourse, prohibition of overfamiliarity	I,4,14
X.5,6,9(G)	Jewish observance of Jewish law, ritual; conversion, methods; status of Jew, toleration, slaves	I,2,3; I,3,17; I,7,6; I,14,1; II,2,2; III,2,3; III,5,2
X.5,6,13(G)	Exclusion from jurisdictions, prohibition on Jews having Christian servants; status of Jew, toleration, slaves; Jews forbidden to insult Christianity; Jewish observance of Jewish law, ritual; Church jurisdiction over Jews, direct	I,2,3; I,4,14; I,7,1; II,3,13; II,8,2; III,3,1

Laws [1]	Themes [2]	Location in *De Iudaeis*
X.5,6,14(G)	Church jurisdiction over Jews, direct; Jews forbidden to insult Christianity	II,8,2; II,3,13
X.5,6,15(G)	Social intercourse, dress regulations, restrictions during Holy Week, prohibition on sexual relations between Jews and Christians	I,4,2; I,7,2; I,13,1; II,3,13
X.5,6,16(G)	Exclusion from jurisdictions; Church jurisdictions over Jews, direct	II,6,1&12; II,8,2
X.5,6,18(G)	Exclusion from jurisdictions	II,6&14
X.5,6,19(G)	Exclusion from jurisdictions, prohibition on Jewish ownership of Christian slaves	II,5,19; II,5,9
X.5,19,3(G)	Usury	I,11,2&7
X.5,19,12(G)	Usury; Church jurisdiction over Jews, indirect excommunication, direct	I,11,3,6&7 II,5,4; II,8,2
X.5,19,18	Usury; Church jurisdiction over Jews, indirect excommunication	II,5,4
X.5,31,17(G)	Church jurisdiction over Jews, direct	
Sext.5,2,13(G)	Conversion, prevarication	II,3,23; II,5,13 &15; III,2,7
Clem.2,8(G)	Restrictions on Jewish witnesses; Church jurisdiction over Jews, direct	I,11,14; II,5,9; II,9,5; II,9,3
Clem.5,5(G) (I)	Usury; Church jurisdiction over Jews, indirect excommunication	I,11,3,6 &14

		Location in
Laws [1]	Themes [2]	*De Iudaeis*

Glosses[4]

D.12,2,5,1	Status; witnesses	
C.1,2,1	Exclusion from jurisdiction; enemies	
C.2,20,6	Social intercourse	
C.6,2,2	Justice; usury	
D.1,c.12	Jews as *cives,* part of Roman people	I,7,5; II,1,3
D.50,c.18	Conversion, improved status of converts	II,5,12
C.1,q.1,c.26	Exclusion from jurisdictions, spiritual	II,6,4
C.1,q.2,c.2	Conversion, methods	III,2,5; III,8,2
C.7,q.1,c.8	Jewish observance of Jewish law, general	II,4,2
C.11,q.3,c.24	Social intercourse, prohibition on dining	I,4,21
C.16,q.3,c.14	Right of Jews to justice	II,2,3
C.31,q.1,c.9	Jewish observance of Jewish law, marital	II,8,4
D.1,c.7 de pen.	Status of Jews, enemies	II,7,3
D.2,c.5 de pen.	Right of Jews to justice, to fair treatment in general	I,2,3; I,5,7
C.34,q.1&2, c.3	Jewish observance of Jewish law, general	II,4,9

---

4. The laws and canons cited in the following list do not apply to Jews. The interpretations of their glosses, however, do apply directly to Jews.

		Location in
Laws [1]	Themes [2]	*De Iudaeis*
D.4,c.63 de cons.	Jews in relation to canons as a whole, exclusion from Christian ritual	I,9,1
D.4,c.99 de cons.	Conversion, methods	III,2,3
D.4,c.102 de cons.	Jews in relation to canons as a whole, exclusion from Christian ritual	III,3,6
D.4,c.108 de cons.	Right of Jews to justice	I,12,1
D.4,c.129 de cons.	Conversion, problems involving children	III,2,7
D.4,c.138 de cons.	Conversion, problems involving children	III,2,7
X.1,2,3	Exclusion from jurisdiction, spiritual	II,6,2&3
X.1,6,34	Jews, as *cives,* part of Roman people	II,6,11
X.2,1,13	Church jurisdiction over Jews, direct	II,9,4
X.2,24,26	Restrictions on Jewish witnesses, Jew's oath	II,5,10
X.3,43,3	Exclusion from jurisdictions, spiritual	II,6,4
X.5,6,10	Status of Jews, inferiority	I,4,21

de Susannis' Interpretations[5]

D.34,5,20	Exclusion from jurisdictions	II,5,23; II,6,14

---

5. The laws and canons cited in the following list do not apply to Jews. (Their glosses do not either.) De Susannis, however, has interpreted these laws and canons to apply to Jews.

Laws [1]	Themes [2]	Location in *De Iudaeis*
D.45,1,34	Restrictions on Jewish witnesses	II,5,11
D.45,1,76,5	Jewish observance of Jewish law, synagogue rebuilding	I,3,10
C.2,7,23	Exclusion from jurisdictions	II,7,3
C.8,17,12	Right of Jews to justice	I,3,3; III,6,2
Nov.109	Conversion, improved status of converts	I,3,3; III,9,5
D.1,c.9	Social intercourse, prohibition of sexual relations between Jews and Christians	I,13,1; II,3,22
D.22,c.2	Exclusion from jurisdictions, spiritual	II,6,4
C.24,q.1,c.29	Exclusion from jurisdictions, spiritual	II,6,4
C.24,q.2,c.6	Exclusion from jurisdictions	II,5,23
D.5,c.6 de pen.	Conversion, conditions for; usury	III,2,4
D.4,c.29 de cons.	Conversion, methods	III,3,8
D.4,c.34 de cons.	Conversion, methods	III,3,7
D.4,c.91 de cons.	Conversion, improved status of converts	III,4,8
X.1,2,7	Jewish observance of Jewish law, general	II,4,1
Sext.5,5,1	Usury	I,11,4
Clem.2,9	Exclusion from jurisdictions, offices	II,6,11

	Location in
Laws [1]	Themes [2]

<table>
<tr><td>Laws [1]</td><td style="text-align:center">Themes [2]</td><td style="text-align:right">Location in
De Iudaeis</td></tr>
<tr><td>Clem.5,2</td><td colspan="2">Title: "De Iudaeis et Sarracenis" deals only with Muslims; is applied to Jews neither by the Gloss nor by de Susannis</td></tr>
</table>

Part II

Commentary on Jewry Law

For each legist and canonist listed here, the following information, apart from his name and appropriate dates, will be given: (1) the title of the work(s) in which he comments on the legal status of the Jews; (2) the date of the edition of the work(s) that was used to check de Susannis' citations (allegations) of these commentaries (full bibliographical and biographical information is found in the three works listed in note 7, and a reference to one of these works, abbreviated as "Sav.," "Sch.," or "Fon.," appears after the name of the individual legist or canonist); (3) the title or location in the work(s) under which the legist or canonist comments on the legal status of the Jews; and (4) the folio numbers indicating where these titles or locations are to be found in the edition used. The lack of a date indicates that no copy of the work was available for reference.

Jurists[6]	Themes[9]
	(for cross-reference with Part III)

1   ALBERICUS DE ROSATE, d. 1354 (Sav.
VI, 127–36)[7] *Commentaria in Codicem*
1545)[8]

---

6. Including civilians (Roman lawyers), canonists, and doctors of both laws, listed alphabetically by first name.

7. The reference to Sav. (F. K. von Savigny, *Geschichte des Römischen Rechts im Mittalalter* [Heidelberg, 1830–50]), Sch. (J. F. von Schulte, *Geschichte*

Jurists[6]	Themes[9]
C.1,9 de Iudaeis, v. item quaeritur (41ᵛ)	justice
C.1,9, de Iudaeis, v. quaero circa (41ᵛ)	Jewish law
Dictionarium (1581)	
v. Iudaeus	conversion

2   ALBERTUS BRUNUS, 16th century (Fon. I, 150)

     Tract. de statutis excludentibus a successione foeminas (1584)

     Article 6, Quest. 3 (*TUJ,* II 55–62)   jurisdiction/ Jewish law

---

der Quellen und Literatur des Canonischen Rechts [Stuttgart, 1875–80]), and/or Fon. (A. Fontana, *Amphitheatrum Legale* [Parma, 1688]) provides both biographical and bibliographical information for both the jurists and the works cited in this index. Titles in this index are generally cited as found in the above three works.

8. The information contained here should be read as follows: The legist (Savigny contains Roman lawyers and Schulte canonists), Albericus de Rosate, who died in 1354, composed a Commentary on the Code of Justinian, published in 1545. There, under the Title *De Iudaeis,* which is title 9 of book 1 of the Code, he commented on the words *item quaeritur* and *quaero circa.* This commentary appears on folio 41, *verso,* of the work.

9. As a rule, *theme* refers to that theme of Jewry law which is both discussed by the jurist under the title or location cited and was also the theme de Susannis was discussing when he cited the jurist. However, it often happens that the jurist discusses a number of themes under one title or location. As much as possible, all these themes have been indicated. Needless to say, there is no reason to assume that de Susannis' allegations are complete. In fact, a significant number of the comments cited in this index are not found in the *De Iudaeis,* but were culled from the indices to the works of the various legists. A complete index of commentary on Jewry law, moreover, would necessitate at the least checking the works of every medieval legist or canonist under each one of the legal titles cited in the entire index. For the sake of brevity, the themes, which are identical with those found in Part I, are abbreviated as follows: (1) status (Status of Jews); (2) justice (Right of Jews to justice); (3) canons (Jews in relation to the canons as a whole); (4) Church jurisdiction (Church jurisdiction over Jews); (5) social intercourse (Restrictions on social intercourse); (6) insult (Jew forbidden to insult Christianity); (7) common law (Jews bound to follow common [Roman] law); (8) *cives* (Jews as *cives*); (9) jurisdiction (Exclusion from jurisdictions); (10) Jewish law (Jewish observance of Jewish law); (11) witnesses (Restrictions on Jewish witnesses); (12) usury (usury); (13) conversion (conversion).

Jurists[6]   Themes[9]

3 ALEXANDER DE NEVO, ca. 1440 (Panziroli, 466)[10]
   Consilia (1560)
   #96   social intercourse/
                                                  cives/
                                                  jurisdiction
   #100–103   Church
                                                  jurisdiction

4 ALEXANDER TARTAGNUS DE IMOLA, d.
   1477 (Sav. VI, 312–19)
   Additiones ad Bartolum (1590)
   D.1, prima constitutio, v. iuramento
   (3[rb])   witnesses
   D.12,1 si certum petatur, 1   Jewish law
   Lecturae in Digestum Novum (1491)
   D.45,1 de verborum obligationibus, 34   status
   multum interest (ccc fol. 7)
   Consilia (1597)
   Vol. 1, #35   witnesses
   Vol. 1, #70, par. 11   witnesses
   Vol. 2, #1, par. 2   usury
   Vol. 2 #3   common law
   Vol. 2, #53   witnesses
   Vol. 2, # 71, par. 2   common law/
                                                   Jewish law
   Vol. 2, #107   Jewish law
   Vol. 2, #161   common law
   Vol. 2 #179, pars. 8–10   witnesses
   Vol. 4, #104   conversion
   Vol. 5, #75   *cives*/ common
                                                   law

---

10. G. Panziroli, *De Claris Legum Interpretibus.* (Venice, 1637).

Jurists[6]	Themes[9]
Vol. 6, #99	status/justice common law/ *cives*
Vol. 6, #233	insult/Jewish law
Vol. 7, #13	canons/social intercourse/ common law
Vol. 7, #130	status/common law

5 ANDREAS ALCIATUS, d. 1550 (Sav. VI, 421)
Annotationes in tres libros Codicis (1582)

De decurionibus, par. generaliter (vol. 3, col. 567)	jurisdiction

Dispunctiones (1582)

Bk. 3, chap. 8 (vol. 4, cols. 213–14)	jurisdiction

6 ANDREAS BARBATIA SICULUS, d. 1479 (Sav. VI,481)
Consilia (1516)

Vol. 1, #15	witnesses/ jurisdiction
Vol. 4, #13	Jewish law
Vol. 4, #16, col. 9	usury
Vol. 4, #63, col. 4	social intercourse/ insult/ common law
Vol. 5, #75, col. 2	common law

7 ANDREAS DE ISERNIA, 1220–1316 (Sav. VI,488)

Jurists[6]   Themes[9]

Commentaria ad constitutiones regni Siciliae (1559)
In rubr., de defensis. imposi., incip.,   witnesses
siquis posterum, par. Iudaeis (p. 31)

8 ANDREAS TIRAQUELLUS, later 16th
century (Fon. II,361)
Tract. de nobilitate (1588)
Cap. 6, nu. 50 (Vol. 1, p. 39)   status
Tract. de iure primogeniorum (1588)
Quest. 66 (Vol. 1, pp. 495–99)   Jewish law

9 ANGELUS DE ARETINUS, d. 1451 (Sav.
VI, 480)
Commentaria in Institutiones (1513)
Inst. 1,10 de nuptiis, 4 duorum autem,   Jewish law
14 (26ᵛ)
Inst. 4,6 de actionibus, 29 fuerat, 31   common law/
(242ʳ)   conversion
Consilia (1576), #33, #36 & #158   common law

10 ANGELUS DE UBALDIS PERUSINUS, d.
1407 (Sav. VI, 249–58)
Commentaria in Digestum Novum
(1579)
D.47,12 de sepulchro violato, 5 utimur   common law
(157ʳ)
D.48,4 ad legem Iuliam maiestatis, 1   common law
(167ᵛ)
Commentaria in Auctenticis
Nov. 8 (Coll. II,3) iusiurandum, quod   conversion
praesta. ab his, par. 1

11 ANTONINUS, Archbishop of Florence,
1389–1459 (Hurter, II, col. 960)[11]

---

11. H. Hurter, *Nomenclator Litterarius,* 3 vols. (Innsbruck, 1906).

Jurists[6]   Themes[9]

> *Juris pontifici et caesari summa* (1740)
> Part II, title 1, chap. 6, par. 1   usury
> (Vol. 2, cols. 74–79)
> Part II, title 12, chap. 3, par. 3   insult
> (Vol. 2, cols. 1151–55)
> Part III, title 3, chap. 2, par. 192   Church
> (Vol. 3, cols. 176–81)   jurisdiction
> Part III, title 3, chap. 6   status
> (Vol. 3, cols. 195–204)

12   ANTONIUS DE BUTRIO, 1338–1408
     (Sch. II, 289)
     Commentaria super Decretalibus
     (1578)
     X.1,4 de consuetudine, 11 quum tanto   Jewish law
     (I,84)
     X.2,20 de test., 21 Iudaei (IV,33)   status /
                                               witnesses
     X.2,28 de appellat., 18 consuluit (IV,   jurisdiction
     141)
     X.3,28 de sepult., 5 ex parte (V,120)   canons
     X.3,33 de convers. infid., 2 ex literis   conversion
     (V,148)
     X.3,34 de voto, 8 quod super his (V,   jurisdiction
     151)
     X.3,42 de bapt., 4 debitum (V,197)   conversion
     X.3,49 de immunitate ecclesia, 6 inter   canons
     alia (V,203)
     X.4,19 de divort., 8 gaudemus (VI,59)   common law/
                                               conversion
     X.5,1 de accusat., 6 de his (VII,3)   conversion
     X.5,6 de Iudaeis, 13 etsi (VII,37–40,   jurisdiction
     whole title)
     X.5,7 de haeret., 9 ad abolendam   status
     (VII,42)

Jurists[6]   Themes[9]

    X.5,9 de apostatis, 4 quidam (VII,47)   conversion
    X.5,19 de usuris, 5 quum tu (VII,62)   usury/
                                               conversion

    X.5,19 de usuris, 12 post miserabilem   common law
    (VII,65)
    X.5,19 de usuris, 18 quanto (VII,66)   canons

13 ANTONIUS CORSETTUS SICULUS, d. ca.
    1500 (Sch. II,348)
    Tract. de potestate ac excellentia regia
    (1584)
    Part 5, quest. 81 (*TUJ, XVI,* 140^v–41^r status
    and 142^v)

14 ANTONIUS FRANCISCUS DE DOCTORIBUS
    Patavinus, d. 1528[12] (Sch. II,366)
    Additiones ad Commentaria Abbatis Si-
    culi (in margins of Panorm.)
    X.2,20 de testibus, 21 Iudaei   witnesses/
                                                conversion

15 ANTONIUS NEGUSANTIUS (Fon. II,7)
    Tract. de pignoribus et hypothecis
    (1584)
    No specific location cited (*TUJ,* VI[1],   common law
    194ff.)

16 AUGUSTINUS BEROIUS, d. 1554 (Sch.
    II,355)
    Consilia (1601)
    Vol. 1, #2   common law/
                                                conversion
    Vol. 3, #209   status

17 AYMO CRAVETTAE A SAVIGLIANO (Fon.
    I,262)

---

12. De Susannis studied under him at the University of Padua.

Jurists[6]   Themes[9]

    Consilia (1575)
    Vol. 1, #73   status/
                                          conversion

18   Azo, d. 1230 (Sav. V,1–44)
      Summa Codicis (1966 photograph of
      1484)
      C.1,9 de Iudaeis (p.7)   conversion
      C.1,12 de his qui ad eccles. confugiunt   canons
      (p.8)

19   Baldus de Ubaldis, 1327–1400 (Sav.
      VI, 209–48)
      Commentaria super Digesto veteri
      (1536)
      D.1,1 de iustitia et iure, 1 (Vol. 1, 6rb)   jurisdiction
      D.1,6 de his qui sui vel alieni iuris sunt,   *cives*/
      4 nam civium (vol. 1, 32vb)   common law
      D.12,2 iureiurando, 5 non erit, 1 (vol.   canons
      1, 38ra)
      D.12.6 de conditione indebiti, 36 servus   justice
      (vol. 2, 64ra)
      D.14,6 de senatus consulto Macedoni-   common law
      ano, 1 (vol. 2, 82ra)
      Commentaria super Infortiato (1536)
      D.27,1 de excusationes, 15 spadonem,   *cives*/common
      6 iam autem (27ra)   law/jurisdiction
      D.32,1 de legatis et fideicommissis, 11   common law
      fideicommissa (124va)
      Commentaria in Codicem (1556)
      C.1,2 de sacrosanctis ecclesiis, 1 (vol.   status
      1, 8va)
      C.1,14 de legibus, 6 quod favore (vol.   Jewish law
      1, 61rb)
      C.2,1 de edendo, 4 qui accusare (vol. 1,   witnesses
      90rb)

Jurists[6]	Themes[9]
C.5,12 de iure Dotium, 14 mater (vol. 2, 192rb)	conversion
C.5,22 rem quam (vol. 2, 193^{va+b})	conversion (I)
C.6,43 communia de legatis, auct., res quae (vol. 2, 156^v–57^r)	common law (I)
Consilia (1575)	
Vol. 1, #315	Church jurisdiction
Vol. 1, #316	status/Jewish law
Vol. 2, #100	Church jurisdiction
Vol. 5, #422	common law
Vol. 5, #428	Church jurisdiction/ jurisdiction/ Jewish law

20 BALDUS NOVELLUS (Bartolini de Perusio) (Fon. I,70)
    Tract. de dotibus (1584) (*TUJ,* IX)

Part 11, col. antepenul. (263, n.15)	common law
Part 11, col. penul. (263, n.16)	conversion
Part 11, col. fin. (264, n.47)	conversion

21 BARTOLOMEO CEPOLLA, d. 1477 (Sav. VI, 320–23)
    Consilia (1515)

#74	common law
Ultimo	common law/ toleration

22 BARTOLOMEO SALICETO, d. 1412 (Sav. VI, 259–69)
    Commentaria in Codicem (1483)

C.1,2 de sacrosanctis ecclesiis, 1 (a7^vb)	jurisdiction

Jurists[6]   Themes[9]

C.1,5 de haereticis, 19 cognovimus   conversion
(e7^{ra})

C.1,9 de Iudaeis, 1 (e7^{vb}–e8^{ra}, whole   jurisdiction
title)

C.1,9 de Iudaeis, 6 ne quis   social
                                       intercourse

C.1,9 de Iudaeis, 7 nemo   Jewish law

C.1,9 de Iudaeis, 15 si qua   jurisdiction

C.1,12 de his qui ad ecclesias, 1 (e8^{rb})   canons

C.5,12 de iure dotium, 14 mater   conversion
(Bb6^{rb})

C.9,13 de raptu virginum, 1 (Nn4^{vb})   social
                                       intercourse

23   BARTOLUS A SAXOFERRATO, 1314–1357
     (Sav. VI, 137–84)
     Commentaria ad Digestum (1590)
     D. praefatio (vol. I,3ra)   canons

     D.12,2 de iureiurando, 2 iusiurandum,   witnesses
     4 iurari (II,22vb)

     D.24,3 soluto matrimonio, 47 cum mu-   status
     lier (III,26rb)

     D.30,1 de legatis et fideicommissis, 41   status
     item Iulianum, 7 constat (IV,12ra)

     D.34,5 de rebus dubiis, 20 cum Senatus   jurisdiction
     (IV,101rb)

     D.39, 1, rubr. de operis novi nuncia-   canons
     tione (V,2ra)

     D.48,4 ad legem Iuliam maiestatis, 1   common law
     (VI,153va)

     D.49,15 de captivis et de postliminio,   common law/
     24 hostes (VI,215ra)   *cives*

     D.50,2 de decurionibus, generaliter, 3   jurisdiction
     fin. (VI,222ra)

     Commentaria ad Codicem (1590)

Jurists[6]   Themes[9]

    C.1,1 de summa trinitate, 1 (VII,3va–   witnesses
4ra)

    C.1, 2 de sacrosanctis ecclesiis, 1 (VII,   jurisdiction
8ra)

    C.1,5 de haereticis, 21 quoniam multi   witnesses
(VII,24vb)

    C.1,9 de Iudaeis, 8 iudaei (VII, 25ra)   Common law/
cives/
jurisdiction/
Jewish law

    C.1,9 de Iudaeis, 18 fin. (VII,25rb)   jurisdiction
    C.1,11 de paganis, 1 (VII,25rb)   status/justice
    C.1,12 de his qui ad ecclesias confu-   canons
giunt (VII,25va)

    C.2,6 de postulando, 1 fin. (VII, 62   jurisdiction
$^{ra+b}$)

    C.10,31 de decurionibus, 49 omnes   jurisdiction
(VIII, 18ra)

    C.12,1 de dignitatibus, 1 (VIII,46ra)   jurisdiction
Commentaria ad Auctenticos (1590)
Nov. 8 (Coll. II,3) iureiurandum, quod   jurisdiction
praestatur ab his (IX,14rb)
Consilia (1590)
Vol. 2, #16 (X,57va)   jurisdiction
Vol. 2, #17 (X,57vb)   jurisdiction
Tract. de testibus (1590)
#20 (X,172rb)   witnesses

24   Bonifacius de Vitalinos, mid-14th
cent. (Sch. II,255)
*Commentarii in Constit. Clementis Pa-
pae V*
Clem. 5,5 de usuris   usury

25   Carolus Molinaeus (Charles Du-
moulin), 1500–1566 (Fon. I, 683)

Jurists[6]   Themes[9]

Annotationes in Decretum (1681, vol. IV)

C.14,q.6,c.2 conperimus nullam   Jewish law
(p. 41, col. 1)

Annotationes in Decretales (1681, vol. IV)

X.2,28 de appellationibus, 18 consuluit   status/social
(130, col.1)   intercourse

X.3,49 de immunitate, 6 inter alia   canons
(162,2)

X.4,5 de conditionibus appositis, 4 ve-   social
rum (171,2)   intercourse

X.5,6 de Iudaeis, 5 Iudaei (181,1)   social
                                      intercourse/
                                      conversion

X.5,6 de Iudaeis, 8 ad haec (181,1)   social
                                       intercourse

26   CAROLUS RUINUS, 16th cent. (Sav.
     VI, 496)
     Consilia (1571)
     Vol. 2, #4   jurisdiction/
                                           Jewish law
     Vol. 5, #13   conversion
     Vol. 5, #159   witnesses

27   CLAUDIUS SEISELLA (Seyssel), d. 1520
     (Sav. VI, 497)
     Commentaria de ordinariis jur. civ. li-
     bris (no date)
     D.1,1 rubr. de iustitia et iure (1[rb])   social
                                                intercourse/
                                                common law/
                                                jurisdiction/
                                                witnesses/
                                                conversion

Jurists[6] Themes[9]

28 COMMODUS (CONRADUS) SUMMEN-
HARTH, 16th cent. (Sch. II,454)
Tract. de contractibus (1580)
Bk.2, quests. 24–28 (pp. 94–123) usury

29 CYNUS DE SINIBALDUS PISTOVIENSIS,
1270–1336 (Sav. VI,71–97)
Lectura ad Codicem (1578)
C.1,2 de sacrosanctis ecclesiis, 1 jurisdiction
(3^{va+b})
C.5,4 de nuptiis, 19 celebrandis Jewish law
293va)

30 DOMINICUS DE SANCTO GEMINIANO,
mid-15th cent. (Sch. II,294ff.)
Super distinctionibus Decreti (1578)
D.1,c.9 ius gentium (7^v) status
D.12,c.12 omnia (27^r) common law/
jurisdictions
D.25 in primum (53^r) conversion
D.30,c.1 si qui (63^r) justice
D.33,c.5 usque adeo (72^r) status
D.45,c.3 qui sincera (90^v–91^r) status
D.45,c.5 de Iudaeis (91^r) conversion
D.54,c.8 mancipium (113^r) social
intercourse
D.54,c.14 nulla (113^v) Church
jurisdiction
D.54,c.15 fraternitatem (114^r) witnesses
D.56,c.8 dominus (118^r) status
Commentarius in libros Decretalium
X.1,33 de maiorit. et obedient., 12 witnesses
dilecta
Commentarius in Sextum (1495)
Sext.5,2 de haereticis, 13 contra (89vb– conversion
90ra)

Jurists[6]   Themes[9]

    Sext.5,5 de usuris, 1 (97rb)   common law/
                                                 usury

31 EGIDIUS BELLAMERA, d. 1392 (Sch.
    II,274)
    Praelectiones in Decretalium libros
    (1548)
    X.1,2 de constitut., 3 translatum (I,21^v)   canons
    X.5,12 de homicid., 6 sicut dignum   justice
    (VII,167^r)

32 FEDERICUS DE SENIS, mid-14th cent.
    (Sch. II, 237 and 275)
    Quaestiones (1545)
    #63   conversion (I)

33 FELYNUS SANDEUS, d. 1503 (Sch. II,
    350–52)
    Lectura in varios titulos libri, I, II, IV,
    V Decretalium (1574)
    X.1,2 de constitutionibus, 1,v. et primo   Church
    (Vol. I, col. 46)   jurisdiction
    X.1,2 de constitutionibus, 1, v. Item   common law
    quo (I,46)
    X.1,33 de maiorit. et obedient., 12 di-   witnesses
    lecta (I,1205)
    X.2,20 de testibus, 21, Iudaei (II,598–   witnesses/
    99)   conversion
    X.2,24 de iureiur., 4 ego (II,1015)   common law
    X.5,1 de accusat., 6 de his (III,691)   conversion (I)
    X.5,6 de Iudaeis (III,951-82, on whole   social
    title)   intercourse/
        c.1   jurisdiction
        c.2 multorum   status
        c.3 Iudaei   canons
        c.4 quia, in prin.   usury

Jurists[6]	Themes[9]
c.4 quia, col. 2	Church jurisdiction/ common law, usury
c.4 quia, ca. fin.	usury
c.5 Iudaei	common law/ *cives*/ conversion
c.5 Iudaei, col. 2	canons/ jurisdictions
c.5 Iudaei, ca. fin.	common law/ conversions
c.6 ita quorundam	justice
c.7 consuluit	Jewish law
c.8 ad haec	social intercourse/ Jewish law
c.9 sicut	conversion
c.14 postulasti	Church jurisdiction
c.15 In nonnullis	social intercourse
c.16 cum sit	witnesses/ conversion
c. 19 fin.	conversion

34 FLORIANUS DE SANCTO PETRO, Floriano Sampieri, d. 1441, (Sav. VI, 295–96) (Fon. II,235)
Commentaria in Digestum (1576)

D.30,1 de legatis, 39 apud Iulianum, par. constat (II,37[rb])	status

Commentaria in Codicem

C.6,28 de liberis praeteritis, 4 maximum vitium	Jewish law

Jurists[6]	Themes[9]
Consilia (1576)	
#11	common law/ witnesses
#17	status/ Church jurisdiction
#18	common law/ jurisdiction/ Jewish law

35 FRANCISCUS ARETINUS DE ACCOLTIS,
d. 1486 (Sav. VI,329–41)
Consilia (1572)

#77, par. 1	*cives*
#157	Church jurisdiction/ common law

36 (GIOV.) FRANCISCUS RIPA, d. 1534
(Sch. III, 444)
Commentaria in Digestum (1586)

D.42,5 de privilegiis creditorum, 24 si ventri, par.divus (II,49ʳᵃ)	common law
D.45,1 de verbor. obligat., 84 si insulam (II,87ᵛᵃ)	common law

Tract. de privilegiis contractuum ulti-marum voluntatum (1586)

#46 (I,62ʳᵃ)	justice
#56 (I,62ʳᵃ)	social intercourse

37 FRANCISCUS SQUILACENCIS, Episcopus
(Fon. II,307)
Tract. de fide catholica (*TUJ*, XIV)

chap. 46 (6ᵛᵃ)	Church jurisdiction

Jurists[6]   Themes[9]

38 Franciscus Zabarella, 1360–1417
    (Sch. II, 283–85)
    Com. in quinque libros Decretalium
    (1518)
    X.3,34 de voto, 8 quod super (III,   conversion
    181rb)
    X.3,42 de baptismo, 3 maiores, par.   conversion
    item quaeritur (III,232rb)
    X.5,6 de Iudaeis, 13 etsi (V,53rb– jurisdiction
    56rb, whole title)
    Lectura super Clementinas (1492)
    Clem.1,4 de renunciatione, in primo no. conversion
    (eii^{ra})
    Clem.2,8 de testibus, 1 Iudaei (kviii^{r+v}) witnesses
    Clem.2,9 de iureiurando, 1 Romani   jurisdiction (I)
    (kix^{ra})
    Clem. 5,2 de Iudaeis (yi^{r+v})   conversion

39 Georg Natan
    Tract. de statuto . . . foeminae non suc-
    cedent. (*TUJ*, II)
    Quest. 2, #105–07 (252$^{rb–va}$)   common law

39a Goffredus de Trano, d. 1245 (Sch.
    II, 88–91)
    Summa super rubricis Decretalium
    (1570)
    X.1,14 de aetate et qualitate (27va) conversion (I)
    X.3,42 de baptismo, v. item quaeritur conversion (I)
    (157rb)
    X.5,6 de Iudaeis (198 and 199^{r})   social
                                          intercourse

40 Gregorius Holoander, 16th cent.
    (Fon. I,474)
    Novellae, Constitutiones Iuris Graecae
    et Latinae (1567)

Jurists[6]	Themes[9]
Nov. 146 (pp. 377–78)	Jewish law

41   GUIDO DE BAYSIO (Archidiaconus), d. 1313 (Sch. II,186f.)
Rosarium super decreto Gratiani (1472) (no folio numbers)

D.33,c.5 usque adeo (col. 2 of D.33)	status
D.45,c.3 qui sincera (col. 2 of D.45)	status/ justice
D.54,c.13 mancipia (col. 7 of . . .)	jurisdiction
D.56,c.8 Dominus (col. 4)	status
D.77,c.3 quicunque (col. 2)	conversion
C.1,q.2,c.2 quam pio (col. 2 of q.2)	conversion
C.3,q.7,c.7 sacerdos (col. 6)	jurisdiction
C.7,q.1,c.8 quam periculosum (col. 7)	Jewish law
C.11,q.3,c.24 ad mensam (col. 11)	status/ justice
C.11,q.3,c.46 cui est (col. 19)	jurisdiction
C.14,q.5,c.15 non sane (col. 5)	conversion
C.17,q.4,c.19 si quis suadente (col. 10)	canons
C.17,q.4,c.31 constituit	jurisdiction
C.23,q.4,c.53 debet homo (col. 26)	conversion
C.23,q.6,c.4 iam nunc (col. 2)	conversion
C.23,q.7,c.2 si de rebus (col. 2)	justice
C.24,q.3,c.1 si habes (col. 2)	justice
C.28,q.1,c.10 iudaei, par., verum (col. 8)	Jewish law
C.28,q.1, c.15 cave (col. 10)	status
C.30,q.1,c.1 pervenit (col. 1)	Jewish law
de cons. D.4,c.93 Iudaei (col. 21 of D.4)	conversion
de.cons. D.4,c.108 rebaptizare (col. 22)	justice

Apparatus ad Sextum (1577)

Jurists[6]	Themes[9]
Sext.3,11 de testamentis, 2 religiosus (110[rb])	conversion
Sext.4,3 de cognatione spirituali, 1 nedum (111[rb])	conversion
Sext.5,2 de haereticis, 13 contra (116[ra])	conversion

42 GUILELMUS BENEDECTI (Fon. I,93)
Repitio in Extra, de testamen., c. Raynutius

In v. eodem testamento., #157	Jewish law/ witnesses

43 GUILELMUS DURANDUS, ca. 1237–1296 (Sch. II, 144–56)
Speculum Iudiciale (1547)

X.1,14 de aetate et qualitate, par. potest; lib.4 (36[ra–b])	jurisdiction
X.2,7 de iuramento calumniae, par. restat; lib.2 (87[va] and 88[ra])	witnesses
X.2,20 de testibus, v. item quod est Iudaeus, par. opponitur; lib.1 (113[vb])	witnesses
X.4,17 qui filii sint legitimi, v. quod si pater, par. in hoc; lib.4 (173[va])	justice
X.5,6 de Iudaeis, par. iura nolunt; lib.4 (183[ra])	status

44 GUILELMUS DE MONTE LAUDUNO, d. 1343 (Sch. II,197)
Lectura super Clementinis (1517)

Clem.5,5 de usuris (154[v])	usury

45 GUNDISALVUS DE VILLADIEGO, ca. 1450–1500 (Sch. II,406)
Tract. de haereticis (*TUJ*, XI[2])

Quest. 5 (33[v])	status (Marranos)

Jurists[6]   Themes[9]

46 HENRICUS BOICH, d. ca. 1350 (Sch.
    II,266–70)
    Distinctiones in libros Decretalium
    (1557)
    X.3 de testamentis, 2 nos quidam (III,   jurisdiction
    224rb)
    X.3,42 de baptismo, 3 maiores, v. prop-   conversion
    ter quod (III, 265ra)
    X.4, 11 de cognatione spirituali, 6 ve-   status
    niens (IV,25rb)
    X.4,19 de divortiis, 8 gaudemus (IV,   Church
    34^{r})   jurisdiction/
                                              common law
    X.5,6 de Iudaeis, 9 sicut (V, 59^{r}–60^{v}) status/
                                              conversion
    X.5,19 de usuris, 8 conquestus (II,   usury
    83ra)

47 HENRICUS DE SEGUSIA (Hostiensis, d.
    1271 (Sch. II,123–29)
    Summa super titulis Decretalium
    (1537)
    X.1,11 de temporibus ordinationum,   justice
    par. et cui (30rb)
    X.3,42 de baptismo, par. quae sit eius   conversion
    forma (186rb)
    X.5,6 de Iudaeis (235vb–237rb)   all themes
    Lectura in Decretales Gregorii (1965
    photograph of 1581)
    X.2,20 de testibus, 21 Iudaei (II, 89ra) status
    X.3,30 de decimis, 26 tua nobis (III,   Church
    103ra)   jurisdiction
    X.3,33 de convers. infidelium, 2 ex lit- status/
    teris (III, 124rb)   Jewish law/
                                              conversion

Jurists[6]	Themes[9]
X.3,34 de voto, 8 quod super, col. 4 (III, 128[vb])	Church jurisdiction/ **jurisdiction**
X.3,42 de baptismo, 4 debitum (III, 170[rb])	conversion
X.4,19 de divortiis, 8 gaudemus (IV, 45[v])	common law/ Jewish law/ conversion
X.5,6 de Iudaeis, 5 Iudaei (V, 30[rb]–34[vb], whole title)	Church jurisdiction/ jurisdiction/ conversion
c.7 consuluit	Jewish law
c.8 ad haec	jurisdiction
c.15 **In nonnullis**	Church jurisdiction/ insult
c.16 cum sit	conversion
X.5,19 de usuris, 12 post miserabilem (V, 57[vb])	Church jurisdiction/ usury

48   HIERONYMUS GIGANS, 16th cent. (Sch. III,456)

Tract. de crimine lesae maiestatis (*TUJ*, XI[1]) lib.2,q.10 (162[vb])	witnesses

49   HIPPOLYTUS DE MARSILIIS, d. 1529 (Sav. VI, 489) (Fon. I,625f.)
Com. ad l. Corneliam (1542)

D.48,8 ad legem Corneliam de sicariis, 3 eiusdem (26[r])	status
D.48,8 ad legem Corneliam de sicariis, 13 ex senatusconsulto, col. fin. (46[r])	canons/ insult

Com. ad tit. de quest. (1564)

Jurists[6]	Themes[9]
D.48,18 de questionibus, 1, par. praeterea (66ʳ)	justice
Consilia (1573)	
#12, par. 14	witnesses
#101	social intercourse/ common law
Singularia (In *Singula Doctorum*, 1579)	
#41 (347ᵛ)	common law
#107, par. 3 (356ʳᵇ)	conversion
#273, par. 7 (381ᵛᵇ)	conversion

50 IACOBUS DE BELVISIO, d. 1335 (Sav. VI,63)
    Lectura summam Auctenticorum et Usus Feudorum elucidans
    Quest.33, v. Iudaeus   conversion

51 IACOBUS DE BUTRIGARIUS, d. 1348 (Sav. VI,68–70)
    Lectura in Codicem (no date)
    C.1,9 de Iudaeis (29ᵛᵃ)   all themes
    C.1,14 de legibus et constitutionibus, 6   Jewish law
    quod favore (31ʳᵇ)

52 IACOBUS DE S. GEORGIO (Fon. I,405)
    Tract. de Feudis (*TUJ, X¹*)
    In verbo, dux, v. ultimo quaero   common law

53 IASON DE MAYNO, d. 1519 (Sav. VI, 397–417)
    Commentaria ad Digestum (1589)
    D.1,1 rubr. de iustitia et iure (I,2ʳᵇ⁻ᵛᵇ)   jurisdiction/ witnesses/ conversion

Jurists[6]	Themes[9]
D.2,11 si quis cautionibus, 8 et si post tres (I,125va)	common law
D.12,1 si certum petatur, 1 (II, 4rb)	Jewish law
D.12,2 de iureiurando, in repeti. 1. 31 admonendi, v. istud iuramentum (II, 91vb–92ra)	common law
D.30,1, de legatis et fideicommissis, 24 apud hostes (IV, 21rb)	*cives*
D.30,1, de legatis et fideicommissis, 39 apud Iulianum, 7 constat (IV,58vb)	status/ justice
D.45,1 de verb. obligat., 84 si insulam (VI,104vb)	common law/ jurisdiction
Commentaria ad Codicem (1589)	
C.1,1 de summa trinitate, 1 (VII, 7^{va+b})	usury
C.3,28 de inofficioso testamento, 11 in arenam (VII,138rb)	conversion
Consilia (1581)	
Bk.4, #124, col. 3	status

54 INNOCENTIUS IV, d. 1254 (Sch. II,91–94)

Apparatus in quinque libros Decretalium (1478, no pagination)

X.2,1 de iudiciis, 13 novit, col. 3 (col. 9 of title 1)	Church jurisdiction (I)
X.2,24 de iureiurando, 26 et si Christus (col. 3)	Church jurisdiction
X.3,34 de voto, 8 quod super, col. 2 (col. 6)	justice Church jurisdiction/ common law/ conversion
X.4,19 de divortiis, 8 gaudemus (col. 4)	Jewish law

Jurists[6]	Themes[9]
X.5,6 de Iudaeis, 5 Iudaei (8 cols.)	all themes
55 IOANNES DE ANANIA, d. 1457 (Sch. II, 320–22)	
Commentaria super V libro Decretalium (1504)	
X.5,1 de accusat., 6 de his (a4^{ra})	conversion
X.5,6 de Iudaeis, rubr. (m7^r–q3^v, whole title)	Church jurisdiction/ jurisdiction
c.3 Iudaei	status/ canons/common law/jurisdiction/ Jewish law
c.4 quia	usury
c.5 Iudaei	justice/Church jurisdiction/ common law/ jurisdiction/ Jewish law/ conversion
c.6 ita quorundam	status
c.8 ad haec	social intercourse
c.9 sicut	status/justice/ conversion
c.13 etsi	status/justice/ canons/common law
c.14 postulasti	Jewish law
c.15 in nonnullis	social intercourse
c.16 sum sit	common law/ jurisdiction/ witnesses/ conversion

Jurists[6]   Themes[9]

    c.18 ex speciali   status
    c.19 nulli Iudaeo   canons/Church
                                                jurisdiction/
                                                common law/
                                                witnesses

    X.5,7 de haereticis, 1 (q3[va])   witnesses
    X.5,19 de usuris, 5 quum tu (o3)[va])   conversion (I)
    X.5,19 de usuris, 8 conquestus (q1[va]) usury
    X.5,19 de usuris, 12 post miserabilem usury
    (q7[r])

56 Ioannes Andreas, d. 1348 (Sch. II,
    205–30)
    Novella in Decretales Gregorii IX
    (1963 photograph of 1581)
    X.2,1 de iudiciis, 13 novit (II,9[vb])   Church
                                                  jurisdiction
    X.2,13 de restitut. spoliat., 13 literas Jewish law
    (II,84[ra])
    X.3,34 de voto, 8 quod super (III,   canons/
    172[v])   Church
                                                  jurisdiction
    X.4,19 de divortiis, 8 gaudemus (IV,   common law/
    67[r])   conversion (I)
    X.5,6 de Iudaeis, 9 sicut (V,40[rb]–46[ra], status/
    whole title)   conversion
    X.5,6 de Iudaeis, 13 etsi   social
                                                  intercourse
    X.5,6 de Iudaeis, 16 cum sit   conversion
    X.5,9 de apostatis, 4 quidam (V,55[rb]) conversion
    Questiones Mercuriales (In *Quaestiones*
    Variae ac Selectae, 1572)
    Questio XVII, super reg. ex eo (p. 604, status/canons
    col. 1)

Jurists[6]   Themes[9]

> *Additiones ad Speculum* (1547 ed. of
> *Speculum*)
> Super rubr. de Iudaeis (IV,182^v–183^r)   status/
>   justice/
>   Church
>   jurisdiction

57 Ioannes Antonius a S. Georgio
    (Card. Alexander), d. 1509 (Sch. II,
    338–41)
    Commentaria super Decretis (1579)
    D.26, c.3 deinde (114va)   jurisdiction (I)
                                                conversion
    D.33,c.5 usque adeo (134ra)   status
    D.42,c.1 si quis (151rb)   conversion
    D.45, c.5 de Iudaeis (157^v–158ra)   conversion

58 Ioannes Calderinus, d. 1365 (Sch.
    II, 247ff.)
    Casus Summarii Decretalium
    X.4,19 de divortiis, 8 gaudemus   conversion
    X.5,1 de accusat., 6 de his   conversion
    Consilia (1550)
    In tit. de constit., n. 10 (#1)   Jewish law
    In tit. de consuetu., n. 2 (#39)   jurisdiction/
                                                Jewish law
    In tit. de iudiciis, n. 11 (#115)   Church
                                                jurisdiction
    In tit. de testamen., n. 30 (#329)   Jewish law
    In tit. de Iudaeis, n. 2 and n. 3 (#487)   status/Church
                                                jurisdiction/
                                                common law/
                                                conversion
    In tit. de Sententia et re iudicata, n.8   common law/
    (#223)   toleration

Jurists[6]   Themes[9]

59 IOANNES CAMPEGIUS (Fon. I,178)
    Tract. de statuto quod stantibus mas-
    culis foeminae non succedent (*TUJ,*
    II
    Quest.36, #158–60 (269[ra])   common law
    Quest.60, #240–41 (271[va])   Jewish law
    Tract. de dote (*TUJ,* IX)
    Part I, quest.47 (281[vb]–282[va])   usury/
                                            conversion

60 IOANNES FABER (Jean Faure de Rous-
    sines), d. 1340 (Sav. VI, 40–45)
    Breviarum in Codicem (1550)
    C.1,2 de sacrosanctis ecclesiis, 1 (p. jurisdiction
    4[a])
    C.1,12 de his qui ad ecclesias confug., canons
    1 (p. 17[b])

61 IOANNES DE FANTUS, d. 1391 (Sch. II,
    265f.)
    Commentaria super Decretum
    C.14,q.4,c.12 ab illo   usury
    C.17,q.4,c.35 diffinivit   canons
    C.23,q.6,c.4 iam nunc   common law

62 IOANNES FRANCISCUS BALBUS (Fon.
    I,56)
    Tract. de praescriptionibus et usuca-
    pionibus (*TUJ,* XVII)
    Part I, quest.5, in fin. (53[rb])   justice/
                                            common law

63 IOANNES DE IMOLA, d. 1436 (Sav. VI,
    279–80) (Sch. II,296–98)
    Commentaria ad Digestum Novum et
    ad Infortiatum (1533)

Jurists[6]	Themes[9]
D.41,3 de usucapionibus, 32 si fur. rem, par. siquis (I,81vb)	common law
D.45, 1 de verb. obligat. 34 multum (II,23va)	status
Commentaria ad Decretales (1575)	
X.1,38 de procurat., 5 tuae (I,326) (I)	common law
X.2,20 de testibus, 1 Iudaei (II,96–97)	status/ witnesses
X.2,28 de appella, 18 consuluit (II, 281)	jurisdiction
Commentaria ad Clementinas (1475)	
Clem. 2,8 de testibus, 1 quum Iudaei (cols. 1–3 of title 8)	witnesses
Clem.5,2 de Iudaeis (cols. 1–3)	common law/ conversion
Clem.5,9 de poenitentis et remissionibus (col. 2)	canons
Consilia	
#1	common law/ Jewish law/ witnesses
#2	witnesses
#3	common law
#5	common law
#6	usury

64   IOANNES LECIRIER (Fon. I,558)
      Tract. de Iure primogeniturae (*TUJ,*
      X^1)

Bk.1,quests.16–18 (31^v–32^v)	common law/ Jewish law

65   IOANNES LOPEZ (Lupus), d. 1496
      (Sch. II,335–36)
      Tract. de libertate Ecclesiastica (*TUJ,*

XIII,1) Quest. ultima, # 1–2 (10$^{rb–va}$)	conversion

Jurists[6]   Themes[9]

66 IOANNES LUPUS DE PALACIIS RUBEIS,
   d. ca. 1503 (Sch. II,337–38)
   Repetitio in Extra. de donat., c. vestrae
   Par. 35, circa prin.   common law

67 IOANNES PETRUS DE FERRARIIS, later
   14th cent. (Sch. II,294)
   Practica Aurea, s. practica de libellis
   col. 7, v. sed hic quaero an liceat   Church
                                              jurisdiction

68 IOANNES DE PLATEA, 16th cent. (Sav.
   VI,492) (Fon. II,106)
   Ad tres ultimos libros Codicis
   C.10,31 de decurionibus, 49 omnes   jurisdiction
   C.12,59 de diversis officiis, 9 proba-   jurisdiction
   torias

69 IOANNES STAPHILEUS (Sch. III,457)
   (Fon. II,309)
   Tract. de gratiis expectativis (*TUJ,*
   XV[1])
   In tit. de rescript. in forma brevium,   jurisdiction
   n.41 (301[va])

70 IOANNES DE TURRECREMATA (Torque-
   mada), d. 1468 (Sch. II,322–27)
   Commentaria ad Decretum Gratiani:
   Decretorum Libri Quinque secundum
   Gregorianos Decretalium Libros
   (Rome, 1728), which is a rearrange-
   ment of the *Decretum* according to the
   titles of the *Decretales* (1728)
   D.45,c.2, qui sincera (569)   conversion
   D.54,c.12 generalis (725) (724–27)   justice
   C.28,q.1,c.15 cave (725) (724–27)   status

Jurists[6]	Themes[9]
71 LAPUS TACTUS, early 14th cent. (Sch. II,238) *Lectura super Clementinis* Clem.5,4 de homicidio; quest.12	conversion
72 LAURENTIUS HISPANIUS, early 13th cent. (Sch. I,190f.) *Apparatus ad Decretum* C.23,q.6,c.4 iam nunc	Church jurisdiction/ conversion
73 LAURENTIUS DE RODULPHIS, d. 1450 (Sch. II,263f.) *Tract. de Usuris* (*TUJ,* VII) Quest.72 (28va) Quest.146 (36vb)	conversion (I) status/usury
74 LAURUS DE PALATIIS, mid-15th cent. (Sch. II,393) *Tract. de statuto . . . foeminae non succedent* (*TUJ,* II) #253-263 (282vb–283ra)	common law
75 LUDOVICO DE GOZADONIS, BONONIENSIS (Fon. I, 438) *Consilia* (1571) #24	Jewish law
76 LUDOVICUS ROMANUS, 1409–39 (Sav. VI,489) *Commentaria de iuris civilis libris* (1580) D.12,2 de iureiur., 3 ait praetor, 4 iurari (I,94^{v}) D.29,2 de adquir. vel omit. her., 38 si duo (II,124^{r})	jurisdiction usury

Jurists[6]   Themes[9]

    D.45,1 de verbor. obligat., 34 multum   status
    interest (III,149^{r+v})
    Singularia (1557)
    #55   conversion
    #679   jurisdiction/
                               conversion
    #687   status/
                               jurisdiction/
                               conversion
    #812   common law (I)
    Consilia (1568)
    #155   canons
    #183   social
                               intercourse/
                               insult
    #489   social
                               intercourse/
                               common law

77   MARTINUS LAUDENSIS, mid-15th cent.
    (Sch. II,395)
    Tract. de principibus (*Volumen Trac-*
    tatuum, XII, 1549)
    Vers. #49 (25ra)   Church
                               jurisdiction
    Vers. #226 (27vb)   canons

78   MATTHEUS DE AFFLICTIS, 1448–1528
    (Sav. IV,479) (Fon. I,7)
    Commentaria in Libris Feudorum
    (1598)
    In rubr. quae sint regalia (p. 740, par.   Church
    6)   jurisdiction
    In rubr. de controversia investiturae usury
    (p.54, par.5)

Jurists[6]   Themes[9]

Neapolitani decisiones (1596)
n.151 serenissimus rex (112[rb]–113[vb])   status/
                                                        conversion

79 NICHOLAUS DE TUDESCHIS (PANORMI-
    TANUS), d. 1445 (Sch. II,312–13)
    Lectura super libros V Decretalium (I,
    1516) (II,1487) (III-V, 1559)
    X.1,3 de rescriptiis, 7 eam te (35[vb])   conversion
    X.2,1 de iudiciis, 13 novit (col. 2 of   status/
    title 1)   justice/
                                                        Church
                                                        jurisdiction/
                                                        cives/usury
    X.2,2 de foro compet., 9 quod clericis   justice/usury
    (col. 7).
    X.2,20 de testibus, 21 Iudaei (col. 1)   status
    X.3,33 de conversione infidelium, 2 ex   common law/
    litteris (III, 173[rb])   conversion
    X.3,34 de voto, 8 quod super (III,   justice/
    177[vb])   Church
                                                        jurisdiction/
                                                        conversion

    X.3,42 de baptismo, 3 maiores (III,   conversion
    215[ra])
    X.3,42, de baptismo, 4 debitum (III,   conversion
    215[rb])
    X.4,19 de divortiis, 8 gaudemus (IV,   Church
    49[r–va])   jurisdiction/
                                                        conversion .

    X.5,3 de simonia, 9 cum in ecclesia   conversion
    (IV,78[vb])
    X.5,6 de Iudaeis (IV,95[r]–99[va], whole
    title)
                c.1   social intercourse/
                                                        jurisdiction

Jurists[6]   Themes[9]

c.5 Iudaei	conversion
c.7 consuluit	Jewish law
c.8 ad haec	social intercourse
c.9 sicut	status/ conversion
c.15 in nonnullis	social intercourse
c.16 cum sit	common law/ jurisdiction
c.18 ex speciali	jurisdiction
X.5,19 de usuris, 5 quum tu (IV, 125rb)	common law/ conversion (I)
X.5,19 de usuris, 12 post miserabilem (IV, 128^r)	Church jurisdiction/ social intercourse
X.5,38 de poenitent. et remiss., 5 quod quidam (IV,173va)	canons
Consilia (1578), #39, lib. 1, col. 2	common law

80 OLDRADUS DE PONTE, d. 1335 (Sav. VI, 55–59)
Consilia (1550)

#36	justice/ Church jurisdiction/ insult
#51	status
#54	canons
#72	status/Church jurisdiction
#87	status/justice
#264	status/justice

Jurists[6]	Themes[9]
#333	social intercouse/ common law

81 PARISEUS DE PUTEO, d. 1493 (Fon. II,128)
    Tract. de Syndicatu (*TUJ,* VII)
    Par. adulterium, n.9 (241va)   Church jurisdiction/ social intercourse

    Consilia
    Bk. 4, #2   common law

82 PAULUS DE CASTRO, d. 1441 (Sav. VI, 281–93)
    Commentaria in Digestum (1582)
    D.34,5, de rebus dubiis, 20 cum senatu   status/ jurisdiction
    (IV,75va)
    Commentaria in IV priores et in VI ac VII libris Codicis (1582)
    C.1,4 de episcopali audientia, 4 mimae   social intercourse
    (VIII,22vb)
    Consilia (1582)
    Vol. 2, #90   common law/ witnesses
    Vol. 2, #109   Church jurisdiction/ usury
    Vol. 2, #317   common law
    Vol. 2, #378   common law/ Jewish law
    Vol. 2, #379   witnesses/ usury
    Vol. 2, #380   common law
    Vol. 2, #397   usury

Jurists[6]   Themes[9]

83   PAULUS DE LEAZARIIS, d. 1356 (Sch.
     II, 246) (Fon. I,308)
     In ius canonicum
     Sext. 5,5 de usuris, 1   status/usury
     Epitome Clementinarum or *Lectura*
     super Clementinis
     Clem.3,7 de sepulturis, 2 dudum   conversion

84   PAULUS GRILLANDUS, 16th cent. (Sch.
     III,456) (Fon. I,450)
     Tract. de poena omnifarii coitus illi-
     citi (TUJ, XI[1])
     Quest. 12, v. quidam tamen fuerunt,   common law/
     col. 3 (305[rb])   social
                                            intercourse

     Quest.12, v. si vero ignoranter, col. common law/
     penul. (305[va])   social
                                            intercourse

85   PAULUS DE MONTE PICO (Sav. VI,
     492) (Fon. I,693)
     Repetitio in l. Titia, ff. de legat. 2
     (D.31,1,34)
     Quest.20, col. 62, de 1. 2   common law

86   PETRUS DE ANCHARANO, d. 1416 (Sch.
     II, 278–82)
     Commentaria in Decretales (III–IV,
     1580) (V,1581)
     X.3,8 de concess. praebend., 2 nulla   status
     (II,88[vb])
     X.3,34 de voto, 8 quod super (II,   justice/
     384[rb])   Church
                                            jurisdiction

     X.4,19 de divortiis, 8 gaudemus (III, Church
     142[vb]–143[v])   jurisdiction/
                                            conversion

Jurists[6]	Themes[9]
X.5,6 de Iudaeis (51^r–58^v, whole title)	all themes
Lectura super Sexto (1583)	
In repetit. Sext. 5,13 de reg. iuris, 26	Church
ea quae (pp. 565–574, esp. 570^a–573^b)	jurisdiction
Lectura super Clementinis (1580)	
Clem.5,1 de magistris, 2 quum sit (235ra)	jurisdiction
Clem.5,9 de poenitent., et remiss. 1 (265rb)	canons
Consilia (1574)	
#15	status/Church jurisdiction/ insult
#195	conversion
#243	usury
#271	Church jurisdiction/ common law
#281	common law
#371	jurisdiction

87 PETRUS DE BELLA PERTICA, d. 1308
    (Sav. VI,27–33)
    Commentaria ad Codicem

C.5,4 de nuptiis, 19 celebrandis	common law/ Jewish law
Com. in Aliquot Cod. Leges (1571)	
C.1,1 Rubr. de sum. trin. (7^r)	status

88 PHILIPPUS CORNEUS, 1420–1492 (Sav.
    VI,485)
    Lecturae ad Digestum vetus et Codicem
    (1553)

D.12,2 de iureiurando, 3 ait praetor (32^r)	canons/ witnesses

Jurists[6]	Themes[9]
C.6,20 de collationibus, 3 pactum (36[r])	witnesses
C.6,28 de liberis praeteritis, 4 maximum vitium (138[r-v])	common law/ Jewish law
C.7,52 Rubr. de re iudicata (300[r])	witnesses
Consilia (1572)	
Vol. 1, #45	witnesses
Vol. 1, #114	insult/ common law
Vol. 2, #65	common law
Vol. 2, #180, pars.5, 12 and 13	common law/ Jewish law
Vol. 3, #19, par.7	Church jurisdiction/ usury
Vol. 3, #260	common law
Vol. 4, #37	witnesses

89 PHILIPPUS DECIUS, 1454–1536 (Sav. VI, 372–96) (Sch. II,350ff.)

In titulum de regulis iuris (1546)	
D.50,17 de reg. iuris, 61 domum suam (pp. 265–66)	Jewish law
Commentaria in Decretales (1579)	
X.1,2 de constitutionibus, 1 (11[v])	status/ common law/ witnesses/ canons
X.1,2 de constitu., 7 quae in ecclesiarum (32[r])	conversion
X.1,3 de rescript., 7 eam te (14[v])	conversion
X.2,1 de iudiciis, 4 at si clerici (200[r])	jurisdiction
X.2,1 de iudiciis, 13 novit (219[v])	Jewish law
X.2,19 de probatio, 1 ex epistolae (235[r])	status/canons/ common law

Jurists[6]   Themes[9]

    X.2,19 de probatio, 4 proposuisti   witnesses
    (251^v)
    X.2,19 de probatio, 8 in presentia   canons
    (263^v)
    X.2,25 de except., 6 quum venerabilis   usury
    (320^v)
    X.2,28 de appellat., 18 consuluit   status/canons/
    (365^{r-v})   social
                                          intercourse/
                                          common law/
                                          jurisdiction

    Consilia (1546)
    Vol. 1, #51, par. 2   common law
    Vol. 1, #130   conversion

90 PIER PAOLO PARISIO, 16th cent. (Sch.
    III,444)
    Consilia (1570)
    Vol. 4, #2   justice/
                                          common law/
                                          conversion

91 PROSDOCIMUS DE COMITIBUS, d. 1438
    (Sch. II,298)
    Tract. de differentiis legum et canonum
    (*TUJ*, I)
    n.146, per tex. c.1 and c. fin. de Iudaeis   social
    (196vb)   intercourse

92 RAPHAEL CUMANUS (FULGOSIUS)
    (RAF. RAIMONDI) d. 1427 (Sav. VI,
    486) (Fon. I, 268)
    Commentaria in Digestum vetus (1544)
    D.1,1, rubr. (6ra)   jurisdiction
    Lecturae in Infortiatum (1544)
    D.34,5 de rebus dubiis, 20 cum Senatus   status/

Jurists[6]	Themes[9]
(134ᵛ) *Consilia* (1576)	jurisdiction
#155	social intercourse

93   ROCCHUS DE CURTE (ROCHUS CUR-
TIUS), late 15th cent. (Sch. II,404)
Tract. de consuetudine (*TUJ*, II)
#752–57 (de Susannis' numbering dif-   common law/
fers from that in *TUJ*)   Jewish law

94   ROFFREDUS EPIPHANII, d. ca. 1243
(Sav. V,185–217)
Libelli iuris civilis (1968 photograph
of 1500)
De constitutione Christianis (159ᵛᵇ–   justice
160ʳ)

95   ROLANDUS A VALLE, 16th cent.
Consilia
Bk. 2, #35   common law/
   cives

96   SOCINI, MARIANUS JR., d. 1556 (Sav.
VI, 343–55, on all 3 Socini)
Commentaria ad Infortiatum (1593)
D.24,3 solut. matri., 1; par.198 (I,   common law
31ᵛᵇ)
Super Decretales, Tract. de foro com-
petenti (1519)
X.2,2 de foro competenti, 8 cum sit   canons
generale, col. 8 (17ᵛᵃ)

97   ———, MARIANUS JR. and BARTO-
LOMEO *Consilia* (1546)
Vol. 1, #62   common law
Vol. 1, #65   witnesses

Jurists[6]	Themes[9]
Vol. 1, #66	Church jurisdiction/ Jewish law/ witnesses
Vol. 1, #70	jurisdiction/ Jewish law
Vol. 1, #71	common law
Vol. 1, #102	insult
Vol. 4, #119	Church jurisdiction/ insult

98 STEPHANUS BERTRANDUS CARPENTO-
    RACTENSIS (Fon. II,466)
    Consilia (1603)

Vol. 1, #233	common law/ witnesses
Vol. 3, #88	usury

99 ULDARICUS ZASIUS, 16th cent. (Sav.
    VI,421)
    De Iudaeis Quaestiones Tres (1550)
    passim (Vol. 5 of *Opera Omnia*, 331–   all themes/
    53)

Part III
Themes[13]
Table of Themes

I. Status
    A. General
    B. Toleration
    C. Enemies
    D. Slaves

---

13. These themes are the same thirteen that are found in Parts I and II of the Index. However, in Part III, as in Part I, the thirteen themes have been broken down into more useful subthemes.

II. Right of Jews to Justice
   A. Explicitly Stated
   B. Right to Fair Treatment in General
III. Jews in Relation to Canons as a Whole
   A. General
   B. Exclusion from Christian Ritual
IV. Church Jurisdiction over Jews
   A. Direct
   B. Indirect (Indirect Excommunication)
V. Social Intercourse
   A. General (esp. Overfamiliarity)
   B. Prohibition on Sexual Relations; Requirement of Special
      Habit
   C. Prohibition on Dining
   D. Holy Week Restrictions
VI. Insult
VII. Jews in Relation to *Ius Commune* (Italian Common Law)
VIII. Jews as *Cives* (Citizens)
IX. Exclusion from Jurisdictions
   A. General
      Prohibition on Legacies to the *Collegia* (Communities)
         of the Jews
      Jurisdiction among Infidels in General
   B. Exclusion from Offices
      Loss of Immunities, with esp. ref. to Curial Offices
   C. Exclusion from Spiritual Jurisdictions
   D. Prohibition on Ownership of Slaves
X. Jewish Law Observance
   A. General
   B. Observance of Jewish Marital Law
   C. Observance of Jewish Ritual Law
   D. Synagogue Building
XI. Restrictions on Witnesses
   A. General
   B. Oaths of Jews

XII. Usury
       Problems Involving Marriage and Usury
XIII. Conversion
       A. Improved Status (New Man)
       B. Separation of Converts from Jews
       C. Problems Involving Children (esp. forced baptism of)
       D. Problems Involving Specifically the Dowry
       E. Methods
       F. Conditions (Prerequisites) for Conversion
       G. Desire (on the part of the Church) for
       H. Prevarication (on the part of Converts)
       I. Conversion to Judaism Prohibited

The themes listed in this table represent the major problems discussed by de Susannis, as well as by all other legists and canonists who devoted attention to the Jews. Their discussions are at once theoretical, in commentary directly on the canons and (Roman) laws appearing in the textbooks and codes used in the Middle Ages, but also practical, in *consilia* and tracts. It is hoped that the divisions made in this table will offer a framework for further research on the specific problems. The order of the divisions here follows in general that used by de Susannis in his exposition, general status, relation to the canons, and relation to *ius commune* (common law), but special problems, such as jurisdictions, witnesses, and observance of Jewish law, whose determination demanded a harmonization of the requirements of both canon and common law, have been put toward the end. Conversion, perhaps fittingly, has been placed last.

In the Index itself, which follows the order of the table, the left-hand column under each subtheme lists the laws, canons, *consilia,* and tracts, in that order (the reader is again referred to the key to legal references at the beginning of the index), in which the sub-themes are found. The right-hand column lists the names of the legists and canonists, if any, who have written a pertinent commentary on the law or canon or in the *consilium* or tract appearing opposite the jurist's name in the lefthand column. To identify precisely any given commentary cited in Part III for the purpose of his own reference, the reader needs simply to look in Part II, first under the name of the jurist and then under the law or title as the entry appears there under his name.

(for cross reference to Part Part II)

I.   STATUS

Locations   Jurists

A.   *General* (I,1,2,5,11, & intro.; II, 3,4, & 7; III,3)[14]

(Laws)

D.30,1,39[15]	Florianus de S. Petro
D.45,1,34	Ioannes de Imola
C.1,1, Rubr.	Petrus de Bellapertica
C.1,2,1	Baldus
C.1,9	Iac. de Butrigarius
	(all topics)
C.1,11,1	Bartolus

(Canons)

D.56,c.8	Dom. de S. Geminiano
	Guido de Baysio
C.11,q.3,c.24	Guido de Baysio
C.28,q.1,c.15	Guido de Baysio
D.1,c.70, de pen.	Guido de Baysio
D.1,c.70, de pen.	Io. de Turre Cremata

---

14. These notations refer to the part and chapters (only) of the *De Iudaeis* in which the themes are discussed.

15. Laws and canons cited in Part III, but not mentioned in Part I, do not themselves bear on Jews either directly or indirectly—only the commentary on them does. Law and canons cited in Part III but with no reference to a jurist are most often laws and canons which de Susannis did not cite, either directly by citing the laws or canons themselves or indirectly by referring to some comment on them.

Locations   Jurists

X.1,2,1	Philippus Decius
X.2,1,13	Panormitanus
X.2,19,1	Phil. Decius
X.2,20,21	Ant. Butrio
X.2,20,21	Io. de Imola
X.2,28,18	Phil. Decius
X.3,8,2	Petrus de Ancharano
X.3,33,2	Hostiensis
X.4,11,6	Henricus Bohic
X.5,6 (*Summa*)	Hostiensis
X.5,6 (*Speculum*)	Guilelmus Durandus
X.5,6 (*Speculum*)	Ioannes Andreas
X.5,6	Petrus de Ancharano (all topics)
X.5,6	Franciscus Zabarella (all topics)
X.5,6,3	Io. de Anania
X.5,6,10	Gloss
X.5,6,10	Io. de Anania
X.5,6,13	Io. de Anania
X.5,6,18	Io. de Anania
X.5,7,9	Ant. Butrio
Sext.5,13 (*Mercuriales*)	Io. Andreas

(Consilia)

Cons. 99, vol. 6	Alex. Tartagnus de Imola
Cons. 130, vol. 7	Alex. Tartagnus de Imola
Cons. 209, vol. 3	Aug. Beroius
Cons. 73, vol. 1	Aymo Cravettae
Cons. 316, vol. 1	Baldus
Cons. ultimo	Bart. Cepolla
Cons. 51	Oldradus de Ponte
Cons. 72	Oldradus de Ponte

Locations	Jurists
Cons. 87	Oldradus de Ponte
Cons. 264	Oldradus de Ponte

(Tracts)

Singularium 689	Ludovicus Romanus
Tract. de nobilitate, car.2, #50	Andr. Tiraquellus
Tract. de haereticis	Gundisalvus de Villadiego
Divini ac humani iuris reperto-rium v. Iudaeus	Io. Calderinus (all topics)

B. *Toleration* (I,2,3,&7; III,5)

(Laws)

D.48,8,3	Hippol. de Marsiliis

(Canons)

C.23,q.8,c.11	
X.2,1,13	Panormitanus
X.2,20,2	Gloss
X.2,28,29	Carol. Molinaeus
X.5,6,9	Gloss
X.5,6,13	Gloss

(Consilia)

Cons. 17	**Florian. de S. Petro**
Cons. 124, bk. 4	Iason de Mayno
Cons. 8(#223)	Ioan. Calderinus

(Tracts)

Tract. de potestate regia, part 5, q.81, col.3	Antonius Corsettus

C. *Enemies* (I,2,7,9, & 13; II,5,6; III,1)

(Laws)

D.12,2,5,1	Gloss

Locations   Jurists

    D.24,3,47   Bartolus
    D.30,1,41,7   Bartolus
    D.30,1,39,7   Iason de Mayno
    D.34,5,20   Paulus de Castro (I)
    D.34,5,20   Raphael Cumanus
    D.45,1,34   Ludovicus Romanus
    D.54,1,34   Alex. Tartagnus
    C.1,1,1

(Canons)
    D.33,c.5   Dominicus de S.
                                        Geminiano
    D.33,c.5   Guido de Baysio
    D.33,c.5   Io. Ant. a S. Georgio
    C.1,q.1,c.37   Gloss
    de pen. D.1,c.7   Gloss
    X.2,20,23
    X.5,6,2   Felynus Sandeus

(Consilia)
    Cons. 2 (#487)   Io. Calderinus
    Cons. 15   Petrus de Ancharno

(Tracts)
    Tract. de potestate regia, part 5, Antonius Corsettus
    q.81

D.   *Slaves* (I,4,7; II,5; III,2,4)

(Laws)
    D.45,1,34   Alex. Tartagnus
    D.45,1,34   Ludovicus Romanus

(Canons)
    D.1,c.9   Dom. de S. Geminiano
    D.45,c.3   Dom. de S. Geminiano
    D.45,c.3   Guido de Baysio
    C.23,q.8,c.11

Locations	Jurists
X.2,20,21	Hostiensis
X.2,20,21	Panormitanus
X.5,6,6	Io de Anania
X.5,6,9	Henr. Bohic
X.5,6,9	Io. de Anania
X.5,6,9	Io. Andreas
X.5,6,9	Panormitanus
X.5,6,13	Gloss
X.5,6,13	Io. de Anania
Summa, Part 3, title 3, chap. 6	St. Antoninus
Decis. 151, col. 3 and 4	Matt. de Afflictis

(Tracts)

Tract. de potest. reg., part 5, q.81	Ant. Corsettus

II. RIGHTS OF JEWS TO JUSTICE

A. *Explicitly stated* (I,2,7,11 and 12; II,5)

D.12,6,36	Baldus
D.30,1,39,7	Iason de Mayno
D.48,18,1	Hippolytus de Marsiliis
C.1,9,14	
C.1,11,1	Bartolus
C.6,2,2	

(Canons)

D.45,c.3*[16]	Guido de Baysio
D.50,c.90	
D.54,c.12	Io. de Turre Cremata
C.16,q.3,c.14	Gloss

---

16. The asterisks in II,A denote that the comments so marked deal with the question of expelling Jews without cause. Strictly speaking, this question belongs under the theme of justice. However, these comments could also be listed under theme I,B, status, toleration.

Locations	Jurists
C.23,q.7,c.1*	Guido de Baysio
C.24,q.3,c.1	Guido de Baysio
D.4,c.108, de cons.	Gloss
D.4,c.108, de cons.	Guido de Baysio
X.2,1,13*	Panormitanus
X.2,2,9	Panormitanus
X.3,34,8*	Innocent IV
X.3,34,8	Panormitanus
X.3,34,8	Petrus de Ancharano
X.5,6 (*Addits. Speculum*)*	Io. Andreas
X.5,6,2	Gloss
X.5,6,5	Io. de Anania
X.5,6,6	Felynus Sandeus
X.5,6,9	Io. de Anania
X.5,6,13*	Io. de Anania
X.5,12,6	Egidius Bellamera

(Consilia)

Cons. 2, vol. 4, col. 2 and 3*	Pier Paolo Parisio
Cons. 36	Oldradus de Ponte
Cons. 87*	Oldradus de Ponte
Cons. 264*	Oldradus de Ponte

(Tracts)

Tract. de peste, #46	Franc. Ripa
Tract. de praescriptionibus, part I, q.5	Io. Franc. Balbus
Libelli iuris civilis, de constitut. Christianis	Roffredus Epiphanii of Benevento

B.   *Right to Fair Treatment in General* (I,2,5; III,4,7)

(Canons)

D.30,c.1	Gloss
D.30,c.1	Dom. de S. Geminiano
D.42,c.2 (I)	

Locations	Jurists
D.86,c.14 (I)	Gloss
D.86,c.21 (I)	
de pen., D.2,c.5	Gloss
X.1,11 (*Summa*)	Hostiensis
X.4,17 (*Speculum*)	Guil. Durandus

(Consilia)

Cons. 99, vol. 6, col. 3	Alex. Tartagnus

III.   JEWS IN RELATION TO CANONS AS A WHOLE

A.   *General* (I,7,8,9 and 10; II,2,3,8 and 12)

(Laws)

D. praefatio	Bartolus
D.12,2,3	Phil. Corneus
D.12,2,5,1	Baldus
D.48,8,13	Hippolytus de Marsiliis
C.1,12 (*Summa*)	Azo
C.1,12,1	Bart. Saliceto
C.1,12,1	Bartolus
C.1,12,1	Io. Faber

(Canons)

C.17,q.4,c.19	Guido de Baysio
C.17,q.4,c.35	Guido de Baysio
C.17,q.4,c.35	Io. de Fantuciis
X.2,2,8	Marianus Socini, Jr.
X.3,48,8	Io. Andreas
X.3,49,6	Antonio de Butrio
X.3,49,6	Carol. Molinaeus
X.4,14,4	Gloss
X.4,19,9	Gloss

Locations	Jurists
X.5,6,3	Felyn. Sandeus
X.5,6,3	Io. de Anania
X.5,6,5	Felyn. Sandeus
X.5,6,13	Io. de Anania
X.5,6,19	Io. de Anania
X.5,19,18	Ant. Butrio
Sext.5,13,38 (*Mercuriales*)	Io. Andreas
Clem.5,9	Io. de Imola
Clem. 5,9	Petrus de Ancharano

(Consilia)

Cons. 75, vol. 5	Alex. Tartagnus
Cons. 13, vol. 7	Alex. Tartagnus
Cons. 155	Ludovicus Romanus
Cons. 54	Oldradus de Ponte

B. *Exclusion from Christian Ritual*
    (I,3,9; III,3,9)

(Canons)

C.24,q.1,c.1 (I)	
D.1,c.27, de cons. (I)	
D.4,c.63, de cons.	Gloss
D.4,c.102, de cons.	Gloss
X.1,2,3	Egid. Bellamera
X.2,19,8	Phil. Decius
X.2,28,18	Phil. Decius
X.3,28,5	Ant. Butrio
X.5,38,5	Panormitanus

(Tracts)

Tract. de principibus, v.226	Martinus Laudensis

IV. CHURCH JURISDICTION OVER JEWS

A. *Direct* (I,7,11; II,2,3,6,8 and 9)

Locations	Jurists
(Feudal Laws)	
Librum Feudorum, in rubr. quae sint reg., col. 4	Matt. de Afflictis*[17]
(Canons)	
D.54,c.14	Dom. de S. Geminiano
C.17,q.4,c.30	Gloss
C.23,q.6,c.4	Laur. Hispanius
C.28,q.1,c.12	
X.1,2,1	Felynus Sandeus
X.2,1,13	Gloss
X.2,1,13	Innocent IV
X.2,1,13	Io. Andreas
X.2,1,13	Panormitanus
X.2,24,26	Innocent IV
X.3,30,26	Hostiensis
X,3,34,8	Franc. Zabarella* [17]
X,3,34,8	Hostiensis*
X,3,34,8	Innocent IV*
X,3,34,8	Io. Andreas
X,3,34,8	Panormitanus*
X,3,34,8	Petrus de Ancharano*
X.4,19,8	Henr. Bohic*
X.4,19,8	Panormitanus*
X.4,19,8	Petrus de Ancharano*
X.5,6,rubr.	Io. de Anania
X.5,6 (*Addits. Speculum*)	Io. Andreas*
X.5,6,4	Felynus Sandeus
X.5,6,5	Io. de Anania
X.5,6,13	Gloss
X.5,6,13	Io. de Anania
X.5,6,14	Felynus Sandeus

---

17. The asterisks in IV,A indicate that the comment deals with the entire theoretical question of Church jurisdiction over infidels besides the specific question of church jurisdiction over Jews. Cf. infra, n. 20.

Locations	Jurists
X.5,6,15	Hostiensis
X.5,6,16	Gloss
X.5,6,19	Io. de Anania
X.5,19,5	Hostiensis
X.5,19,12	Gloss
X.5,31,17	Gloss
X.5,31,17	Panormitanus*
Sext. 5,13,26	Petrus de Ancharano (I)
Clem. 2,8	Gloss
Summa, part 3, title 3, chap, 2, pars. 1 and 2	St. Antoninus*

(Consilia)

Cons. 96	Alexander de Nevo
Cons. 315, vol. 1	Baldus
Cons. 100, vol. 2	Baldus
Cons. 428, vol. 5	Baldus
Cons. 18	Florian. de S. Petro
Cons. 157	Franc. Aretinus de Accoltis
Cons. 2 (#487)	Io. Calderinus
Cons. 11 (#115)	Io. Calderinus
Cons. 36	Oldradus de Ponte
Cons. 72	Oldradus de Ponte
Cons. 109, vol. 2	Paulus de Castro (I)
Cons. 15	Petrus de Ancharano
Cons. 271	Petrus de Ancharano
Cons. 19, vol. 3	Philippus Corneus
Cons. 66, vol. 1	Socini
Cons. 119, vol. 4	Socini

(Tracts)

Tract. de fide Catholica, chap. 46	Franc. Squilacencis
Tract. de principibus, v.49	Mart. Laudensis*
Tract. de Syndicatu, par. adulterium, #9	Pariseo de Puteo

Locations	Jurists
Practica Aurea, de libellis, col. 7	Io. Petr. de Ferrariis*

B. *Indirect (Indirect Excommunication) (II,5)*

(Canons)

X.3,30,16	Gloss
X.5,6,5	Hostiensis
X.5,19,12	Gloss
X.5,19,18	
Clem.5,5	Gloss

V. SOCIAL INTERCOURSE

A. *General (esp. Overfamiliarity)*
(I,3,4,5; II,5,7; III,5)

(Laws)

D.1,1, rubr.	Claudius Seyssel
C.2,20,6	Gloss

(Canons)

D.54,c.8	Dom. de S. Geminianus
C.2,q.1,c.18	
C.28,q.1,c.13	
X.2,1,4	Panormitanus
X.2,28,18	Carol. Molinaeus
	Phil. Decius
X.5,6,1	Panormitanus
X.5,6,8	Gloss
X.5,6,8	Felyn. Sandeus
X.5,6,8	Io. de Anania
X.5,6,8	Panormitanus
X.5,6,8	Carol. Molinaeus
X.5,6,13	Io. Andreas
X.5,9,12	Panormitanus

Locations	Jurists
(Consilia)	
Cons. 13, vol. 7	Alex. Tartagnus
Cons. 489, col. 7	Ludovicus Romanus
(Tracts)	
Tract. de differentia, #146	Prosdocimus de Comitibus

B. *Prohibition on Sexual Relations;*
   Requirement of Special Habit
   (I,4,7, and 13; II,2,3 and 7)

(Laws)	
C.1,4,4	Paulus de Castro
C.1,9,6	Bart. Saliceto
C.9,13,1	Bart. Saliceto
(Canons)	
C.28,q.1,c.15	Gloss
C.28,q.1,c.16 (I)	
C.28,q.1,c.17	
X.2,28,18	Philippus Decius
X.4,5,4	Carol. Molinaeus
X.5,6,15	Gloss
X.5,6,15	Felynus Sandeus
X.5,6,15	Io. de Anania
X.5,6,15	Panormitanus
(Consilia)	
Cons. 13, vol. 7	Alex. Tartagnus
Cons. 63, vol. 4, col. 4	Andr. Barbatia Siculus
Cons. 101, vol. 2	Hippolytus de Marsiliis
Cons. 183, col. 1	Ludovicus Romanus
Cons. 333	Oldradus de Ponte
Cons. 115	Raphael Fulgosius

Locations   Jurists

(Tracts)

    Tract. de peste, tit. de remediis,   Franciscus Ripae
    #56

    Tract. de syndicatu, par. adult.,   Pariseo de Puteo
    #9

    Tract. de poena, q.12   Paulus Grillandus

C. *Prohibition on Dining* (I,4)

(Canons)
    C.11,q.3,c.24   Gloss
    C.28,q.1,c.14
    X.5,6 (*Summa*)   Goffredus de Trano

(Consilia)
    Cons. 96   Alexander de Nevo

D. *Holy Week Restrictions* (I,4; II,3)

(Canons)
    X.5,6,4
    X.5,6,15   Gloss

VI. INSULT[18] (I,2,7 and 9; II,3,6,9; III,3,9)

    D.48,8,13   Hippolytus de
                                      Marsiliis

    C.1,9,11
    C.1,9,14
    C.1,9,19
    Nov.37
    Nov.131, chap. 14

---

18. Included here are items dealing *explicitly* with insult. In fact, many, if not most, entries under Themes III, IV, and V belong to the general category of insult and its prevention.

Locations	Jurists
(Canons)	
D.21,c.1 (I)	
D.25,c.1 (I)	
D.54,c.14	
C.1,q.1,c.35	Gloss
X.5,6,4	
X.5,6,13	Gloss
X.5,6,14	
X.5,6,15	Hostiensis
Sext.5,13,26	Petrus de Ancharano
Summa, Part 2, tit. 12, chap. 3, par. 3	St. Antoninus
(Consilia)	
Cons. 233, vol. 6	Alex. Tartagnus
Cons. 63, vol. 4	Andr. Barb. Siculus
Cons. 100, vol. 2	Baldus
Cons. 183	Ludovicus Romanus
Cons. 15	Petrus de Ancharano
Cons. 114, vol. 1	Phil. Corneus
Cons. 102, vol. 1	Socini
Cons. 119, vol. 4	Socini

VII. JEWS IN RELATION TO IUS COMMUNE
(I,7,11 and 14; II,1–9; III,2,4,8)

(Laws)	
Inst.4,6,29	Angelus de Aretinus
D.1,1,rubr.	Claudius Seyssel
D.1,6,4	Baldus
D.2,11,8	Iason de Mayno
D.12,2,31 (repetit.)	Iason de Mayno
D.14,6,1	Baldus
D.24,3,1	Marianus Socini, Jr.

Locations	Jurists
D.27,1,15,6	Baldus
D.31,1,34 (repetit.q.20)	Paulus de Monte Pico
D.32,1,11	Baldus
D.41,3,32	Io. de Imola
D.42,5,24,1	Franc. Ripa
D.45,1,34	Alex. Tartagnus
D.45,1,84	Franc. Ripa
D.45,1,84	Iason de Mayno
D.47,12,5	Angelus de Ubaldis
D.48,4,1	Angelus de Ubaldis
D.48,4,1	Bartolus
D.49,15,24	Bartolus
C.1,9,7	
C.1,9,8	Bartolus
C.1,9,9	
C.5,4,19	Petrus de bella Pertica
C.6,28,4	Phil. Corneus
C.6,43, auct. res quae	Baldus
C.10,76 (I)	
Nov.45	

(Canons)	
D.12,c.12	Dom. de S. Geminianus
C.23,q.6,c.4	Io. de Fantus
X.1,2,1	Felynus Sandeus
X.1,38,5	Io. de Imola
X.2,19,1	Phil. Decius
X.2,24,4	Felynus Sandeus
X.2,28,18	Phil. Decius
X.3,33,2	Panormitanus
X.3,34,8	Innocent IV
X.4,19,8	Ant. de Butrio
X.4,19,8	Henr. Bohic
X.4,19,8	Hostiensis
X.4,19,8	Io. Andreas

Locations	Jurists
X.5,6,3	Io. de Anania
X.5,6,4	Felynus Sandeus
X.5,6,5	Felynus Sandeus
X.5,6,5	Io. de Anania
X.5,6,13	Io. de Anania
X.5,6,16	Io. de Anania
X.5,6,16	Panormitanus
X.5,6,19	Io. de Anania
X.5,19,5	Panormitanus
X.5,19,12	Ant. Butrio
Sext.5,5,1	Dom. de S. Geminiano
Clem.5,2	Io. de Imola
Repetitio rubr. X. de Donatio., par. 35	Io. Lupus
Singularia 41, Iudaeus	Hippolytus de Marsiliis

(Consilia)	
Cons. 3, vol. 2	Alex. Tartagnus
Cons. 71, vol. 2	Alex. Tartagnus
Cons. 161, vol. 2	Alex. Tartagnus
Cons. 75, vol. 5	Alex. Tartagnus
Cons. 99, vol. 6	Alex. Tartagnus
Cons. 13, vol. 7	Alex. Tartagnus
Cons. 130, vol. 7	Alex. Tartagnus
Cons. 63, vol. 4	Andr. Barb. Siculus
Cons. 76, vol. 5	Andr. Barb. Siculus
Cons. 158 + 33 + 36	Angelus Aretinus
Cons. 2, vol. 1	Aug. Beroius
Cons. 422, vol. 5	Baldus
Cons. 74 + ultimo	Bart. Cepolla
Cons. 18 + 11	Flor. de S. Petro
Cons. 101, vol. 2	Hippolytus de Marsiliis
Cons. 70	Io. de Anania

Locations	Jurists
Cons. 3, (#487) + n.8 (#223)	Io. Calderinus
Cons. 1 + 3 + 5	Io. de Imola
Cons. 489	Ludovicus Romanus
Cons. 333	Oldradus de Ponte
Cons. 39, vol. 1	Panormitanus
Cons. 2, vol. 4	Pariseo de Puteo
Cons. 90, vol. 2	Paulus de Castro
Cons. 377, vol. 2	Paulus de Castro
Cons. 378, vol. 2	Paulus de Castro
Cons. 271 + 281	Petrus de Ancharano
Cons. 114, vol. 1	Phil. Corneus
Cons. 65, vol. 2	Phil. Corneus
Cons. 180, vol. 2	Phil. Corneus
Cons. 260, vol. 3	Phil. Corneus
Cons. 51, vol. 1	Phil. Decius
Cons. 2, vol. 4	Pier Paolo Pariseo
Cons. 35, vol. 2	Rolandus a Valle
Cons. 62, vol. 1	Socini
Cons. 70, vol. 1	Socini
Cons. 71, vol. 1	Socini
Cons. 233, vol. 1	Steph. Bertrandus

(Tracts)

Tract. de pignoribus	Ant. Negusantius
Tract. de dotibus, part 2, col. 1	Baldus Novellus
Tract. de feudis, v. dux, ult. quaero	Iac. d. S. Georgio
Tract. de statuto exclu. foemi., q.2	Georg Natan
Tract. de statuto exclu. foemi., q.36	Io. Campegiis
Tract. de statuto exclu. foemi., q.36 #253-63	Laurus de Palatiis
Tract. de praescriptionibus, part 1, q.5	Io. Franc. Balbus

Locations   Jurists

    Tract. de iure primogeniturae, bk.   Io. Lecirier
    1,q.6
    Tract. de poena, q.1,col.3   Paulus Grillandus
    Tract. de consuetudine, #752-57 Rochus de Curte

VIII.   JEWS AS CIVES (I,5,7; II,1,2 and 6)

(Laws)
    D.1,6,4   Baldus
    D.27,1,15,6   Baldus
    D.30,1,24   Iason de Mayno
    D.49,15,24   Bartolus
    C.1,9,8   Bartolus

(Canons)
    D.1,c.12   Gloss
    X.1,6,34   Gloss
    X.2,1,13   Panormitanus
    X.5,6,5   Felynus Sandeus

(Consilia)
    Cons. 96   Alex. de Nevo
    Cons. 75, vol. 5   Alex. Tartagnus
    Cons. 77, par. 1   Franc. Aret. de Accoltis

IX.   EXCLUSION FROM JURISDICTIONS

A.   *General* (I,7; II,5,6, and 7)

(Laws)
    D.1,1, rubr.   Claud. Seyssel
    D.27,1,15,6   Baldus
    C.1,2,1   Gloss
    C.1,4,5 (I)

Locations   Jurists

    C.1,5,12,4-14
    C.1,9,15   Bart. Saliceto
    C.1,9,17
    C.1,9,18-19
    C.2,6,8 (I)   Gloss

(Canons)
    C.2,q.6,c.32 (I)
    X.3,26,3   Henr. Bohic
    X.5,6,5   Hostiensis
    X.5,6,16   Gloss
    X.5,6,18   Gloss

Prohibition on Legacies to the Collegia of the Jews[19] (II,5)

(Laws)
    D.34,5,20   Bartolus
    D.34,5,20   Paulus de Castro
    D.34,5,20   Raph. Cumanus
    C.1,2,1   Ant. de Butrio
    C.1,2,1   Bart. Saliceto
    C.1,2,1   Bartolus
    C.1,2,1   Cynus
    C.1,2,1   Io. Faber
    C.1,9,1   Bart. Saliceto

(Canons)
    X.5,6,5   Felynus Sandeus
    X.5,6,5   Hostiensis
    X.5,6,5   Io. de Anania

---

19. Bart. Saliceto, on C.1,9,1 states explicitly that this prohibition exists because the sect (Judaism) is reprobate, and thus its members (Jews) have no corporate status and therefore no jurisdictional rights or privileges. The numerous comments on this prohibition make it worthwhile to list them in one block.

Locations	Jurists
Jurisdiction among infidels in General[20] (II,6)	
D.26,c.3	Io. Ant. a S. Georgio
C.3,q.7,c.7	Guido de Baysio
C.11,q.3,c.46	Guido de Baysio
X.3,34,8	Ant. de Butrio
X.3,34,8	Franc. Zabarella

B. *Exclusion from Offices* (II,5,6, and 7)

(Laws)

D.1,1	Baldus
D.1,1	Bartolus
D.1,1	Iason de Mayno
D.1,1	Raph. Fulgosius
D.12,2,34	Ludovicus Romanus
D.27,1,15,6	Baldus
D.34,5,20	Bartolus
D.34,5,20	Paulus de Castro (I)
D.45,1,84	Iason de Mayno
D.50,2,3,3	Bartolus
C.1,9,8	Bartolus
C.1,9,18	Bartolus
C.2,6, fin.	Bartolus
C.10,31,49	Bartolus
C.10,31,49	Io. de Platea
C.21,1,1	Bartolus
C.12,59,9	Io. de Platea
Nov. 8	Angelus de Ubaldis

20. This theme clearly has reference to Jews, although the comments do not necessarily refer to Jews specifically. In addition, the theme, IV,A, of Church jurisdiction over infidels derives from the question of infidel jurisdiction in general. Thus to study either theme, one must examine both the entries in IV,A and also those about to be listed here. I am listing five entries, although they could have been included in IV,A, simply to alert the reader to the fact that the entries in both IV,A and IX,A each cover two themes.

Locations	Jurists
(Canons)	
D.54,c.14	
C.17,q.4,c.31	Gloss
C.17,q.4,c.31	Guido de Baysio
C.23,q.8,c.21	
D.1,c.7, de pen. (I)	Gloss
X.1,6,34	Doctores
X.5,6, rubr.	Io. de Anania
X.5,6,1	Felynus Sandeus
X.5,6,3	Io. de Anania
X.5,6,3	Panormitanus
X.5,6,16	Io. de Anania
X.5,6,16	Panormitanus
X.5,6,18	Panormitanus
Clem.2,9,1	Franc. Zabarella (I)
Clem. 5,1,2	Petrus de Ancharano (I)
(Consilia)	
Cons. 96	Alex. de Nevo
Cons. 15, vol. 1	Andr. Barb. Siculus
Cons. 428, vol. 5	Baldus
Cons. 16 + 17, vol. 2	Bartolus
Cons. 4, vol. 2	Carol. Ruinus
Cons. 18	Flor. de S. Petro
Cons. 2 (#39)	Io. Calderinus
Cons. 371	Petrus de Ancharano
Cons. 70, vol. 1	Socini
(Tracts)	
Tract. de statu. exclu. foemi., art. 6,q.1	Albertus Brunus
Tract. de gratiis, tit. de rescript., #41	Io. Staphileus
Singularia 679	Ludovicus Romanus
Singularia 687	Ludovicus Romanus

Locations   Jurists

    Loss of Immunities, with esp. ref.
    to Curial Offices (II,6)

(Laws)
    D.50,2,3,3
    C.10,31,49   Gloss
    C.10,31,49   Andr. Alciatus
    C.10,31,49   Bartolus
    Nov.45
    Dispunctiones, bk.3,chap.8   Andr. Alciatus

C. *Exclusion from Spiritual Jurisdic-*
    tions (II,6; III,2)

(Canons)
    D.12,c.12   Dom. de S. Geminianus
    D.32,c.6 (I)
    C.1,q.1,c.26 (I)   Gloss
    X.1,2,3   Gloss
    X.1,14 (Speculum)   Guil. Durandus
    X.3,43,3   Gloss

D. *Prohibition on Ownership of*
    Slaves[21] (I,4; II,5,6; III,2,5)

(Laws)
    C.1,3,54,8-10
    Nov.37

(Canons)
    D.54,d.p.c.12
    D.54,c.13   Gloss
    D.54,c.13   Guido de Baysio

---

21. Although in the *De Iudaeis* de Susannis discussed "slaves" mainly under the headings of prohibitions on social intercourse and the necessity for Jews to be inferior to Christians in status, I feel that the theme is most closely related to loss of jurisdiction; that is, possession of slaves, like possession of offices, grants Jews jurisdiction over Christians.

Locations	Jurists
D.54,c.15	
D.54,c.16	
D.54,c.17	
D.54,c.18 (I)	
X.2,1,4	Phil. Decius
X.2,28,18	Ant. Butrio
X.2,28,18	Io. de Imola
X.2,28,18	Phil. Decius
X.5,6,1	Gloss
X.5,6,2	
X.5,6,8	Gloss
X.5,6,8	Hostiensis
X.5,6,13	Gloss
X.5,6,13	Ant. de Butrio
X.5,6,13	Franc. Zabarella
X.5,6,19	

X.   JEWISH LAW OBSERVANCE

A.   *General* (I,2; II,2,4; III,1)

(Laws)

D.5,4,1	Alex. Tartagnus
D.12,1,1	Iason de Mayno
C.6,28,4	Florianus de S. Petro
C.6,30,19	Phil. Corneus
Nov.146	Greg. Holoander

(Canons)

C.7,q.1,c.8	Gloss
C.7,q.1,c.8	Guido de Baysio
C.34,q.1 and 2,c.3	Gloss
X.1,4,11	Ant. de Butrio
X.3,33,2	Hostiensis
X.4,14,4	Gloss

Locations	Jurists
X.4,17,18	Gloss
X.4,19,9	Gloss
X.5,6,5	Io. de Anania
Repetitio, X. de testamen., c. Ray- nutius, #157	Guilelmus Benedecti

(Consilia)

Cons. 107, vol. 2	Alex. Tartagnus
Cons. 15, vol. 1	Andr. Barb. Siculus
Cons. 316, vol. 1	Baldus
Cons. 4, vol. 2	Carol. Ruinus
Cons. 18	Flor. de S. Petro
Cons. 10 (#1)	Io. Calderinus
Cons. 2 (#39)	Io. Calderinus
Cons. 30 (#329)	Io. Calderinus
Cons. 1	Io. de Imola
Cons. 377, vol. 2	Paulus de Castro
Cons. 378, vol. 2	Paulus de Castro
Cons. 380, vol. 2	Paulus de Castro
Cons. 180, vol. 2	Phil. Corneus

(Tracts)

Tract. de statu. exclu. foemi., art. 6,q.3	Albertus Brunus
Tract. de iure primogeniturae, q. 66,#32	Andr. Tiraquellus
Tract. de statu. exclu. foemi., q.60	Io. Campegius
Tract. de iure primogen., bk.1, q.16	Io. Lecirier
Tract. de consuetudine, #754-57	Rochus de Curte

B.   *Observance of Jewish Marital Law*
      (I,4; II,1,3,4, and 8; III,4)

(Laws)

C.1,9	Albericus de Rosate
C.1,9,7	Bart. Saliceto

Locations	Jurists
C.5,4,19	Cynus
C.5,4,19	Petrus de bella Pertica

(Canons)

D.26,q.3 (I)	
C.28,q.1,c.10	Guido de Baysio
C.30,q.1,c.1	Guido de Baysio
C.31,q.1,c.9	Gloss
X.2,13,13	Io. Andreas
X.4,14,4	Gloss
X.4,19,8	Gloss
X.4,19,8	Hostiensis
X.4,19,8	Innocent IV
X.5,6,8	Felynus Sandeus
X.5,6,14	Io. de Anania

(Consilia)

Cons. 71, vol. 2	Alex. Tartagnus
Cons. 65, vol. 2	Andr. Barb. Siculus
Cons. 13, vol. 4	Andr. Barb. Siculus
Cons. 316, vol. 1	Baldus
Cons. 428, vol. 5	Baldus
Cons. 24	Ludovicus de Gozadinis
Cons. 66, vol. 1	Socini

(Tracts)

Tract. de dote, q. ult.	Io. Campegius

C.   *Observance of Jewish Ritual Law*[22]
    (I,23; II,6,9; III,5,8)

(Laws)
    D.48,8,34

---

22. It can be argued that this topic belongs under: status, toleration. Thus de Susannis follows the general statement of toleration in *De Iudaeis* 1,2 with a statement on ritual toleration (I,3). However, the theme more strictly falls under the heading of observance of Jewish law.

Locations   Jurists

    C.1,9,8   Bartolus
    C.1,9,13
    C.1,14,6   Baldus
    C.1,14,6   Iac. de Butrigarius

(Canons)
    D.45,c.3   Gloss
    C.14,q.6,c.2   Carol. Molinaeus
    X.5,6,3   Gloss
    X.5,6,7   Gloss
    X.5,6,7   Felynus Sandeus
    X.5,6,9   Gloss
    X.5,6,13   Gloss

D.   *Synagogue Building* (I,3)

(Laws)
    Inst.2,1
    D.50,17,61   Phil. Decius
    C.1,9,4
    C.1,9,19
    Nov.131, chap. 14

(Canons)
    X.2,1,13   Phil. Decius
    X.5,6,3   Io. de Anania
    X.5,6,5   Io. de Anania
    X.5,6,7   Felynus Sandeus
    X.5,6,7   Hostiensis
    X.5,6,7   Panormitanus

XI. RESTRICTIONS ON WITNESSES

A.   *General* (I,1,2 and 11;II,5,9; III, 6)

Locations	Jurists
(Laws)	
D.1,1 (*Addits. ad Bart.*)	Alex. Tartagnus
D.1,1	Claud. Seyssel
D.1,1	Iason de Mayno
D.12,2,51	Gloss
C.1,1,1	Bartolus
C.1,5,21	Bartolus
C.2,1,4	Baldus
C.3,28,11	
Nov.45	
(Canons)	
D.54,c.15	Dom. de S. Geminiano
C.2,q.7,c.24	
C.2,q.7,c.25	
C.2,q.7,c.26 Palea (I)	
C.6,q.1,c.6	
X.2,19,4	Phil. Decius
X.2,20,2	Gloss
X.2,20,21	Ant. Franc. de Doctoribus
X.2,20,21	Ant. Butrio
X.2,20,21	Felynus Sandeus
X.2,20,21 (*Speculum*)	Guil. Durandus
X.2,20,21	Io. de Imola
X.2,20,23	
X.5,6,16	
X.5,6,16	Io. de Anania
X.5,7,1	Io. de Anania
Clem. 2,8,1	Franc. Zabarella
Clem. 2,8,1	Io. de Imola
(Consilia)	
Cons. 35, vol. 1	Alex. Tartagnus
Cons. 70, vol. 1	Alex. Tartagnus
Cons. 179, vol. 2	Alex. Tartagnus

Locations	Jurists
Cons. 11	Flor. de S. Petro
Cons. 379, vol. 2	Paulus de Castro

(Tracts)

Tract. de crim. 1. maj., bk.2,q.10	Hieron. Gigans

B. *Oaths of Jews* (II,5,7 and 8)

(Laws)

D.1,1 rubr.	Claud. Seyssel
D.12,2,2,4	Bartolus
D.12,2,2,4	Phil. Corneus
C.6,20,3	Phil. Corneus
C.7,52 rubr.	Phil. Corneus

(Canons)

C.22,q.1,c.11	
X.1,2,1	Phil. Decius
X.1,33,13	Dom. de S. Geminiano
X.1,33,13	Felynus Sandeus
X.2,7 (*Speculum*)	Guil. Durandus
X.2,24,26	Gloss
X.5,6,19	Io. de Anania
Clem. 2,8,1	Io de Imola
Repetitio, c. Raynutius, #289	Guil. Benedecti

(Sicilian Law)

Const. Regni Siciliae, rubr. de defen., #31	Andr. de Isernia

(Consilia)

Cons. 15, vol. 1	Andr. Barb. Siculus
Cons. 159, vol. 5	Carol. Ruinus
Cons. 1	Io. de Imola
Cons. 2	Io. de Imola
Cons. 90, vol. 2	Paulus de Castro
Cons. 45, vol. 1	Phil. Corneus
Cons. 37, vol. 4	Phil. Corneus

Locations	Jurists
Cons. 65, vol. 1	Socini
Cons. 66, vol. 1	Socini
Cons. 233, vol. 1	Steph. Bertrandus

XII.   USURY   (I,2,11; II,5)

(Laws)

D.29,2,38	Ludovicus Romanus
C.1,1,1	Iason de Mayno

(Canons)

C.14,q.4,c.12	Gloss
C.14,q.4,c.12	Guido de Baysio
C.14,q.4,c.12	Io. de Fantus
X.2,2,9	Panormitanus
X.2,25,6	Phil. Decius
X.5,6,4	Io. de Anania
X.5,6,4	Felynus Sandeus
X.5,19,3	Gloss
X.5,19,5	Ant. de Butrio
X.5,19,5	Hostiensis
X.5,19,8	Henr. Bohic
X.5,19,8	Io. de Anania
X.5,19,12	Gloss
X.5,19,12	Hostiensis
X.5,19,12	Io. de Anania
Sext. 5,5	Dom. de S. Geminiano
X.3,33,2	Gloss
X.3,33,2	Ant. Butrio
X.3,33,2	Panormitanus
X.3,42,3	Franc. Zabarella
X.5,6,9	Felynus Sandeus
X.5,6,9	Henr. Bohic
X.5,6,9	Io. de Anania

Locations	Jurists
X.5,6,9	Io. Andreas
X.5,6,9	Panormitanus
Clem.5,2,1	Franc. Zabarella
(Consilia)	
Cons. 3 (#487)	Io. Calderinus
Cons. 2, vol. 4	Pier Paolo Pariseo
Decisio 151	Matt. de Afflictis

Problems Involving Marriage and Usury
    (II,8; III,3,7, and 9)

(Canons)	
C.28,q.1,c.2	Gloss
C.28,q.11,c.7	Gloss
X.3,32,20	Gloss
X.4,14,4	Gloss
X.4,14,4	Panormitanus
X.4,17,14	Gloss
X.4,19,7 (I)	Gloss
X.4,19,8 (I)	
X.4,19,9	Gloss
Sext.4,3,1	Guido de Baysio
Sext.5,5	Paulus de Leazariis
Clem.5,5	Gloss
Clem.5,5	Bonifacius de Vitalinos
Clem.5,5	Guil. de Monte Lauduno
Summa, title 1, chap. 6, par. 1	St. Antoninus

(Consilia)	
Cons. 100–103	Alex. de Nevo
Cons. 1, vol. 2	Alex. Tartagnus
Cons. 2, vol. 2	Alex. Tartagnus
Cons. 107, vol. 2	Alex. Tartagnus
Cons. 16, vol. 4	Alex. Tartagnus
Cons. 8, vol. 6	Alex. Tartagnus
Cons. 80, vol. 7	Alex. Tartagnus

Locations	Jurists
Cons. 15, vol. 4	Andr. Barb. Siculus
Cons. 6	Io. de Imola
Cons. 109, vol. 2	Paulus de Castro (I)
Cons. 379, vol. 2	Paulus de Castro
Cons. 397, vol. 2	Paulus de Castro
Cons. 243	Petrus de Ancharano
Cons. 19, vol. 3	Phil. Corneus
Cons. 88, vol. 3	Steph. Bertrandus

(Tracts)

Tract. de contractibus illicitis, bk. 2,q.24-28	Commodus Summenharth
Tract. de dote, part 1, q.47	Io. Campegius
Tract. de usuris, q.146	Laur. de Roduphis

XIII.   CONVERSION

A. *Improved Status* (*New Man*)
   (I,12; II,1,5; III,2,4,5,6,8, and 9)

(Laws)

D.1,1,rubr.	Claud. Seyssel
D.24,2,1	Iason de Mayno
C.3,28,11	Iason de Mayno
C.5,12,14	Baldus
C.5,12,18–22	Bart. Saliceto

(Canons)

D.26,c.3	Io. Ant. a S. Georgio
D.26,c.4 (I) and d.p.c.4 (I)	
D.48,c.1	
D.50,c.18	Gloss
D.77,c.3	Guido de Baysio
X.1,2,7	Phil. Decius
X.1.3,7	Gloss

Locations	Jurists
X.1.3,7	Panormitanus
X.1.3,7	Phil. Decius
X.1,29,38	Doctores
X.2,20,21	Ant. Franc. de Doctoribus
X.2,20,21	Felynus Sandeus
X.3,33,2	Panormitanus
X.3,34,8	Innocent IV
X.4,19,8	Ant. de Butrio
X.4,19,8	Hostiensis
X.4,19,8	Io. Calderinus
X.4,19,8	Panormitanus
X.5,1,6	Ant. de Butrio
X.5,1,6	Felynus Sandeus (I)
X.5,1,6	Io. de Anania
X.5,1,6	Io. Calderinus
X.5,6,5	Carol. Molinaeus
X.5,6,5	Felynus Sandeus
X.5,6,5	Innocent IV
X.5,6,5	Io. de Anania
X.5,6,5	Panormitanus
X.5,6,16	Felynus Sandeus
X.5,6,16	Hostiensis
Clem.5,4	Lapus Tactus

(Consilia)

Cons. 104, vol. 4	Alex. Tartagnus
Cons. 13, vol. 5	Carol. Ruinus
Cons. 679	Ludovicus Romanus
Cons. 130, vol. 1	Phil. Decius
Cons. 2, vol. 4	Pier Paolo Pariseo
Singularia 107	Hippolytus de Marsiliis
Singularia 273	Hippolytus de Marsiliis

Locations	Jurists
Singularia 679	Ludovicus Romanus
Singularia 687	Ludovicus Romanus

(Tracts)

Tract. de dote, q.47	Io. Campegius

B. *Separation of Converts from Jews* (III,2)

(Canons)
C.28,q.1,c.12

C. *Problems Involving Children (esp. forced baptism of)* (III,2,4, and 8)

(Laws)
C.1,5,18 (I)
C.1,5,19 (I)

(Canons)

C.28,q.1,c.10	Gloss
C.28,q.1,c.11	Gloss
D.4,c.129, de cons.	Gloss
D.4,c.138, de cons.	Gloss

D. *Problems Involving Specifically the Dowry* (III,4,8, and 9)

(Laws)

Inst.4,6,29	Ang. de Aretinus
C.5,12,22	Baldus (I)

(Canons)

X.4,19,8	Io. Andreas
X.4,19,8	Panormitanus
X.4,19,8	Petrus de Ancharano
X.5,6,5	Io. de Anania

Locations	Jurists
X.5,6,16	Hostiensis
X.5,19 (*Summa*)	Hostiensis
X.5,19,5	Hostiensis
X.5,19,5	Io. de Anania (I)
X.5,19,5	Panormitanus
X.5,38 (*Summa*)	Hostiensis
Sext.3,11,2	Guido de Baysio

(Consilia)

Cons. 63	Federicus de Senis

(Tracts)

Tract. de dotibus, part 11, col. fi.	Baldus Novellus
Tract. de dotibus, part 1, q.47	Io. Campegius
Tract. de usuris, q.72	Laur. de Rodulphis

E.   *Methods* (I,7,14; III,1,2,3, and 8)

(Laws)

C.1,9,3 (*Summa*)	Azo

(Canons)

D.37,c.13 (I)	
D.42,c.2	Io. Ant. a S. Georgio
D.45,c.3	Gloss
D.45,c.5	Gloss
D.45,c.5	Dom. de S. Geminiano
D.45,c.5	Io. Ant. a S. Georgio
D.50,c.40	
C.1,q.2,c.2	Gloss
C.1,q.2,c.2	Guido de Baysio
C.23,q.4,c.53	Gloss
C.23,q.4,c.53	Guido de Baysio
C.23,q.5,c.33	Gloss
C.23,q.6,c.4 (I)	Gloss
C.23,q.6,c.4 (I)	Guido de Baysio
C.23,q.6,c.4 (I)	Laurentius Hispanius

Locations	Jurists
D.4,c.24, de cons.	Gloss
D.4,c.93, de cons.	Gloss
D.4,c.98, de cons.	Gloss
D.4,c.99, de cons.	Gloss
X.1,4,4	Doctores
X.1,14 (*Summa*)	Goffredus de Trano (I)
X.3,33,2	Hostiensis
X.3,42 (*Summa*)	Goffredus de Trano
X.3,42 (*Summa*)	Hosteinsis
X.3,42,3 (I)	Gloss
X.3,42,3 (I)	Henr. Bohic
X.3,42,3	Panormitanus
X.3,42,4	Gloss
X.3,42,4	Hostiensis
X.5,3,9	Panormitanus
X.5,6,9	Gloss
X.5,6,9	Io. de Anania
X.5,6,19	Felynus Sandeus
X.5,9,4	Ant. Butrio
Clem.1,4	Franc. Zabarella
Summa, v. Iudaeus, q.33	Iac. de Belvisio
Dictionarium, v. Iudaeus	Albericus de Rosate

(Consilia)

Cons. 2, vol. 1	Aug. Beroius
Cons. 195	Petrus de Ancharano
Cons. 2, vol. 4	Pier Paolo Pariseo
Libellus de Iudaeis	Uldaricus Zasius
Sing. 55	Ludovicus Romanus

F.   *Conditions (prerequisites) for Conversion* (I,8; III,2,5, and 8)

(Laws)
   C.1,12,1

Locations	Jurists
(Canons)	
D.25, in primum	Dom. de S. Geminiano
C.14,q.5,c.15	Guido de Baysio
D.4,c.93, de cons.	Guido de Baysio
X.3,42,4	Ant. Butrio
X.3,42,4	Panormitanus
X.5,6,5	Io. de Anania
X.5,6,9	Panormitanus
X.5,6,16	Hostiensis
X.5,6,16	Io. Andreas
Sext.3,11,2	Guido de Baysio
Clem.3,7,2	Paulus de Leazariis

G. *Desire (on the part of the Church)*
    for (I,7; II,5; III,9)

(Canons)	
D.45,c.2	Io. de Turrecremata
D.1,c.67, de cons.	
X.1,3,7	Panormitanus
X.3,34,8	Panormitanus
Clem.5,2	Io. de Imola

(Tracts)	
Tract. de lib. eccles., q. ult.	Io. Lopez

H. *Prevarication (on the part of con-*
    verts)   (II,1,5 and 9; III,2,5,
    and 6)

(Canons)	
C.1,q.4,c.7	Gloss
X.5,6,16	Io. de Anania
X.5,9,4	Io. Andreas
Sext.5,2,13	Gloss
Sext.5,2,13	Dom. de S. Geminiano
Sext.5,2,13	Guido de Baysio

Locations	Jurists
(Consilia)	
Cons. 73, vol. 1, vol. 3	Aymo Cravettae
Sing. 107	Hippolytus de Marsiliis
Sing. 203	Hippolytus de Marsiliis
Sing. 687	Ludovicus Romanus

I.   *Conversion to Judaism Prohibited*

(Laws)
    C.1,9,16

(Canons)
    D.54,c.14

BIBLIOGRAPHY

MANUSCRIPTS

Jerusalem: National Library, Institute for MS Photography.
    Film #324 (Bibl. Vat. Ebr. 267), A Romano, *Vikhuaḥ*.
      #12508 (Paris, B.N. Hebr. 753/1 & 2), L.
      Karrito and J. Schacki, *Lettres*.
      #18518 (Bibl. Vat. Neofiti 38), A del. Monte.
      Confusione de Giudei.
      #18519 (Bibl. Vat. Neof. 37), A del. Monte.
      Lettere di Pace.
      #22290 (Bodl. MS 2587), *Vikhuaḥ*, Ferrara 1617.
Rome: *Archivio della Comunità di Roma*.
    ITb, ITc, ITd. *Bolle e editti Papali*, secs. 13–18.
    IZd, *Nota di spese inviata dalla Casa dei Catecumini*.
    ASV: *Arm*. 41 vol. 29, nn. 10, 90, 107, 117, 140, 195, 197, 221.
      Arm. 41, vol. 37, nn. 586, 658, 659, 664.
      Arm. 41, vol. 60, nn. 426, 443, 448, 449.
      Arm. 42, vol. 6, nn. 140, 183.
      Arm. 42, vol. 8, nn. 375.
      Div. Cam. vol. 200, f. 36, 38.
      Instr. Misc. 7480, 7481. *Forma Procedendi in Romana Curia* and *Formularium Card. Camerarii*.
    BAV: *Barb. Lat*. 5697, ff. 1–10. 132, 136.
      Ottob. 2532, f. 72.
      Vat. Lat. 6189, ff. 687, 772, 788, 805, 811, 819.
      Vat. Lat. 6792, ff. 81, 89, 106, 109–15, 170.
    Archivio del Vicariato. Fond. Pia casa dei catecumeni e neofiti, Filze, 121, *Copie delle Bolle*
Udine: *Archivio di Stato di Udine*.
    MS 2294, *Raccolta del Torso*, #1309; *Archivio Susanna, Busta*, 76; #1266, *Busta* 18.
    Biblioteca Comunale, Vincenzo Joppi
    MS 640, MS 1054, MS 1236 passim, and esp. n. 15.
    MS Joppi 359, MS Joppi, 710.
    Susanna, Tavola 4, *Genealogia del Torso*.

SOURCES

Agathius Guidacerius. *Ad Paulum III . . . in tres . . . Davidicos Psalmos . . .* (*contra Mahometistas, Haereticos, Iudaeosque . . .*) *. . . summa . . .* Paris, 1537.

Alberigo, J., et al. *Conciliorum Oecumenicorum Decreta.* Basle, 1962.

Almosnino, Moses. *Sefer Ma'amatz Khoaḥ.* Venice, 1588.

Andreae Alciati . . . Operum. Basle, 1582.

Antoninus. *Historiarum Domini.* Lyons, 1517.

Aquilino, Raffaele. *Ma'amar Ḥasidi.* Pesaro, 1571.

Aquinas, Thomas of. *Summa Theologica.* Translated by Fathers of the English Dominican Province. New York, 1947.

Augustine. *The City of God.* Translated by M. Dods. New York, 1950.

Aziqri, Eliezer. *Sefer Ḥaredim.* Venice, 1601.

Baer, Y. F. *Die Juden im Christlichen Spanien.* Berlin, 1936.

Baldus de Ubaldis. *Consilia.* Vol. 5. Venice, 1608.

Bartoli a Saxoferrato omnium iuris interpretum . . . commentaria. Venice, 1590.

Bartolus a Saxoferrato. *Super prima parte Codicis secundum lecturam.* 1510.

Bellarmine, Robert, *Opera Omnia.* Edited by Justinus Fèvre. Vols. 10–11. Paris, 1874.

Benedict XIII. "Etsi doctoris gentium." In *Beiträge zur politischen, kirchlichen, und Kultur-Geschichte der sechs letzten Jahrhunderte,* edited by I. Döllinger, vol. 2. pp. 383–93. Regensburg, 1863.

Blau, L., ed. *Leo Modenas Briefe und Schriftstücke.* Budapest, 1905.

Blumenkranz, B., ed. *Gisliberti Crispini Disputatio Iudei et Christiani.* Utrecht, 1956.

Bucer, Martin, "Judenratschlag." In *Martin Bucers Deutsche Schriften,* edited by R. Stupperich, vol. 7. Gütersloh, 1964.

Bullarium Diplomatum et Privilegiorum Taurensis Editio. Vols. 4–10. Turin, 1857–72.

Caraccioli, Antonio. *De Vita Pauli Quarti.* Coloniae Ubiorum, 1612.

Chrysostom, John. "Homily on the Gospel of John and the Epistle to the Hebrews." In *The Nicene and Post-Nicene Fathers,* edited by P. Schaff, vol. 14. New York, 1906.

Concilium Tridentinum: Concilii Tridentini Diariorum, edited by S. Merkle, vol. 2. Freibourg, 1911. *Concilii Tridentini Actorum,* edited by S. Ehses, vols. 4–9. Freibourg, 1904–24. *Concilii Tridentini Epistularum,* edited by G. Buschbell, vol. 11. Freibourg, 1936. *Concilii Tridentini Tractatuum,* edited by Schweitzer, vol. 12. Freibourg, 1930.

Contarini, G. *Gegenreformatorische Schriften* (*1530–1542*). Edited by F. Hünermann. *Corpus Catholicorum,* vol. 7. Münster, 1923.

Corpus Iuris Canonici. Lyons, 1606. ("Editio Romana").

Corpus Iuris Canonici. Edited by E. Friedberg. 2 vols. Leipzig, 1879, 1881.

Corpus Iuris Civilis. Paris, 1550. Paris, 1576. Lyons, 1569. Lyons, 1604. Lyons, 1612.

Corpus Iuris Civilis. Edited by P. Krueger and Th. Mommsen. 3 vols. Berlin, 1905, 1906, 1928.

de Castro, Paulus. *Pauli Castrensis, In primam Codicis partem Commentaria.* Venice, 1582.

Dejob, Ch. "Documents tirés des papiers du Cardinal Sirleto et des quelques autres manuscrits de la Vaticane sur les Juifs des États Pontificaux." *Revue des Études Juives* 9 (1884): 77–91.

del Bene, David. *Sefer Khisoth le-Veth David.* Verona, 1597.

De Letter, P., trans. and notes. *St. Prosper of Aquitaine: The Call of All Nations.* London, 1952.

de Mayno, Jason. *Iasoni Mayni Mediol., In primam Digesti Veteris Partem Commentaria.* Venice, 1598.

de Pomis, David. *Enarratio Apologica.* Venice, 1588.

de Susannis, Marquardus. *De Iudaeis et aliis Infidelibus.* Venice, 1558.

————. *De Iudaeis et aliis Infidelibus. Tractatus universi iuris.* Vol. 14, Venice, 1584.

de Torres, Francisco. *De Sola Lectione Legis, et Prophetarum Iudaeis cum Mosaico Ritu et, Cultu Permittenda, et de Jesu in Synogogis Eorum ex Lege, ac Prophetis Ostendendo et Annunciando. Ad Reverendissimos Inquisitores. Libri Duo.* Rome, 1555.

de Trano, Goffredus. *Summa Goffredi de Trano . . . in titulos Decretalium omnibus.* Venice, 1570.

Donovan, J., trans. *The Catechism of the Council of Trent: Published by the Command of Pope Pius the Fifth.* New York, 1829.

Dynus de Mugillo. *Tractatus de Praescriptionibus.* In *Tractatus Universi Iuris,* vol. 17, pp. 50–52. Venice, 1584.

Felynus Sandeus. *Commentariorum Felini Sandei Ferrariensis in Decretalium, Libros V.* Venice, 1574.

Fichardus, Io *Elenchus omnium auctorum sive scriptorum qui in iure tam civili quam canonico . . . claruerunt.* Frankfurt am Main, 1579.

Ficino, Marsilio. *De Christiana Religione Liber. Opera Omnia.* Vol. 1. Basle, 1576.

Fioghi, Fabiano. *Dialogo fra il Cathecumino e il Padre Cathechizante.* Rome, 1582.

Foa, Eliezer N. *Midrash be-Ḥidush,* Tel-Aviv, 1965.

Fontana, Agostino. *Amphitheatrum legale . . . seu Bibliotheca legalis amplissima in qua recensentur omnes authores cum omnibus eorum operis in iure editis.*

Friedlieb, J. H., trans. and ed. *Oracula Sibyllina.* Leipzig, 1852.

Fulgosius, Raphaelus. *Consilia . . . Raphaelis Cumani nempe et Fulgosii.* Venice, 1576.

Gherardus, Petrus, ed. *In foedus et victoriam contra Turcos . . . Poemata varia.* Venice, 1572.

Grayzel, S. *The Church and the Jews in the XIIIth Century.* Philadelphia, 1933.

————. "References to the Jews in the Correspondence of John XXII." *Hebrew Union College Annual* 23 (1950–51): 37–80.

Hagiz, Samuel, *Sefer Mvaqesh Adonai.* Venice, 1596.

Ha-Kohen, Joseph. *'Emeq ha-Bakha'.* Edited by M. Letteris. Cracow, 1895.

————. *Emeq ha-Bakha de Yosef ha-Kohen.* Translated into Spanish and notes by Pilar Leon Tello. Madrid, 1964.

Hardouin. *Acta Conciliorum.* Vols. 8–10. Paris, 1714.

Henry of Susa (Hostiensis). *Summa aurea.* Lyons, 1542.

ibn Yaḥya, Gedaliah. *Sefer Shalshelet ha-Qabbalah.* Jerusalem, 1962.

Imbonati, C. J. *Bibliotheca Latino-Hebraica.* Rome, 1694.

Innocent IV. *Apparatus quinque librorum decretalium.* Edited by Ant. Hartmanni. Argentinae, Eggesteyn, 1478.

Jellinek, A., ed. "*Ḥaqiroth 'al 'Inyan Ha-Notzrim.*" *Ha-Shaḥar* 2 (1870):17–23.

Jerome. *S. Hieronymi Presbyteri Opera, Commentariorum in Danielem Libri III [IV], Corpus Christianorum, Series Latina, LXXV,* A. Turnhoult, 1964.

Joachim of Flora. *Adversus Iudaeos di Gioacchino da Fiore.* Edited by Arsenio Frugoni. Rome, 1957.

Josephus, Flavius. *The Complete Works of Flavius Josephus.* Translated by W. Whiston. Boston, 1847.

Justiniani, Paulus, and Quirini, Petrus. *Libellus ad Leonem Decem.* Edited by J. B. Mittarelli et A. Costadoni. *Annales Camuldulenses.* Vol. 9. Venice, 1773.

Kahl Johannis., alias Calvini. *Magnum Lexicon Juridicum.* Coloniae Allobrogum, 1759.

Katzenellenbogen, Samuel b. Judah. *Shtaim 'Esre Drashoth.* Venice, 1588.

Laderchio, G. *Annales Ecclesiastici ab anno quo . . . desinit Odoricus Raynaldus.* Vol. 35 (for 1566–67). Cologne, 1733.

Langlois, E. *Les Registres de Nicolaus IV.* Paris, 1886.

Lattes, Isaiah. Introduction to *Sefer ha-Zohar.* Mantua, 1558.

Lipens, Martin. *Martini Lipenii Bibliotheca realis iuridica.* Leipzig, 1757.

Luther, Martin. "Against the Sabbatarians." In *Luther's Works,* ed. and trans. by M. H. Bertram, vol. 47, pp. 59–98. Philadelphia, 1971.

————. "Concerning the Jews and Their Lies." In *Luther's Works,* ed. and trans. by M. H. Bertram, vol. 47, pp. 121–306. Philadelphia, 1971.

————. "That Jesus Christ Was Born a Jew." In *Luther's Works,* ed. and trans. by W. I. Brandt, vol. 45, pp. 195–229. Philadelphia, 1971.

Maimonides, Moses. *Mishneh Torah.* Jerusalem, 1964.

Mansi, J. D. *Sacrorum Conciliorum nova et amplissima Collectio.* Venice, 1779–82, and Paris, 1902.

Martini, Raymundus. *Pugio Fidei Adversus Mauros et Iudaeos.* Leipzig, 1687.

Mocenigo, Luigi. "Relazione di Roma (1560)." In *Relazioni degli Ambasciatori Veneti al Senato,* edited by Alberi, ser. 2, tom 4, vol. 10. Florence, 1857.

Moscato, Judah. *Kol Yehudah,* in *Sefer HaKhuzari.* Venice, 1594.

Navagero, B. "Relazione di Roma (1558)." In *Relazioni degli Ambasciatori Veneti al Senato,* edited by Alberi, ser. 2, tom. 3, vol. 9. Florence, 1846.

Neubauer, A. "The *Shilte Giborim* of Jacob b. Joab of Fano" (Hebrew). *Letterbode* 10 (1884): 124 ff.

Nicholas of Lyra. *Bibliorum Sacrorum cum glossa ordinaria et N. Lyrani expositionibus.* Lyons, 1545.

Panziroli, Guido, *De claris legum interpretibus.* Venice, 1637.

Paul IV. "Cum ex apostolatus officio." In *Quellen zur Geschichte des Papsttums und des Romischen Katholizmus,* edited by C. Mirbt, 3d ed. Tübingen, 1911.

Perez de Valentia, Jacobus. *Centum ac quinquaginta psalmi Davidici, cum . . . expositione Iacobi Perez de Valentia. Accessit ad haec tractatus contra Iudaeos.* Lyons, 1514.

Perlmann, M., ed. and trans. *"Samu'al al-Magribi Ifḥam al-Yahud (Silencing the Jews)." Proceedings of the American Academy for Jewish Research* 33 (1964).

Pius V. *Apostolicarum Pii Quinti P. M. Epistolarum. Libri Quinque.* Edited by F. Goubau. Antwerp, 1640.

Possevin, Antonius. *Apparatus Sacri.* Vol. 2. Venice, 1606.

————. *Bibliotheca selecta . . . ad salutem omnium gentium procurandum.* Cologne, 1607.

Potthast, A. *Regesta Pontificum Romanorum.* Berlin, 1874–75.

Raba, Menahem. *Beth Mo'ed.* Venice, 1605.

Rawdon-Brown. *Calendar of State Papers, Venetian.* Vol. 6. London, 1881.

Raynaldus, Odoricus. *Annales Ecclesiastici ab anno MCXCVIII ubi desinit Card. Baronius.* Edited by J. D. Mansi. Vol. 9. Lucca, 1752.

Reusch, F., ed. *Die Indices Librorum Prohibitorum*. Tübingen, 1886.
Ripae, Joannis Franc. *In primam et secundae ff. Novi*. Venice, 1636.
Rosenthal, J., ed. *Ḥerev Pifioth of Yair b. Shabbtai* (Hebrew). Jerusalem, 1958.
Schwab, Moïse. "Une supplique de la communauté de Rome à Pie V." *Revue des Études Juives* 25 (1892): 113–16.
Sefer Yossipon. Ed. Hominer. Jerusalem, 1956.
Sessa, Joh. *Tract. de Iudaeis*. Turin, 1712.
Sixtus Senensis. *Bibliotheca Sancta*. 2 Vols. Venice, 1566.
Sonne, Is., ed. *Mi-Pavolo ha-Revi'i 'ad Pius ha-Ḥamishi*. Jerusalem, 1954.
Stern, Moritz., ed. *Urkundliche Beiträge Über die Stellung der Päpste zu den Juden*. Kiel, 1893.
Summa 'Elegantius in iure divino' seu Coloniensis. Edited by S. Kuttner and G. Fransen. Vol. 1. New York, 1969.
Tudeschis, Nicolaus (Panormitanus). *Panormitani in quartum et quintum decretalium commentaria*. Lyons, 1559.
Venier, Sebastiano, *Relazione*. Edited by Prospero Antonino. *Del Friuli ed in particolare dei Trattati da cui ebbe Origine*. Venice, 1873.

SECONDARY WORKS

Ancel, R. "L'Activité réformatrice de Paul IV." *Revue des Questions Historiques* 86 (1909); 67–103.
Assaf, S. *Texts and Studies in Jewish History* (Hebrew). Jerusalem, 1946.
Baer, Y. F. *A History of the Jews in Christian Spain*. Translated by Leibowitz and Halkin. 2 Vols. Philadelphia, 1966.
Balletti, Andrea. *Gli Ebrei e gli Estensi*. Modena, 1913.
Barni, G. "Notizie del Giurista e Umanista Andrea Alciato, sur manoscritti non glossati delle Pandette." *Bibliothèque d'Humanisme et Renaissance* 20 (1958): 542–55.
Baron, S. W. "Medieval Nationalism and Jewish Serfdom." In *Studies and Essays in Honor of Abraham A. Neuman*, edited by M. Ben-Horin et al. Leiden, 1962.
———. "Plenitude of Apostolic Powers and Medieval Jewish Serfdom" (Hebrew). In *Sefer Yovel le-Yitzchak Baer*. Jerusalem, 1960.
———. *A Social and Religious History of the Jews*. 2d ed. 14 vols. Philadelphia, 1952–69.
H. Beinart. *Conversos on Trial before the Inquisition* (Hebrew). Tel Aviv. 1965.
Benrath, K. *Geschichte der Reformation in Venedig*. Halle, 1887.

Ben-Sasson, H. H. "Jewish-Christian Disputation in the Setting of Humanism and Reformation in the German Empire." *Harvard Theological Revue* 59 (1966): 369–90.

————. "Ha-Yehudim mul Ha-Reformatziah." *Proceedings of the Israel Academy of Arts and Sciences* 5 (1970).

Berliner, A. *Geschichte der Juden in Rom.* Frankfurt, 1893.

Blau, J. *The Christian Interpretation of the Cabala in the Renaissance.* New York, 1944.

Bloomfield, M. W. "Joachim of Flora: A Critical Survey of His Canon, Teachings, Sources, Biography, and Influence." *Traditio* 12 (1957): 249–312.

Blumenkranz, B. "Anti-Jewish Polemics and Legislation in the Middle Ages: Literary Fiction or Reality." *Journal of Jewish Studies* 15 (1964): 125–40.

————. *Les Auteurs Chrétiens Latins du Moyen Age sur les Juifs.* Paris, 1963.

————. *Juifs et Chrétiens dans le Monde Occidental (430–1096).* Paris, 1960.

————. "Nicholas de Lyre et Jacob ben Reuben." *Journal of Jewish Studies* 16 (1965): 47–51.

Bouwsma, Wm. J. *Venice and the Defense of Republican Liberty.* Berkeley, 1968.

Braudel, Fernand. *La Mediterranée et le monde mediterranéen à l'époque de Philippe II.* Paris, 1963.

Bromato, Carlo. *Storia di Paolo IV.* 2 Vols. Ravenna, 1748.

Browe, P. *Die Judenmission im Mittelalter und die Päpste.* Rome, 1942.

————. "Die religiöse Duldung der Juden im Mittelalter." *Archiv für katholisches Kirchenrecht* 118 (1938): 1–76.

Buschbell, G. *Reformation und Inquisition in Italien um die mittel des XVI Jahrhunderts.* Paderborn, 1910.

Calasso, Francesco. *Medio Evo del Diritto, I. Le Fonti.* Milan, 1954.

Cantimori, Delio. *Eretici Italiani del cinquecento.* Milan, 1947.

————. *Prospettive di storia ereticale italiana del cinquecento.* Bari, 1960.

Cantù, C. *Les hérètiques d'Italie.* Translated by A. Digard and E. Martin. Vols. 2–4. Paris, 1869.

Caperan, Louis. *Le problème du salut des infidèles.* 2d ed. Paris, 1932.

Capodagli, Gio: Giuseppe. *Udine Illustrata.* Udine, 1665.

Cassuto, Umberto. *Gli Ebrei a Firenze nell'età del Rinascimento.* Florence, 1918.

Chastel, A. "L'Antechrist à la Renaissance." In *L'Umanesimo e il Demoniaco nell'Arte,* edited by E. Castelli. *Cristianesimo e regione di stato,* vol. 2. Milan, 1952.

Christiani, L. *L'Église à l'époque du Concile de Trente*. Histoire de l'Église, edited by A. Fliche and Martin, vol. 17. Paris, 1948.
Cohen, G. D. "Esau as Symbol in Early Medieval Thought." In *Jewish Medieval and Renaissance Studies,* edited by A. Altmann. Cambridge, Mass., 1967.
―――. Review of *The Marranos of Spain,* by B. Netanyahu. *Jewish Social Studies* 29 (1966–67): 178–84.
―――. "The Soteriology of R. Abraham Maimuni." *Proceedings of the American Academy for Jewish Research* 35 (1967): 75–98, and 36 (1968): 33–56.
Colorni, V. *Gli Ebrei nel sistema del diritto comune*. Milan, 1956.
―――. *Legge ebraica e leggi locali*. Milan, 1945.
Cortese, Ennio. *La Norma Giuridica*. Milan, 1962.
Daniel, N. *Islam and the West*. Edinburgh, 1962.
Daniel-Rops, Henri. *The Catholic Reformation*. Translated by J. Warrington. 2 Vols. New York, 1964.
Delumeau, J. *Vie Économique et Sociale de Rome, dans la seconde moitié du XVIᵉ siècle*. Vol. 1. Paris, 1957.
de Maulde, R. "Les Juifs dans les États Français du Pape." *Revue des Études Juives* 10 (1885): 180–81.
de Renaldis, Girolamo Conte. *Memorie storiche dei tre ultimi secoli del Patriarcato d'Aquileia, 1411–1751*. Udine, 1888.
De Rossi, J. B. *Bibliotheca Judaica Antichristiana*. Parma, 1800.
Dictionnaire de Théologie Catholique. Paris, 1920.
Dimitrovsky, H. Z. "Rabbi Yaakov Berab's Academy" (Hebrew). *Sefunot* 7, (1963): 41–103.
Eisenstein-Barzilay, I. *Between Reason and Faith: Anti-Rationalism in Italian Jewish Thought, 1250–1650*. Paris, 1967.
Élie, Hubert. "Contribution à l'étude du statut des Juifs en Italie aux XVᵉ et XVIᵉ siècles: L'opinion de Bernardin de Busti." *Revue de l'Histoire des Religions* 142 (1952): 67–96.
Elton, G. R. *Reformation Europe, 1517–1559*. London, 1963.
Enciclopedia Cattolica. Vatican City, 1949.
Encyclopedia Hebraica. Jerusalem, 1952.
Engelmann, Woldemar. *Die Wiedergeburt der Rechtskultur in Italien*. Leipzig, 1938.
Erler, L. "Die Juden des Mittelalters. Die Päpste und die Juden." *Archiv für katholisches Kirchenrecht* 53 (1885): 1–70.
Feine, Hans Erich. *Kirchliche Rechtsgeschichte, Die Katholische Kirche*. 4th ed. Köln Graz, 1964.
Ferorelli, N. *Gli Ebrei nell'Italia Meridionale, dall'età romana al secolo XVIII*. Turin, 1915.

Feroso, C. *Gil Ebrei Portoghesi Giustiziati in Ancona sotto Paolo IV.* Foligno, 1889.

Ferrari, L. *Onomasticon, Repertorio Biobibliografico degli scrittori Italiani dal 1501 al 1850.* Milan, 1947.

Finkelstein, L. *Jewish Self-Government in the Middle Ages.* New York, 1924.

Franklin, Julian H. *Jean Bodin and the Sixteenth-Century Revolution in the Methodology of Law and History.* New York, 1963.

Friedenwald, H. *The Jews and Medicine.* 2 vols. Baltimore, 1944.

Funkenstein, A. "Changes in the Patterns of Christian Anti-Jewish Polemics in the 12th Century" (Hebrew). *Zion* 33 (1968): 125–44.

Galliner, H. "Agathius Guidacerius, 1477–1540." *Historia Judaica* 2 (1940): 85–110.

Grayzel, S. "The Avignonese Popes and the Jews." *Historia Judaica* 2 (1940): 1–12.

———. "The Papal Bull Sicut Judeis." In *Studies and Essays in Honor of Abraham A. Neuman,* edited by M. Ben-Horin et al. Leiden, 1962.

Grundmann, H. *Religiöse Bewegungen im Mittelalter.* Darmstadt, 1961.

Haliczer, S. "The Castilian Urban Patriciate and the Jewish Expulsions." *American Historical Review* 78 (1973): 35–58.

Harris, Alan C. "La demografia del ghetto in Italia, 1516–1797 circa." In *La Rassegna Mensile di Israel.* Rome, 1967.

Helmio, A. K. *The Lutheran Reformation and the Jews.* Hancock, Mich., 1949.

Hoffmann, K. W. *Ursprung und Anfängstatigkeit des ersten päpstlichen Missioninstituts.* Münster, 1923.

Holtzmann, W. "Zur päpstlichen Gesetzgebung über die Juden im 12 Jahrhundert." In *Festschrift Guido Kisch.* Stuttgart, 1955.

Horn, N. *Aequitas in den Lehren des Baldus.* Cologne, 1968.

Humbert, A. *Les Origines de la théologie moderne, I. La Renaissance de l'Antiquité Chrétienne (1450–1521).* Paris, 1911.

Hurter, Hugo. *Nomenclator Literarius Recentioris Theologiae Catholicae.* 5 Vols. Innsbruck, 1892–99.

H. Inalcik. "Capital Formation in the Ottoman Empire." *Journal of Economic History* 29 (1969): 97–140.

"Inquisitionsverfahren gegen die Juden in Bologna im Jahre 1568." *Monatsschrift für Geschichte und Wissenschaft des Judentums* 20 (1871): 378–81.

G. Jackson. *The Making of Medieval Spain.* New York, 1972.

Jedin, H. *A History of the Council of Trent.* Translated by E. Graf. 2 Vols. St. Louis, 1957–61.

Jemolo, A. C. *Stato e Chiesa negli scrittori politici italiani del seicento e del settecento.* Turin, 1914.

Jewish Encyclopedia. New York, 1901–6.

Jung, Eva-Marie. "On the Nature of Evangelism in Sixteenth-Century Italy." *Journal of the History of Ideas* 14 (1953): 511–27.

Kasher, H. M. *Sarei Ha-Elef.* New York, 1959.

Katz, J. "The Controversy on the Semikha (Ordination) between Rabbi Yacob Bei-Rav and the Ralbaḥ" (Hebrew), *Zion* 16 (1951): 28–45.

Kaufmann, D. "Les Martyrs d'Ancone." *Revue des Études Juives* 11 (1893): 149–53.

Kayser, F. "Papst Nicholaus V und die Juden." *Archiv für katholisches Kirchenrecht* 53 (1885): 209–20.

Kelly, D. R. "Budé and the First Historical School of Law." *American Historical Review* 72 (1967): 807–34.

Kerker. "Die kirchliche Reform in Italien unmittelbar vor dem Tridentinum." *Theologische Quartalschrift* 41 (1859): 1–56.

Kisch, G. *Zasius und Reuchlin.* Stuttgart, 1961.

Kristeller, P. O. *The Philosophy of Marsilio Ficino.* Translated by Virginia Conant. New York, 1943.

Kunkel, P. *The Theatines in the History of the Catholic Reform before the Establishment of Lutheranism.* Washington, 1941.

Kuttner, S. *Harmony from Dissonance.* Latrobe, Pa., 1961.

Landauer, G. "Zur Geschichte der Judenrechtswissenschaft." *Zeitschrift für die Geschichte der Juden in Deutschland* 2 (1930): 255–61.

Langmuir, G. "The Jews in the Archives of Angevin England: Reflections on Medieval Anti-Semitism." *Traditio* 19 (1963): 183–244.

———. " 'Judei nostri' and the Beginnings of Capetian Legislation." *Traditio* 16 (1960): 201–40.

Lauchert, F. *Die italienischen literarischer Gegner Luthers.* Freiburg im Breisgau, 1912.

Le Bras, G. *Prolégomènes. Histoire du Droit et des Institutions de l'Église en Occident,* vol. 1. Paris, 1955.

Le Bras, G.; Rambaud, J.; and Lefebvre, Ch. *L'Age classique (1140–1378). Histoire du Droit et des Institutions de l'Église en Occident,* vol. 7. Paris, 1965.

Lexikon für Theologie und Kirche. Vols. 2 and 5. Freiburg, 1958, 1960.

Lieberman, S. "Raymund Martini and His Alleged Forgeries." *Historia Judaica* 5 (1943): 87–102.

———. *Shkiin.* Jerusalem, 1939.

Liruti, Gian Giuseppe. *Notizie della vita ed opere scritte dei Letterati del Friuli.* Vols. 2 and 4. Venice, 1830.

Luzzatto, Federico. *Cronache storiche della università degli Ebrei di San Daniele del Friuli.* Rome, 1964.

Luzzatto, Gino. *I Banchieri Ebrei in Urbino.* Verona, 1903.

Maccarrone, Michele. *Vicarius Christi, Storia del titolo papale.* Rome, 1952.

Maffei, Domenico. *Alessandro d'Alessandro, giureconsulto umanista (1461–1523).* Milan, 1956.

Martines, L. *Lawyers and Statecraft in Renaissance Florence.* Princeton, 1968.

Mattingly, G. *The Armada.* Boston, 1960.

Merchavia, Ch. *The Church versus Talmudic and Midrashic Literature* (Hebrew). Jerusalem, 1970.

————. "The Talmud in the Additions of Paul of Burgos." *Journal of Jewish Studies* 16 (1965): 115–34.

Milano, A. "Battesimi di Ebrei a Roma dal Cinquecento all'Ottocento." In *Scritti in Memoria di Enzo Sereni.* Jerusalem, 1970.

————. *Il Ghetto di Roma.* Rome, 1964.

————. "L'Impari lotta della comunità di Roma contro la casa dei catecumeni." *La Rassegna Mensile di Israel* 16 (1950): 355–68.

————. *Storia degli Ebrei in Italia.* Turin. 1963.

————. "Sugli Ebrei a Viterbo." In *Scritti sull'Ebraismo in Memoria di Guido Bedarida.* Florence, 1966.

Monti, G. M. *Ricerche su Papa Paolo IV Carafa.* Benevento, 1923.

Neppi-Ghirondi. *Toldoth Gdolé Yisraèl Ve-Geone Italiah.* Trieste, 1853.

Netanyahu, B. *The Marranos of Spain.* New York, 1966.

Ohrenstein, R. P. "Academic Opinion on the Jews and on Their Activities in Germany" (Hebrew), *Zion* 12 (1947): 24–36.

O'Malley, J. W. *Giles of Viterbo on Church and Reform.* Leiden, 1968.

Palladio, Gio: Francesco. *Historie della Provincia del Friuli.* Udine, 1660.

Pastor, L. *The History of the Popes.* Translated by K. Paul, Trench, and Trubner. 40 vols. London, 1938.

Perles, J. *Beiträge zur Geschichte Aramaischem und Hebraischen Studien.* Munich, 1855.

Perugini, R. "L'Inquisition Romaine et les Israélites." *Revue des Études Juives* 3 (1881): 94–108.

Phelan, J. L. *The Millennial Kingdom of the Franciscans in the New World: A Study of the Writings of Geronimo de Mendieta, 1525–1604.* Berkeley, 1956.

Piano-Mortari, V. *Ricerche sulla teoria dell'interpretazione del diritto nel secolo XVI.* Milan, 1956.

Pilati, G. *Stato e Chiesa nei primi quindici secoli.* Rome, 1961.

Polman, Pontien. *L'Élément historique dans la controverse religeuse au XVIᵉ siècle.* Gembloux, 1932.

Popper, Wm. *The Censorship of Hebrew Books.* New York, 1899.

Poznanski, A. *Schiloh: Ein Beitrag zur Geschichte der Messiaslehre.* Leipzig, 1904.

Rabinowicz, R. N. *Ma'amar 'al Hadpasath ha-Talmud.* Edited by M. Haberman. Jerusalem, 1952.

Radin, M. "An Unknown Letter of Pius IV." *Jewish Quarterly Review* 1 (1910): 113–21.

Reeves, M. "The Abbot Joachim and the Society of Jesus." *Medieval and Renaissance Studies* 5 (1961): 163–81.

———. *The Influence of Prophecy in the Later Middle Ages.* Oxford, 1969.

———. "Joachimist Expectations in the Order of Augustinian Hermits." *Recherches de Théologie Ancienne et Médiévale* 25 (1958): 111–41.

Riesenberg, P. "The Consilia Literature: A Prospectus." *Manuscripta* 6 (1962): 3–22.

Rodochanachi, E. *La réforme en Italie.* 2 vols. Paris, 1920–21.

———. *Le St. Siège et les Juifs.* Paris, 1891.

Roth, C. *A History of the Jews in Italy,* Philadelphia, 1946.

———. *A History of the Marranos.* Philadelphia, 1941.

———. *The House of Nasi: Doña Gracia.* Philadelphia, 1946.

———. *The Jews in the Renaissance.* Philadelphia, 1959.

Schmidlin, J. "Reformation und Gegenreformation in ihrem Verhältnis zur Mission." *Zeitschrift für Missionwissenschaft* 7 (1917): 257–69.

Scholem, G. *Ursprung und Anfänge der Kabbala.* Berlin, 1962.

Scult, Melvin M. "The Conversion of the Jews and the Origins of Jewish Emancipation in England." Ph.D. dissertation, Brandeis University, 1968. University Microfilms, Ann Arbor, 1969.

Secret, F. "Les Dominicains et la Kabbale Chrétienne à la Renaissance." *Archivum Fratrum Praedicatorum* 27 (1957): 319–36.

———. "Les Jésuites et le Kabbalisme Chrétien à la Renaissance." *Bibliothèque d'Humanisme et Renaissance* 20 (1958): 542–55.

Sheedy, Anna T. *Bartolus on Social Conditions in the Fourteenth Century.* New York, 1942.

Short Title Catalog of Books Printed in Italy and of Books in Italian Printed Abroad, 1501–1600 Held in Selected North American Libraries. Boston, 1970.

Shulvass, Moses A. *Jewish Life in Renaissance Italy* (Hebrew). New York, 1955.

Sicroff, A. A. *Les Controverses des Statuts de "Pureté de Sang" en Espagne du XVe au XVIIe Siècle.* Paris, 1960.

Simonsohn, Max. *Die Kirchliche Judengesetzgebung im Zeitalter der Reformkonzilien von Konstanz und Basel.* Breslau, 1912.

Simonsohn, S. "Ha-Ghetto be-Italiah u-Mishtaro. In *Sefer Yovel le-Yitzchak Baer*. Jerusalem, 1960.

──────. *Toldoth ha-Yehudin be-Dukhsuth Mantovah*. 2 vols. Jerusalem, 1962–64.

Smalley, B. *The Study of the Bible in the Middle Ages*. Notre Dame, 1964.

Sommervogel, Carlos. *Bibliothèque de la Compagnie de Jesus*. Paris, 1898.

Song, R. *The Sacred Congregation for the Propagation of the Faith*. Washington, 1961.

Sonne, I. "Le-Toldoth K'hillath Boloniah be-Thilath ha-Me'ah ha-Tet-zayin." *Hebrew Union College Annual* 16 (1941): 35–98.

Stow, K. "The Burning of the Talmud in 1553, In the Light of Sixteenth-Century Catholic Attitudes toward the Talmud." *Bibliothèque d'Humanisme et Renaissance* 34 (1972): 435–59.

Streit, Robert, *Bibliotheca Missionum*. 26 vols. Münster, 1916.

Synan, E. *The Popes and the Jews in the Middle Ages*. New York, 1965.

Tacchi-Venturi, P. *Storia della Compagnia di Gesù in Italia*. 2 vols. Rome, 1922–31.

Ullmann, W. *The Medieval Idea of Law as Represented in Lucas de Penna*. London, 1946.

──────. *Medieval Papalism*. London, 1949.

Vendrell, F. "La actividad proselitista de San Vincente Ferrer durante el reinado de Fernando I de Aragón." *Sefarad* 13 (1953): 87–104.

──────. "La politica proselitista del rey D. Fernando I de Aragón." *Sefarad* 10 (1950): 349–66.

──────. "En torno a la confirmacion real, en Aragón, de la Pragmatica de Benedicto XIII." *Sefarad* 20 (1960): 319–51.

Vernet, F. "Le Pape Martin V et les Juifs." *Revue des Questions Historiques* 51 (1892): 409–23.

Villicrosa, José Mª Millas. "San Vincente Ferrer y el antisemitismo." *Sefarad* 10 (1950): 182–84.

Vogelstein, H. *Rome*. Translated by M. Hadas. Philadelphia, 1940.

von Savigny, F. K. *Geschichte des Römischen Rechts im Mittelalter*. 7 vols. Heidelberg, 1830–50.

von Schulte, J. F. *Geschichte der Quellen und Literatur des Canonischen Rechts*. 3 vols. Stuttgart, 1875–80.

Weinstein, D. "Savonarola, Florence, and the Millennarian Tradition." *Church History* 27 (1958): 291–305.

Werblowsky, R. J. Z. "Crispin's Disputation." *Journal of Jewish Studies* 11 1960: 67–77.

Wilks, M. *The Problem of Sovereignty in the Later Middle Ages*. Cambridge, 1963.

Willaert, L. *La Restauration Catholique, 1563–1648 Histoire de l'Église,* edited by Fliche and Martin, vol. 18. Paris, 1960.

Williams, G. H. *The Radical Reformation.* Philadelphia, 1962.

Yaari, A. *Srefath ha-Talmud be-Italiah.* Tel-Aviv, 1954.

Yerushalmi, Y. H. "The Inquisition and the Jews of France in the Time of Bernard Gui." *Harvard Theological Review* 63 (1970): 317–76.

INDEX OF PERSONS

For an index of laws and legists, the reader is referred to Parts I and II of Appendix II.